# THE EVERYDAY MAKERS OF INTERNATIONAL LAW

This book offers a unique insight into the inner workings of international courts and tribunals. Combining the rigour of the essay and the creativity of the novel, Tommaso Soave narrates the invisible practices and interactions that make up the dispute settlement process, from the filing of the initial complaint to the issuance of the final decision. At each step, the book unravels the myriad activities of the legal experts running the international judiciary – judges, arbitrators, agents, counsel, advisors, bureaucrats, and specialized academics – and reveals their pervasive power in the process. The cooperation and competition among these inner circles of professionals lie at the heart of international judicial decisions. By shedding light on these social dynamics, Soave takes the reader on a journey through the lives, ambitions, and preoccupations of the everyday makers of international law.

TOMMASO SOAVE is an assistant professor of law at Central European University. Previously, he practiced international law for almost a decade, first as an attorney with Sidley Austin LLP, then as a dispute settlement lawyer at the World Trade Organization. His research focuses on the socio-professional dimensions of global governance.

CAMBRIDGE STUDIES IN INTERNATIONAL
AND COMPARATIVE LAW: 170

Established in 1946, this series produces high quality, reflective and innovative scholarship in the field of public international law. It publishes works on international law that are of a theoretical, historical, cross-disciplinary or doctrinal nature. The series also welcomes books providing insights from private international law, comparative law and transnational studies which inform international legal thought and practice more generally.

The series seeks to publish views from diverse legal traditions and perspectives, and of any geographical origin. In this respect it invites studies offering regional perspectives on core *problématiques* of international law, and in the same vein, it appreciates contrasts and debates between diverging approaches. Accordingly, books offering new or less orthodox perspectives are very much welcome. Works of a generalist character are greatly valued and the series is also open to studies on specific areas, institutions or problems. Translations of the most outstanding works published in other languages are also considered.

After seventy years, Cambridge Studies in International and Comparative Law sets the standard for international legal scholarship and will continue to define the discipline as it evolves in the years to come.

*Series Editors*

Larissa van den Herik

*Professor of Public International Law, Grotius Centre for International Legal Studies, Leiden University*

Jean d'Aspremont

*Professor of International Law, University of Manchester and Sciences Po Law School*

A list of books in the series can be found at the end of this volume.

# THE EVERYDAY MAKERS
# OF INTERNATIONAL LAW

From Great Halls to Back Rooms

TOMMASO SOAVE
*Central European University*

# CAMBRIDGE
## UNIVERSITY PRESS

University Printing House, Cambridge CB2 8BS, United Kingdom

One Liberty Plaza, 20th Floor, New York, NY 10006, USA

477 Williamstown Road, Port Melbourne, VIC 3207, Australia

314–321, 3rd Floor, Plot 3, Splendor Forum, Jasola District Centre, New Delhi – 110025, India

103 Penang Road, #05–06/07, Visioncrest Commercial, Singapore 238467

Cambridge University Press is part of the University of Cambridge.

It furthers the University's mission by disseminating knowledge in the pursuit of education, learning, and research at the highest international levels of excellence.

www.cambridge.org
Information on this title: www.cambridge.org/9781009248006
DOI: 10.1017/9781009248013

© Tommaso Soave 2022

This publication is in copyright. Subject to statutory exception and to the provisions of relevant collective licensing agreements, no reproduction of any part may take place without the written permission of Cambridge University Press.

First published 2022

*A catalogue record for this publication is available from the British Library.*

ISBN 978-1-009-24800-6 Hardback

Cambridge University Press has no responsibility for the persistence or accuracy of URLs for external or third-party internet websites referred to in this publication and does not guarantee that any content on such websites is, or will remain, accurate or appropriate.

A Irene

By doing something a half centimetre high, you are more likely to get a sense of the universe than if you try to do the whole sky.

Alberto Giacometti

# CONTENTS

*Preface*     *page* ix
*List of Abbreviations*     xx

1  Carnegieplein 2, 10:00 AM     1
2  Coffee, Cigarettes, and International Judicial Practices     22
3  A New Generation of Litigators     54
4  Telling a Story     79
5  The Invisible Army     102
6  The Three Wise Monkeys     137
7  The Lyophilization of Life     153
8  The Memo     163
9  To Capture the World     174
10  Bricolage     185
11  The Explorer     201
12  A Four-Letter Word     224
13  What Does It Mean…     245
14  The Stage     256
15  The Moment of (Constructed) Truth     276
16  Truth Woven Together     303
17  Spijkermakersstraat 9, 8:00 PM     335

*Index*     339

# PREFACE

*Any Resemblance Is Purely Intentional*

This book, like most books, tells a story. As it happens, a story of international law. To be more precise, this is an account of the everyday lives of the legal experts who populate international courts and tribunals; an exploration of their routine interactions and internal dynamics; and an exposé of how their tireless work, often carried out behind the scenes, steers the course of judicial proceedings and shapes the final outcomes of international disputes. In other words, this is resolutely a *law* book, written by an international lawyer for international lawyers.

So why the disclaimer? Well, because the way the story is told may be a little different from what you expect. Traditional legal scholarship 'is characterized by a pseudo-scientific neutral voice'[1] that speaks the language of rules, principles, procedures, and institutions. This book, by contrast, teems with people, activities, communications, and practices that cannot be tackled solely through 'rational discourse',[2] but require a bit of 'undisciplined writing'.[3] Its point is precisely to show that, beneath the smooth surface of the law, international judicial processes bubble with socio-professional struggles, clashing worldviews, unpredictable contingencies, and occasional humour.

More surprising, however, may be the style of storytelling. The narrative intersperses academic analysis with frequent forays into literary fiction. Its protagonists are not real persons, but archetypal characters who exemplify the various actors in the field. Each character has a background story, occupies a specific position, is moved by certain ideals or preoccupations – but none actually exists, not even those you think you recognize. The events chronicled in the book are equally fictional, as they concern

---

[1] A. Matasar, 'Storytelling and Legal Scholarship' (1992) 68(1) Chi-KentLRev 353.
[2] Ibid.
[3] J. Harris, 'Undisciplined Writing', in K. Blake Yancey (ed.), *Delivering College Composition: The Fifth Canon* (Boynton/Cook, 2006), 155.

judicial disputes that have not (yet) arisen in real life.[4] At best, they closely *resemble* the real-life situations that regularly confront international courts. In fact, a lot of effort went into making the action as credible and its setting as authentic as possible.

To facilitate reading, the academic and the literary passages are clearly signposted. The former are introduced by an asterisk (*) and the latter by a black circle (•). This typographical device enables you to exercise a fundamental right of the reader: the right to skip pages.[5] Be mindful, though, that the two sides of the narrative mirror each other and are meant to form a coherent whole. To every episode that moves the plot forward corresponds a description grounded in scholarly research, and vice versa. Neither side is inherently more 'true' than the other, and both contribute to portraying a full picture of the everyday making of international adjudication. Incidentally, the dual voice explains why the narrator refers to themselves as 'we'.

Before you say it – yes, this is a tricky sell. Experiments in (non-)fiction may be increasingly popular among novelists[6] but remain an unusual approach to *academic* production. The choice to narrate legal processes and institutions in those terms constitutes a radical departure from canon and, as such, entails a measure of risk. At best, it can offer a fresh, genre-bending take on the study of international courts and tribunals. At worst, it can alienate the more orthodox reader and relegate this book to the curio shelf of international law libraries.

For instance, you may legitimately wonder about the research methodology behind the story. What source material was used to support the analysis? How was it collected? And what makes it comprehensive and reliable rather than selective and anecdotal? Or, more fundamentally, you may question the value of literary writing when it comes to informing, reporting, or commenting on real life. If the narrative blends 'factual discourse' with 'fictional moves and liberties',[7] how can you tell what is real from what is fantasy? How can you distinguish the rigour of the essay from the unruliness of the novel? In short, how can you *trust* the narrator?

---

[4] But sometimes reality moves faster than fiction. The trade case imagined in the book concerns Indonesia's complaint against the European Union's regulations on palm oil. In November 2019, Indonesia *actually* initiated proceedings, which are currently ongoing. *European Union – Certain Measures Concerning Palm Oil and Oil Palm Crop-Based Biofuels*, WT/DS/593.
[5] D. Pennac, *Comme un Roman* (Gallimard, 1992), 79–80.
[6] See e.g. R. Langbaum, 'Capote's Nonfiction Novel' (1966) 35(3) AmSch 570.
[7] L. Pocci, '"Io So": A Reading of Roberto Saviano's "Gomorra"' (2011) 126(1) MLN 224, 226.

I believe some explanation is in order. Before the story kicks off and I turn into an impersonal 'we', let me spend a few words about the research and writing process that got me here. In this preface, I detail how I gathered information from the relevant sources, verified its completeness and accuracy, and analysed it under a unified framework. Then, I address the issue of style and discuss why I decided to present my findings in the form of plausible fiction. These clarifications do not have the ambition to question the politics of method in international legal scholarship. More modestly, they show that what could be mistaken as an act of subversion is, in fact, the result of meticulous investigation, careful reflection, and acute self-doubt. Think of it, if you will, as a making of the making of international law.

\*

My interest in the inner workings of the international judicial community arose from being part of it. From 2011 to 2019, I practiced international trade dispute settlement first as an attorney with a US law firm, then as a legal officer at the World Trade Organization (WTO). Those experiences initiated me to the myriad activities that punctuate the preparation, filing, litigation, deliberation, and resolution of international cases.

I quickly realized that the visible part of the process, which culminates in the issuance of a judgment, was the tip of an iceberg of invisible connections, networked interactions, and recursive practices. Astonishingly, international judges seemed to play a relatively minor role, entangled as they were in a close-knit fabric of socio-professional relations. Their solemn statements of the law were not *just* theirs but rather echoed the voices of countless other actors, including the litigants' counsel and representatives, the legal bureaucrats assisting the bench, and the academics critiquing the court's decisions. Communication, cooperation, and competition among these experts pervaded every corner of the court, yet remained largely off the radar of scholars and commentators.

Why such silence? How could literature on international adjudication be so preoccupied with foreground phenomena and so oblivious of background routines? I was intrigued. At the time, I was fresh from my studies at Harvard, where I had had an eye-opening encounter with Critical Legal Studies. My take-home was a certain curiosity about the soft tissue of supranational institutions, the power of discourse and ideology in the construction of normative orders, and the 'role of expertise and professional practice in the routine conflicts through which global political and economic life takes shape'.[8] Meanwhile, I had enrolled in a PhD at the Graduate Institute and was looking for ways to give my dissertation a critical edge.

An idea came to me. I would combine my insider knowledge as a practitioner with my outsider perspective as a researcher to shed a new light on the mundane, the quotidian, and the unextraordinary aspects of life at the court. I would trace the mysterious and circuitous paths that lead to the formation of seemingly unassailable judicial truths. I would describe, in 'micro-level detail',[9] what happens in the back rooms of international justice.

There came the first challenge: how, exactly, would I go about the exercise? By using which tools? The obvious starting point was to use my eyes and ears. As a participant-observer in the WTO community, I was in a privileged position to witness the exchanges that went on around me and make sense of how they were socially and culturally organized. The deployment of ethnography – if not as a 'hard' research method, at least as a 'soft' analytical posture[10] – guided my initial exploration of the field. I started taking notes of the meetings I attended, the conversations I had, the documents I read, and the gossip I was told. I frequently asked my peers and supervisors about their ambitions and preoccupations, paying attention to what they said and what they left unsaid. At the end of the working day, I would review my minutes and annotate them with additional questions and observations. The more I watched my co-workers' interactions, the more fascinated I grew. A hidden social world was unfolding before me with its own structures, logics, assumptions, and exclusionary mechanisms.

For all its excitement, however, this method of inquiry soon began to show its drawbacks. Unlike other participant-observers, I was not a temporary visitor to the trade law profession but sought to make an actual *career* in it. Not only did I have to work overtime to reconcile my official duties with field observation, but also I experienced the paradox of building relationships and friendships while studying them from a certain distance. Some of my colleagues were aware of being 'test subjects', but others were not. The more responsibilities I took on, the more

---

[8] D. Kennedy, *A World of Struggle: How Power, Law, and Expertise Shape Global Political Economy* (Princeton University Press, 2016), 2.
[9] G. A. Sarfaty, 'Corporate Actors as Translators in Transnational Lawmaking' (2021) 115 AJIL Unbound 278.
[10] See M. Halme-Tuomisaari, 'Toward Rejuvenated Inspiration with the Unbearable Lightness of Anthropology' (2021) 115 AJIL Unbound 283, 287.

people perceived me as one of them – and the guiltier I felt for spying on their reflexes and idiosyncrasies. My career progression was a problem in itself. By becoming increasingly embedded in the community, I was gradually gaining access to its innermost secrets, but also losing the ability to critically discern its invisible frameworks and ingrained presuppositions – much like David Foster Wallace's parable of the fish that does not know what water is.[11]

Worse still, my vantage point was severely limited. I was discovering the backstage of WTO dispute settlement, but my confidentiality obligations prevented me from disclosing those discoveries to the public. What happened in the rooms where litigation teams discussed strategies with their clients, where WTO secretariat officials wrote internal memoranda, and where judges reached their decisions had to stay in those rooms. Besides, I had little clue about the functioning of *other* international judicial institutions, like the International Court of Justice (ICJ) or regional human rights mechanisms. My occasional involvement in investor–state dispute settlement provided some pointers, but not enough to draw a proper comparison with the trade regime. Did those other institutions have the same division of labour among counsel, bureaucracies, adjudicators, and academics? Was litigation equally concentrated in the hands of few legal entrepreneurs? Did judicial assistants play a role equivalent to the WTO secretariat in advising their respective judges and drafting their rulings? In short, was the trade field unique or could my analysis extend to international adjudication at large?

Direct observation was no longer sufficient. I had to corroborate my findings by other means. The next thing I did was dig out all the information I could find in policy papers and scholarly articles. After all, I thought, we international legal practitioners are a vain bunch, and surely someone had to have written about their professional experiences. I was right. Academic journals – especially those boasting a 'practical' approach – were rife with the memoirs of sitting and retired judges,[12] top-tier litigators,[13] and

---

[11] See J. Krajeski, 'This Is Water', New Yorker, 19 September 2008, www.newyorker.com/books/page-turner/this-is-water.

[12] See e.g. the interviews contained in D. Terris, C. P. R. Romano, and L. Swigart, *The International Judge: An Introduction to the Men and Women Who Decide the World's Cases* (Oxford University Press, 2007), 39–48 (Navi Pillay), 92–101 (Thomas Buergenthal), 131–46 (Georges Abi-Saab), 180–90 (Cecilia Medina Quiroga), and 212–20 (John Hedigan).

[13] See e.g. A. Pellet, 'The Role of the International Lawyer in International Litigation', in C. Wickremasinghe (ed.), *The International Lawyer as a Practitioner* (British Institute of International and Comparative Law, 2000), 147.

senior registry officials,[14] who took stock of their time at court and shared juicy details about their day-to-day business. These writings offered a window into the secret workings of various tribunals, including the modes of appointment of adjudicators, the internal preparation of case files, and the basic features of deliberations. More importantly, they made it easier for me to avoid confidentiality issues and rely on statements published by others. In fact, a good portion of the material contained in this book comes from publicly available sources.

The question was how to *read* those sources. By their nature, the accounts of embedded practitioners tended to be selective, uncritical, and self-congratulatory. Their hints on the life of judicial communities were often buried under layers of coded language and professional affectation. Few bothered to mention the duller moments of their daily grind. Even fewer questioned the image of international justice as an emancipatory project, lest they be seen as biting the hand that fed them. The goal then became to see past the rose-tinted glasses and take a closer look at the underlying realities. My first-hand exposure to practice helped me separate the wheat from the chaff, but I needed additional data to complete my record.

Thus, I set out to conduct a series of semi-structured interviews with professionals working for international courts and tribunals. It took months to identify people with the right profiles and qualifications. The ideal candidates would not only have direct knowledge of the inner processes of adjudication but also be willing to talk about them openly. I expected judges, arbitrators, and government representatives to be tight-lipped, so I focused my search on private attorneys, clerks, and court bureaucrats. Thanks to my network, I eventually reached out to four lawyers affiliated with the ICJ registry, three employed at the registry of the European Court of Human Rights (ECtHR), two serving at the secretariat of the Inter-American Court of Human Rights (IACtHR), three assisting investment arbitrators as tribunal secretaries, and five acting as counsel in state-to-state and investor–state proceedings. About two-thirds of my prospective interviewees were in the early to mid stages of their careers, while the rest were senior practitioners. Ten were men and seven were women.

Preparing the questions was a delicate task. On the one hand, I wanted to give my interlocutors a safe space to share their views freely and

[14] See e.g. H. Thirlway, 'The Drafting of ICJ Decisions: Some Personal Recollections and Observations' (2006) 5(1) CJIL 15.

without withholding crucial bits of information. On the other hand, I was mindful that much of that information was covered by confidentiality, the breach of which could entail serious disciplinary consequences.[15] To balance these concerns, I negotiated the terms of each interview and incorporated them into a signed agreement. I undertook to protect the anonymity of my sources and not to make them directly or indirectly identifiable by name, title, specific tasks performed, gender, nationality, or other similar qualification. The interviewees would be entitled, upon request, to check the relevant parts of the manuscript. Three of them have asked to see the draft, and none has raised any objections.

With these precautions in place, my informants felt more comfortable speaking up. Intriguingly, their degree of openness seemed to vary by affiliation. For instance, IACtHR secretariat officers were quite relaxed and forthcoming, whereas ICJ clerks and ECtHR registry lawyers sounded more tense and circumspect. Every personality was unique and required a tailored approach. Sometimes I would offer breadcrumbs about my own experiences and see whether they resonated with the interviewee's. Other times I would express my guesses as statements of knowledge and check whether the interviewee confirmed or denied them. Often, I would simply try to establish a connection, a sense of camaraderie: 'Judge so-and-so wrote that deliberations happen this way. Now let's be serious: how do things *really* work?'.

As I compared and cross-checked the testimonies, the puzzle finally started to come together. Yes, the sample size paled in comparison to the almost 300 interviews conducted by Yves Dezalay and Bryant Garth for *Dealing in Virtue*.[16] And yes, one had to account for institutional differences across judicial regimes. However, the answers I collected presented striking commonalities. They pointed to similar social structures, patterns of practice, perceptions of competence, and standards of legal argument. They seemed to validate rather than refute the dynamics I had observed in the WTO community. They demonstrated, beyond any doubt, that there is more to international judicial processes than first meets the eye. By the end of the talks, I knew this was a story worth telling.

\*

All I had to do was organize the information, take a deep breath, and… get stuck. Suddenly, putting my findings in writing looked like an

---

[15] See *infra*, Chapter 6.
[16] Y. Dezalay and B. G. Garth, *Dealing in Virtue: International Commercial Arbitration and the Construction of a Transnational Legal Order* (University of Chicago Press, 1996), 9.

insurmountable challenge. The material I had gathered through ethnographic fieldwork, desk research, and interviews was rich and fascinating, but lacked the force of hard data. The secrecy surrounding courts and tribunals prevented me from offering conclusive evidence in support of my claims without giving out the identities of my sources. Hence, no matter how I turned the narrative, I would be unable to produce the measurable empirics[17] and actionable indicators[18] that contemporary scholarship values so highly.

*Quoi faire?* I turned to the classics for inspiration. Seminal essays like *Dealing in Virtue* and John Flood's *Barristers' Clerks*[19] relied heavily on the input of interviewees. To protect confidentiality, all quotes were anonymized and each source was referred to by a number (e.g. 'interviewee 17') or by a generic identifier (e.g. 'one clerk', 'another clerk', etc.). In *La Fabrique du Droit*, Bruno Latour took a slightly different approach to describe the judicial function of the French Conseil d'État: he redacted the case file numbers and modified names of the lawyers handling them, such that his chronicles read like '*des fictions vraisemblables*'.[20]

Going through these works assuaged my concerns. Other authors, faced with the same dilemmas, had traded off the verifiability of data for greater access to restricted material. In one way or another, all invited the reader to suspend disbelief and place their confidence in the narrator. Even more reassuring was the authors' composure. They did not bend over backwards to justify their choices, did not claim to remove 'all the messy juxtapositions and color combinations',[21] did not scramble to 'achieve relevance'[22] with the audience – but serenely stood by their 'hazy methodology'[23] in the face of critics.[24] There it was, my inspiration. I would follow their example. If I could not demonstrate my hypotheses by solid proof, I would come up

---

[17] See e.g. G. Shaffer and T. Ginsburg, 'The Empirical Turn in International Legal Scholarship' (2012) 106(1) AJIL 1.

[18] See M. Halme-Tuomisaari, 'Toward a Lasting Anthropology of International Law/Governance' (2016) 27(1) EJIL 235, 242.

[19] J. Flood, *Barristers' Clerks: The Law's Middlemen* (Manchester University Press, 1983).

[20] B. Latour, *La Fabrique du Droit: Une Ethnographie du Conseil d'État* (La Découverte, 2002), 9.

[21] Dezalay and Garth, *Dealing in Virtue*, 14.

[22] G. Simpson, 'The Sentimental Life of International Law' (2015) 3(1) LondRevIntlL 3, 28.

[23] Halme-Tuomisaari, 'Rejuvenated Inspiration', 287.

[24] And criticism there was indeed. See e.g. E. A. Schwartz, 'Book Review of "*Dealing in Virtue*"' (1997) 12(1) ICSID Rev/FILJ 229, 230 (lamenting that Dezalay and Garth's 'anecdotal' approach painted a 'misleading portrait of the world of international

with another solution, however '*boiteuse et bricolée*',[25] to gain the trust of my readers. Incidentally, wasn't that precisely what international courts do? Don't they ask the public to trust a process of truth production without knowing too much about it?

My doubts gone, I laid the foundations of the narrative. I knew what I wanted to write, but the how was still vague. Finding a credible voice as a storyteller was as crucial as the content of the story to be told. The '"feel" of professional competence is the outcome of style, more particularly of linguistic style'.[26] For several weeks I wondered about possible ways of representing the judicial backstage, the reactions they would elicit, and the imaginations they would engender.

The socio-legal classics I had consulted were masterful but somehow burdened by their own weight. The gaze of the social scientist was driven (and constrained) by the availability of empirics, their prose set on orderly patterns and structured phenomena. The rendering I had in mind was something else. I wished the audience to share my sense of discovery, my 'culture shock'[27] at the beliefs and behaviour of legal professionals. I needed a vocabulary that would capture the passions and the fears, the enthusiasm and the disillusionment, and the ideals and the cynicism that agitate international courts. I wanted to pepper the action with a bit of irony and *souplesse*.

Then, one day, it dawned on me. Why not replace the abstractions of academic discourse with the 'radically personalizing language'[28] of literary fiction? If confidentiality kept me from writing about real actors, why not imagine my own characters and let them take centre stage? Why not take the notion of *emplotment*, which is proper to any form of legal reasoning, and push it to its limits? The more I toyed with the idea, the more a novelesque approach seemed to fit my purpose. The appeal of that approach was twofold. First, it would add explanatory force and critical bite to the analysis. By focusing on what my characters did, said, and thought in their daily routines, I could weave together their material practices and inner

---

commercial arbitration'); S. Landsman, 'The Servants' (1985) 83(4) MichLRev 1105, 1112 (noting that Flood's '[c]oncentration on detail and anecdote' prevented his study from being 'systematic').

[25] Latour, *La Fabrique du Droit*, 9.
[26] M. Koskenniemi, 'Letter to the Editors of the Symposium' (1999) 93(2) AJIL 351, 357.
[27] A. Riles, 'Introduction to the Symposium on the Anthropology of International Law' (2021) 115 AJIL Unbound 268, 269.
[28] Koskenniemi, Symposium, 361.

processes, thus grasping nuances that would get lost in aggregate data. Second, it would make my arcane topic accessible to a wider readership, bridging the language barriers that separate law, social studies, and political theory.

I just needed the courage to take the plunge. I was not – I am not – a novelist, especially not in a language other than my native tongue. Concepts like *mise-en-scène* and *dramatis personae* were completely foreign to me. I had little guidance from existing scholarship, no comfort zone to fall back on. A warning echoed in my head: '[t]he pseudo-poet who writes his thesis in poetry is a pitiful writer (and probably a bad poet)'.[29] This could end up in a disaster. And yet, I was drawn to the prospect of pushing my thoughts in this direction, of continuing the line of '"critical" inventions which belong to literature while deforming its limits'.[30]

It has been four years since I decided to follow those instincts, and I do not regret a moment of it. Sure, the writing was tough slogging and faced me with new obstacles almost every day. A vignette was superfluous, another underdeveloped. This line of dialogue sounded stilted, that scene did not go anywhere. The most daunting issue was my own relationship with the story's protagonists. In order to be credible, each character would be *situated* in the narrative, that is, be endowed with a distinct personality and agenda, but also with blind spots and epistemic limitations. Only I, the narrator, would have the advantage of *distance* – the detachment necessary to see the ties that bound the characters together, imparted meaning and direction to their actions, and informed their experiences consciously and unconsciously.

Yet, it turned out, not even the narrator could be truly objective. For one thing, I was very much part of the community under scrutiny and, as such, carried my own assumptions and presuppositions. For another, my 'outside' perspective was still, by all purposes, a *chosen* perspective that modified the object of the narrative. The very act of taking up a point of view on the action, withdrawing from it to observe it from a distance, *constitutes* the action as a '*representation*'.[31] Hence, all I could do was to straddle the line between pure phenomenology – the primary and unmediated experience

---

[29] U. Eco, *How to Write a Thesis*, trans. C. Mongiat Farina and G. Farina (MIT Press, 2015), 150.
[30] J. Derrida, cit. in S. Muecke, 'The Fall: Fictocritical Writing' (2002) 8(4) *Parallax* 108.
[31] P. Bourdieu, *Outline of a Theory of Practice*, trans. R. Nice (Cambridge University Press, 1977), 2.

of the actors – and pure objectivism – the 'hypostatize[d] systems'[32] to which the actors respond. Hopefully, this 'middle ground' approach does justice to the complexity of each character, revealing them as *both* a player and an observer, an agent and a reagent, and a speaker and a listener.

Likewise, I was unsure what to make of the intersectional identities of my protagonists. At first, I thought that aspects like nationality, ethnicity, gender, sexuality, social status, education, and political beliefs should feature prominently as drivers of action and communication. As I progressed, however, I started to worry that too much emphasis on personal traits would end up obscuring the *collective* traits of the international judicial world. Indeed, this world perpetuates its cohesiveness precisely by depotentiating the individual and diluting personal positions to a pastiche of habits and conditioned reflexes.[33] Eventually, I stayed true to my focus on community dynamics, and left the baggage of privilege and oppression of each character at the door of courts and tribunals.

Despite these insecurities, the labour was made more joyful by the support of those around me. My doctoral supervisor, Andrea Bianchi, provided constant guidance and advice. The more I tinkered with narrative solutions, the more he encouraged me to press ahead. Thomas Schultz and Jean d'Aspremont, who read multiple iterations of the draft, believed in the project and offered valuable suggestions to improve its quality. The three anonymous readers who reviewed the book proposal delivered a thorough and constructive critique. To each of them does my deepest gratitude. I was also delighted to see many friends and colleagues eager to share insights and perspectives, some of which stand out as true eye-openers. Heartfelt thanks to Anne Coulon, Brian McGarry, Fuad Zarbiyev, Josef Ostřanský, Klara Polackova van der Ploeg, León Castellanos-Jankiewicz, Luca Pasquet, María de la Colina, Michele Potestà, Miguel Villamizar, Mikael Rask Madsen, and Shashank Kumar. Finally, I would be remiss not to mention my wife Federica, my parents Fedela and Roberto, my brother Filippo, and my sister Camilla. Without their unwavering love and care, perhaps this work would still have come about – but it would be a different work, for the author would be a different man.

Writing a story is a difficult business, and it is only for you, the reader, to decide if this book comes any close to success. If you are willing to give it a chance, you might perhaps find some truth in it. Even better – but this would really go beyond expectations – you might have some fun.

---

[32] Bourdieu, *Theory of Practice*, 72.
[33] See *infra*, Chapter 13.

# ABBREVIATIONS

## Abbreviations in the Book

| | |
|---|---|
| ABS | Appellate Body Secretariat |
| ACHR | Organization of American States, *American Convention on Human Rights* (22 November 1969), UNTS 1144, 123 |
| ACWL | Advisory Centre on WTO Law |
| BIT | Bilateral investment treaty |
| CJEU | Court of Justice of the European Union |
| DLM | Department of Legal Matters |
| DSU | *Dispute Settlement Rules: Understanding on Rules and Procedures Governing the Settlement of Disputes*, Marrakesh Agreement Establishing the World Trade Organization, Annex 2 (15 April 1994), UNTS 1869, 401 |
| ECHR | Council of Europe, *European Convention for the Protection of Human Rights and Fundamental Freedoms, as amended by Protocols Nos. 11 and 14* (4 November 1950), ETS 5 |
| ECtHR | European Court of Human Rights |
| FTA | Free-trade agreement |
| GATS | *General Agreement on Trade in Services*, Marrakesh Agreement Establishing the World Trade Organization, Annex 1B (15 April 1994), UNTS 1869, 183 |
| GATT | *General Agreement on Tariffs and Trade* (30 October 1947), UNTS 55, 194 |
| IACHR | Inter-American Commission on Human Rights |
| IACtHR | Inter-American Court of Human Rights |
| ICJ | International Court of Justice |
| ICSID | International Centre for Settlement of Investment Disputes |
| ICTY | International Criminal Tribunal for Former Yugoslavia |
| ILC | International Law Commission |
| ILO | International Labour Organization |
| ISDS | Investor–state dispute settlement |
| ITLOS | International Tribunal for the Law of the Sea |
| LCIA | London Court of International Arbitration |
| MPIA | Multi-Party Interim Appeal Arbitration Arrangement |

| | |
|---|---|
| MSEN | Multi-sourced equivalent norm |
| NGO | Non-governmental organization |
| PCA | Permanent Court of Arbitration |
| PCIJ | Permanent Court of International Justice |
| PJP | Pilot judgment procedure |
| QC | Queen's Counsel |
| RSPO | Roundtable on Sustainable Palm Oil |
| TBT | Agreement *Agreement on Technical Barriers to Trade*, Marrakesh Agreement Establishing the World Trade Organization, Annex 1 (15 April 1994), UNTS 1868, 120 |
| UN | United Nations |
| UNCITRAL | United Nations Commission on International Trade Law |
| VCCR | United Nations, *Vienna Convention on Consular Relations* (24 April 1963), UNTS 500, 95 |
| VCLT | United Nations, *Vienna Convention on the Law of Treaties* (23 May 1969), UNTS 1155, 331 |
| WTO | World Trade Organization |

## Academic Journals

| | |
|---|---|
| AJIL | American Journal of International Law |
| AJIL Unbound | American Journal of International Law Unbound |
| AmJJurisprud | American Journal of Jurisprudence |
| AmJPolSci | American Journal of Political Science |
| AmPolSciRev | American Political Science Review |
| AmSch | The American Scholar |
| AmUIntlLRev | American University International Law Review |
| AnnuRevAnthropol | Annual Review of Anthropology |
| ArbIntl | Arbitration International |
| ASILPROC | American Society of International Law Proceedings |
| AustYBIL | Australian Yearbook of International Law |
| BaltYIL | Baltic Yearbook of International Law |
| BerkeleyJIntlL | Berkeley Journal of International Law |
| BrJPolSci | British Journal of Political Science |
| BrJSociol | British Journal of Sociology |
| BrookLRev | Brooklyn Law Review |
| BYBIL | British Yearbook of International Law |
| CAAJ | Contemporary Asian Arbitration Journal |
| CalLRev | California Law Review |
| CILJ | Cambridge Journal of International and Comparative Law |

| | |
|---|---|
| CardozoLRev | Cardozo Law Review |
| CaseWResLRev | Case Western Reserve Law Review |
| ChiJIntlL | Chicago Journal of International Law |
| Chi-KentLRev | Chicago-Kent Law Review |
| CJIL | Chinese Journal of International Law |
| ColumJTransnatlL | Columbia Journal of Transnational Law |
| CompPolStud | Comparative Political Studies |
| CornellIntlLJ | Cornell International Law Journal |
| CLP | Current Legal Problems |
| CritInq | Critical Inquiry |
| DenvJIntlL&Pol | Denver Journal of International Law and Policy |
| DispResIntl | Dispute Resolution International |
| DispResJ | Dispute Resolution Journal |
| DukeLJ | Duke Law Journal |
| EHRLR | European Human Rights Law Review |
| EJST | European Journal of Social Theory |
| ELJ | European Law Journal |
| EmoryJIntlDispRes | Emory Journal of International Dispute Resolution |
| Ethics&IntlAff | Ethics and International Affairs |
| EurJIntlRel | European Journal of International Relations |
| EurJLegStud | European Journal of Legal Studies |
| FlaLRev | Florida Law Review |
| FordhamIntlLJ | Fordham International Law Journal |
| FordhamLR | Fordham Law Review |
| GeogrZ | Geographische Zeitschrift |
| GeoJIntlL | Georgetown Journal of International Law |
| GeoLJ | Georgetown Law Journal |
| GTCJ | Global Trade and Customs Journal |
| HarvIntlLJ | Harvard International Law Journal |
| HarvLRev | Harvard Law Review |
| HastingsIntl&CompLRev | Hastings International and Comparative Law Review |
| HastingsLJ | Hastings Law Journal |
| HRLRev | Human Rights Law Review |
| HumRtsQ | Human Rights Quarterly |
| ICLQ | International and Comparative Law Quarterly |
| ICLR | International Community Law Review |
| ICON | International Journal of Constitutional Law |
| ICSID Rev/FILJ | ICSID Review/Foreign Investment Law Journal |
| IJHR | International Journal of Human Rights |

| | |
|---|---|
| IntlJLContext | International Journal of Law in Context |
| IntlLawyer | The International Lawyer |
| IntlOrg | International Organization |
| IntlOrgLRev | International Organization Law Review |
| IntlPolSciRev | International Political Science Review |
| IntlStudQ | International Studies Quarterly |
| IntlTheory | International Theory |
| IsLR | Israel Law Review |
| ItYBIL | Italian Yearbook of International Law |
| JapanYBIL | Japanese Yearbook of International Law |
| JEP | Journal of Economic Perspectives |
| JIDS | Journal of International Dispute Settlement |
| JIEL | Journal of International Economic Law |
| JIntlArb | Journal of International Arbitration |
| JIntlL&Econ | Journal of International Law and Economics |
| JITLP | Journal of International Trade Law and Policy |
| JL&Society | Journal of Law and Society |
| JLegEduc | Journal of Legal Education |
| JTransnatLawPol | Journal of Transnational Law and Policy |
| JWIT | Journal of World Investment and Trade |
| L&ContempProbs | Law and Contemporary Problems |
| L&Crit | Law and Critique |
| L&Phil | Law and Philosophy |
| L&SocRev | Law and Society Review |
| LegTheory | Legal Theory |
| LJIL | Leiden Journal of International Law |
| LondRevIntlL | London Review of International Law |
| LoyLAIntl&CompLRev | Loyola of Los Angeles International and Comparative Law Review |
| LPICT | The Law and Practice of International Courts and Tribunals |
| MarqueeLRev | Marquee Law Review |
| MJECL | Maastricht Journal of European and Comparative Law |
| MichJIntlL | Michigan Journal of International Law |
| MichLRev | Michigan Law Review |
| MLN | Modern Language Notes |
| MLR | Modern Law Review |
| NILR | Netherlands International Law Review |
| NQHR | Netherlands Quarterly of Human Rights |

| | |
|---|---|
| NWULR | Northwestern University Law Review |
| NYIL | Netherlands Yearbook of International Law |
| NYUJILP | New York University Journal of International Law and Politics |
| NYULRev | New York University Law Review |
| NYURevL&SocChange | New York University Review of Law and Social Change |
| OhioNULRev | Ohio Northern University Law Review |
| Oñati Socio-Leg Ser | Oñati Socio-Legal Series |
| OrLRev | Oregon Law Review |
| OttawaLRev | Ottawa Law Review |
| PaceYBIntlL | Pace Yearbook of International Law |
| PeenYBArb&Med | Penn Yearbook on Arbitration and Mediation |
| PennStIntlLRev | Penn State International Law Review |
| PeppDispResLJ | Pepperdine Dispute Resolution Law Journal |
| PerspPolitics | Perspective on Politics |
| Phil&PubAff | Philosophy and Public Affairs |
| QJPolSci | Quarterly Journal of Political Science |
| RAE | Review of Artistic Education |
| RBDI | Revue Belge de Droit International |
| RegentJL&PubPol | Regent Journal of Law and Public Policy |
| ResL&Soc | Research in Law and Sociology |
| RevIntlStud | Review of International Studies |
| RevIntPolitEcon | Review of International Political Economy |
| RGDIP | Revue Générale de Droit International Public |
| RIEJ | Revue Interdisciplinaire d'Études Juridiques |
| RMUE | Revue du Marché Unique Européen |
| SCalLRev | Southern California Law Review |
| Signs | Signs: Journal of Women in Culture and Society |
| SociolTheory | Sociological Theory |
| SocSciInf | Social Science Information |
| StanLRev | Stanford Law Review |
| SydLRev | Sydney Law Review |
| TDR | The Drama Review |
| TexIntlLJ | Texas International Law Journal |
| Theory&Soc'y | Theory and Society |
| TL&D | Trade Law and Development |
| TransAmPhilSoc | Transactions of the American Philosophical Society |
| TransnatlL&ContempProbs | Transnational Law and Contemporary Problems |
| TulJIntl&CompL | Tulane Journal of International and Comparative Law |

| | |
|---|---|
| UCinLRev | University of Cincinnati Law Review |
| UNYB | Max Planck Yearbook of United Nations Law |
| UPaLRev | University of Pennsylvania Law Review |
| URichLRev | University of Richmond Law Review |
| USFLRev | University of San Francisco Law Review |
| VaJIntlL | Virginia Journal of International Law |
| VandJTransnatlL | Vanderbilt Journal of Transnational Law |
| VillanovaLRev | Villanova Law Review |
| WashUJurRev | Washington University Jurisprudence Review |
| WorldEcon | The World Economy |
| YaleJIntlL | Yale Journal of International Law |
| YaleLJ | Yale Law Journal |
| YaleRev | Yale Review |
| YaleStudWorldPubOrd | Yale Studies in World Public Order |
| ZaöRV | Zeitschrift für ausländisches öffentliches Recht und Völkerrecht |

# 1

## Carnegieplein 2, 10:00 AM

'*La Cour!*'
Despite an optimistic weather forecast, it is a cold and gloomy morning in The Hague. A faint sunlight filters through the stained glass windows of the Great Hall of Justice and reflects off the brass chandeliers hanging from the vault. Resplendent at the centre of a large oil painting, the Goddess of Peace gazes upon the room packed with people. The attendees are all in business attire, except a handful of attorneys wearing the formal garments of their national bars. The tension is palpable, the atmosphere almost rarefied. Someone in the front row lets out a raucous cough; someone in the back is nervously clicking a pen.

In a few moments, the Goddess' wishes will be granted. The International Court of Justice (ICJ) is about to render its judgment in a complex territorial dispute between the Philippines and Malaysia. After decades of heated controversy, bitter confrontation, and even deadly skirmishes, this matter will be settled once and for all. The Law will be said, as per the ancient meaning of 'jurisdiction'. Or, if you prefer, the Law itself will make its eternal voice heard through the temporal mouth of the Court's President, Judge José Ignacio Rosas.

Upon hearing the bailiff's stentorian announcement – '*La Cour!*' – the whole crowd stands up. Fourteen men and three women, all in black robes and white jabots, slowly emerge from a small side door. One by one, they take their assigned seats at the podium. After a moment of silence, President Rosas clears his throat:

> *Bonjour, veuillez vous asseoir. La séance est ouverte. La Cour se réunit aujourd'hui, conformément à l'Article 58 de son Statut, pour rendre son arrêt dans l'affaire relative à la souveraineté sur le Territoire de Sabah, Bornéo du Nord (Philippines contre Malaisie) ....*
>
> Good morning, please take your seats. The sitting is open. The Court meets today, pursuant to Article 58 of its Statute, to render its judgment in the case concerning the sovereignty over the Territory of Sabah, North Borneo (Philippines/Malaysia) ....

The rite is beginning. It will go on for about two hours, during which the President will read out the Court's lengthy decision almost verbatim, before turning the floor to the Registrar for the statement of the *dispositif* (the operative provisions of the judgment). Everyone is ready to join in this communion, this celebration of the triumph of Reason and Fairness over the irrationality and cynicism of Politics. The Great Hall of Justice is transfiguring, once again, into the inner sanctum of international law, under the Goddess' benevolent watch.

Amid the solemnity of the ceremony, no one notices a young lady sitting in the overhead balcony, next to the press. Fiddling with her red curls, Sophie contemplates the scene from above, her pale green eyes searching for familiar faces in the crowd. She immediately recognizes her boss, Judge Jürgen Lehmann, sitting to the right of President Rosas. Sophie has not spoken to her mentor for days, precisely since the text of the judgment went out for the final editing. She realizes, with some surprise, that this is the longest silence between them since the dispute kicked off, over three years ago. If one were to count, Sophie has since spent more time with Judge Lehmann than with anyone else, her girlfriend Norma included. The old 'German Lion' – a nickname Jürgen Lehmann pretends to dislike – looks proud and relaxed today. Who wouldn't be, after emerging victorious from a fight over the outcomes of a case? Sophie is equally satisfied, but her satisfaction is tinged with pensiveness. All the battles they fought together, their shared struggles to cement the majority opinion, and the evenings spent trying to overcome unexpected stumbling blocks, will be forgotten as soon as the ritual ends.

As she is about to get lost in her thoughts, Sophie spots her friend Filibert N'Diaye, a senior associate with Burnham & Hutz LLP, sitting next to the Philippines' lead counsel (what's his name? Liam? Leonard? Sophie can't remember). Filibert looks exhausted. He must be relieved that this whole business is finally coming to an end. No matter the final result – and Sophie already knows the result will *not* be in his client's favour – Filibert's late shifts in the office are over. Soon, he will be free to take holidays, spend some long overdue time with his family, and eventually turn to a new dossier, already waiting on his desk. Sophie remembers the conversations they had in their law school days, sipping coffee at a Starbucks near Astor Place. The future was uncertain back then, as New York University (NYU) tuition fees had left them both in need of decently paying jobs. Still, Sophie and Filibert were confident that, one day, they would join the 'invisible college of international lawyers'[1] – the exclusive club of women and men who sit at the centre of the international legal order. Little did they know that their journey would be that quick and that, only a few years later, they would find themselves together in *that* room.

Sophie's mind keeps wandering. Some of her former teachers and fellow PhDs are probably watching the live webcast. As soon as the judgment becomes public, legions of scholars will start appraising its merits, dissecting its every technical detail, and filling in the blanks in the Court's reasoning with deep theoretical understanding. The more traditional pundits will no doubt lament a certain lack of clarity in the Court's analysis. In particular, they may argue that the Court's reading of a crucial legal source – an ancient deed signed by His Majesty the Sultan of Sulu – lacks the rigour required under the Vienna Convention on the Law of Treaties (VCLT).[2] Other commentators will take a less technical and more normative stance. They may praise the Court's willingness to move past the colonial history of South-East Asia, or trace the evolution of the Court's views on statehood from 1947 to date. Yet other observers will focus on the discursive elements of the opinion. They may, for example, count the number of times the Court has referred to the decisions of other international tribunals, in order to test whether, in recent years, the ICJ has been striving to reunify a fragmented legal system.[3] Whatever the angle, today's decision will dominate international law blogs for quite some time: 'the Court meant this'; 'the Court meant that'; 'long live the Court'.

Sophie bets that the inevitable plethora of articles and case notes will all share one essential feature: they will take today's judgment as the *starting point* of the analysis – the irreducible building block upon which to develop their hypotheses. Only a few will dare to peek behind the curtain and investigate the processes that led to the formation of the judgment. And even those who seek to discern the true *'intention ... du juge'* (usually to prove either its *'liberté ... radicale'* or, conversely, its being *'logiquement ... déterminée'*[4]) will concentrate their efforts on the text that President Rosas is now reading before his distinguished audience.

---

[1] O. Schachter, 'The Invisible College of International Lawyers' (1977) 72(2) NWULR 217.
[2] United Nations, *Vienna Convention on the Law of Treaties* (23 May 1969), UNTS 1155, 331.
[3] See e.g. M. Andenas, 'Reassertion and Transformation: From Fragmentation to Convergence in International Law' (2015) 46(3) GeoJIntlL 685.
[4] E. Jouannet, 'La Motivation ou le Mystère de la Boîte Noire', in H. Ruiz Fabri and J.-M. Sorel (eds.), *La Motivation des Décisions des Juridictions Internationales* (Pedone, 2008) 251, 271.

Who could blame them? After all, that text constitutes the sole tangible result of international adjudication. That orderly series of words, sentences, and paragraphs is the artefact that embodies the ethos and aspirations of our discipline. If you deconstruct the artefact, its magic vanishes. A believer cannot question the manner in which the scriptures came about, lest they lose faith in the voice of God. A respectable international lawyer cannot unravel the hidden ways the Court's 'holy writs'[5] were cobbled together, lest they destroy the very foundation of their inquiry and undermine the possibility to say anything meaningful. In law, as in religion, you are supposed to play with what you are given. Right?

Well, not quite. At least for Sophie, today's judgment is not the starting point, but *the end* of a strenuous journey that began over three years ago, when the Philippines decided to turn its political grievances against Malaysia into a set of legal claims. Considering what has happened since, that seems like a lifetime ago. As she silently watches the ceremony unfold, Sophie cannot but grin and ponder:

> If only they knew what a ride it was to get here …. If they knew how many people worked behind the scenes to shape the content of this decision, they would think twice before praising or faulting those seventeen folks at the podium. If they had any idea of the conversations, confrontations, and doubts that punctuated the process, maybe they would pause before calling the ruling a mere elucidation of the law. If they could get a glimpse of the endless series of choices through which certain elements of the case made it to the final text, while others ended up in the dustbin of discarded possibilities, they would probably share the slight vertigo I am experiencing now.

For a split second, Sophie's eyes cross those of the Goddess of Peace. Perhaps due to the emotion of the moment, or perhaps because of the fatigue accumulated, Sophie could swear that the Goddess is winking at her.

What a three years it has been.

\*

The story you are about to read is the story of those three years. Or, more accurately, it is the story of the practices, the interactions, and the confrontations that occur every day within the international judicial community. Throughout the long and winding path that leads to an international judgment, countless people work incessantly to promote their competing

---

[5] R. Jennings, 'The Role of the International Court of Justice' (1998) 68(1) BYBIL 1, 41.

views about the persuasiveness of legal argument,[6] assert their authority over the issues at stake,[7] and maximize their capital within their professional field.[8] These endogenous dynamics, so often overlooked in scholarly accounts, are not a corollary to the judicial process – they *are* the process. We can hardly understand the results of an international case without inquiring into the discrete operations that marked its every step. Likewise, we cannot explain the behaviour of international courts and tribunals by focusing on the judges alone, in isolation from the professional milieu that surrounds them. Agents, counsel, advisers, scientific experts, clerks, registries, secretariats, and academics – they all partake in the development of legal discourse and the definition of judicial outcomes.

The idea behind this book, simply put, is that the ways in which these inner circles of legal professionals interact, cooperate, and clash in their everyday routines have a crucial impact on international judgments: *more so*, dare we say, than the substantive norms that adjudicators are called upon to interpret and apply; and *more so* than the external political pressure exerted on international courts and tribunals.

Some of you may dismiss this idea as obscene. We would agree. The word 'obscene' comes from the Latin *ob scaena*, meaning 'off stage'. Indeed, this story seeks to mark a symbolic movement away from the ceremonial courtroom setting where the decision is read – where international law is *said* – towards the muted ambience of deliberation rooms, the buzz of printers in the backroom offices, the friendly chatter of cafeterias – where international law is *constructed*.

The plot will take us to the seats of five international adjudicative bodies: the ICJ, the European Court of Human Rights (ECtHR), the Inter-American Court of Human Rights (IACtHR), the World Trade Organization (WTO) dispute settlement system, and an ideal-typical

---

[6] See e.g. A. Bianchi, 'Textual Interpretation and (International) Law Reading: The Myth of (In)Determinacy and the Genealogy of Meaning', in P. Bekker, R. Dolzer, and M. Waibel (eds.), *Making Transnational Law Work in the Global Economy: Essays in Honour of Detlev Vagts* (Cambridge University Press, 2010) 34, 49; I. Venzke, *How Interpretation Makes International Law: On Semantic Change and Normative Twists* (Oxford University Press, 2012), 5; J. d'Aspremont, 'The Multidimensional Process of Interpretation: Content-Determination and Law-Ascertainment Distinguished', in A. Bianchi, D. Peat, and M. Windsor (eds.), *Interpretation in International Law* (Oxford University Press, 2015) 111, 114.

[7] See e.g. K. T. Gaubatz and M. MacArthur, 'How International Is "International" Law?' (2001) 22(2) MichJIntlL 239, 246; G. Shaffer and J. P. Trachtman, 'Interpretation and Institutional Choice at the WTO' (2011) 52(1) VaJIntlL 103, 122.

[8] P. Bourdieu, 'The Force of Law: Toward a Sociology of the Juridical Field' (1987) 38(5) HastingsLJ 805, 817.

investment arbitral tribunal. There, we will trace the unfolding of judicial proceedings from the preparatory stages, when the complaining party starts to put together its case, to the closing moment, when the final judgment is issued to the public. At every turn, we will reveal the myriad ways in which Sophie, Filibert, Judge Lehmann, and various other members of the international judicial community contribute to the process. We will see, among other things, how counsel help their clients transform amorphous masses of facts and grievances into structured sets of claims and arguments; how institutional bureaucracies shape the adjudicators' decisions by conducting legal research, preparing memoranda, and drafting the rulings; and how specialized scholars systematize case law and develop a common grammar for a shared understanding of the discipline.

Be warned: in the pages that follow, you will not find an exhaustive review of the official powers vested in those actors, nor a treatise on the formal rules that govern their procedures. What you *will* find is a detailed account of the social structures, the professional relationships, the shared assumptions, the tacit understandings, and the sites of struggle that make up the international judicial field. By the end of the book, most of you will have discovered a wealth of 'otherwise hidden activities that illuminate international tribunals' inner workings'.[9] Some of you may have come to appreciate the 'vascularization' and the numerous connections that allow judicial institutions to breathe.[10] All of you will have been reminded, time and again, that '[i]nternational law is a group of *people* pursuing projects in a common professional language.'[11]

\*

If you are still debating whether to continue reading, let us say that we are neither the first nor the last storyteller to attempt such a feat. In recent years, numerous voices have emerged that stress the need to open the 'black box' of international courts and tribunals and shed light on their inner workings.[12] This call to arms does not arise in a vacuum but marks the next step in the evolution of scholarly sensibilities, eager to investigate the role of international adjudication in contemporary world affairs.

---

[9] J. L. Dunoff and M. A. Pollack, 'International Judicial Practices: Opening the "Black Box" of International Courts' (2018) 40(1) MichJIntlL 47, 49.

[10] B. Latour, *The Making of Law: An Ethnography of the Conseil d'État*, trans. M. Brilman and A. Pottage (Polity Press, 2010), 5.

[11] D. W. Kennedy, 'One, Two, Three, Many Legal Orders: Legal Pluralism and the Cosmopolitan Dream' (2007) 31(3) NYURevL&SocChange 641, 650 (original emphasis).

[12] See e.g. Dunoff and Pollack, 'International Judicial Practices'.

The literature on the topic has come a long way and nowadays offers a rich menu of approaches drawing from international law, international relations, organization theory, and social studies. Yet, we would argue, most observers still conceive of international courts as 'reified collectives forming separate and self-standing units of analysis',[13] thereby remaining oblivious to the socio-professional communities in which adjudicators are immersed. A brief overview of the main narratives may help elucidate this argument and better explain why we see merit in telling this story.

Traditional scholars moved from the 'uncontroversial' (!) premise that the international legal system was nothing but 'the aggregate of the legal norms governing international relations'.[14] That system was populated by abstract entities, such as sovereign states and the other formal 'subjects' of international law,[15] seeking protection of their rights before 'apersonal' adjudicative bodies.[16] International judges were seen – and, perhaps, still see themselves – as the impartial 'guardians of the law'.[17] Herculean individuals of 'superhuman intellectual power and patience',[18] they were tasked with *ascertaining* the preordained meaning of the relevant norms,[19] *clarifying* their ambiguities,[20] and mechanically *applying* them to

---

[13] A. Vauchez, 'Communities of International Litigators', in C. P. R. Romano, K. J. Alter, and Y. Shany (eds.), *The Oxford Handbook of International Adjudication* (Oxford University Press, 2014) 655–6.

[14] P. Weil, 'Towards Relative Normativity in International Law?' (1983) 77(3) AJIL 413.

[15] A. Bianchi, 'The Game of Interpretation in International Law: The Players, the Cards, and Why the Game Is Worth the Candle', in A. Bianchi, D. Peat, and M. Windsor (eds.), *Interpretation in International Law* (Oxford University Press, 2015) 34, 39.

[16] G. Messenger, 'The Practice of Litigation at the ICJ: The Role of Counsel in the Development of International Law', in M. Hirsch and A. Lang (eds.), *Research Handbook on the Sociology of International Law* (Edward Elgar, 2018) 208, 210.

[17] Terris, Romano, and Swigart, *The International Judge*, xix. See also e.g. E. U. Petersmann, 'Multilevel Judicial Governance as Guardian of the Constitutional Unity of International Economic Law' (2008) 30(3) LoyLAIntl&CompLRev 367, 378; A. Føllesdal, 'To Guide and Guard International Judges' (2014) 46(3) NYUJILP 793–5.

[18] R. Dworkin, *The Law's Empire* (Harvard University Press, 1986), 239.

[19] J. Klabbers, 'Virtuous Interpretation', in M. Fitzmaurice, O. Elias, and P. Merkouris (eds.), *Treaty Interpretation and the Vienna Convention on the Law of Treaties: 30 Years On* (Martinus Nijhoff, 2010) 17, 23. See also I. Johnstone, *The Power of Deliberation: International Law, Politics and Organizations* (Oxford University Press, 2011), 35; I. Venzke, 'The Role of International Courts as Interpreters and Developers of the Law: Working Out the Jurisgenerative Practice of Interpretation' (2011) 34(1) LoyLAIntl&CompLRev 99–100; Latour, *The Making of Law*, 142.

[20] H. Lauterpacht, *The Development of International Law by the International Court* (Steven and Sons, 1958), 66.

the disputed facts.[21] To better carry out these duties, judges could resort to a host of codified doctrines, such as the methods of treaty interpretation set out in Articles 31 and 32 of the VCLT, which offered objective and neutral guidance on how to read legal sources. Rigorous and uniform adherence to those doctrines would enable the interpreter to '*deduce* the meaning exactly of what ha[d] been consented to' and reach logical and unassailable conclusions.[22]

This formalist conception, rooted in 'classical legal thought',[23] knew its peak in the aftermath of the Cold War. That is the moment when international law entered its 'post–ontological era',[24] that is when its effectiveness and 'lawness' ceased to be questioned. Indeed, the fall of the Berlin Wall was accompanied by the explosive expansion of international adjudication. Within the span of a decade, dozens of new judicial mechanisms were established, including the WTO dispute settlement system, its homologue under the North-American Free Trade Association (NAFTA), the International Tribunal for the Law of the Sea (ITLOS), the International Criminal Tribunals for Former Yugoslavia (ICTY) and Rwanda, the International Criminal Court, and the mixed tribunals for Lebanon and Sierra-Leone. Investor–state dispute settlement (ISDS), which had remained dormant throughout the 1980s, suddenly rose to prominence as a central governance node.[25] Preexisting mechanisms, like the ECtHR, were overhauled to facilitate the filing of complaints and broaden the pool of potential applicants. As a result, the current landscape of international adjudication sees the simultaneous operation of roughly thirty standing

---

[21] C. Wells, 'Situated Decisionmaking' (1990) 63 SCalLRev 1727, 1732–3.

[22] A. Orakhelashvili, *The Interpretation of Acts and Rules in Public International Law* (Oxford University Press, 2008), 286 (emphasis added). See also Venzke, *How Interpretation Makes International Law*, 50; J.-M. Sorel and V. Boré-Eveno, 'Article 31', in O. Corten and P. Klein (eds.), *The Vienna Conventions on the Law of Treaties: A Commentary* (Oxford University Press, 2011) 804, 806.

[23] D. Kennedy, 'Towards a Historical Understanding of Legal Consciousness: The Case of Classical Legal Thought in America, 1850–1940' (1980) 3 ResL&Soc 3.

[24] T. M. Franck, *Fairness in International Law and Institutions* (Clarendon Press, 1995), 6. See also J. d'Aspremont, 'The Professionalisation of International Law', in J. d'Aspremont et al. (eds.), *International Law as a Profession* (Cambridge University Press, 2017) 19, 23.

[25] According to the statistics of the United Nations Conference on Trade and Development (UNCTAD), by the end of 2011, states had signed 3,164 international investment agreements – comprising 2,833 bilateral investment treaties (BITs) and 331 other investment agreements. UNCTAD, World Investment Report 2012, UN Doc. No. UNCTAD/WIR/2012, 84 (2012). See also B. E. Allen and T. Soave, 'Jurisdictional Overlap in WTO Dispute Settlement and Investment Arbitration' (2014) 30(1) ArbIntl 1, 4.

courts and hundreds of ad hoc tribunals.[26] Together, these bodies have rendered almost 40,000 rulings on a wide array of contentious political, economic, and security issues.[27]

As the dockets filled up, international lawyers rejoiced. At last, international law had teeth.[28] At last, they could focus on 'real law' – real cases decided by real judges – on par with domestic law specialists.[29] The 'new terrain'[30] of international adjudication led to the proliferation of treatises systematizing the case law of the various courts, evaluating the quality and rigour of their reasoning, and exploring a variety of jurisdictional and procedural matters.[31] Long relegated to the margins of scholarly analysis, judicial interpretation suddenly became the obsession of international lawyers, playing out as 'the functional equivalent of truth' in international legal discourse.[32]

To be sure, some feared that the proliferation of adjudicatory bodies, each with its own focus on a sectoral subject matter (human rights, trade, investment, law of the sea, etc.), might give rise to conflicting rulings and threaten the coherence of 'general' international law.[33] Yet, these were but 'anxieties'[34] that could be easily assuaged by resort to

---

[26] For a more comprehensive account, see C. P. R. Romano, K. J. Alter, and Y. Shany (eds.), *The Oxford Handbook of International Adjudication* (Oxford University Press, 2014), annexed taxonomic timeline. See also J. I. Charney, 'Third Party Dispute Settlement and International Law' (1998) 36(1&2) ColumJTransnatlL 65, 69–70; T. Buergenthal, 'Proliferation of International Courts and Tribunals: Is It Good or Bad?' (2001) 14(2) LJIL 267, 271–2.

[27] See K. J. Alter, *The New Terrain of International Law: Courts, Politics, Rights* (Princeton University Press, 2014), 4; Dunoff and Pollack, 'International Judicial Practices', 47.

[28] See generally J. I. Charney, 'The Impact on the International Legal System of the Growth of International Courts and Tribunals' (1999) 31(4) NYUJILP 697; G. Hafner, 'Pros and Cons Ensuing from Fragmentation of International Law' (2004) 25(4) MichJIntlL 859; G. Abi-Saab, 'Fragmentation or Unification: Some Concluding Remarks' (1999) 31(4) NYUJILP 919.

[29] J. E. Alvarez, 'The New Dispute Settlers: (Half) Truths and Consequences' (2003) 38(3) TexIntlLJ 405, 406.

[30] Alter, *The New Terrain*.

[31] Dunoff and Pollack, 'International Judicial Practices', 48.

[32] Klabbers, 'Virtuous Interpretation', 18 (quoting D. W. Kennedy, 'The Turn to Interpretation' (1985) 58 SCalLRev 251, 265).

[33] See e.g. Buergenthal, 'Proliferation of International Courts', 272; J. Calamita, 'Countermeasures and Jurisdiction: Between Effectiveness and Fragmentation' (2010) 42(2) GeoJIntlL 1.

[34] M. Koskenniemi and P. Leino, 'Fragmentation of International Law? Postmodern Anxieties', 15(3) LJIL 553 (2002).

conflict-management techniques like 'systemic integration',[35] *lex posterior, lex specialis*,[36] *res judicata, lis pendens,* judicial comity,[37] and the like.[38] A careful use of these tools would enable courts to 'interpret away' most potential frictions.[39] At any rate, the international community had little time to waste with these qualms: it was too busy celebrating the judicialization of international relations,[40] the victory of the international rule of law over the cynicism of state politics,[41] and the new normalcy where 'the rules of civilised behaviour would come to govern international life'.[42]

Along this triumphal march, some prophesied that international judges would coalesce into an 'integrated and interconnected system'[43] forged more by their 'common function' than by the differences in the sectoral rules they applied and the parties appearing before them.[44] The emergence of this 'global community of courts' would ultimately lead to a 'global jurisprudence' based on common values like due process and universal human rights.[45] Amid the general enthusiasm, those who dared questioning the objectivity of law or alluded its underlying ideologies

---

[35] See e.g. M. McLachlan, 'The Principle of Systemic Integration and Article 31(3)(c) of the Vienna Convention', 54(2) ICLQ 279 (2005).

[36] See e.g. M. Akehurst, 'The Hierarchy of the Sources of International Law' (1975) 47(1) BYBIL 273; M. E. Villiger, *Customary International Law and Treaties* (Martinus Nijhoff, 1985), 36; J. Pauwelyn, *Conflict of Norms in Public International Law: How WTO Law Relates to Other Rules of International Law* (Cambridge University Press, 2003), 327–436; H. Thirlway, 'The Sources of International Law', in M. Evans (ed.), *International Law* (2nd edn., Oxford University Press, 2006) 132.

[37] See e.g. Allen and Soave, 'Jurisdictional Overlap', 20–5, 43–7.

[38] The most exhaustive exploration of these conflict-management techniques is contained in the International Law Commission's 2006 report titled *Fragmentation of International Law: Difficulties Arising from the Diversification and Expansion of International Law*, A/CN.4/L.682 (13 April 2006) ('ILC Fragmentation Report').

[39] J. Pauwelyn, 'The Role of Public International Law in the WTO: How Far Can We Go?' (2001) 95(3) AJIL 535, 550.

[40] See e.g. A. Stone Sweet, 'Judicialization and the Construction of Governance' (1999) 32(2) CompPolStud 147, 163–4.

[41] See e.g. J. Hillman, 'An Emerging International Rule of Law? The WTO Dispute Settlement System's Role in Its Evolution' (2011) 42(2) OttawaLRev 269.

[42] M. Koskenniemi, '"The Lady Doth Protest Too Much": Kosovo, and the Turn to Ethics in International Law' (2002) 65(2) MLR 159, 160.

[43] W. W. Burke-White, 'International Legal Pluralism' (2004) 25(4) MichJIntlL 963, 971.

[44] A.-M. Slaughter, 'A Global Community of Courts' (2003) 44(1) HarvIntlLJ 191, 192.

[45] Ibid., 202, 217. See also A.-M. Slaughter, 'A Typology of Transjudicial Communication' (1994) 29(1) URichLRev 99, 134.

were dismissed as regressive, outmoded, and opposed to the enthronement of Reason.[46]

Thankfully, it did not take long before more critical accounts of international adjudication saw the light of day. In the 2000s, a new cohort of scholars began to look beyond the formal features of international norms and procedure, and expanded the inquiry to include the political environment where international courts operate. Inspired by international relations, these analyses sought to establish 'correlations between inputs (such as the identity and relative power of the parties, or the backgrounds of the judges) and outputs (who wins, who loses)', while 'exploring judicial independence and institutional design'.[47]

For instance, the recent wave of scholarship concerning the legitimacy[48] and authority[49] of international courts examines how adjudicators command respect for and compliance with their decisions. The core claim is that a court's 'right to rule'[50] depends on whether the addressees of its decisions are willing to accept their legal authority even when they are adversely affected by them.[51] Several metrics have been proposed to measure legitimacy. Some metrics relate to factors intrinsic to the courts themselves, like the formal delegation of powers by their constituent states[52] or the degree

---

[46] This is reminiscent of the internal debate between traditionalists and realists in the 1930s. See J. Frank, 'Are Judges Human? Part One: The Effect on Legal Thinking of the Assumption that Judges Behave like Human Beings' (1931) 80(1) UPaLRev 17 (lamenting the use of 'verbal brickbats' by traditional lawyers as a reaction to his realist account of judicial decision-making).

[47] Dunoff and Pollack, 'International Judicial Practices', 48.

[48] See e.g. K. J. Alter, L. R. Helfer, and M. R. Madsen, 'How Context Shapes the Authority of International Courts' (2016) 79(1) L&ContempProbs 1; H. G. Cohen et al., 'Legitimacy and International Courts: A Framework', in N. Grossman et al., *Legitimacy and International Courts* (Cambridge University Press, 2018), 1.

[49] See e.g. N. Roughan, 'Mind the Gaps: Authority and Legality in International Law' (2016), 27(2) EJIL 329.

[50] D. Bodansky, 'Legitimacy in International Law and International Relations', in J. L. Dunoff and M. A. Pollack (eds.), *Interdisciplinary Perspectives on International Law and International Relations: The State of the Art* (Cambridge University Press, 2013) 321, 324.

[51] On the notion of legitimacy as 'diffuse support', see e.g. J. L. Gibson and G. A. Caldeira, 'The Legitimacy of Transnational Legal Institutions: Compliance, Support, and the European Court of Justice' (1995) 39(2) AmJPolSci 459; Bodansky, 'Legitimacy in International Law', 326–7.

[52] See e.g. Alter, Helfer, and Madsen, 'Context', 3; C. P. R. Romano, K. J. Alter and Y. Shany, 'Mapping International Adjudicative Bodies, the Issues and Players', in C. P. R. Romano, K. J. Alter, and Y. Shany (eds.), *The Oxford Handbook of International Adjudication* (Oxford University Press, 2014) 1, 5–6; A. Buchanan and R. O. Keohane, 'The Legitimacy of Global Governance Institutions' (2006) 20(4) Ethics&IntlAff 405, 412–13.

of impartiality and fair treatment of the parties.[53] Other metrics concern the reception of judgments by the audience: the sensible application of the relevant rules; the economy and clarity of the reasoning; the ability to solve pressing problems and set viable precedents; the type and quantum of remedies granted; etc.[54] Along similar lines, some have discussed the recent backlash against international adjudication from political actors and member states.[55]

This new focus on the relationship between courts and their environment led to a number of important discoveries. First, adjudicators were no longer seen as mere guardians of the law but, instead, as political actors constantly reacting to the pressure of various stakeholders (governments, business conglomerates, civil society, etc.). These 'external constraints'[56] would force courts to adopt judicial strategies and interpretive postures that 'promote the expression of certain types of interests' and 'suppress that of others'.[57] Decisions perceived as erratic or contrary to the audience's expectations would likely face greater resistance, lower compliance rates, or even the threat of dissolution of the courts.

Second, the pluralism of the environment recast the fragmentation of international law as a political problem. In a disaggregated world, sectoral constituencies create specialized legal regimes to push their partial interests onto the global arena. Trade law, for instance, rests on the premise, typical of *mercatores* from developed countries, that the liberalization of commerce is a crucial component of development and prosperity.[58] Socioeconomic human rights are meant to protect the poor and the marginalized, with a 'collectivist' flavour to them.[59] Investment arbitration is a

---

[53] See e.g. Franck, *Fairness*, 7.
[54] See Cohen et al., 'Legitimacy and International Courts'; Y. Shany, 'Assessing the Effectiveness of International Courts: A Goal-Based Approach' (2012) 106(2) AJIL 225; A. von Bogdandy and I. Venzke, 'In Whose Name? On the Functions, Authority, and Legitimacy of International Courts' (2012) 23(1) EJIL 7; Alter, Helfer, and Madsen, 'Context', 4.
[55] See e.g. M. R. Madsen, P. Cebulak and M. Wiebusch, 'Backlash Against International Courts: Explaining the Forms and Patterns of Resistance to International Courts' (2018) 14(2) IntlJLContext 197.
[56] S. Dothan, *Reputation and Judicial Tactics: A Theory of National and International Courts* (Cambridge University Press, 2015), 87.
[57] B. de Sousa Santos, 'Law: A Map of Misreading. Towards a Postmodern Conception of Law' (1987) 14(3) JL&Society 279, 297.
[58] For a critical discussion of this premise, see e.g. A. Orford, 'Beyond Harmonization: Trade, Human Rights and the Economy of Sacrifice' (2005) 18(2) LJIL 179.
[59] See e.g. B. S. Chimni, 'Third World Approaches to International Law: A Manifesto' (2006) 8(1) ICLR 3, 17.

means to depoliticize the frictions between multinational corporations and host states by conferring direct rights to investors and bypassing the hurdles of diplomatic protection.[60] And so on. Seen from this angle, the proliferation of sectoral regimes and the attendant courts is the vehicle through which political differentiation is transposed from the domestic sphere onto the international plane.[61]

This, the argument continues, has profound repercussions on judicial interpretation, and calls into question the possibility of universality and coherence across different fora. A court or tribunal with a sectoral focus will be more preoccupied with preserving its 'internal legitimacy' – that is, catering to the interests of the sector's insiders – than with its 'external legitimacy' – that is, giving purchase to the beliefs of outsiders.[62] So, for example, a human rights court will be institutionally 'programmed'[63] to prioritize the promotion of fundamental freedoms over, say, rational resource allocation; a WTO panel will be more inclined towards the imperative of trade liberalization than towards environmental protection; an investment arbitral tribunal will tend to maximize the protection of investors to the detriment of the regulatory autonomy of the host state; etc. Hence, for the proponents of radical pluralism, the pressure exerted on each sectoral court by its political environment determines the emergence of a 'structural bias'[64] that largely *predetermines* the outcomes produced in the international world.

So where does all this leave us? Actually, we would argue, in a bind. Most of the aforementioned literature focuses on the *output* of international adjudication, that is, the judgments themselves. Conversely, few authors dare to explore the *input* of adjudication, that is, the series of intermediate

---

[60] See e.g. I. Shihata, 'Toward a Greater Depoliticization of Investment Disputes: The Roles of ICSID and MIGA', in K. W. Lu et al. (eds.), *Investing with Confidence: Understanding Political Risk Management in the 21st Century* (World Bank, 2009) 2.

[61] See M. Koskenniemi, 'The Fate of Public International Law: Between Technique and Politics' (2007) 70(1) MLR 1, 4; A. Lang, 'Legal Regimes and Professional Knowledges: The Internal Politics of Regime Definition', in M. A. Young (ed.), *Regime Interaction in International Law: Facing Fragmentation* (Cambridge University Press, 2012) 113.

[62] J. H. H. Weiler, 'The Rule of Lawyers and the Ethos of Diplomats: Reflections on the Internal and External Legitimacy of WTO Dispute Settlement' (2001), 35(2) JWT 191, 193. See also Cohen et al., 'Legitimacy and International Courts'.

[63] ILC Fragmentation Report, para. 488.

[64] M. Koskenniemi, 'The Politics of International Law: 20 Years Later' (2009) 20(1) EJIL 7, 9. See also M. Koskenniemi, *From Apology to Utopia: The Structure of International Legal Argument – Reissue with New Epilogue* (Cambridge University Press, 2006), 600–15; Lang, 'Legal Regimes and Professional Knowledges', 113.

steps that lead to the formation of those judgments. To this day, we know surprisingly little about 'the everyday practices and social relationships through which international judicial decisions are produced'.[65] What happens behind the closed doors of deliberation rooms? How are opinions formulated, drafted, revised, and translated? How do adjudicators structure their relationship with their registries, secretariats, clerks, and other court officials? How much do they respect or fear the critiques of journalists and academics? With some notable exceptions,[66] these questions remain largely unanswered. The few attempts to open the black box tend to focus on judges alone[67] – who they are, where they come from, etc. – without paying the same attention to the multitude of professional actors that surround them in their daily work.

As we will argue,[68] this oversight may not be completely unintentional. For now, let us just say that existing scholarship suffers from a number of blind spots. For one, it does not tell us much about the way international courts and tribunals *actually* function: which actors contribute to the judicial process, how labour is allocated among them, what strategies they pursue... The spotlight remains firmly on the Herculean adjudicator, a 'loner' who 'converses with no one' and 'has no encounters'[69] except with their colleagues on the bench.

But there is another, more insidious problem with treating international courts as 'unitary actors'[70] that speak only through their decisions. It is the risk of painting a reified, 'deterministic'[71] picture of the factors that drive judicial outcomes. The decisions of international adjudicators are explained by reference to some *other* reality, invisible to their eyes, that guides their every action. For traditionalists, that reality is the law itself: a concrete entity with its own inherent logic

---

[65] Dunoff and Pollack, 'International Judicial Practices', 48.
[66] See e.g. J. Meierhenrich, 'Foreword: The Practices of the International Criminal Court' (2013) 76(3&4) L&ContempProbs i; Romano, Alter, and Shany, *Oxford Handbook of International Adjudication*; F. Baetens (ed.), *Legitimacy of Unseen Actors in International Adjudication* (Cambridge University Press, 2019); J. Pauwelyn and K. Pelc, *Who Writes the Rulings of the World Trade Organization? A Critical Assessment of the Role of the Secretariat in WTO Dispute Settlement*, IHEID Working Paper (2019).
[67] See e.g. Terris, Romano, and Swigart, *The International Judge*.
[68] See *infra*, Chapter 6.
[69] F. I. Michelman, 'The Supreme Court 1985 Term' (1986) 100(1) HarvLRev 4, 76. See also J. Habermas, *Between Facts and Norms: Contributions to a Discourse Theory of Law and Democracy* (MIT Press, 1996), 224.
[70] Dunoff and Pollack, 'International Judicial Practices', 48.
[71] Messenger, 'The Practice of Litigation', 211.

and rationality, somehow independent of the people that routinely create, interpret, apply, resist, and are bound by it.[72] For critics, it is the political environment – the set of 'deeper, impersonal forces'[73] – that exerts its ineluctable pressure on courts and pushes them towards predetermined results. In either case, the actual *people* involved exercise little agency, squeezed as they are between the Scylla of formal law and the Charybdis of structural bias. Whatever they think, say, or do, they will eventually have to surrender to a higher voice. When taken to an extreme, both formalist and critical narratives freeze the process into a static image.

\*

This is where our story kicks in. When matter looks inert, it is sufficient to place it under a microscope to realize that its molecules are still moving, interacting, colliding. We, too, are going to place international adjudication under a microscope and observe the movement, the interactions, the collisions that agitate it.

The word 'microscope' is used deliberately and should not be misread. When we zoom in on an object, we are not merely watching that object close-up: we are seeing something *new* while *losing sight* of something else. 'Each scale reveals a phenomenon and distorts or hides others'.[74] Likewise, the plot that is about to unfold does not simply provide more detail about the international judicial process, or merely augment the resolution of the image we already have. Instead, its focus on the small-scale, the mundane, and the everyday casts the whole process in a different light and brings to the fore aspects that would otherwise remain 'unmarked'.[75] A proper use of the microscope requires certain analytical shifts, certain adjustments to the angle of vision, which we might find unfamiliar – or even uncomfortable – given our common disciplinary sensibilities as international lawyers.

The first shift concerns the *identity of the actors* involved in the process. From our usual vantage point, we tend to equate those actors with the official subjects of international law. When we observe an ICJ hearing, we see a confrontation between, say, the Philippines and Malaysia. When

---

[72] See e.g. P. Schlag, *The Enchantment of Reason* (Duke University Press, 1998), 100–4.
[73] D. W. Kennedy, 'Challenging Expert Rule: The Politics of Global Governance' (2005) 27(1) SydLRev 1, 4.
[74] de Sousa Santos, 'A Map of Misreading', 284.
[75] See W. Brekhus, 'A Sociology of the Unmarked: Redirecting Our Focus' (1998) 16(1) SociolTheory 34.

we gaze at the Court itself, we see a monolithic body that speaks with 'one institutional voice'.[76] Individuals and social groups are relegated to the margins of our field of vision. They become visible only when vested with the official standing to participate in proceedings (as with individuals in human rights cases or investors in ISDS).

But what if, looking more closely, we saw the same ICJ hearing as a professional contest among *agents*, *advisors*, and *counsel*? What if, instead of one cohesive institution, the Court suddenly appeared as a bundle of social relations that tie together – and sometimes pit against each other – *judges*, *clerks*, *experts*, and *registry officials*? And what if, rather than the embodiment of legal abstractions, individuals were revealed as *players*[77] who engage in a game, deploy strategies, and advance interests in a dynamic social space?

You get the gist: viewed through the optics of the microscope, the official actors of international law slip into the background, whereas the socio-professional actors that incarnate them come into focus. Seen from this angle, the system looks less like a grid of legal entities, and more like a network of individuals 'engaged in a shared enterprise with broadly similar understandings of what they are doing and why they are doing it'.[78] This network, which we call the *international judicial community*, comprises the 'mutually recognised professionals' who are intimately familiar with the practice and the study of international adjudication.[79]

Judges and arbitrators are, of course, the most visible of these professionals – visible enough not to require a microscope at all. However, the community also encompasses a panoply of other actors who occupy less conspicuous positions: agents, counsel, advisors, court officials, specialized scholars, and the like. Together with the adjudicators, these professionals are in charge of running the judicial machinery in its routine operations. Each from their own position, they contribute to all phases of the process: the preparation of written and oral pleadings; the formulation

---

[76] T. Soave, 'European Legal Culture and WTO Dispute Settlement: Thirty Years of Socio-Legal Transplants from Brussels to Geneva' (2020) 19(1) LPICT 107, 114.
[77] See Bianchi, 'The Game of Interpretation'.
[78] Johnstone, *The Power of Deliberation*, 41. See also e.g. Klabbers, 'Virtuous Interpretation', 31; Bianchi, 'Textual Interpretation', 51–4; S. Fish, *Is There a Text in This Class? The Authority of Interpretive Communities* (Harvard University Press, 1980), 338–55; Shaffer and Trachtman, 'Interpretation and Institutional Choice', 120–3; E. Adler and V. Pouliot, 'International Practices' (2011) 3(1) IntlTheory 1, 8.
[79] d'Aspremont, 'Professionalisation', 20.

of legal arguments; the collection and assessment of factual evidence; the allocation of evidentiary burdens; deliberations; the writing of opinions; and the critical appraisal of jurisprudence.[80]

As we will see,[81] the international judicial community is not coextensive with the 'immense'[82] group of people involved in international law. Rather, if courts and tribunals stand 'at the centre of the world of the professional international lawyer',[83] then the community constitutes the innermost circle of that world, that which inhabits the immediate vicinity of the centre. Its members are uniquely placed to shape judicial outcomes, and zealously defend their position from outside interference. Indeed, much of the output of international courts is explained by the *internal* properties of this 'social universe ... which is in practice relatively independent of external determinations and pressures'.[84] Pointing the microscope at the community means shedding light on its social structures, its professional dynamics, the forms of cooperation and competition among its participants, and more generally the 'relations of mutual engagement by which they can do whatever they do'.[85]

The second optical effect is about the *nature* of the process and the operations that define it. Thanks to years of studies and disciplinary acculturation, we international lawyers are trained to see legal outcomes as a result of the interplay of rules, principles, and procedures. We are used to parsing through the sources of international law listed in Article 38 of the ICJ Statute;[86] discussing the meaning of treaty terms through the lens of the VCLT; scrutinizing the procedures set out in the ICJ Rules of Court[87] or the WTO Dispute Settlement Understanding (DSU);[88] and dissecting judicial opinions to test their persuasiveness and coherence. Of course, we come to these tasks from different places, different traditions,

---

[80] See Dunoff and Pollack, 'International Judicial Practices', 73.
[81] See *infra*, Chapter 2.
[82] J. d'Aspremont et al., 'Introduction', in J. d'Aspremont et al. (eds.), *International Law as a Profession I* (Cambridge University Press, 2017) 1, 2.
[83] I. Brownlie, 'The Calling of the International Lawyer: Sir Humphrey Waldock and His Work' (1983) 54(1) BYBIL 7, 68.
[84] Bourdieu, 'The Force of Law', 816.
[85] É. Wenger, *Communities of Practice: Learning, Meaning and Identity* (Cambridge University Press, 1998), 73.
[86] United Nations, *Statute of the International Court of Justice* (18 April 1946) ('ICJ Statute').
[87] ICJ, *Rules of Court* (14 April 1978), last amended on 14 April 2005 ('ICJ Rules of Court').
[88] *Dispute Settlement Rules: Understanding on Rules and Procedures Governing the Settlement of Disputes*, Marrakesh Agreement Establishing the World Trade Organization, Annex 2 (15 April 1994), UNTS 1869, 401.

and different levels of technical prowess. Debate and disagreement about normative constructs are inherent – not to mention lucrative – to our profession. Yet, those constructs remain firmly anchored in official documents and formal sources. The legal objects that capture our attention tell us how legal processes are 'supposed to operate', not 'how they actually operate'.[89]

But if, once again, we observe this landscape through the microscope, we see formal rules and principles fade into the distance, replaced by a myriad of socio-professional *practices*. The official normativity of legal sources gives way to the discursive normativity of narratives, strategies of persuasion, expert vernaculars, and modes of world sense-making.[90] Behind the unified and apodictic interpretation of a treaty, we discover a plurality of competing arguments, logics, and postures, whose relative merits – their being 'correct' or 'incorrect' – depend on the standards of acceptability collectively held by the community.[91] In lieu of court procedures on paper, we glimpse the 'competent performances' and the 'socially meaningful patterns of action'[92] that give materiality and breathe life into the various stages of litigation. And rather than a conclusive and coherent text, the international judgment is revealed as 'the product of a symbolic struggle between professionals possessing unequal technical skills and social influence'.[93]

This analytical shift from norms to practices helps answer questions that have long vexed legal theorists. First, as will be argued,[94] practices are a key driver of constraint and freedom, structure and contingency, continuity and change in international adjudication. On the one hand, intersubjective socialization and patterned repetition allow for shared assumptions and expectations to crystallize and become embedded in the community, thereby ensuring certainty and predictability in judicial outcomes at any

---

[89] See Dunoff and Pollack, 'International Judicial Practices', 52.
[90] See e.g. Kennedy, 'Challenging Expert Rule'; A. Lang, 'Rethinking Trade and Human Rights' (2007) 15(2) TulJIntl&CompL 335, 357–8; T. Soave, 'Three Ways of Looking at a Blackbird: Political, Legal, and Institutional Perspectives on Pharmaceutical Patents and Access to Medicines' (2016) 8(1) TL&D 137, 172–3.
[91] See J. Gross Stein, 'Background Knowledge in the Foreground: Conversations about Competent Practice in "Sacred Space"', in E. Adler and V. Pouliot (eds.), *International Practices* (Cambridge University Press, 2011) 87; T. Schultz, 'Secondary Rules of Recognition and Relative Legality in Transnational Regimes' (2011) 56(1) AmJJurisprud 59, 62.
[92] Adler and Pouliot, 'International Practices', 6.
[93] Bourdieu, 'The Force of Law', 827.
[94] See *infra*, Chapter 2.

given point in time. On the other hand, the endless struggles among community members – which, in turn, reflect their power relations and relative social capital – enable the contestation of pre-established patterns, the opening of paths to resistance, and the creation of avenues for the gradual evolution of judicial systems.

Second, practices explain the level of fragmentation and convergence among sectoral regimes in international law (human rights, trade, investment, etc.). Each such regime orbits around a specific sub-community with its own internal dynamics, preoccupations, and biases. As the habits and worldviews of the various sub-communities develop largely independently of each other, they often end up colliding over cross-cutting themes. Yet, the degree of operational 'closure' or 'openness'[95] of a sectoral regime is not carved in stone, but evolves over time as a result of the internal struggles and negotiations of the participants in each sub-community.[96]

Our microscope calibrated, we are ready to pick up where we left Sophie – immersed in her thoughts in the Great Hall of Justice – and narrate her (non-)adventures up to that moment. Of course, this story is not hers alone, but involves a multitude of characters that will be introduced along the way. We will meet zealous diplomats, ambitious attorneys, industrious bureaucrats, promising clerks, astute academics and, of course, a fair number of judges and arbitrators. Everyone has a part to play, an agenda to pursue, a constellation of beliefs and idiosyncrasies. As the plot unfolds, the threads will become increasingly interwoven, slowly revealing the web of invisible ties that gives international law its mysterious force.

The events are narrated more or less chronologically. Chapter 2 flashes back to the first days of Sophie's employment at the ICJ registry, and sees her and her girlfriend Norma mull over the concepts that lie at the core of this book: the international judicial community, its social structures, and its everyday practices. This initial discussion helps set the stage, refine the theoretical coordinates of the story, provide some context for the actions of its protagonists, and foreshadow their trajectories through the judicial process. From there, the plot follows the main steps of a typical set of international judicial proceedings: the complainant's decision to initiate the dispute and the establishment of its legal team (Chapter 3); the parties' filing of written submissions and rebuttals (Chapter 4); the processing of the case file by the court's legal bureaucracy (Chapters 5 and 6), including

---

[95] The terms are borrowed from N. Luhmann, 'Operational Closure and Structural Coupling: The Differentiation of the Legal System' (1992) 13(5) CardozoLRev 1419.
[96] See generally Lang, 'Legal Regimes and Professional Knowledges'.

the summarization of the parties' arguments (Chapter 7), the preparation of internal memoranda (Chapter 8), the examination of the state conduct at issue (Chapter 9), the preliminary assessment of the disputes facts and evidence (Chapter 10), the identification of the norms applicable to the case (Chapter 11), and the interpretation of the meaning of those norms (Chapters 12 and 13); the conduct of hearings (Chapter 14); the court's deliberations (Chapter 15); and the drafting and revision of the final judgment (Chapter 16). Chapter 17 closes the circle. If the story opened with a solemn view of the Great Hall of Justice, it ends in the quiet of a living room on the other side of The Hague.

Of course, the selection of these steps as particularly noteworthy is the fruit of a deliberate choice. These are the moments where the power of the international judicial community is most keenly felt, and where its background practices contribute most directly to the definition of judicial outcomes. Inevitably, the selection obscures other aspects of life at the court and neglects many actors who, in a way or another, play a more indirect role in the process. Think, for instance, of state delegates negotiating the appointment of international judges; interpreters and translators dealing with multilingualism in the proceedings; support staff physically handling case files and maintaining the correspondence between the court and the parties; website managers aggregating and organizing case law to make it more easily accessible to the public; and so forth.

Equally selective is the choice of the ICJ, the ECtHR, the IACtHR, the WTO, and an investor–state arbitral tribunal as the five scenarios in which the story unfolds. Why only those five? What about the ITLOS, international criminal tribunals, and regional courts? Fair point: again, we make no claim of exhaustiveness. Not only are we being selective in the choice of our case studies but we are also assuming the possibility to discern common patterns across them. The courts and tribunals examined in this book differ widely in terms of jurisdictional powers, areas of competence, and institutional design. Some adjudicative bodies (like the ICJ and the WTO) handle disputes between sovereign states, while others (like human rights and ISDS tribunals) typically hear complaints brought by private persons and entities. The jurisdiction of some courts (e.g. the ICJ) is subject to the consent of both parties,[97] whereas that of other courts (e.g. the WTO and the ECtHR) is automatic and unconditional.[98]

---

[97] See Articles 36 and 37 of the ICJ Statute.
[98] See Article 23 of the DSU.

Finally, the procedures of standing courts are governed by their respective statutes and rules, while the procedures of ISDS tribunals are tailored to the specifics of each case. Following initial consultations with the parties and the co-arbitrators, the president of the tribunal prepares so-called Procedural Order No. 1, a document that sets forth the fundamental procedural aspects of the dispute, including the applicable law and arbitration rules; the place of the arbitration and the location of hearings; the possible bi- or trifurcation of the proceedings into jurisdictional issues, merits, and *quantum*; the arbitrators' fees; etc.

These and other distinctions have obvious repercussions on the daily activities of the professional sub-communities concerned. Accordingly, we will take them into due account whenever appropriate. However, our analysis of the various systems will also reveal striking *recurrences* in the patterns of structured practice, the perceptions of competence, the argumentative techniques, and the social dynamics of our professional field. A modicum of blurriness may even help the story gather pace. After all, is it even 'always an advantage to replace an indistinct picture by a sharp one? Isn't the indistinct one often exactly what we need?'[99]

---

[99] L. Wittgenstein, *Philosophical Investigations*, trans. G. E. M. Anscombe (Basil Blackwell, 1958), para 71.

# 2

## Coffee, Cigarettes, and International Judicial Practices

Many months later, as she nervously taps her foot on the office floor, Sophie will remember the question Norma asked her on that late summer afternoon. It must have been their second or third date. They were sitting at an outdoor café in Grote Markt, two large lattes in front of them. Norma was comically struggling to roll a cigarette – of course, mused Sophie, a researcher in sociology couldn't but *roll* her cigarettes – while trying to keep her round glasses from sliding down her nose. Around them, the square bustled with life. Students drank pale ale to celebrate the beginning of the term, young professionals laid out their plans for the fall, and flocks of pigeons congregated around breadcrumbs and abandoned leftovers. Sophie enjoyed that quiet chaos and glanced around with mild curiosity. All was good and well in the capital of international law.

She had recently started her clerkship at the International Court of Justice (ICJ) and was still inebriated with pride. A week earlier, the Court's Registrar had summoned the new recruits in his office and profusely congratulated them on their appointment. In his words, this cohort included some of the 'brightest international lawyers on Earth' – second only, the Registrar felt compelled to specify, to 'our distinguished Judges and myself'. (Polite chuckles.) Each newcomer had then been invited to introduce themself in a few minutes. Sophie had chosen to deliver her brief address in French. Despite a few syntactic stumbles and her thick German accent, the Registrar's visible satisfaction had attested to a moderate success.

It was, then, with a certain self-assuredness that she reacted when Norma, having finally managed to light her cigarette, casually asked her:

'So, tell me, Sophie Richter: what is it *exactly* that you do?'

Sophie had been waiting for that moment. Telling Norma about her new job would have sounded like bragging when they first met. But now, once asked, it was time to thoroughly impress her date.

'Well, I do international law.' Pause for effect.

'... Which means?'

'It's the law that governs the conduct of states and their relations to one another. You see, when you say "international law," laypersons sometimes confuse it with ...'

Norma stopped her in the tracks.

'Wait a sec, that's an exclusionary term right there. I may be a "layperson," as you say, but I know what international law is. Took a couple of classes in uni. What I was asking is ... what it means for you to "*do*" international law.'

That was unexpected. Normally, all it took Sophie to gain the awe of an interlocutor was a generic description of the international legal system (yes, there are rules constraining state behaviour), a cursory overview of the institutions enforcing it (yes, there are courts and tribunals with the authority to judge states), and a benevolent acknowledgement of existing challenges (yes, politics are still a thing, but we are slowly moving towards a world governed by the Rule of Law).

Norma had just made it clear that these niceties would not be enough. Her quip about 'laypersons' forced Sophie to reflect, albeit momentarily, on the distinction between the inside and the outside of her professional community. Who is part of that community? What criteria determine membership in it, and where does one draw its boundaries? How is the community organized? Is it cohesive or fragmented? Does it have a centre and a periphery? How do the participants in the community relate to one another? Are their relations hierarchical, horizontal, or networked? Of course, none of these questions arose in Sophie's mind so explicitly – more as vague doubts on how to continue the conversation.

But somehow, Norma had managed to raise an even trickier set of issues. What does it mean to *do*, or to *practice*, international law? How do the members of the community run their daily business? What degree of agency does each actor exercise in the process? To what extent is practice constrained by pre-existing structures? Sophie had never really thought this through. A brilliant academic record (understated, of course, as 'my time in Greenwich Village') had persuaded her of the inherent emancipatory force of international law and sparked her ambition to be part of it. The prospect of using rules and principles to resolve grievous conflicts meant more to her than a simple practice: it meant partaking in a higher *vision*, learning to speak the 'vocabularies of justice and goodness, solidarity, responsibility and – faith'.[1] Was she supposed to believe otherwise, a week into the job?

Sophie's eyes lingered on the square for a brief moment, then resolutely met Norma's. This date was going to be a bit more challenging than expected.

*

Whether Sophie managed to secure another date, we shall see at the end of the chapter. For now, let us reflect for a moment on the fundamental issues that Norma raised with such economy of words.

The first set of issues relates to the nature and the boundaries of the international judicial community – the professional milieu whose inner dynamics this book seeks to explore. Throughout the chapter, we will outline the core characteristics of the community and the criteria that distinguish it from the broader group of international lawyers. We will also identify the key actors that participate in the community and discuss the structures that govern their relations. Having outlined the main features of the community, we will then set it in motion and provide an initial account of its practices. In particular, we will see how the social structures of the community produce a set of shared assumptions among its participants, which in turn come to define their standards of competence and incompetence. Based on these premises, we will then argue that community practices serve as the vehicle of both continuity and change in international judicial outcomes.

At this point, you may protest: Why the theoretical detour? Why not let the characters themselves carry the plot forward? The golden rule of fiction is 'show, don't tell'!

The reason is simple. While practice is always performed by individuals, 'it acquires meaning only through collectively shared understandings of competency, of what is well done or poorly done'.[2] Without those understandings, it would be difficult to 'construe individual "doing" as practice'.[3] International adjudication is, by definition, a collective enterprise. No one actor is in full command of the myriad activities that punctuate the process. No single mind, not even the most searching, could exhaustively map all the threads that run through the fabric of the community. In fact, it is likely that Sophie's account, hastily delivered over a coffee in Grote

---

[1] Koskenniemi, 'The Fate of Public International Law', 30.
[2] Gross Stein, 'Background Knowledge', 89.
[3] Ibid. See also Wenger, *Communities of Practice*, 47.

Markt, would reflect her subjective experience of a familiar environment. That experience would, in turn, be shaped by the tacit assumptions that govern her world – the truths that are so deeply ingrained as to become invisible. In other words, Sophie's 'practical mastery'[4] would hardly comprise any knowledge of its own structuring principles. Norma would not hear the whole story but only the *part* of the story that Sophie is able to tell given the specific position she occupies in the field.

So back to Norma's questions.

The idea of a professional community devoted to the practice and study of international law is not novel. In 1977, Oscar Schachter coined the famous metaphor of an 'invisible college of international lawyers'.[5] As originally formulated, the notion referred to a small elite of academics hailing from the most prestigious law schools of Europe and the Americas, as well as a handful of government officials who 'maintain[ed] intellectual contact with the scholarly side of the profession'.[6] According to Schachter, the members of the college were dedicated to the 'common intellectual enterprise' of promoting international law as a unified discipline able to transcend state borders[7] and strove to serve as the '*conscience juridique*'[8] of the world. The law of the college was a law of professors.

Some 45 years later, this idyllic image is thoroughly outdated. The college, if it ever truly existed, has given way to a full-blown profession that attracts ever-growing numbers of individuals and institutions. The object of international regulation has exploded in both scope and reach. What once was 'a thin net of rules' thrown over the anarchic sea of international relations has evolved into a multilayered set of norms, standards, and guidelines covering most aspects of political, economic, and social life. Today, we find international 'law and regulation and rule at every turn'.[9] The thickening of the system's 'normative density' has resulted in a proportional increase in the 'institutional density necessary to sustain the norms'.[10] Inter- and non-governmental organizations (NGOs)

---

[4] See Bourdieu, *Theory of Practice*, 19.
[5] Schachter, 'Invisible College', 217.
[6] Ibid.
[7] Ibid.
[8] Ibid., 224.
[9] D. W. Kennedy, 'The Mystery of Global Governance' (2008) 34(3) OhioNULRev 827, 848.
[10] G. Abi-Saab, *Cours Général de Droit International Public* (Volume 207), in Collected Courses of the Hague Academy of International Law, The Hague Academy of International Law (Martinus Nijhoff, 1987), 93.

have proliferated; most state governments have permanent teams or departments tasked with handling international legal affairs; the number of students in the field has grown well beyond the system's absorption capacity; and, most importantly, a variety of new actors – politicians, civil servants, military commanders, business conglomerates, advocacy networks, journalists, and opinion-makers – have become conversant in the vernacular of the discipline.[11]

In some ways, this expansion bears the hallmarks of Marcuse's 'desublimation' of higher culture.[12] In Schachter's days, the keys to the temple remained firmly in the hands of a privileged minority who embodied the progressive, emancipatory, and counter-hegemonic aspirations of international law. The recent broadening of the profession has, so to speak, 'flattened out' those aspirations – not through their denial and rejection but 'through their wholesale incorporation into the established order' and their 'reproduction and display on a massive scale'.[13] If yesteryear's international law was 'a tradition and a political project',[14] today's international law is also a *business*.

While international legal actors are now aplenty, only a few of them are involved in the *judicial* settlement of international disputes. In fact, adjudication traditionally accounted for a minuscule portion of international legal practice. For the best part of the twentieth century, the Permanent Court of International Justice (PCIJ) and its successor, the ICJ, remained the only state-to-state courts, each issuing no more than a couple of decisions per year. The professionals orbiting around those institutions were few and far between. Even to this day, 'only a tiny percentage' of international controversies end up before a judge. The vast majority 'are still resolved the old-fashioned way: through diplomacy behind closed doors if we are lucky, through more confrontational and even violent forms when we are not'.[15] In other words, the professional world of international lawyers has always been broader than courts alone and comprises a rich and diverse palimpsest of discourses and expert knowledges.

Yet, the protagonists of this story inhabit a small segment of that world – a segment we call the *international judicial community*. Around

---

[11] See e.g. A. Bianchi, 'The International Legal Regulation of the Use of Force' (2009), 22(4) LJIL 651, 653–4.
[12] H. Marcuse, *One-Dimensional Man: Studies in the Ideology of Advanced Industrial Society* (Routledge, 1964), 59.
[13] Ibid., 60.
[14] Koskenniemi, 'The Fate of Public International Law', 1.
[15] Alvarez, 'The New Dispute Settlers', 411.

the turn of the century, the expansion of courts and tribunals led a group of practitioners and intellectuals to differentiate themselves from their peers and specialize in the various aspects of international litigation. Relying on international law as background knowledge, they mastered the procedures of the different adjudicative institutions, honed their skills in the art of judicial persuasion and, crucially, reached out to public officials and private entities that may be interested in resorting to adjudication or arbitration to settle their differences. Long relegated to the margins of the discipline, the group has progressively come to occupy its centre – to the point of becoming a synecdoche for the whole international legal profession.

This rise in relevance is readily apparent. Forty years ago, if you had asked a young international lawyer about their professional ambitions, they would have probably mentioned the UN Office of Legal Affairs or the International Law Commission (ILC); today, they are more likely to indicate the ICJ, the European Court of Human Rights (ECtHR), or the World Trade Organization (WTO) as ideal duty stations. Back then, private practitioners would lament a lack of business opportunities in international dispute settlement; today, they can comfortably list the many multinational law firms that have set up dedicated offices in the strategic hubs of the system. Universities around the globe would treat international judicial practice as an exotic appendix to their curricula; today, they offer a wealth of specialized courses on the topic. Doctoral researchers would typically write about substantive rules and principles of international law, invariably acknowledging their aspirational and unenforceable character; today, they turn their attention to the jurisprudential trends of this or that tribunal, trying to discern 'what courts have actually decided'.[16]

As its influence grew, the international judicial community sought to erect external boundaries to protect its niche from competing social sectors. Defining the precise contours of those boundaries is admittedly difficult. The membrane that separates the 'outside' and the 'inside' of the community remains rather porous, and many of its participants cross it back and forth during the course of their careers. What matters, in our opinion, is the degree of *proximity* to the routine functioning of international courts and tribunals – which, we shall see, roughly corresponds to the degree of *influence* on judicial outcomes.

---

[16] J. Frank, *Law and the Modern Mind* (Brentano's, 1930), 46.

Let us explain.

In a broad sense, a wide variety of actors have direct or indirect stakes in international adjudication. Government representatives spend years defining the institutional design of each new court, debating its powers and jurisdiction, and eventually ratifying its founding treaty. Later, diplomats periodically engage in complex negotiations for the appointment or renewal of judges and set the agenda for institutional reform. Meanwhile, national politicians praise or blame judicial decisions to advance domestic or foreign policy agendas; NGOs submit *amicus curiae* briefs or sponsor complaints in pursuit of advocacy strategies; multinational corporations take jurisprudence into account when setting out trade or investment plans; journalists cover the most significant rulings and disseminate them to the general public; etc. These forms of engagement ensure the continued goodwill of political stakeholders towards international adjudication,[17] thereby making them the ultimate arbiters of the system's legitimacy.

In practice, however, these stakeholders have a relatively limited say on the day-to-day unfolding of the international judicial process. The pressure they exert on courts and tribunals occurs either *before* the start of proceedings – through institutional design and the appointment of judges – or *after* their completion – through the appraisal and the (non-)implementation of judgments. What happens *in between* is usually none of their concern: after all, the procedural rules that govern international proceedings aim to shield the content of decisions from overt political interference. Thus, if anything, external stakeholders serve as the *mediate* audience of international courts: a looming presence that observes the unfolding of dispute settlement from a certain distance and intervenes only when the circumstances so require.[18]

By contrast, the international judicial community operates within and in the immediate surroundings of courts and tribunals. This inner circle of legal professionals is in charge of running the judicial machinery in its routine operations, and its recursive practices shape and inform every stage of the proceedings. Telling exactly *who* is part of the community can be daunting. Tentatively, we could say that it extends to whoever

---

[17] See e.g. A.-M. Slaughter and L. R. Helfer, 'Why States Create International Tribunals: A Response to Professors Posner and Yoo' (2005) 93(3) CalLRev 899, 946–9.

[18] See T. Soave, 'Who Controls WTO Dispute Settlement? Socio-Professional Practices and the Crisis of the Appellate Body' (2020) 29(1) ItYBIL 13, 17.

possesses sufficient expertise, capital, and interest to repeatedly participate in the adjudicative process.[19]

Obviously, international judges and arbitrators fit the bill: they are the most recognizable actors in the community, vested with the official authority to interpret and apply the relevant norms to resolve the cases at hand. Other repeat players include the government departments tasked with litigating cases, as well as the private counsel representing the parties and submitting arguments on their behalf. In addition, the community includes a panoply of actors whose roles are less apparent. For instance, each court or tribunal provides its adjudicators with a set of legal bureaucrats (called clerks, registry or secretariat officials, or arbitral secretaries depending on the institution concerned) who assist in the preparation, deliberation, and drafting of judgments; outside of courts, specialized scholars critically appraise judicial outcomes, identify patterns and inconsistencies in jurisprudence, and suggest solutions going forward; universities organize conferences and symposia bringing together practitioners from multiple judicial regimes; and so on.

Ostensibly, these various members of the community occupy distinct and well-defined positions. However, the boundaries between their roles are blurrier than they first appear. Throughout their careers, community members swap roles frequently – and sometimes even don multiple hats at once.[20] Prominent academics may take a break from their faculty chairs to serve on an international court;[21] arbitrators in one investor–state dispute settlement (ISDS) case may appear as counsel in another; the legal officers working for a registry or secretariat may later be recruited by government departments or specialized law firms. All combinations are possible.[22]

---

[19] See e.g. E. Adler, *Communitarian International Relations: The Epistemic Foundations of International Relations* (Routledge, 2005), 24 (describing communities as being 'determined by people's knowledge and identity and the discourse associated with a specific practice').

[20] See d'Aspremont et al., 'Introduction', 8.

[21] According to some estimates, 40 per cent of the judges sitting on permanent international courts 'have significant academic credentials' (Terris, Romano, and Swigart, *The International Judge*, 20) and one-third of investment arbitrators are former or current scholars (J. A. Fontoura Costa, 'Comparing WTO Panelists and ICSID Arbitrators: The Creation of International Legal Fields' (2011) 1(4) Oñati Socio-Leg Ser 1, 17). Recently, the President of the ICJ has taken steps to reduce so-called 'moonlighting', i.e. the practice of ICJ Judges serving as arbitrators in their spare time. See e.g. C. Musto, 'New Restrictions on Arbitral Appointments for Sitting ICJ Judges', EJIL Talk!, 5 November 2018, www.ejiltalk.org/new-restrictions-on-arbitral-appointments-for-sitting-icj-judges/.

[22] See d'Aspremont et al., 'Introduction', 8; Vauchez, 'Communities of International Litigators', 661.

This revolving door among the bench, the bureaucracy, the bar, and the academe helps strengthen bonds and forge ties. Indeed, while external stakeholders are diffused and scattered across the world, the inner circle is a tight network of *habitués* who walk the corridors of international courts on a regular basis, maintain first-name personal contacts, and cultivate friendly professional relationships.[23]

Overall, community members are driven by different interests from external stakeholders. The latter play the game of adjudication in pursuit of goals *other* than the game itself – be they a country's perceived national interest, a multinational company's trade or investment opportunities, an individual's fundamental freedoms, etc. The former, conversely, derive their standing, prestige, and income *from the very functioning* of the adjudicative mechanism.[24] For them, the complexities of dispute settlement are not the means to an ulterior result – but an end in itself, and the specific focus of their expertise. It follows that community members share an enormous self-interest in defending international judicial institutions as such, extending the reach and pervasiveness of their powers and constantly reasserting their 'courtness'.[25]

Thanks to this cohesiveness, the community has gradually secured its control on the everyday functioning of international courts and tribunals, while managing to insulate its internal operations from outside interference. In its routine unfolding, international adjudication takes place 'at a considerable remove from … political and diplomatic institutions'.[26] As we will see throughout the book, the same handful of counsel appear at most hearings alongside their clients. The importance of registries and secretariats as the 'guardians of jurisprudence' has steadily grown over time. And scholarly production in the field is densely populated by authors who have direct or indirect stakes in the system.

Being an 'insider' in the game means being familiar with its rules, adopting strategies that resonate with other players, and ultimately shaping the outcomes of the adjudicative process to an extent that is usually precluded to 'outsiders'. With a little stretch of the imagination,

---

[23] See Weiler, 'The Rule of Lawyers', 195; K. Hopewell, 'Multilateral Trade Governance as Social Field: Global Civil Society and the WTO' (2015) 22(6) RevIntPolitEcon 1128, 1142–3.

[24] See Soave, 'Who Controls WTO Dispute Settlement?', 18.

[25] M. Shapiro and A. Stone Sweet, *On Law, Politics and Judicialization* (Oxford University Press, 2002), 175.

[26] R. Howse, 'The World Trade Organization 20 Years On: Global Governance by Judiciary' (2016) 27(1) EJIL 9, 25.

one could say that the community has replaced external stakeholders as the *immediate* audience of international adjudication. When a court or tribunal issues a decision, it is often 'speaking' more directly to the legal professionals gravitating around it than to its broader political constituency or the general public.[27]

Such a degree of socio-professional closure contributes to the independence and impartiality of international courts and ensures that extraneous factors and preoccupations are kept at bay. Yet, it can also give rise to frictions between the inner circle of community members and the outer circle of external stakeholders, especially when the latter feel unfairly marginalized in the day-to-day operations of judicial institutions. When this happens, one can witness a temporary re-entry of external forces into the community's dynamics.

The recent downfall of the WTO Appellate Body is a good case in point. Once considered one of the most powerful international courts, since 2017 the Appellate Body has been facing the United States' veto on the appointment of new adjudicators, eventually leading to a complete paralysis of its proceedings in December 2019.[28] Officially, the United States justified its blockade by accusing the Appellate Body of overstepping its judicial mandate in a number of ways.[29] However, it soon became clear that there was more at stake than a simple normative disagreement or a raw assertion of diplomatic might: the attack on the Appellate Body was a radical attempt by US political stakeholders to regain control of a process that they believed was slipping out of their hands.[30]

In pursuit of this goal, the US delegation tried to persuade the WTO Director-General to sack the director of the Appellate Body Secretariat (ABS),[31] the legal bureaucracy that provides support to appellate adjudicators. It also threatened to freeze the WTO's annual budget for 2020 unless other states agreed to draconian cuts to the Appellate Body's funding.[32]

---

[27] See Soave, 'Who Controls WTO Dispute Settlement?', 18–19.
[28] See ibid., 14–15.
[29] See e.g. Office of the United States Trade Representative, *Report on the Appellate Body of the World Trade Organization* (2020), https://ustr.gov/sites/default/files/Report_on_the_ Appellate_Body_of_the_World_Trade_Organization.pdf ('USTR Report').
[30] See Soave, 'Who Controls WTO Dispute Settlement?', 30–1.
[31] See S. Charnovitz, 'The Attack on the Appellate Body: Events of 5 December 2019', International Economic Law and Policy Blog, 5 December 2019, https://ielp.worldtradelaw .net/2019/12/the-attack-on-the-appellate-body-events-of-5-december-2019.html.
[32] See B. Baschuk, 'A US Offer to Keep the WTO Alive Comes with Painful Conditions', Bloomberg, 26 November 2019, www.bloomberg.com/news/articles/2019-11-26/a-u-s-offer-to-keep-the-wto-alive-comes-with-painful-conditions.

No one was fired eventually, but ABS staff were reallocated to other WTO divisions. As evidenced by these moves, the offensive on the Appellate Body was *also* an offensive on the inner circle of professional WTO litigators, aimed at disrupting their monopoly over the conduct of appellate proceedings.

This backlash poses a formidable threat to the club of trade practitioners, which has been in turmoil since the beginning of the crisis. Professional feuds both inside and outside the WTO[33] are reshuffling alliances and reconfiguring the community, whose participants are mobilizing to mitigate the impact on their career prospects. For instance, in 2020, a number of WTO member states (excluding, of course, the United States) have agreed to the Multi-Party Interim Appeal Arbitration Arrangement (MPIA), designed to temporarily replace ordinary appellate proceedings. It remains to be seen how this new mechanism will work in practice. However, it bears mentioning that the MPIA proposal was developed jointly by a state delegation *and* a preeminent trade law firm based in Geneva.[34]

Similar tensions between insiders and outsiders can be witnessed in the ongoing discussions of the institutional reform of ISDS.[35] Since its inception, this area of international law has been dominated by a select elite of practitioners enjoying a wide reputation and possessing highly concentrated professional capital. When, in 2017, the UN Commission on International Trade Law (UNCITRAL) was tasked with working on ISDS reform, it became apparent that the negotiating states would not let the arbitration 'mafia'[36] infiltrate the debate and perpetuate their dominance.

Faced with this hostility from outside political stakeholders, the inner circle of arbitration practitioners had mixed reactions. Some strove to maintain control over the system, warning that the UNCITRAL project would 'bring termites into [the] wooden house of investor state dispute

---

[33] See B. Baschuk, 'WTO Faces Cliff-edge Crisis Next Week as Mediator Eyes Departure', Bloomberg, 2 December 2019, www.bloomberg.com/news/articles/2019-12-02/wto-faces-cliff-edge-crisis-next-week-as-mediator-eyes-departure.

[34] S. Andersen et al., *Using Arbitration under Article 25 of the DSU to Ensure the Availability of Appeals*, CTEI Working Paper 2017–17 (2017).

[35] See generally A. Roberts, 'Incremental, Systemic, and Paradigmatic Reform of Investor-State Arbitration' (2018) 112(3) AJIL 410.

[36] Dezalay and Garth, *Dealing in Virtue*, 10; C. A. Rogers, 'The Vocation of the International Arbitrator' (2005) 20(5) AmUIntlLRev 957, 967; S. Puig, 'Social Capital in the Arbitration Market' (2014) 25(2) EJIL 387, 423.

resolution'.[37] Others showed a greater ability to adapt to the new environment and secure a seat at the negotiating table. For instance, two papers co-authored by a leading arbitrator and one of her closest collaborators offered the technical basis for the UNCITRAL discussions and are largely credited for catalysing the reform process.[38] Thanks to their efforts, the two authors were included in Switzerland's delegation and are now key actors in the debate.

•

'That's pretty cool,' said Norma, lighting a second cigarette. 'So, basically, you're one of a few dozen people running this whole ICJ business on a daily basis. You must feel quite proud.'

Sophie blushed. As tiring as it was to sustain the barrage of questions, she was flattered by her date's curiosity. Norma's eyes, almost as pale as hers, narrowed imperceptibly at every answer, as if to digest it. Then, they widened warmly as the interrogation resumed. It had been one hour since they had finished their coffees, and the sun was setting behind the buildings along Jan Hendrikstraat. For a moment, Sophie thought to ask for the check. The rest of the conversation could wait for another day. Norma called the waiter but, instead of paying, she ordered some tortilla chips and a bottle of white wine.

'So, do you feel proud?' She insisted, showing her intention to continue the discussion.

'Yes, I do. Let's put it this way: if international adjudication is an art, then I'm part of the art world.'[39]

'Or, if international adjudication is a crime, you're part of the mafia.'

'That's ... that's another way to put it, I guess ...'

Noticing Sophie's sudden unease, Norma was quick to lighten the mood.

---

[37] L. Pelucacci, 'Hon. Charles N. Brower Delivers Keynote Address at International Arbitration Conference', Fordham Law News, 27 November 2017, https://news.law.fordham.edu/blog/2017/11/27/hon-charles-n-brower-delivers-keynote-address-international-arbitration-conference/.

[38] G. Kauffman-Kohler and M. Potestà, *Can the Mauritius Convention Serve as a Model for the Reform of Investor-State Arbitration in Connection with the Introduction of a Permanent Investment Tribunal or an Appeal Mechanism?*, CIDS Working Paper (3 June 2016); G. Kauffman-Kohler and M. Potestà, *The Composition of a Multilateral Investment Court and of an Appeal Mechanism for Investment Awards*, CIDS Supplemental Report (15 November 2017).

[39] H. Becker, *Art Worlds* (Berkeley University Press, 1984).

'Oh, I'm sorry. That was a lame joke. But you guys must make fun of your clique from time to time, right? I mean, where's your Judge Lehning's sense of humour?'

'It's "Lehmann." And no, I'd never dare comparing him to a mafioso. I don't think he'd take it well.'

'No sense of humour, then?'

'It's not that. It's that I am ... I'm too junior to afford those jokes. Maybe another judge could say something like that. Or maybe one of my professors in New York. But I can't, not yet.'

'I see.' Norma's eyes narrowed again. 'So, this workplace of yours is quite hierarchical ...'

'... And competitive, too! Promotion opportunities are scarce enough without me coming across as disrespectful. If I want to stay at the Court after my clerkship, or to find a job at another international tribunal, I'd better keep my head down.'

'Are you saying that if your contract is not renewed, you could transition to another court? Like, Strasbourg? There is the human rights court in Strasbourg, right?'

'Right, but it's not that easy. I know my folks here in The Hague, but I don't know anybody in Strasbourg, or Geneva, or Hamburg. I couldn't name a single lawyer working at the registry of the European Court of Human Rights. I don't remember ever reading a WTO report cover to cover. And I don't know the names of all ITLOS judges. You see, we don't interact much with people working for other courts. We all do international law, we all do dispute settlement, and yet we ... live on different planets. Long story short: no, it's not that easy to land a job elsewhere. Conversion costs and all that.'

'Ok. So, the clique is not only hierarchical, but also fragmented. Interesting.'

'Well, we meet at conferences sometimes. The other day, Judge Lehmann had lunch with a group of colleagues from the Permanent Court of Arbitration, and I went with him to do some networking. Deep down, there is some shared sense of belonging that ties us all together. But in our routines, we go our separate ways: human rights lawyers with human rights lawyers, trade lawyers with trade lawyers, etc.'

'In my discipline, we would call that "polycentricity." Scattered poles of authority, loose coordination, competing allegiances.'

'I guess so.'

Norma's eyes widened.

'See? Just like the mafia.'

\*

This further exchange between Sophie and Norma adds several layers of complexity to our description of the international judicial community. So far, we have focused on its *esprit de corps* and its successful attempts to achieve autonomy from both politics and the rest of the international legal profession. These tight external boundaries may suggest that the community is internally homogeneous, heterarchical, and peaceful. But nothing would be farther from the truth.

In fact, the community is agitated by a fierce contest among its members, who strive to assert their dominance and to consolidate their position relative to one another. Borrowing from Pierre Bourdieu's notion of *juridical field*, we could think of the community as the site of a 'confrontation among actors possessing a technical competence which is inevitably social' and which consists essentially in 'the socially recognized capacity to interpret a corpus of texts sanctifying a correct or legitimized vision of the social world'.[40] This shift in focus from cooperation to competition is key to a number of discoveries.

The first discovery is that various species of capital – influence, prestige, social relationships, economic resources, technical prowess, etc.[41] – are *unevenly distributed* across the community. Not all views carry the same weight and not all voices are equally listened to.[42] Powerful hierarchical structures, both formal and informal, shape the social relationships among community members,[43] with a handful of professionals sitting at the top of the pyramid and the majority slowly crawling up from the bottom. The most eminent actors in the field are widely recognizable throughout the international legal world, and some of them even break through with the general public. The rest of the lot is virtually unknown, relegated to the underbelly of the judicial machinery.

These hierarchies occur, first, *within* each cluster of community actors. Inside a court, judges enjoy an exalted position compared to their supporting legal staff. Yet, not all judges are created equal. Most courts and tribunals attach formal significance to the role of presidents or chairpersons, who often exercise greater powers and bear additional responsibilities than the rest of the bench. Some judicial institutions, like the ECtHR and the WTO, contemplate two levels of jurisdiction, therefore placing first-instance adjudicators in a subordinate position

---

[40] Bourdieu, 'The Force of Law', 817 (emphasis omitted). See also U. Özsu, 'International Legal Fields', 5(2) *Humanity* 277 (2014).
[41] See P. Bourdieu, 'The Forms of Capital', in G. Richardson (ed.), *Handbook of Theory and Research for the Sociology of Education* (Greenwood Press, 1986) 241, 248.
[42] See Bianchi, 'The Game of Interpretation', 40–2.
[43] d'Aspremont, 'Professionalisation', 35.

vis-à-vis their appellate counterparts. Official prerogatives aside, certain judges possess informal qualities (experience, fame, fluency in the court's working languages) that make them perceived as more authoritative, more capable, or more reliable than others, thus becoming the object of admiration – or envy – by their colleagues.[44]

The supporting legal bureaucracy, too, can be formally organized in descending tiers of seniority (as with the ABS) or be more horizontal (as with ICJ clerks and arbitral secretaries). Administrative personnel, translators, interpreters, and other non-lawyers usually come last in the court's ranks. At the informal level, bureaucrats with a long-standing record of service are more familiar with a court's practice than their more junior colleagues, thereby wielding greater power in the conduct of proceedings. Meanwhile, at law firms, the earnings of partners (usually calculated on the basis of equity) are several times higher than those of associate attorneys (usually taking the form of salaries). De facto, partners are in charge of pleading in the courtroom (thereby making themselves known to the bench), while associates tend to take the backseat, provide support, and pass notes (thus going mostly unnoticed).

As for academia, well, most readers will know already.

But hierarchies exist also *across* clusters, that is, community-wide, with certain professional profiles garnering more recognition than others. Predictably, judges tend again to occupy the most prestigious spot. Given the symbolic power accorded to judicial interpretation,[45] being appointed to an international court is widely regarded as the acme of one's career in the field. Actually, it would perhaps be improper to speak of a full-fledged career. The total number of available positions on permanent courts is estimated at around 300[46] – a small figure compared to the size of the community. When states nominate their candidates to the bench, they seldom do so based on standardized selection procedures. Often, a successful candidate owes the privilege to an inscrutable set of factors such as possessing the right nationality, cultivating personal and professional relationships, and more generally being at the right place at the right time.[47] Under these

---

[44] See Terris, Romano, and Swigart, *The International Judge*, 66–7.
[45] See Bianchi, 'The Game of Interpretation', 40–2.
[46] See L. Swigart and D. Terris, 'Who Are International Judges?', in C. P. R. Romano, K. J. Alter, and Y. Shany (eds.), *The Oxford Handbook of International Adjudication* (Oxford University Press, 2014) 619, 621; Terris, Romano, and Swigart, *The International Judge*, 17.
[47] See Terris, Romano, and Swigart, *The International Judge*, 17; Swigart and Terris, 'Who Are International Judges?', 633.

conditions, it would be difficult for anyone, even the most accomplished lawyer, to deliberately *plan* to become an international judge.

Similar reverence is paid to top-tier investment arbitrators, who constitute an even smaller group. As we will discuss,[48] social capital in the ISDS arena is particularly concentrated, with 20–30 arbitrators securing most appointments to tribunals and leaving the rest of their peers fighting for the scraps. The status acquired by the arbitration elite is the object of intense scrutiny and scholarly analysis.[49] As evidence of that status, the United States bestows the title of 'Honorable' on its nationals sitting on the US-Iran States Claims Tribunal, thereby equating them to federal judges. While most US members of the Tribunal do not make much of this title, some proudly sport it on their professional webpages.[50]

University professors and prominent litigators compete for the second position in the hierarchy. Both clusters of actors are highly visible within the field, and both produce a steady pool of candidates for international courts and tribunals. However, the types of capital that scholars and counsel deploy are quite different. The former advance their position by disseminating their ideas across the community. Academics are in a 'co-constitutive'[51] relationship with judicial practice: on the one hand, it is that practice that creates the object of their studies; on the other, it is their theories, commentaries, and systematizations that generate the background knowledge necessary to structure the epistemic categories and the expert vernacular of practitioners.[52] Ideas legitimate judicial power and judicial power enforces ideas. Counsel, for their part, mobilize economic resources and channel clients into the dispute settlement process, thereby acting as 'brokers' that connect the demands of the parties with the legal supply of the courts.[53] Indeed, it is largely thanks to their initiative and entrepreneurship that international adjudication has expanded from a fragile political project to a robust node of global governance.

---

[48] See *infra*, pp. 62–5.

[49] See e.g. Dezalay and Garth, *Dealing in Virtue*; Puig, 'The Arbitration Market'; J. Pauwelyn, 'The Rule of Law without the Rule of Lawyers? Why Investment Arbitrators Are from Mars, Trade Adjudicators from Venus' (2015) 109(4) AJIL 761.

[50] See e.g. Twenty Essex website, *The Honorable Charles N. Brower*, https://twentyessex.com/people/charles-brower/.

[51] G. I. Hernández, 'The Responsibility of the International Legal Academic: Situating the Grammarian within the "Invisible College"', in J. d'Aspremont et al. (eds.), *International Law as a Profession* (Cambridge University Press, 2017) 160.

[52] See D. W. Kennedy, 'The Politics of the Invisible College: International Governance and the Politics of Expertise' (2001) 5 EHRLR 463; Hernández, 'The International Legal Academic', 160–1.

[53] Vauchez, 'Communities of International Litigators', 657.

At the bottom of the hierarchy we find the legion of clerks, secretariat and registry staff, and arbitral secretaries assisting the adjudicators. As will become clear,[54] this cluster of actors constitutes the backbone of international courts and tribunals. Yet, its manifold activities take place mostly off the radar, concealed behind the closed doors of judicial institutions and largely neglected by external commentators. Faceless by definition, judicial bureaucrats seldom enjoy the visibility necessary to rise to fame. Some of them relish their *in*visibility and take great pleasure in the influence they wield behind the scenes. Their vocation, as well as the source of their capital, resides in what Max Weber described as 'technical superiority[,] [p]recision, speed, unambiguity, knowledge of the files, continuity, [and] discretion'.[55] For others, employment with the bureaucracy is a mere entry point into the community and, hopefully, a springboard towards more visible positions.

Interestingly, the 'conversion rate'[56] between social and economic capital, or between recognition and income, is not 1:1. In fact, if we were to rank community members based on their earnings, the hierarchy would look a bit different. At the top, we would find big law firm partners and elite arbitrators. The former can charge in excess of USD 1,000 per hour, especially when working on large trade or investment cases.[57] The latter's fees are capped at USD 3,000 per day when the arbitration takes place under the auspices of the International Centre for Settlement of Investment Disputes (ICSID), and can rise up to USD 6,000 per day if the arbitration is governed by the rules of the London Court of International Arbitration.[58] Next we would find permanent judges, whose remuneration, while varying across courts, easily exceeds USD 200,000 per annum.[59] Judicial bureaucrats

---

[54] See *infra*, Chapter 5.
[55] M. Weber, *Economy and Society: An Outline of Interpretive Sociology*, edited by G. Roth and C. Wittich (University of California Press, 1978), 973.
[56] Bourdieu, 'The Forms of Capital', 248.
[57] See e.g. Aceris Law LLC website, *International Arbitration Information*, www.international-arbitration-attorney.com/icsid-arbitration-cost-calculator-2/.
[58] See e.g. D. Rosert, *The Stakes Are High: A Review of the Financial Costs of Investment Treaty Arbitration* (International Institute for Sustainable Development, 2014), 10–11.
[59] See e.g. M. Simons, 'In The Hague's lofty judicial halls, judges wrangle over pay', New York Times, 20 January 2019, www.nytimes.com/2019/01/20/world/europe/hague-judges-pay.html (reporting that ICJ Judges are paid USD 230,000/annum as of 2019); O. Bowcott, 'UK nominees for judge at European court of human rights revealed', The Guardian, 28 April 2016, www.theguardian.com/law/2016/apr/28/uk-nominees-for-judge-at-european-court-of-human-rights-revealed (estimating the net annual salary of ECtHR Judges at EUR 200,000).

would come a distant third. Their net annual salaries differ widely depending on institutional affiliation and level of seniority, and indicatively range from USD 60,000 (for newcomers) to 150,000 (for top officials).[60] Finally, academic remuneration is highly dependent on the salary structure of each university, but would normally land in the lower regions of the chart. Of course, the fact that community participants may don multiple hats at once enables them to combine different sources of income.

The second discovery is that the distribution of capital within the community is not only uneven, but indeed *inseparable from the substance* of legal activity. Ostensibly, the 'ultimate object' of the game of international adjudication is to persuade one's audience that a legal opinion or solution to a given problem is 'correct'. The 'winner', in principle, is he or she who succeeds in securing adherence to a own views.[61] However, 'victory' is not merely a source of personal gratification – it is *also* a means to strengthen one's position in the field. Therefore, any sharp distinction between purely 'legal' and purely 'socio-professional' debates is purely artificial. The various normative positions taken by community members can never be reduced to mere technical arguments or abstract opinions. Instead, those positions always combine dispassionate normative beliefs with the positioning, the agendas – not to mention the sheer 'careerism'[62] – of the actors involved.

For instance, when a counsel pursues a sophisticated line of argument in court, they do merely wish to advance their client's interests; they also seek to impress the judges with their *interprétation savante* and, possibly, secure a precedent they can exploit in future cases with *other* clients. Likewise, when a scholar develops a new legal theory or taxonomy, they often undertake a 'marketing campaign' to disseminate it across courts and tribunals; this way, they may hope that practitioners will adopt it as their own, or even that adjudicators will cite it in their rulings.[63] Each

---

[60] See e.g. ICJ website, *Vacancy announcement: Associate Legal Officer*, www.icj-cij.org/files/vacancy-announcements/2018-11-EN.pdf (accessed 29 August 2020) (fixing the indicative minimum net annual remuneration for ICJ clerks at USD 63,806); WTO Committee on Budget, Finance and Administration, *2019 WTO Salary Survey*, WT/BFA/W/471 (7 March 2019) (indicating that gross annual salaries range from CHF 90,881 for G7 officers to CHF 216,168 for G11 directors).

[61] See Bianchi, 'The Game of Interpretation', 36.

[62] P. Schlag, 'US CLS' (1999) 10(3) L&Crit 199, 210. See also P. Schlag, 'Normativity and the Politics of Form' (1991) 139(4) UPaLRev 801, fn 125.

[63] Of course, this opens the door to a plethora of shallow doctrine, eager to 'imitate judicial discourse'. P. Schlag, 'Spam Jurisprudence, Air Law, and the Rank Anxiety of Nothing Happening: A Report on the State of the Art' (2009) 97(3) GeoLJ 803, 819.

actor's endowment of capital dictates, at any given moment, the strength of their persuasiveness and the deference accorded to their views. Thus, a reputable judge will think twice before following the advice of a new recruit to the supporting bureaucracy; a junior associate will have to work extra hard to include a certain argument in a submission against the opinion of a seasoned partner; and so on.

The inextricable link between legal argument and social positioning brings us to the third and final discovery. The social configurations of the community are not static, but rather *evolve over time* as a result of the endless struggle among its participants. Competition and conflict pervade literally every corner of international courts and tribunals, from hearing rooms to backroom corridors, from deliberation tables to cafeterias. Day after day, case after case, the members of the community strive against one another to assert their authority, increase their capital, and impose their competing visions of the law as the dominant paradigm. Every step of the judicial process sees a confrontation among judges, bureaucrats, agents, and counsel, each resorting to schemes, postures, and strategies that, depending on the circumstances, may be 'risky or cautious, subversive or conservative'.[64] The incumbents will have a natural tendency to perpetuate their dominance. The challengers will have to come up with other plans, ranging from opportunistic deference to overt defiance, to get the upper hand. At every turn, old alliances may break down and new ones may emerge, in a continuous process of assertion, contestation, and restructuring.

The twofold structure of the community – externally autonomous and internally conflictive – will become more apparent as the story progresses. For now, let us focus on another point made by Sophie: the problem of dispute settlement professionals 'living on different planets'.

The exponential growth of the international legal profession at the turn of the century was accompanied by its progressive specialization into sectoral areas of expertise such as human rights, trade, investment, territorial delimitation, and international criminal law. The international judicial community is no stranger to this trend, and has been 'fragmenting'[65] into

---

[64] P. Bourdieu and L. Wacquant, *An Invitation to Reflexive Sociology* (University of Chicago Press, 1992), 98.

[65] H. G. Cohen, 'Finding International Law, Part II: Our Fragmenting Legal Community' (2012) 44(4) NYUJILP 1049. See also e.g. A. Bianchi, 'Looking Ahead: International Law's Main Challenges', in D. Armstrong (ed.), *Routledge Handbook of International Law* (Routledge, 2009) 392, 404; M. Waibel, 'Interpretive Communities in International Law', in A. Bianchi, D. Peat, and M. Windsor (eds.), *Interpretation in International Law* (Oxford University Press, 2015) 147.

several 'sub-communities'[66] that operate largely independently of one another. According to some, this centrifugal tendency ought not to be overstated. After all, judicial professionals from different regimes are still 'coming together in all sorts of ways', from 'seminars to training sessions', on 'the Internet, through clerks', etc.,[67] thereby fostering cross-fertilization and the development of common adjudicative practices.[68] For others, fragmentation runs much deeper. In their view, the various sub-communities are bound to clash with their agendas, preoccupations, sensibilities, and vocabularies, thus foreclosing any possibility to find universal meaning and breaking up 'the very center of global law, where courts and arbitration tribunals are located'.[69]

Who is right? Echoing Sophie's metaphor,[70] we would say that the international judicial community resembles a constellation. Each court or tribunal is a star exerting its gravitational pull on the various planets – government departments, law firms, academic centres, and so on – that orbit around it in concentric circles, from centre to periphery. Some gravitational fields may be stronger than others. Specialized knowledge may be more concentrated in certain sub-communities (e.g. the WTO, characterized by a highly sectarian expertise) than in others (e.g. the ICJ, which takes great pride in its 'generalist' outlook). Moreover, the trajectories of some planets may be attracted to the gravitational fields of more than one star, therefore creating overlaps between different sub-communities.[71] For instance, ICJ experts often cross into ISDS territory by appearing as arbitrators or counsel; European Union law specialists have progressively come to infiltrate the WTO arena, with repercussions on the ethos, style, and tone of trade adjudicators;[72] regional human rights courts maintain strong relationships among their judges and legal bureaucracies, and carefully read each other's judgments;[73] and so on.

Yet, none of the stars – not even the ICJ – can be deemed to sit at the centre of the constellation. No sub-community can lay claim to a truly neutral and universal outlook on the international legal world, which has

---

[66] d'Aspremont, 'Professionalisation', 32.
[67] Slaughter, 'A Global Community of Courts', 192.
[68] See e.g. Abi-Saab, 'Fragmentation or Unification'; A. Stone Sweet and J. Mathews, 'Proportionality Balancing and Global Constitutionalism' (2008) 47(1) ColumJTransnatlL 73.
[69] A. Fischer-Lescano and G. Teubner, 'Regime-Collisions: The Vain Search for Legal Unity in the Fragmentation of Global Law' (2004) 25(4) MichJIntlL 999, 1014.
[70] Which, in turn, reminds of B. Simma and D. Pulkowski, 'Of Planets and the Universe: Self-Contained Regimes in International Law' (2006) 17(3) EJIL 483.
[71] See Cohen, 'Finding International Law, Part II', 1068.
[72] See generally Soave, 'European Legal Culture'.
[73] See e.g. Terris, Romano, and Swigart, *The International Judge*, 120.

become too vast and too pluralistic for anyone to master it all. Instead, as we shall see,[74] the position that each sub-community occupies in the constellation shapes its epistemic categories, its social dynamics, and its operational boundaries. Unfortunately for Sophie, this polycentricity entails entry barriers and conversion costs for professionals wishing to transition from one sub-community to another. A senior lawyer trained in the practice of the WTO may struggle to land an equally senior position at a firm specializing in ISDS. A preeminent scholar in the field of European human rights law may not enjoy the same reputation in ICJ circles. And so forth. Hence, the members of a sub-community do not only seek autonomy from the broader international legal profession – they also guard their turf from *other* sub-communities.

•

After dusk, the atmosphere of Grote Markt had changed. The afternoon bustle had quieted down, and some cafés had closed. A few students lingered in a corner of the square, beer cans in hand, playing trap music from a portable speaker. The pigeons had disappeared. The air was getting chilly, but Sophie and Norma were too tipsy to notice it. The first bottle was gone, and Norma had just ordered a second one. The conversation had momentarily moved away from Sophie's job and hopped from Lebanese wine to the Israel-Palestine conflict, to Mediterranean music, to Spaghetti Western movies, to the myth of the lone American cowboy, to Donald Trump, to Brexit, to Jonathan Coe's novel about Brexit, which they were both reading. As Sophie was finally beginning to relax, Norma suddenly brought the discussion back to where it started.

'You're still avoiding my question,' she smirked.

'Huh?'

'You haven't answered the question I asked you three hours ago.'

'Which was …?'

'… What it means for you to do what you do.'

'I thought I had just told you.'

'You told me the who, not the what. I now understand more or less who the folks in your field are, but not what they do all day.'

'That's top secret. Sorry.'

'Are you kidding me?'

'Yeah, I'm kidding.' Sophie grinned at Norma's bemusement. 'But I'd hate to bore you.'

---

[74] See *infra*, pp. 214–18.

Hopefully, you did not get too bored as we sketched the structure of the international judicial community. Our description has focused on its main participants, their quest for autonomy from the broader international legal profession, and their internal hierarchies and competitive dynamics. Yet, the sketch remains somewhat incomplete: the outline is in place, but it is lacking in colour. To complete the picture, it now bears asking: how does the community operate? How do its members go about their daily business? What activities, interactions, and discourses make up their professional universe? In short: what are *international judicial practices*?

For a full answer to these questions, you will have to read the whole book. The 'gigantic maze of practices and arrangements'[75] that enliven international courts and tribunals is too intricate to explore in a few pages. We can, however, try to provide at least an initial account of international judicial practices, relate them to the underlying social structures, and explore their impact on international legal outcomes.

The first step is to understand the notion of 'practices'. In recent years, social theory has attempted to overcome the 'rationalist' and 'norm-based' traditions that had dominated the discipline for much of the twentieth century.[76] Instead of focusing on the preordained intentions and preferences of individual actors or the objectified norms to which they respond, practice theory seeks to appraise social action as 'an actual, contingent, evolving and productive set of activities'.[77] Those activities are informed by 'symbolic structures of knowledge' that 'enable and constrain the agents to interpret the world according to certain forms, and to behave in corresponding ways'.[78] In turn, structures are not dictated only by official discourse or peremptory commands, but rather encompass 'the explicit and the tacit'; 'what is said and what is left unsaid'; 'what is represented and what is assumed'; 'the language, tools, documents, ... regulations, and contracts' that instantiate the shared dispositions of a social group.[79]

---

[75] T. Schatzki, 'Keeping Track of Large Phenomena' (2016) 104(1) GeogrZ 4, 6.
[76] See e.g. A. Reckwitz, 'Toward a Theory of Social Practices: A Development in Culturalist Theorizing' (2002) 5(2) EJST 243; Dunoff and Pollack, 'International Judicial Practices', 52.
[77] N. M. Rajkovic, T. E. Aalberts, and T. Gammeltoft-Hansen, 'Introduction', in N. M. Rajkovic, T. E. Aalberts, and T. Gammeltoft-Hansen (eds.), *The Power of Legality: Practices of International Law and Their Politics* (Cambridge University Press, 2016) 1, 12.
[78] Reckwitz, 'A Theory of Social Practices', 245–6.
[79] Wenger, *Communities of Practice*, 47.

As applied to international governance, practices have been famously – and laconically – defined as 'competent performances'.[80] More precisely, practices 'are socially meaningful patterns of action which, in being performed more or less competently, simultaneously embody, act out, and possibly reify background knowledge and discourse in and on the material world'.[81] This definition has known considerable success among international law and international relations scholars,[82] and has recently been used to describe some of the activities of international courts and tribunals.[83]

Drawing from this theoretical framework, we can identify four main attributes that distinguish international judicial practices from (and make them something more than) simple action.

*First*, practices are 'performances'. At its simplest, this means that international adjudication entails 'a process of doing' that has 'no existence other than in [its] unfolding'.[84] Thus understood, this attribute is self-evident. The various members of the community engage in a variety of activities throughout the litigation process. Chief among these is the interpretation of the international legal norms applicable to the case at hand. According to many, this is *the* activity that, more than any other, defines the essence of adjudication. Indeed, all community participants compete, in one way or another, for interpretive authority: agents and counsel through their briefs and arguments, judicial bureaucrats through their advice and internal memoranda, scholars through their articles, and adjudicators through their decisions. As discussed, securing control over legal interpretation is the ultimate prize of community struggles.[85]

However, legal interpretation does not exhaust the scope of international judicial practices. In fact, a large swathe of life at the court is taken up by tasks that are not of 'interpretive' in nature. For instance, state agents coordinate with their political principals to define the goals and the modes of litigation. Counsel spend time and energy reaching out to potential

---

[80] Adler and Pouliot, 'International Practices', 4.
[81] Ibid.
[82] See e.g. J. Brunnée and S. Toope, *Legitimacy and Legality in International Law: An Interactional Account* (Cambridge University Press, 2013); T. E. Aalberts and I. Venzke, 'Moving beyond Interdisciplinary Turf Wars: Towards an Understanding of International Law as Practice', in J. d'Aspremont et al. (eds.), *International Law as a Profession* (Cambridge University Press, 2017) 287.
[83] Dunoff and Pollack, 'International Judicial Practices'. See also F. Mégret, 'International Criminal Justice as a Juridical Field' (2016) 13 *Champ pénal*.
[84] Adler and Pouliot, 'International Practices', 6.
[85] Bourdieu, 'The Force of Law', 818.

clients, devising litigation strategies, and cultivating friendly relationships with the bench. Court bureaucrats digest vast amounts of information, summarize the litigants' legal and factual submissions, and provide logistical support throughout the proceedings. Academics seek to secure chairs, funding, and visibility within their respective universities. Adjudicators often engage in extra-judicial activities such as lecturing, publishing, and outreach. And so on.[86]

Whether interpretive or not, every act of 'doing' leaves a trace, or produces a discrete object, that contributes to the overall conduct of judicial proceedings. Some traces are tangible: a counsel's written submission, a bureaucrat's memo, a folder of documentary evidence and, of course, the court's final judgment are all embodied in the physical medium of printed paper. The corporeal properties of the object are not a mere wrap for content: in many instances, they take on a significance of their own. For instance, a *thick* dossier, one that contains lengthy party memorials and voluminous amounts of evidence, will typically make for a '*big* case' requiring the allocation of additional time and staff resources to be processed; the *length* of a decision will be read as a proxy for the complexity of the issues addressed, the degree of harmony or discord among the judges, etc. Other traces are physically intangible, but no less material: oral pleadings, deliberations, and conference presentations all generate a web of meaning that carries a certain *weight*, informs the behaviour of both speakers and listeners, and imparts direction to subsequent action.

But there is more to the word 'performances' than first meets the eye. One cannot think about that word without thinking about theatre.[87] From artists to semioticians, from literary critics to philosophers, many see everyday life as rife with instances of theatrical performance.[88] As Umberto Eco once noted, '[i]t is not theatre that is able to imitate life; it is social life that is designed as a continuous performance and, because of this, there is a link between theatre and life.'[89] Or, as new wave rock star David Byrne puts it, 'there [are] lots of unacknowledged theater forms

---

[86] For a more comprehensive typology of international judicial practices, see e.g. Dunoff and Pollack, 'International Judicial Practices', 65–85.
[87] See P. Auslander, *From Acting to Performance: Essays in Modernism and Postmodernism* (Routledge, 1997), 4.
[88] See e.g. U. Eco, 'Semiotics of Theatrical Performance' (1977) 21(1) TDR 107, 113; D. Byrne, *How Music Works* (McSweeney's, 2012), 64.
[89] Eco, 'Theatrical Performance', 113.

going on all around' that 'have been so woven into our daily routine that the artificial ... aspect has slipped into invisibility'.[90]

International judicial practices are no exception. The adjudicative process is a succession of carefully *staged* acts carried out by certain *actors*, directed at a certain *audience*, and following a *script*. Some steps of the process are more explicitly 'performative' than others. In the first pages of this book, for example, we emphasized the ceremonial nature of the delivery of an ICJ judgment. Similarly, as we will see later,[91] court hearings are tightly choreographed events that publicly display the courtroom as the centre-stage of peaceful dispute resolution. Yet, theatrics and rituals permeate many other corners of life at the court.

*Second*, practices are 'patterned', meaning that they tend to exhibit 'certain regularities over time and space'.[92] Their repetition 'reproduce[s] similar behaviors with regular meanings', and 'structures interaction' within a socially organized context.[93] This attribute comports well with the iterative nature of international adjudication. Although every dispute is unique in the legal issues it raises, the procedural steps that mark its unfolding are standardized. Every case invariably begins with the submission of written memorials by the complainant and the respondent, often followed by rejoinders and counter-rejoinders. These written filings are then processed by the bureaucrats assisting the court or tribunal, who circulate internal memoranda to summarize their analyses and help the adjudicators prepare for the next steps. After the written phase, most courts and tribunals hold one or more hearings, where the merits of the case are discussed orally. After the hearing(s), the adjudicators convene for deliberations and cast their decisions about the issues at stake. Based on the adjudicators' instructions, the final judgment is drafted, reviewed, approved, translated, and issued to the parties and the public.

Iteration is not limited to the procedural steps of litigation, but extends to the social interactions among the actors involved. As discussed, the international judicial community is a close-knit network whose participants know each other well, communicate regularly, and entertain long-term professional relationships. In the game of adjudication, repeat players are the norm and one-shotters are the exception. Indeed, the

---

[90] Byrne, *How Music Works*, 64.
[91] See *infra*, Chapter 14.
[92] Adler and Pouliot, 'International Practices', 6.
[93] Ibid.

capital of each player stems in part from their experience and recurring participation in judicial proceedings. It follows that international judicial practices occur within a 'highly organized context'[94] and present a strong measure of systematic repetition.

*Third*, international judicial practices can be 'performed more or less competently' depending on the shared 'background knowledge' of the actors carrying them out.[95] This means, in a nutshell, that the hallmarks of (in)competence in the community are not inherent in the abstract quality of the work performed, but are socially attributed by the community itself based on collectively held standards. Through education, training, and work experience, community members are initiated to the way things are done.[96] Over time, they master the doctrines, the argumentative techniques, the ethos, the aesthetics, and the mythologies of their peers and superiors,[97] and reproduce them through communication and transmission of knowledge. Newcomers quickly internalize the *habitus* – the set of 'durable, transposable dispositions'[98] – of the community, and tend to conform to it in order to cement their status.

These channels of socialization contribute to the perpetuation of the structures of the system, which 'condense and are confirmed as a result of the system's own operations'.[99] *Habitus* is not only a source of *constraint* for those who play the game of adjudication; it also *enables* them to make statements and express positions that will be accepted as 'true' or 'valid' by other players.[100]

The outer limits of the game, the boundaries beyond which no respectable player can venture, are dictated by *doxa*, that is, the set of unquestioned truths that define the universe of possible practices and discourses

---

[94] Dunoff and Pollack, 'International Judicial Practices', 62.
[95] Adler and Pouliot, 'International Practices', 6–7 (emphasis omitted).
[96] Gross Stein, 'Background Knowledge', 89. Anthea Robert's work shows the power of international legal education(s) in shaping our vision of the discipline and our self-perception as members of the community. A. Roberts, *Is International Law International?* (Oxford University Press, 2017).
[97] See e.g. d'Aspremont, 'Professionalisation', 33–4; D. W. Kennedy, 'The Disciplines of International Law and Policy' (1999) 12(1) LJIL 9; P. Schlag, 'The Aesthetics of American Law' (2002) 115(4) HarvLRev 1047.
[98] Bourdieu, *Theory of Practice*, 72.
[99] Luhmann, 'Operational Closure', 1424.
[100] See e.g. S. B. Ortner, *Anthropology and Social Theory: Culture, Power and the Acting Subject* (Duke University Press, 2006), 3; Dunoff and Pollack, 'International Judicial Practices', 54.

in the field.¹⁰¹ International adjudication has no short supply of doxic beliefs: that law is better than politics; that politics is better than war; that judicialization fosters the security and predictability of behaviour on the world stage; and the like. Incidentally, those beliefs aggrandize the self-perception of the international judicial community as indispensable to international affairs. Many of its members have become blind to the irreducible pluralism of global society. From their vantage point, it is easy to forget that there are more things in heaven and earth than are dreamt of in their philosophy.¹⁰²

Background knowledge informs every aspect of the judicial process, including – and perhaps especially – the interpretation of international legal norms. This idea was first explored by Stanley Fish in his seminal work on interpretive communities¹⁰³ and is now increasingly popular among international law scholars.¹⁰⁴ Moving from the premise that the meaning of words resides in their use in language,¹⁰⁵ several authors have highlighted that the meaning of a legal text is not inherent in the text itself, but rather reflects the categories of understanding, the ways of organizing experience, and the stipulations of relevance and irrelevance shared by the community tasked with interpreting that text.¹⁰⁶ The consensus of the community determines, at any given moment, whether the reading of a given norm is or is not acceptable, whether a specific interpretative posture is or is not viable, and whether a particular legal argument is or is not persuasive.¹⁰⁷ Thus conceived, interpretation becomes 'an act of authority dependent on its ability to induce acceptance by way of argument or persuasion'.¹⁰⁸

---

[101] See e.g. P. Bourdieu, 'Structures, Habitus, Power: Basis for a Theory of Symbolic Power' in N. B. Dirks, G. Eley, and S. B. Ortner (eds.), *Culture/Power/History: A Reader in Contemporary Social Theory* (Princeton University Press, 1994) 164.

[102] Forgive us, Shakespeare. W. Shakespeare, *The Tragedy of Hamlet, Prince of Denmark* (ca. 1600), 1.5.187-8.

[103] See Fish, *Is There a Text*.

[104] See e.g. I. Johnstone, 'Treaty Interpretation: The Authority of Interpretive Communities' (1991) 12(2) MichJIntlL 371; Bianchi, 'Textual Interpretation'; Klabbers, 'Virtuous Interpretation'; Shaffer and Trachtman, 'Interpretation and Institutional Choice'; Venzke, *How Interpretation Makes International Law*; d'Aspremont, 'The Multidimensional Process of Interpretation'; Waibel, 'Interpretive Communities'.

[105] Wittgenstein, *Philosophical Investigations*, para. 43.

[106] S. Fish, *Doing What Comes Naturally: Change, Rhetoric, and the Practice of Theory in Literary and Legal Studies* (Duke University Press, 1990), 141.

[107] See e.g. Bianchi, 'Textual Interpretation', 39–40; d'Aspremont, 'The Multidimensional Process of Interpretation', 114.

[108] d'Aspremont, 'The Multidimensional Process of Interpretation', 114.

Yet, the shared assumptions and dispositions of the community also inform non-interpretive practices. When a legal counsel calibrates their argument so as to avoid potential conflicts with prospective clients; when a newly appointed judge accedes to the views of a senior colleague out of deference; when a scholar acquires visibility and semantic authority thanks to their astute positioning on the academic market; in all those instances, the structures of the system are at play. This is due to the *fourth* and final attribute of international judicial practices: their ability to weave together the 'discursive' and the 'material world'. As mentioned, the technical discourses that develop within the community cannot be divorced from the professional strategies and social positioning of the actors involved. Communication may take 'the form of legal discourse', but inevitably bears 'material consequences for the litigants'.[109]

In this sense, international judicial practices differ from those of an 'epistemic community', first defined by Peter Haas as 'a network of professionals with recognized expertise and competence in a particular domain and an authoritative claim to policy-relevant knowledge within that domain'.[110] According to Haas, an epistemic community is animated by 'normative and principled beliefs, which provide a value-based rationale for ... social action', and pursues a 'common policy enterprise'.[111]

While this account helpfully places the accent on the power of expert vernaculars and worldviews,[112] it also overplays the values and ideals shared by the actors involved in a community. The practices of the international judicial community can hardly be explained by reference to cohesive sets of principles or grand normative theories. The judicial process resembles nothing like an orderly endeavour, guided by an overarching rationality. Instead, it is akin to a hesitant, uncertain, and painstaking knitting process throughout which community actors

---

[109] Dunoff and Pollack, 'International Judicial Practices', 62.
[110] P. M. Haas, 'Introduction: Epistemic Communities and International Policy Coordination' (1992) 46(1) IntlOrg 1, 3. See also e.g. D. Pulkowski, *The Law and Politics of International Regime Conflict* (Oxford University Press, 2014), 16; M. Noortmann, 'The International Law Association and Non-State Actors: Professional Network, Public Interest Group or Epistemic Community?', in J. d'Aspremont (ed.), *Participants in the International Legal System: Multiple Perspective on Non-State Actors in International Law* (Routledge, 2015) 233.
[111] Haas, 'Epistemic Communities', 3. See also e.g. T. S. Kuhn, *The Structure of Scientific Revolutions* (2nd edn., University of Chicago Press, 1970), 175 (speaking to the 'constellation of beliefs, values, techniques' that govern community practice); A. Wendt, *Social Theory of International Politics* (Cambridge University Press, 1999), 215–20.
[112] See Waibel, 'Interpretive Communities', 149–50.

'grapple with a file';[113] assemble, disassemble, and reassemble claims and arguments; single out the salient facts among the plethora of evidence on record; assert, resist, and test their interpretive choices and moral instincts; until, eventually, the patchwork takes the form of a coherent whole.[114] The contribution of each actor to the process can hardly be defined as purely principled or ideational. Rather, it responds to 'a form of mastery that is expressed in the capacity to carry out a social and material activity'.[115]

Having outlined the main attributes of international judicial practices, it is almost time to go back to Grote Markt and see how Sophie and Norma are doing. But before, let us raise one last question that will resurface time and again throughout this book: the question of freedom. If practice is socially shaped by the community, and if the community is rigidly structured, what room is left for personal agency? How can Sophie, Filibert, Judge Lehmann, and the other protagonists of this story leave their personal marks on the adjudicative process?

Again, practice theory offers an answer: practices are not 'merely descriptive "arrows" that connect structure to agency and back', but rather 'the dynamic material and ideational processes that enable structures to be stable or to evolve, and agents to reproduce or transform structures'.[116] Stated otherwise, our characters operate under a condition of *structured contingency*.

'Contingency', because the path that leads to the formation of an international judgment is not predetermined, but open-ended. Every step of the process contemplates choices and purposeful actions on the part of the professionals involved. (Why else would we speak of judicial *decisions*?) Each actor has countless opportunities to voice their opinion, assert and resist claims, and consciously exercise a discrete portion of agency to steer the course of proceedings.

'Structured', because while existing arrangements can be changed, 'change unfolds within a context that includes systematic constraints and pressures'.[117] Departing too abruptly from the tacit rules of the game

---

[113] Latour, *The Making of Law*, 192.
[114] See Wells, 'Situated Decisionmaking', 1734–6.
[115] D. Nicolini, *Practice Theory, Work and Organization: An Introduction* (Oxford University Press, 2012), 5.
[116] E. Adler and V. Pouliot, 'International Practices: Introduction and Framework', in E. Adler and V. Pouliot (eds.), *International Practices* (Cambridge University Press, 2011) 3, 4–5.
[117] S. Marks, 'False Contingency' (2009) 62(1) CLP 1, 2.

would lead to professional reprimand, public derision, or outright expulsion from the game itself. As Karl Marx would put it, our characters 'make their own history, but they do not make it just as they please in circumstances they choose for themselves; rather they make it in present circumstances, given and inherited'.[118]

Seen through the lens of structured contingency, the practices of the international judicial community are both the vehicle of reproduction that ensures predictability in international judicial outcomes and the source from which legal change originates.[119]

The stabilizing function stems essentially from patterned repetition and intersubjective socialization. The community plays its stabilizing role in both an active and a passive way. Throughout the adjudicative process, it pushes and forces adjudicators by expressing views as to how certain issues should be addressed, how certain legal terms should be interpreted, and what bodies of rules should be considered to solve the case. Once the judgment is rendered, it carefully tests its persuasiveness, ascribes competence and incompetence based on its collective knowledge, and acts as the ultimate arbiter of professional recognition. At each step, community expectations determine the continued validity of legal standards and ensure jurisprudential predictability in a system without formal *stare decisis*. While a decision that slightly departs from established practice will normally be tolerated, an abrupt change of direction will encounter resistance and be attacked as an anomaly, a deviation, or – heaven forbid! – an 'irrational' decision.[120] Hence, the community serves as the anchor that prevents adjudicators from sailing adrift, reaching 'extreme' conclusions, and ripping the underlying social fabric apart.

---

[118] K. Marx, 'The Eighteenth Brumaire of Louis Bonaparte' in T. Carver (ed.), *Marx: Later Political Writings* (Cambridge University Press, 1996), 32.

[119] See Adler and Pouliot, 'International Practices', 18.

[120] For example, Harm Schepel and Rein Wesseling described how a decision of the European Court of Justice that deviated from well-established case law was lambasted as being '"inexplicable and contradictory", without "convincing or sufficient motivation", leaving ... a "worrisome jurisprudential void"'. H. Schepel and R. Wesseling, 'The Legal Community: Judges, Lawyers, Officials and Clerks in the Writing of Europe' (1997) 3(2) ELJ 165, 185–6 (citing A . Mattera, 'De l'Arrêt "Dassonville" à l'Arrêt "Keck": L'Obscure Clarté d'une Jurisprudence Riche en Principes Novateurs et en Contradictions' (1994) 1 RMUE 117, 153).

But the community, is not only a source of stability. Its practices also help explain how legal outcomes *evolve* over t ime.[121] After all, stability is only 'an illusion created by the recursive nature of practice', whereas change 'is the ordinary condition of social life'.[122] Given the struggles that that endlessly roil the community, the boundaries, priorities, and preoccupations of judicial regimes are 'never inherently fixed or stable', but are 'constantly being renegotiated' among community members.[123] The expert vocabularies in use in international courts are 'sites of controversy and compromise where prevailing "mainstreams" constantly clash against minority challengers'.[124] Each agent modifies the form taken by arguments and the salience of texts, and traces 'a set of divergent paths, mobilizing clans who confront each other with facts, precedents, understandings, opportunities or public morality, all of which are used to stoke the fire of the debate.'[125]

These tensions create paths of contestation and open the door to new legal approaches, new interpretive postures, new ways of doing things. Innovations are seldom presented as radical, lest they be dismissed out of hand. They will usually creep in through the backdoor – discussed as a side point during a meeting, inserted in the paragraph of a submission or memo, etc. The most successful will then slowly grow in the system – first as obscure footnotes buried in a judgment, then as *obiter dicta* in the main text, and finally as the new standard against which the community measures the persuasiveness of legal reasoning. Ultimately, change occurs when the dominant assumptions embedded in a judicial regime are successfully challenged and replaced by new assumptions, as a result of the piecemeal evolution of the power relationships among competing actors. Whenever the judicial process culminates in a final decision, 'it is never because pure law has triumphed, but because of the internal properties of these relations of force or these conflicts between heterogeneous multiplicities.'[126]

•

---

[121] See N. Stappert, 'Practice Theory and Change in International Law: Theorizing the Development of Legal Meaning through the Interpretive Practices of International Criminal Courts', (2020) 12(1) IntlTheory 33.
[122] Adler and Pouliot, 'International Practices', 18.
[123] Ibid.
[124] Koskenniemi, '20 Years Later', 12.
[125] Latour, *The Making of Law*, 192.
[126] Ibid.

'You are *exhausting*, you know?' proclaimed Sophie as she crossed the street holding Norma's hand. The waiter had unceremoniously asked them to leave at 11 PM and started mopping the floor of the terrace as they stood up. The intersection of Brouwersgracht and Spijkermakersstraat was deserted when they arrived at the door of Norma's apartment.

'Exhausting? That was a lot of fun! You can be quite talkative if only one presses you enough.'

'Jeez, and aren't you the presser. All of your sociology shenanigans gave me a headache. Or maybe it was the crappy wine you ordered, who knows.'

Both giggled.

'Look, honey,' Norma continued, 'you told me what you do for a living, and I showed you what *I* do. You have a real job. Mine consists of digging into other people's jobs. What's not to love?'

'It was fun, I'll give you that. I'd never thought about things in those terms. Wait, did you just call me "honey"?'

Norma did not answer. She was searching for the bag of rolling tobacco in the pockets of her coat.

'I must have left my smokes at the café. Oh well. Would you like to come upstairs for the last drink?'

Sophie smiled and shook her head. 'I have to be in the office early tomorrow to prepare for my first case. Big day. But I'll tell you more about it if you do me the honour of another marathon coffee session.'

Norma pouted, jokingly, like a little kid caught past her bedtime. Then, her eyes widened even more than usual.

'I can't wait to hear more. Next time you pick the wine,' she said, and kissed Sophie goodnight.

3

# A New Generation of Litigators

A good international dispute should start with a bang. This one, more modestly, starts with a pop. The pop in question is produced by the cork of a bottle of Moët, which barely misses Filibert's right eye and flies straight into the ceiling. The ceiling in question separates the third and fourth floors of a Haussmanian building located in avenue Victor Hugo, 8th arrondissement. The building in question hosts the Paris offices of Burnham & Hutz LLP, a US law firm whose local branch specializes in ICJ litigation. The law firm in question operates under the supervision of managing partner Lionel Blum, who is now pouring champagne from the aforementioned bottle into the glasses of six other lawyers in the corner office with a view on the Arc de Triomphe.

The morale of the troops is sky-high, and not only because of the free drink. Lionel has just been officially mandated by the government of the Philippines to coordinate the legal team in charge of initiating ICJ proceedings against Malaysia. A high-profile case that Lionel was all too happy to accept. Ok, perhaps the hourly rate is less generous than would be offered by more affluent clients. But the visibility that the firm will gain from this dispute makes up for the modest financial prospects.

Burnham & Hutz opened its public international law branch in Paris in 2006. Since then, it has tried to establish its presence in an arena dominated by powerhouses like Foley Hoag, Freshfields, and White & Case. The new office reported net losses for its first few fiscal years and was kept afloat by the firm's more 'traditional' practice areas (mergers and acquisitions, white collar crime, etc.). Given the relatively modest volume of state-to-state dispute settlement practice, entry barriers remain quite high. Only those actors with sufficient initial capital can set a firm foothold in the field.[1]

---

[1] See e.g. M. Galanter, 'Why the "Haves" Come Out Ahead: Speculations on the Limits of Legal Change' (1974) 9(1) L&SocRev 95, 98.

Thanks to a combination of careful market positioning and discounted rates for early clients, the Paris office quickly overcame those initial hiccups. Lionel and his team began to secure deals with states appearing before the Permanent Court of Arbitration (PCA) and a couple of ISDS tribunals. As the team's reputation grew, some state delegations required its assistance for their third-participant interventions before the World Court. Now, the time has finally come for the big leap. Representing the Philippines as a main party in the *North Borneo* dispute against Malaysia will surely make Burnham & Hutz an entity to be reckoned with.

Hence the Moët.

Besides this collective achievement, each of the lawyers now raising their glasses has important personal gains at stake. Take Lionel, for instance. After years spent as a sidekick for more experienced colleagues, the 49-year-old Queen's Counsel (QC) now sees a unique chance to crack one of the most exclusive cartels in the international judicial community: the bar of ICJ litigators. As we will see in a moment, this handful of professionals affiliated with law firms, universities, and state departments pleads the majority of cases before the World Court. Entering the magic circle will greatly boost Lionel's reputation – and, hopefully, help him overcome his inferiority complex due to a lack of academic activity. If this case goes well, others will almost certainly follow. Who knows, within a few years, Lionel's name may even move up a rank or two on the dedicated page of the Chambers & Partners website[2] – the ultimate sign of professional recognition. 'Lionel Jacob Blum, III: Global-wide, Public International Law: Band 1'. Oh, sweet dreams!

Despite almost losing an eye to the cork, Filibert rejoices, too. As one of Lionel's most trusted supervisees, he now has a precious opportunity to accelerate his rise through the ranks. Since his recruitment as a junior associate, Filibert has done the heavy lifting in three cases, one before an ISDS tribunal and two before the PCA: providing first drafts of submissions, checking references, sifting through the files in search for evidence, passing notes during hearings, and so forth. He cannot remember the last day he did not work 12 hours, the nightmare of billables always looming large.

All worth it, of course. As local media did not fail to report, Filibert is one of the few Malians ever to be hired by a US firm, and one of even fewer to successfully enter the field of state-to-state litigation. From the day Lionel took him under his wing, Filibert made it his goal to serve his

---

[2] www.chambersandpartners.com/.

boss to the very best of his abilities. Over time, the two have developed a bond that extends beyond office hours, often exchanging invitations for family dinners and spending their little spare time talking about this or that case. An optimist may call it a friendship. A realist would call it a mutually profitable mentor–pupil relationship.

Surely, neither Filibert nor Lionel is consciously aware of the contradictions that bond is fraught with. Were he to dig deeper, Filibert may sense some tension between, on the one hand, his youthful dream of using international law to foster the aspirations of sub-Saharan peoples and, on the other hand, his co-optation into the beating heart of a system built on colonial expansion.[3] Lionel, for his part, may have to acknowledge that his predilection for Filibert stems partly from the reconciliatory power of inclusion.[4] The symbolic capital of international justice 'builds on the contradictory form of complementarity between … *jurisconsultes* from the North … and a legal elite of lawyer-statesmen from the South … through their belief in the universal'.[5] Fortunately for both, such thoughts have never crossed their minds.

Cheers, everyone!

\*

The celebratory toast at Burnham & Hutz is one of many that take place around the world every year. Litigation before international courts and tribunals has evolved from a narrow *niche* of legal practice to a fully recognized specialty with substantial revenue capacity. As mentioned,[6] the rapid expansion of the international judiciary in the aftermath of the Cold War quickly captured the attention of multinational firms, headquartered mostly in the United Kingdom and the United States, which discovered new and lucrative opportunities in the field and established dedicated offices in cities like London, Paris, Washington DC, Brussels, Geneva, The Hague, and Singapore.

---

[3] See A. Anghie, 'Finding the Peripheries: Sovereignty and Colonialism in Nineteenth-Century International Law' (1999) 40(1) HarvIntlLJ 1.
[4] On the difficult reconciliation between African countries and the ICJ, see e.g. A. Pellet, 'Remarques Cursives sur les Contentieux "Africains" Devant la CIJ', in M. Kamga and M. M. Mbengue (eds.), *Liber Amicorum en l'Honneur de Raymond Ranjeva: L'Afrique et le Droit International: Variations sur l'Organisation Internationale* (Pedone, 2013) 277, 282–3.
[5] S. Dezalay and Y. Dezalay, 'Professionals of International Justice: From the Shadow of State Diplomacy to the Pull of the Market for Commercial Arbitration', in J. d'Aspremont et al. (eds.), *International Law as a Profession* (Cambridge University Press, 2017) 311, 322.
[6] See *supra*, pp. 26–7.

Actually, 'discovered' is a reductive term. The dissemination of professional expertise brought about by these global legal entrepreneurs has contributed to the *making* of modern international dispute settlement. If, nowadays, many sovereign states have overcome their traditional reluctance towards supranational adjudication,[7] it is not only because of their purported commitment to the rule of law.[8] It is *also* because of their increased exposure to a network of professional litigators, who forged alliances with government departments, academic circles, and civil society organizations to promote their discourse and foster their agendas.

Think, for instance, of the ISDS field: there, in the 1980s and 1990s, a handful of pioneering practitioners developed the very legal doctrines that, a decade later, would be used to consolidate the system and make it thrive.[9] Another example is international criminal justice, where NGOs and legal advocacy groups played a key role in the negotiation of the Rome Statute.[10] In other judicial regimes, too, the professional capital accumulated collectively by the agents of the global legal market has determined an increase in demand for legal expertise, while at the same time fostering the credibility and recognition of the very carriers of that expertise.[11] The lawyers 'created the clients as often as the clients [created] the lawyers'.[12]

---

[7] See e.g. L. Gross, 'Compulsory Jurisdiction under the Optional Clause: History and Practice', in L. F. Damrosch (ed.), *The International Court of Justice at a Crossroads* (Transnational, 1987) 19; L. F. Damrosch, 'The Impact of the Nicaragua Case on the Court and Its Role: Harmful, Helpful or In Between?' (2012) 25(1) LJIL 137.

[8] See e.g. H. Thirlway, 'The Proliferation of International Judicial Organs: Institutional and Substantive Questions', in N. Blokker and H. Schermers (eds.), *Proliferation of International Organizations* (Kluwer Law International, 2001) 251, 255.

[9] A good case in point is Jan Paulsson's elaboration of the doctrine of 'arbitration without privity', whereby an investor's right to sue the host state stems from the BIT between the home and the host state rather than from contract-specific arbitral clauses. J. Paulsson, 'Arbitration without Privity' (1995) 10(2) ICSID Rev/FILJ 232. This construction of state consent offered a way around the obstacles traditionally raised by state sovereignty, thereby enabling the explosion of arbitration. See e.g. S. Schill, 'W(h)ither Fragmentation? On the Literature and Sociology of International Investment Law' (2011) 22(3) EJIL 875, 876.

[10] See e.g. S. Sur, 'Vers une Cour Pénale Internationale: La Convention de Rome entre les ONG et le Conseil de Sécurité' (1999) RGDIP 29; Z. Pearson, 'Non-Governmental Organizations and the International Criminal Court: Changing Landscapes of International Law' (2006) 39(2) CornellIntlLJ 243.

[11] See e.g. Dezalay and Dezalay, 'Professionals of International Justice', 313.

[12] M. Shapiro, 'Judicialization of Politics in the United States' (1994) 15(2) IntlPolSciRev 101, 109. See also Vauchez, 'Communities of International Litigators', 657.

The historical vicissitudes that led to the growth, specialization, and rise in influence of international litigators have been explored elsewhere[13] and would require a book of its own. For our purposes, it is enough to look at how those vicissitudes affected the current landscape of international adjudication. The most visible consequence is that, today, almost every international court or tribunal is surrounded by a specialized bar of counsel, whose members master the particular subject matter and judicial style of the institution at hand.[14] These bars are not formally recognized institutions. To this day, there exist no official requirements or qualifications for someone to represent a party before an international judicial body.[15] Instead, bars coalesce as a result of the reputational structures and the recursive nature of legal practice. Social capital in international litigation is concentrated in the hands of a surprisingly small cluster of individuals. Indeed, most international judicial regimes see a handful of highly experienced counsel signing most written submissions and taking the floor in most hearings.

The ICJ bar that Lionel Blum covets so avidly stands out as a prime example. Flip through the front pages of World Court judgments, where the parties' counsel are listed, and you will find the same names recurring over and over. Between 1986 and 1998, a total of 54 lawyers appeared before the Court, only 14 of whom handled three or more cases.[16] The period 1999–2012 saw a little more variety, with 63 lawyers pleading in the Great Hall of Justice twice or more.[17] These repeat players are mostly

---

[13] See e.g. D. M. Trubek et al., 'Global Restructuring and the Law: Studies of the Internationalization of Legal Fields and the Creation of Transitional Arenas' (1993) 44(2) CaseWResLRev 407; Y. Dezalay and B. G. Garth, 'Merchants of Law as Moral Entrepreneurs: Constructing International Justice from the Competition for Transnational Business Disputes' (1995) 29(1) L&SocRev 27; Dezalay and Garth, *Dealing in Virtue*; H. H. Koh, 'Why Transnational Law Matters' (2006) 24(4) PennStIntlLRev 745; S. Quack, 'Legal Professionals and Transnational Law-Making: A Case of Distributed Agency' (2007) 14(5) Organization 643; Y. Dezalay and B. G. Garth, 'Corporate Law Firms, NGOs and Issues of Legitimacy for a Global Legal Order' (2011) 80(6) FordhamLR 2309; Dezalay and Dezalay, 'Professionals of International Justice'.
[14] See Vauchez, 'Communities of International Litigators', 656–7.
[15] See e.g. M. Kazazi, 'Commentary on the Hague Principles of Ethical Standards for Counsel Appearing before International Courts and Tribunals' (2011) 10(1) LPICT 17, 18; J. Crawford, 'The International Law Bar: Essence before Existence?', in J. d'Aspremont et al. (eds.), *International Law as a Profession* (Cambridge University Press, 2017) 338.
[16] Pellet, 'The Role of the International Lawyer', 147–62; E. Sthoeger and M. Wood, 'The International Bar', in C. P. R. Romano, K. J. Alter, and Y. Shany (eds.), *The Oxford Handbook of International Adjudication* (Oxford University Press, 2014) 639, 647–51.
[17] S. P. Kumar and C. Rose, 'A Study of Lawyers Appearing before the International Court of Justice, 1999–2012' (2014) 25(3) EJIL 893, 902.

white Western men drafted from the highest levels of the international law academe.[18] A few more come from the top ranks of private firms, provided they have a scholarly record sufficient to validate their credentials – hence Lionel's inferiority complex. Access to the club requires long and strenuous training (few make it before their late 40s or early 50s), a good measure of chance, and – crucially – the mentorship of an incumbent member.

These high entry barriers, coupled with a relatively limited docket, enable the ICJ bar to perpetuate its social hierarchies and its clout over the Court's operations. Of course, life inside the club is anything but peaceful. Rivalries often arise among its members, who compete with one another for authority, influence, and prestige. The fault lines of these conflicts are ever shifting. Some, for instance, have contrasted counsel coming from OECD and non-OECD countries to show a lack of geographical representativeness in the bar.[19] Others have emphasized the distinction between scholars and practitioners,[20] the former leaning towards theory and the latter towards the casuistry of concrete situations.[21]

Assisting a state before the World Court involves a delicate division of labour among a diverse team of actors. First there is the agent, usually a high-ranking government official, who is in charge of formally representing the state throughout the proceedings.[22] Typically, the agent does not handle the legal aspects of the case,[23] but rather serves as the link between the state client and the legal team. He or she is responsible for coordinating with officials in the state's capital and convey their political decisions down the chain of command.[24]

Second, the agent almost invariably hires one or more counsel affiliated with the ICJ bar to prepare and deliver the oral pleadings.[25] As we

---

[18] See Pellet, 'The Role of the International Lawyer', 150; Sthoeger and Wood, 'The International Bar', 648.
[19] See e.g. Gaubatz and MacArthur, 'How International Is "International" Law?', 252–60; Kumar and Rose, 'ICJ Lawyers', 902–4.
[20] Dezalay and Dezalay, 'Professionals of International Justice', 317–23.
[21] Bourdieu, 'The Force of Law', 824.
[22] Article 42.2 of the ICJ Statute.
[23] At most, the agent 'book-end[s] the oral proceedings by opening their party's pleadings with a brief historical and factual background to the dispute' and 'by concluding the pleadings with a reading of their party's final submissions'. Kumar and Rose, 'ICJ Lawyers', 897. See also S. Rosenne, 'International Court of Justice: Practice Directions on Judges ad hoc; Agents, Counsel and Advocates; and Submission of New Documents' (2002) 1(2) LPICT 223, 226.
[24] See Pellet, 'The Role of the International Lawyer', 154.
[25] See ibid., 155.

will see,[26] ICJ hearings are largely ceremonial, and the Court typically allows counsel to speak virtually uninterrupted for several days. Why, then, should a party deploy such distinguished (and costly) jurists in the courtroom, when it could simply hire them as consultants behind the scenes? The answer is reputation. To have a big name appear before the judges is to borrow their prestige, thereby buttressing the weight and credibility of the litigant's position.

Third, groundwork tasks like the collection of documents, the production of evidence, and the preparation of communications with the ICJ registry are often entrusted to a law firm such as Burnham & Hutz.[27] These menial duties are usually carried out by associate attorneys under the partners' supervision. In recent years, however, some of the largest firms have expanded their role to the coordination of the legal team, the brokerage of divergent views, and the preparation of the first drafts of memorials.

Work on the memorials is one of the most sensitive aspects of the legal team's work. The content of a memorial is typically the fruit of collective labour, whereby the various participants in the team – the agent, the counsel, and the law firm attorneys – come up with a shared outline, internally allocate the drafting of sections, and test each other's views on this or that point of reasoning.[28] Throughout the process, tensions and competition may arise. Some team members may wish to pursue a line of argument that others find unconvincing; the agent may wish to abstain from making undiplomatic claims that a counsel, by contrast, sees as decisive; and so forth. These disagreements reflect not only personal inclinations but also the specific position that each actor occupies in the process.

Other international judicial regimes, such as WTO dispute settlement, have witnessed a similar concentration of counsel work in the hands of a few dozen lawyers. Private counsel made a relatively late debut in the multilateral trade arena. During the Uruguay Round, some delegates had expressed scepticism about the participation of law firms in WTO proceedings, fearing that private attorneys would prove too aggressive and unamenable to compromise.[29] As a result, in early disputes, WTO member states usually appointed diplomatic attachés as their representatives in court.

---

[26] See *infra*, pp. 267–8.
[27] See Pellet, 'The Role of the International Lawyer', 155–6.
[28] See ibid., 157–60. See also M. N. Shaw, 'The International Court of Justice: A Practical Perspective' (1997) 46(4) ICLQ 831.
[29] See e.g. P. D. Ehrenhaft, 'The Role of Lawyers in the World Trade Organization' (2001) 34(4) VandJTransnatlL 963, 964.

In 1998, however, the Appellate Body ruled that nothing in the WTO Agreement or in general international law prevented WTO member states from determining for themselves the composition of their delegations in dispute settlement proceedings.[30] This opening of WTO adjudication to private practitioners encouraged some multinational law firms – including Sidley Austin, Steptoe & Johnson, White & Case, King & Spalding, and Akin Gump – to establish their presence in Geneva and other trade capitals, like Brussels and Washington. At the same time, the Advisory Centre on WTO Law (ACWL) was established to assist developing- and least-developed-country members at reduced rates.

Soon enough, some WTO member states began to resort to external counsel to manage their disputes, often requesting them to draft their written submissions and enlisting them in their delegations to hearings. This trend was particularly pronounced among emerging players (e.g. Brazil, Korea, and Mexico), which lacked the expertise necessary to engage in the burgeoning WTO forum. By contrast, incumbent players (e.g. the United States, the European Union, Canada, and Australia) continued to rely mostly on in-house counsel.[31]

The initiative of these early legal entrepreneurs paid off, as they gained a significant edge over competitors and secured a de facto oligopoly on WTO litigation.[32] Today, private attorneys and ACWL lawyers intervene in WTO proceedings as frequently as (if not more frequently than) government officials. Similar to the ICJ bar, the magic circle is protected by high entry barriers, but new entrants stand a slightly better chance here than at the World Court. First, the WTO docket is more voluminous than the ICJ's, with over 600 disputes initiated from 1995 to date.[33] Second, the number of states having regular recourse to WTO dispute settlement has expanded. While some developing-country governments have built enough capacity to handle cases without private assistance,[34] the accession of juggernauts like China

---

[30] Appellate Body Report, *European Communities – Regime for the Importation, Sale and Distribution of Bananas*, WT/DS27/AB/R (9 September 1997), para. 10.
[31] The mammoth disputes concerning subsidies to large civil aircraft are a notable exception. In those cases, the team of European Commission legal advisers has been backed up by private attorneys from a leading firm in the field.
[32] See Soave, 'Who Controls WTO Dispute Settlement?', 23.
[33] WTO website, *Chronological list of disputes cases*, www.wto.org/english/tratop_e/dispu_e/dispu_status_e.htm (accessed 23 August 2021).
[34] See A. Santos, 'Carving Out Policy Autonomy for Developing Countries in the World Trade Organization: The Experience of Brazil and Mexico' (2011) 52(3) VaJIntlL 551, 608–12.

(2001) and Russia (2011) has brought about new business opportunities. Third, the practice of WTO counsel often extends beyond dispute-related matters and encompasses advice to private clients. Hence, while marginal gains may be diminishing, the market for legal services in the trade arena has not yet reached saturation.

Overall, the members of the WTO bar are less academically inclined than their ICJ counterparts. Although professors of international economic law may occasionally serve as of counsel for law firms or pro-bono centres, they tend to remain at the margins of litigation. Most of them keep their ambitions for the bench of the Appellate Body (and now, possibly, the MPIA).

This allocation of relative capital between academics and practitioners can be traced to the early years of the General Agreement on Tariffs and Trade (GATT). The group of professionals that took seat in Geneva in 1947 comprised pragmatic individuals with little connection to scholarly circles. The GATT secretariat comprised a few dozen officers 'on loan' from the Interim Commission for the International Trade Organization.[35] State delegates, for their part, were typically drafted from the lower ranks of the foreign service. The group did not see itself as an emergent hub of international law, but as a network devoted to the lowering of tariff barriers and the liberalization of trade across countries. Its marginalization within national diplomacies, coupled with the technical nature of its mandate, left the group free to develop the core tenets of the GATT regime away from media attention and political controversy.

The advent of the WTO in 1995 partly disrupted this sense of 'clubiness' and sparked the interest of politicians, activists, and journalists. In particular, the establishment of the Appellate Body awoke academics to the potential of an effective judicial forum with almost universal coverage.[36] However, these developments were not sufficient to upend the habits that had crystallized during the GATT era. To this day, the WTO field remains rather parochial and maintains little contact with general international legal scholars.

Litigation expertise in the ISDS field is, if possible, even more concentrated than at the ICJ and the WTO. Indeed, like Norma in the previous

---

[35] See R. Hudec, 'The Role of the GATT Secretariat in the Evolution of the WTO Dispute Settlement Procedure', in J. Bhagwati and M. Hirsch (eds.), *The Uruguay Round and Beyond: Essays in Honor of Arthur Dunkel* (University of Michigan Press, 1998) 101, 105.

[36] For in-depth analysis, see Howse, 'Governance by Judiciary'.

chapter, some commentators have called the inner circle of arbitration professionals a 'mafia'.[37]

That mafia emerged as a result of the cooperation and competition between, on the one hand, a group of prominent European academics specialized in public international law and, on the other hand, a group of Anglo-American litigators who sought to expand their business beyond commercial arbitration.[38] Throughout the 1990s, this hybrid culture managed to carve out its *niche* in international law debates, thanks to a skilful combination of result-oriented pragmatism and a series of strategic publications forging and popularizing the foundational concepts of the new discipline. For instance, early ISDS practitioner-scholars called for 'arbitration without privity',[39] decried the politicization of diplomatic protection,[40] stated their aversion to the Calvo doctrine,[41] and underlined the importance of delocalized dispute settlement for the promotion of foreign direct investment in developing countries.[42]

The 'mutual constitution'[43] of practitioners and academics contributed to the affirmation of the nascent legal field. The boom of investment arbitration in the 2000s – due in part to exogenous shocks like the Argentine crisis of 2001[44] – led to the 'mainstreaming' of its core doctrines[45] and to the normalization of dedicated scholarship in international law discourse. Arbitral tribunals increasingly referred to each other's jurisprudence to

---

[37] See e.g. Dezalay and Garth, *Dealing in Virtue*, 10; Rogers, 'The Vocation', 967; Puig, 'The Arbitration Market', 423.

[38] See generally Dezalay and Garth, *Dealing in Virtue*; Puig, 'The Arbitration Market', 388–9. On the 'dual' nature of the ISDS community, see also Schill, 'W(h)ither Fragmentation?', 878–83; A. Roberts, 'Clash of Paradigms: Actors and Analogies Shaping the Investment Treaty System' (2013) 107(1) AJIL 45.

[39] See Paulsson, 'Arbitration without Privity'.

[40] See e.g. J. K. Lelewer, 'International Commercial Arbitration as a Model for Resolving Treaty Disputes' (1989) 21(2) NYUJILP 379, 390–9.

[41] See e.g. P. Lalive, 'Some Threats to International Investment Arbitration' (1986) 1(1) ICSID Rev/FILJ 26, 34.

[42] W. M. Reisman, 'The Breakdown of the Control Mechanism in ICSID Arbitration' (1989) DukeLJ 1989(4), 750–5.

[43] The expression is borrowed from G. Teubner, 'The Two Faces of Janus: Rethinking Legal Pluralism' (1991) 13(5) CardozoLRev 1443, 1451. For similar uses, see e.g. A. Leander and T. E. Aalberts, 'The Co-Constitution of Legal Expertise and International Security' (2013) 26(4) LJIL 783; Hernández, 'The International Legal Academic', 160.

[44] Puig, 'The Arbitration Market', 396.

[45] See generally S. Schill, 'Mainstreaming Investment Treaty Jurisprudence: The Contribution of Investment Treaty Tribunals to the Consolidation and Development of General International Law' (2015) 14(1) LPICT 94.

support their rulings.[46] Countless treatises appeared that appraised and systematized case law for the benefit of specialists and students alike.[47] Numerous research centres devoted their curricula to ISDS law and practice.[48]

This expansion of ISDS as a central global governance node did not coincide with an even distribution of professional recognition across the field. While many new players have jumped aboard the ship, the pioneers remain firmly at the helm. Thanks to their original accumulation of capital, some 20 or 30 individuals – unsurprisingly, mostly white men with strong credentials in either private practice or academia – still sit on a major portion of all arbitral tribunals, earn fees that rival those of law firm partners,[49] and leave newcomers with little more than peanuts. So far, these heavyweights have managed to protect their clique by routinely appointing one another as co-arbitrators or tribunal presidents, frequently shifting hats between counsel and adjudicator work, and constantly interacting in academic venues.

Such centripetal tendencies, which are common in reputation-based networks, are compounded by the lack of an institutional framework able to mediate and redistribute capital. Although many arbitration proceedings occur under the auspices of the ICSID or the UNCITRAL, the credibility and legitimacy of the process rests with the arbitrators themselves.[50] As we will see,[51] the ICSID and UNCITRAL secretariats often play an ancillary role in investment cases and leave tribunal members free to internally organize their work as they see fit.

---

[46] See generally S. Schill, *The Multilateralization of International Investment Law* (Cambridge University Press, 2009), 278–361.

[47] See e.g. C. McLachlan, L. Shore, and M. Weiniger, *International Investment Arbitration: Substantive Principles* (Oxford University Press, 2007); A. Newcombe and L. Paradell, *Law and Practice of Investment Treaties: Standards of Treatment* (Kluwer Law International, 2009); J. W. Salacuse, *The Law of International Investment Treaties* (Oxford University Press, 2010); K. Vandevelde, *Bilateral Investment Treaties: History, Policy and Interpretation* (Oxford University Press, 2010).

[48] Examples include the Master on International Dispute Settlement (MIDS) in Geneva, the School of Arbitration of the Queen Mary University of London, and the LLM in Transnational Arbitration and Dispute Settlement at SciencesPo Paris.

[49] See e.g. Puig, 'The Arbitration Market', 398, 407; T. Ginsburg, 'The Culture of Arbitration' (2003) 36(4) VandJTransnatlL 1337; Rogers, 'The Vocation', 1120; Fontoura Costa, 'WTO Panelists and ICSID Arbitrators'; Pauwelyn, 'Mars and Venus', 791.

[50] Pauwelyn, 'Mars and Venus', 795–8.

[51] See *infra*, p. 135.

This level of polarization has exposed the ISDS system to harsh criticism in recent years.[52] In particular, it is claimed, systemic decisions concerning the welfare of entire nations rest with an exceedingly small pool of elite lawyers who 'operate largely separate from any local political process or investment decisions'.[53] Furthermore, the fact that arbitrators wear several hats simultaneously has given rise to concerns about potential conflicts of interest and the continued neutrality of the system.[54] Despite ongoing efforts, a prohibition on double-hatting is yet to come.

Admittedly, not all international bars are as exclusive as those of the ICJ, the WTO, or ISDS. In regional human rights systems, for instance, litigation expertise is more diffuse and involves a wider range of practitioners. This is partly due to the nature of cases brought before regional human rights courts. Access to the ECtHR is available to any person subject to the jurisdiction of a member state of the Council of Europe, provided that certain threshold requirements are met.[55] In practice, this adds up to almost a billion potential complainants from 46 countries. Similarly, the IACtHR has jurisdiction to hear individual claims against any of the 23 member states. Unlike the European system, the Inter-American Commission on Human Rights (IACHR) remains in charge of filtering those claims and representing the complainants before the Court.[56] In both systems, the number, geographical distribution, and demographic diversity of potential clients prevent the concentration of legal expertise in the hands of few.

Moreover, the financial gains to be reaped from human rights cases are modest in comparison with other sectors of international litigation. While ICJ, WTO, or ISDS counsel are hired by sovereign states or wealthy companies, human rights litigators are more likely to assist inmates lamenting police abuse, refugees resisting *refoulement*, or destitute tenants facing

---

[52] See generally M. Waibel et al. (eds.), *The Backlash against Investment Arbitration: Perceptions and Reality* (Kluwer Law International, 2010).

[53] Puig, 'The Arbitration Market', 397.

[54] See e.g. A. Kaushal, 'Revisiting History: How the Past Matters for the Present Backlash against the Foreign Investment Regime' (2009) 50(2) HarvIntlLJ 491.

[55] Council of Europe, *European Convention for the Protection of Human Rights and Fundamental Freedoms, as amended by Protocols Nos. 11 and 14* (4 November 1950), ETS 5, Articles 34–35.

[56] Organization of American States, *American Convention on Human Rights* (22 November 1969), UNTS 1144, 123, Articles 48–51, 61.

forced eviction.[57] Frequently, the attorneys who represent complainants before national courts take care of the continuation of proceedings before the ECtHR. Similarly, cases before the IACHR are usually brought by the same counsel who assisted the complainants at the domestic level. Whenever the Commission refers a dispute to the Court, Commission lawyers take over the representation.

Responding states, by contrast, seldom hire external counsel to handle human rights proceedings, preferring instead to rely on dedicated government departments. Besides lowering the costs of repeat appearance in court, resort to high-ranking officials also serves as a display of the symbolic force of state authority, which towers over the humble ambitions of complainants and their lawyers. Seeing a minister or an attorney-general step into the courtroom is likely to send chills down the spine of even the most seasoned litigator.

These considerations notwithstanding, it would be premature to conclude that a human rights bar does not exist at all. In recent years, a number of attorneys and barristers from the United Kingdom, France, Italy, and Switzerland have gained traction in their respective jurisdictions as 'go-to' ECtHR litigators. Working in close contact with regional human rights networks and pro-bono advisory centres, these counsel are using their knowledge of the Court's procedures and working languages (French and English) to get ahead of the competition. Moreover, famous scholars sometimes make their appearance before the Court as external advisors for the parties or third parties.[58] Their presence in the courtroom highlights the importance of the case at hand and sometimes

---

[57] Of course, there are important exceptions. First, the ECtHR is competent, pursuant to Article 33 of the ECHR, to hear cases between member states of the Council of Europe. Second, the pool of potential complainants encompasses affluent companies that may afford high-level counsel. Third, the Court is sometimes called upon to decide on state-sponsored individual applications, that is cases where the applicant's attorney fees are covered by their home state. For instance, Cyprus had high stakes in the outcomes of the *Loizidou v. Turkey* case, which might explain why a claimant of modest economic means could afford to hire Ian Brownlie as counsel. See *Loizidou v. Turkey*, Merits, Judgment of 18 December 1996, No. 15318/89, ECHR-1998 ('*Loizidou* judgment on the merits'), para. 5; *Loizidou v. Turkey (Article 50)*, Judgment of 28 July 1998, No. 15318/89, ECHR-1998, para. 8. Similarly, Azerbaijan might have had a sufficient interest in the *Chiragov and others v. Armenia* dispute to hire Malcolm N. Shaw as its third-party litigator. See *Chiragov and others v. Armenia*, Judgment of 16 June 2015, No. 13216/05, ECHR-2015, para. 10.

[58] See e.g. *Lautsi and others v. Italy*, Grand Chamber Judgment of 18 March 2011, No. 30814/06, ECtHR-2011, para. 9; *Perinçek v. Switzerland*, Grand Chamber Judgment of 15 October 2015, No. 27510/08, ECtHR-2015, para. 9; *Al-Dulimi and Montana Management Inc. v. Switzerland*, Grand Chamber Judgment of 21 June 2016, No. 5809/08, ECtHR-2016, para. 9.

mitigates the symbolic power imbalance between the individual complainant and the responding state.

Similarly, the Inter-American regime sees a number of advocates – usually affiliated with top Latin American universities or continental human rights networks – appearing as repeat players before the Commission and/or being frequently consulted by the Court as independent experts on the law of the Convention or the human rights framework in force in the responding state.

\*

As this long digression shows, Lionel, Filibert, and their homologues scattered across the globe are part of a new generation of international litigators. Throughout the first half of the twentieth century, the task of handling disputes before international courts was the *domaine réservé* of diplomats and scholars raised in domestic legal traditions – and often having the same nationality as the states they represented.[59] By contrast, the new generation consists largely of 'purebred' international lawyers. Their expertise focuses *primarily* on international norms and they bear no particular allegiance to any municipal legal system. The modern international counsel has typically taken every international law class during their law school days, before enrolling in master or doctoral programmes devoted to the study of trade, investment, or human rights law. Their career incentives do not reside in fostering a particular national vision of the global order, but rather in their ability to move gracefully in a highly cosmopolitan, delocalized, and close-knit socio-professional space.

The uprooting of international litigation from domestic legal traditions has produced some fascinating paradoxes. The first paradox relates to the degree of geographical diversity in the international judicial community. When we look at the field from the standpoint of its official actors, we see that diversity is rapidly increasing. An ever-growing number of states, companies, and individuals seek enforcement of their rights before international courts and tribunals. The range of responding states extends well beyond the handful of European nations that once appeared before the PCIJ, and encompasses developed and developing countries from almost every continent.

However, once we shift the focus from official actors to the individuals that represent them in court, we discover a different reality – one where

---

[59] See e.g. S. Neff, *Justice among Nations: A History of International Law* (Harvard University Press, 2014), 303–4; d'Aspremont, 'Professionalisation', 21.

the level of relative diversity has in fact *decreased*. Albeit based on incomplete data, our overview of the different international bars suggests that the new players in the international judicial arena tend to outsource their legal representation to a small cluster of white Western men, without bringing their own local culture and expertise to bear in the proceedings.[60] The trend is particularly visible in the ICJ and the WTO regimes, where developing countries hire external counsel more frequently than their developed counterparts.

This peculiar configuration is not without its perks, as it ensures a certain equality of arms in international adjudication. No matter how poor, a developing country will often have the means to rely on the services of some elite bar members – especially if the latter are willing to work at a discounted rate in exchange for visibility. Conversely, the transparency and public spending constraints typical of advanced economies may prevent developed countries from paying large sums to outside counsel.[61]

However, the current state of affairs also naturalizes the position of incumbents and undermines the possibility of introducing new faces and unorthodox viewpoints. Over time, the stagnation in the pool of litigators and the scarcity of fresh approaches may lead to intellectual sclerosis, and thus to a deterioration in the quality of pleadings. Furthermore, the lack of national allegiance between a counsel and their client sometimes makes their relationship somewhat ambiguous. While the client seeks only to win the case, the latter *also* aims at consolidating their standing among their peers, developing a cordial relationship with the bench, and securing future hiring opportunities. In other words, counsel's principal source of social capital 'is the recognition of judges, not clients (who are merely *proximate* sources of capital)'.[62] This peculiar double game – or, to paraphrase George Scelle, this *dédoublement fonctionnel*[63] – has tangible repercussions on the way a case is presented. When forced to make patently untenable points, counsel will secretly hope that the court rejects them; when the position of one client is at variance with that of another,

---

[60] See P. Reichler. 'Preparation of Cases before International Courts and Tribunals' (2012) 106 ASILPROC 158; Sthoeger and Wood, 'The International Bar', 648.

[61] See Messenger, 'The Practice of Litigation', 220.

[62] Ibid. (emphasis added).

[63] For a discussion of the original meaning of the notion, see e.g. A. Cassese, 'Remarks on Scelle's Theory of "Role Splitting" (dédoublement fonctionnel) in International Law' (1990) 1 EJIL 210.

counsel will tread carefully to avoid jeopardizing the coherence of their argumentation across multiple cases; etc.

This inherent tension famously emerged in an ICJ case where a developing-country litigant did not even try to pair its foreign counsel with a national agent. One of the judges questioned 'whether the case [had been] brought to the Court in the interest of the State involved or for some other reason'.[64] Similarly, in a recent WTO case, the United States' counsel requested the Appellate Body to review the panel's reading of the terms contained in a domestic US memorandum.[65] This request was strikingly at odds with the United States' diplomatic position that the Appellate Body is precluded from interpreting the meaning of municipal law.[66] Besides these extreme examples, the legal fees incurred by clients may not always 'correlate with their expected outcomes', but feed into the game of practitioners.[67]

The second paradox concerns the form and structure of the international legal argument. Thanks to the autonomization and delocalization of their practice, modern litigators are more adroit at catering to their audience than their predecessors ever were. By setting up their offices in (or routinely travelling to) the capitals of international dispute settlement, new-generation counsel have come to know 'their' judges quite well. Through repeated interactions with the bench, competent lawyers get a sense of each adjudicator's personality, sensibilities, and idiosyncrasies, and learn how to adjust their argumentative strategies accordingly.

The strong ties between the bar and the bench are reinforced by the existence of a revolving door between the two. As already mentioned, the ISDS field knows virtually no boundary between the role of arbitrator and that of counsel.[68] A person sitting on an arbitral tribunal may *simultaneously* represent a client before another tribunal, provided that no conflicts of interest arise. Similar dynamics can also be observed in

---

[64] See *Armed Activities on the Territory of the Congo (Democratic Republic of the Congo v. Uganda)*, Provisional Measures, Order of 1 July 2000, ICJ Rep. 2000, 111, Declaration of Judge Oda, para. 8. For discussion, see Messenger, 'The Practice of Litigation', 217.
[65] United States' appellant's submission in *United States – Countervailing Duty Measures on Certain Products from China (Recourse to Article 21.5 of the DSU by China)*, WT/DS437 (27 April 2018), https://ustr.gov/sites/default/files/enforcement/DS/US.Appellant.Sub.fin.%28public%29.pdf, paras. 36–79.
[66] See Soave, 'Who Controls WTO Dispute Settlement?', 25.
[67] Messenger, 'The Practice of Litigation', 229.
[68] See M. Langford, D. Behn, and R. H. Lie, 'The Revolving Door in International Investment Arbitration' (2017) 20(2) JIEL 301.

standing courts. Senior counsel are often appointed to judgeship; former adjudicators and legal bureaucrats are regularly recruited by the very firms litigating before the court; and so on.[69] Admittedly, the degree of mutual acquaintance may vary depending on the size of the bench: profiling the seven members of the WTO Appellate Body or the seven judges of the IACtHR may be easier that getting to know all 47 judges sitting on the ECtHR. The exclusivity of each bar is also relevant: a concentrated cluster of litigators has more frequent access to the courtroom than a diffuse one.

Familiarity with the court is a very valuable currency. The reputation of a lawyer and the fees that ensue do not stem only from technical prowess, but *also* from being 'well-known to the Judges and the Registrar', knowing 'how things work out in practice', and understanding by experience 'the difficulties, pitfalls and tricks of the trade'.[70] When adjudicators recognize an attorney appearing before them as a friendly face, they might be more likely to pay keen attention to their pleadings, or be readier to forgive a momentary stumble. Compared to a one-shotter, a repeat litigator has better chances to discern which claims are more likely to stick and to concentrate their resources on 'rule-changes that are likely to make a tangible difference'.[71]

Crucially, an intimate knowledge of the bench also enables experienced counsel to better tailor their arguments, take calculated risks, and test creative lines of reasoning. The court is more likely to engage with a novel or unusual claim when it comes from a well-established litigator than from an inexperienced pleader. If successful, innovative approaches will lead prospective litigants to adopt similar strategies and move the ball forward. Case after case, these recursive interactions contribute to a piecemeal increase in the sophistication of legal argument, which in turn opens the door to more complex disputes. A good example is the WTO

---

[69] For instance, international trade law firms routinely hire former WTO secretariat officials, panelists, and sometimes even Appellate Body members. See Soave, 'Who Controls WTO Dispute Settlement?', 24 and fn 46.

[70] K. Highet, 'A Personal Memoir of Eduardo Jiménez de Aréchaga' (1994) 88 ASILPROC 577, 579.

[71] Galanter, 'Why the "Haves" Come out Ahead', 100. Of course, a repeat litigator also has higher reputational stakes than a one-shotter, for they must 'maintain credibility as a combatant'. Ibid., 99. Their every move will be carefully scrutinized and connected to past practice. When going through the submission of a well-known counsel, the adjudicators will not merely read 'what state X is arguing', but also 'what good old Lionel came up with this time around'. If, at some point in the past, the repeat litigator has written or said something that contradicts their current position, the adjudicators will notice and probably ask questions about the mismatch.

regime, where early cases against 'basic' import measures gradually gave way to elaborate cases about technical regulations, labelling requirements, sanitary and phytosanitary standards, consumer protection laws, and environmental subsidies.[72] Many observers attribute this rise in complexity to the evolving dynamics of world trade. However, that was also the fruit of the initiative of skilled litigators who, thanks to their social capital, were in a position to advance more sophisticated claims and persuade WTO adjudicators to entertain their positions.

Where is the paradox, then? Is it not normal that experience and professional connections yield better results?

The paradox is that, for all their practical mastery of international legal regimes, new-generation litigators have actually become *less knowledgeable* about other areas of law and governance. Typically, early twentieth century practitioners would trace their views and arguments back to the legal principles of their home jurisdictions. They would readily understand the intricacies of political discourse at the national level and would not lightly discount their cultural and social origins. By contrast, modern litigators tend to scoff at domestic law, policy, and culture as relics of a bygone era, foreign to their area of expertise, and largely irrelevant to their career prospects.

Sometimes this obliviousness borders on the comical. Filibert still remembers the day he had to remind Lionel that a certain conduct may be unlawful even if it does not constitute a crime under domestic law. Filibert was careful to introduce the reminder with the polite phrase: 'At the risk of the stating the obvious ....' Yet, for weeks afterwards, he chuckled at the thought that his boss would fail a first-year law school exam. Another day, during coffee break, Filibert tried to elicit Lionel's views on Brexit. The answer:

'What can I say? People are stupid. Let's hope this sends some work our way.'

Filibert decided that, from that moment on, he would stick to small talk about holiday destinations, a topic that invariably got Lionel's attention. (It goes without saying that Filibert was *never* asked about the political situation in Mali.)

The '*docta ignorantia*'[73] of modern counsel does not concern only municipal law and politics. Similar treatment is reserved for unfamiliar

---

[72] On the incremental complexification of WTO disputes, see e.g. N. Meagher, 'Regulatory convergence and dispute settlement in the WTO' (2015) 14(3) JITLP 157, 158.
[73] Bourdieu, *Theory of Practice*, 19.

areas of *inter*national law. Indeed, the increasing specialization of counsel in highly compartmentalized practice areas like human rights, trade, investment, territorial delimitation, etc. has fragmented their expertise and fostered epistemics biases and tunnel visions. If yesteryear's practitioners disagreed over, say, the virtues of common law vs. civil law,[74] their successors quarrel over the relevance of modes of reasoning pertaining to competing specialized regimes.

Ask a WTO expert, and they will tell you that human rights are a lofty ideal with no bearing on trade disputes. Mention environmental principles to an investment lawyer, and they will probably dismiss them as 'interesting' material for a research paper.[75] Tell an ECtHR specialist that the unlawful expropriation of investments is a human rights violation, and they will retort that the Convention was not conceived to protect the greed of multinationals.[76] Mention any of the above to a member of the ICJ bar, and they will look askance at your attempt to pollute their 'generalist' outlook. As we will see,[77] this compartmentalization of knowledge and expertise does not prevent a few brave lawyers from acting as brokers and borrowing concepts pertaining to unfamiliar legal fields. However, by and large, the site of epistemic competition within the profession has shifted from state borders to sectoral lines.

•

It has been just a few days since the toast, and the corridors of Burnham & Hutz are already bustling with people. Representatives of the Philippine government, diplomats, technical experts, geographers, historians, lobbyists: Lionel's schedule of meetings is booked to the minute. Filibert patiently follows his mentor wherever he goes, always carrying a voluminous folder where he collects minutes and whatever papers are exchanged during the talks. He is rarely given a chance to speak. One day, before receiving the Philippine ambassador to France, Lionel puts a hand on his shoulder:

'Remember: when I call someone by their first name, you call them Mr. So-and-so. When I call someone Mr. So-and-so, you call them Sir. When I call someone Sir, you don't speak to them.'[78]

---

[74] See e.g. Q. Wright, 'Due Process and International Law' (1946) 40(2) AJIL 398.
[75] In our professional lingo, few adjectives are more disdainful than 'interesting'.
[76] For analysis, see e.g. D. Spielmann, 'Companies in the Strasbourg Courtroom' (2016) 5(3) CILJ 404.
[77] See *infra*, pp. 99–101.
[78] John Flood nailed this point. See Flood, *Barristers' Clerks*, 66.

Filibert is happy to abide. For the first time, he can witness the preparation of a dispute from scratch: in the past, he used to receive the case files only after the partners and the client had agreed on the litigation strategy. Best of all, this dispute sounds quite intriguing.

The bone of contention between the Philippines and Malaysia is sovereignty over Sabah (North Borneo). Apparently, tensions over that remote territory began in the early 1960s, when the Federation of Malaysia was formed and North Borneo became part of it. Since then, the two governments have confronted each other across multiple channels, from diplomatic negotiations to domestic political rallies. Both nations passed bills recognizing the disputed territory as their own and took whatever action they deemed necessary to 'protect' its population. A momentary detente came in 1977, when the Philippine president declared that his country would withdraw its sovereign claim in order to lift a political burden from the Association of South-East Nations. However, that declaration was never followed through, and tensions rose again.[79] In 2002, the Philippines unsuccessfully filed a third-party intervention request with the ICJ, which was dismissed on grounds of lack of a sufficient interest.[80] Finally, in 2013, a standoff between an armed group of protesters and Malaysian security forces left 68 people dead or missing.[81] The massacre precipitated the Philippine's decision to press a new case before the World Court.

At least, this is what Filibert understands from the conversations between Lionel and his interlocutors. Each talk addresses certain aspects of the controversy while leaving others obscure. In the evenings, the legal team meets and tries to piece the puzzle together. As days go by, Filibert starts wondering what the Philippines *really* wants from the case. What are the claims? Are they based on treaty or custom? Is there a reason no one has yet mentioned international law?

The answers to Filibert's questions arrive all together, on the day of the first meeting with the Philippines' agent. A retired diplomat and exquisite-looking gentleman, the agent slowly walks into the conference room at

---

[79] See M. L. Quezon III, 'North Borneo (Sabah): An annotated timeline 1640s-present', Inquirer.net, 2 March 2013, http://globalnation.inquirer.net/66281/north-borneo-sabah-an-annotated-timeline-1640s-present.

[80] *Sovereignty over Pulau Ligitan and Pulau Sipadan (Indonesia* v. *Malaysia)*, Application for Permission to Intervene, Judgment of 23 October 2001, ICJ Rep. 2001, 575 ('*Pulau* judgment on third-party intervention'), para. 93.

[81] See N. Najib, 'Lahad Datu Invasion: A Painful Memory of 2013', Astro Awani, 30 December 2013, http://english.astroawani.com/malaysia-news/lahad-datu-invasion-painful-memory-2013-27579.

2 PM, holding a cup of tea courtesy of the firm's secretary. After exchanging some pleasantries with Lionel (who calls him 'Your Excellency', therefore cutting Filibert off), the agent takes his seat at the head of the table.

'Good afternoon, everyone. Let's keep this short and sweet. My folks in Manila are after the return of Sabah to the Philippines. Personally, I think they're crazy. That will never happen. But you know what *could* happen? That the Court hesitates. That its decision contains a statement that casts doubt on Malaysia's sovereignty over Sabah. That statement is all I'm asking of you. Even if the Court eventually rules against us, please make sure you get that statement. I'm entirely in your hands on how to get there. Anything you achieve above and beyond that is a bonus.'

In that exact moment, Filibert makes three discoveries. First, he finds out that his client, plainly and simply, does not care much about international law. By suing Malaysia before the ICJ, the Philippines is not trying to contribute to the development of the international legal system or to signal its commitment to the judicialization of world affairs.[82] Instead, the Philippines is playing out its 'foreign legal policy',[83] which in turn reflects its domestic political arrangements. Should international law 'develop' as a result of this case, it will be only an *incidental* development – one that derives from 'the choices of counsel made in concert with the representatives of their client', with the judges 'transposing particularised claims to the universal'.[84]

Second, the agent's disagreement with his political masters in Manila teaches Filibert that a state is not a 'unified self' able to express a monolithic position,[85] but an aggregate of competing structures and trajectories. National interests 'are not just "out there" waiting to be discovered', but are rather 'constructed through social interaction'.[86] This

---

[82] See J. Merrills, 'The Place of International Litigation in International Law', in N. Klein (ed.), *Litigating International Law Disputes: Weighing the Options* (Cambridge University Press, 2014) 3, 15.

[83] The expression is borrowed from G. de Lacharrière, *La Politique Juridique Extérieure* (Economica, 1983).

[84] Messenger, 'The Practice of Litigation', 209.

[85] K. Knop, 'Feminism and State Sovereignty in International Law' (1993) 3(2) TransnatlL&ContempProbs 293, 333. See also R. Malley, J. Manas, and C. Nix, 'Constructing the State Extra-Territorially: Jurisdictional Discourse, the National Interest, and Transnational Norms' (1990) 103(6) HarvLRev 1273, 1285.

[86] M. Finnemore, *National Interests in International Society* (Cornell University Press, 1996), 2. See also A. Wendt, 'Collective Identity Formation and the International State' (1994) 88(2) AmPolSciRev 384, 385.

means, Filibert ponders, that international adjudication is neither the centre of the universe nor a goal in itself, but simply *one* of many platforms for political action.

By engaging in ICJ litigation, governments pursue objectives way more complex than (and often having little to do with) winning the case. Some may wish to rebalance a weak bargaining position and obtain a better outcome than they could obtain through diplomatic negotiations.[87] Some others may be forced to pursue a losing case because they cannot look weak in the eyes of their domestic constituencies.[88] For yet others, the goal may be to 'ease domestic opposition to unpopular policies' or to 'signal to their domestic audiences that their policies are appropriate or have international support'.[89] All permutations are possible.

The same holds true for litigants appearing before other international courts. States engaging in WTO dispute settlement, for example, may do so on behalf of their domestic industries or other interest groups. Faced with a threat of commercial injury, domestic producers are likely to lobby their governments into initiating trade cases, cooperate with government representatives in the pursuit of claims, and sometimes even bear the cost of the proceedings.[90] Other WTO members may consciously bring losing cases to show their constituencies that their hands are tied to the mast, thereby resisting domestic calls for protectionism.[91] Again, there are endless possibilities.

---

[87] See R. B. Bilder, 'International Third Party Dispute Settlement' (1988) 17(3) DenvJIntlL&Pol 471, 478–9; P. R. Hensel, 'Contentious Issues and World Politics: The Management of Territorial Claims in the Americas, 1816–1992' (2001) 45(1) IntlStudQ 81, 89; S. Fang, 'The Strategic Use of International Institutions in Dispute Settlement' (2010) 5(2) QJPolSci 107, 110.

[88] See e.g. R. B. Bilder, 'Some Limitations of Adjudication as an International Dispute Settlement Technique' (1982) 23(1) VaJIntlL 1, 7–9; Bilder, 'Third Party Dispute Settlement', 489–90.

[89] Fang, 'The Strategic Use', 110.

[90] See e.g. G. Shaffer, *Defending Interests: Public-Private Partnerships in WTO Litigation* (Brookings, 2003), 1–9, 143–53; J. P. Trachtman and P. M. Moremen, 'Costs and Benefits of Private Participation in WTO Dispute Settlement: Whose Right Is It Anyway?' (2003) 44(1) HarvIntlLJ 221; C. Gibson, 'A Look at the Compulsory License in Investment Arbitration: The Case of Indirect Expropriation' (2010) 25(3) AmUIntlLRev 357, 408.

[91] See e.g. See P. C. Mavroidis, G. A. Bermann and M. Wu, *The Law of the World Trade Organization: Documents, Cases and Analysis* (1st edn., West, 2010), 46; T. Soave, 'The Politics of Time in Domestic and International Lawmaking', in K. Polackova Van Der Ploeg, L. Pasquet, and L. Castellanos-Jankiewicz (eds.), *International Law and Time: Narratives and Techniques* (Springer, forthcoming 2022).

And what about individuals bringing claims before the ECtHR and the IACtHR, or multinationals suing their host states before ISDS tribunals? Are these not 'simple' complainants seeking financial reparation for the harm they suffered? Well, yes and no. While compensation is usually the end-goal, some human rights claims might also be backed by states or civil society networks wishing to obtain a systemic precedent.[92] Likewise, some investors may use the threat of ISDS litigation to induce or prevent regulatory reform in the host state.

If this looks complex enough, just think about *multi-regime* litigation. The most influential actors on the global scene – be they governments, economic conglomerates, or advocacy networks – have learnt how to strategically juggle among multiple forums at both the national and the international level in order to maximize their odds of success and tailor litigation as best suits their needs.[93] The fragmented configuration of the global judiciary offers expert players a wealth of opportunities for forum shopping, which give them a competitive edge over their opponents and skew the game in their favour.[94]

---

[92] See *supra*, p. 66, note 57.

[93] Consider, for instance, the parallel proceedings against Australia's tobacco plain packaging regulation of 2011. This complex litigation saw the tobacco industry act in concert to challenge the measure before a host of domestic and international tribunals. First, Japan Tobacco brought the case before the Australian judiciary all the way up to the High Court, which dismissed the complainant's claims of unconstitutionality (*JT International SA v. Commonwealth of Australia*, [2012] HCA 43 (5 October 2012)). Next, Philip Morris initiated a case before an investment arbitral tribunal (*Philip Morris Asia Limited (Hong Kong) v. The Commonwealth of Australia*, UNCITRAL Case No. 2012-12) and persuaded a couple of friendly governments to promote its cause at the WTO (*Australia – Certain Measures Concerning Trademarks, Geographical Indications and Other Plain Packaging Requirements Applicable to Tobacco Products and Packaging*, WT/DS434, WT/DS435, WT/DS441, WT/DS467). By engaging in this double game, Philip Morris sought to obtain both financial compensation *and* the withdrawal or modification of the plain packaging regulation. Finally, British American Tobacco and other companies brought claims before British courts in respect of the UK plain packaging regulation of 2015. The complainants argued, among other things, that the regulations infringed their human rights under Article 1 of Protocol 1 of the ECHR. (*R (British American Tobacco and others) v. Secretary of State for Health* [2016] EWCA Civ 1182). For discussion, see e.g. Allen and Soave, 'Jurisdictional Overlap', 19; L. Curran and J. Eckhardt, 'Smoke Screen? The Globalization of Production, Transnational Lobbying and the International Political Economy of Plain Tobacco Packaging' (2017) 24(1) RevIntPolitEcon 87.

[94] For discussion of forum shopping as a litigation strategy, see e.g. G. R. Delaume, 'Economic Development and Sovereign Immunity' (1985) 79(2) AJIL 319, 344; Y. Shany, *The Competing Jurisdictions of International Courts and Tribunals* (Oxford University Press, 2003), 79–80; E. Benvenisti and G. Downs, 'The Empire's New Clothes: Political Economy and the Fragmentation of International Law' (2007) 60(2) StanLRev 595, 610, 615;

Fortunately for Filibert, the third discovery is a bit more comforting. The agent's words, 'I am entirely in your hands', suggest that the legal team will enjoy considerable latitude to shape the course of the proceedings. Not only will the lawyers be in charge of selecting the claims and arguments to include in the written memorials and the oral pleadings; they will also contribute to the definition of the client's interests before the Court.

That is right, concludes Filibert: the legal team in the *North Borneo* dispute is not a random group of professionals thrown into international litigation by their client's demand, but rather the *mirror* the client needs to better define its own interests and priorities over the issue at stake. Filibert, Lionel, and their colleagues are not only the 'transmission belt[]', but also the *motor* that moves the belt.[95] Thanks to its high concentration of capital, the team will channel the client's position as needed; broker compromises among the various positions on the table; frame both the input – from social facts to 'legal strategies' – and the output – from the raw decision to consolidated 'jurisprudence'.[96] Quite intriguing, indeed.

Two weeks later, Filibert is already short on sleep. Research for the memorial has not even started and he already longs for a break. After the last exhausting meeting, he and Lionel find themselves on the terrace, staring absently at the cars driving down the boulevard and inhaling the breeze of a late-spring evening. Lionel is first to break the silence.

'I am spent.'

'Me too. It was good though, huh?'

'Painful, you mean. I can't stand all this blah-blah anymore. Your Excellency here, Ma'am Secretary there … Give me a break. Thank God it's over now. We can start talking real business.'

'Personally, I discovered quite a few interesting things.'

'Such as …?'

'Well, law school doesn't prepare you for all the political implications of this job.'

'Screw that. We are here to do law, not to write PhDs. A good legal strategy, a good memorial, a good set of pleadings. *That*'s our job. The rest is fluff. By the way, well done during those meetings. Speaking when requested and leaving the rest to me. We'll make a good team.'

---

J. Pauwelyn, 'Legal Avenues to "Multilateralizing Regionalism": Beyond Article XXIV', in R. Baldwin and P. Low (eds.), *Multilateralizing Regionalism: Challenges for the Global Tradin System* (Cambridge University Press, 2009) 368, 386.

[95] Vauchez, 'Communities of International Litigators', 657.

[96] Ibid.

'Thanks. By the way, what do you think of the team?'

'The *ad hoc* judge, this Felipe Jimeno, sounds like a decent choice. He's the dean of Ateneo de Manila, and was one of the government advisors that pushed for a detente on North Borneo back in the 1970s. As they say around here, *un citoyen au-dessus de tout soupçon.*'

'Agree. What about the other lead counsel?'

'He's a good bloke. We cordially hate each other. He thinks I'm an insufferable yuppie and I think he's a hopeless bookworm. We'll get along just fine.'

Filibert remains silent for a moment.

'Lionel ... This is a hard case, right?'

'Yep. Go and convince the Court that a peaceful and prosperous territory should suddenly change owner after more than 50 years. That won't be a walk in the park, for sure.'

'Any bright ideas?'

'We'll see. The agent kept mentioning this ancient deed by the Sultan of Sulu, which apparently will give us the answers we need ... Gosh, I sound like Indiana bloody Jones.'

Both laugh before Lionel gets pensive again.

'Let's just hope they don't decide to go for a settlement.'

'Why not? Wouldn't a friendly solution be better than a contentious judgment?'

'Are you kidding me? Stop playing the goody-goody!'

'...'

'Alright, sleep tight. Tomorrow we get this ball rolling.'

# 4

## Telling a Story

As an international lawyer, Jasper Schoonraad has always found it quite fitting that his business address is Rue de la Loi 200, Brussels. The Berlaymont building, which houses the headquarters of the European Commission, towers over its surroundings with its 14 stories and 240,000 m² floor area.

Jasper's office is located on the seventh floor, which hosts the Commission's Legal Service. A graduate of the University of Leuven, he joined the Service six years ago, after a three-year stint with a leading trade law firm in Geneva. The reasons for Jasper's return home are readily explained: his wife and two children had stayed in Brussels during his sojourn in Switzerland, and he was tired of commuting every weekend. Sure, the move entailed a significant salary drop, but the life quality improvement was priceless. If anything, Jasper's hesitation about leaving the firm and sitting for the Commission's *concours* stemmed from the fear of getting caught in a mindless bureaucracy and losing the opportunity to provide top-notch legal advice.

These doubts dissipated the moment Jasper met his new boss, Mr. Duncan Doyle, Deputy Director of the Commission's WTO litigation team. Duncan's knowledge of WTO dispute settlement easily rivals that of the best private practitioners. Over the period 1995–2018, he was the chief litigator in half of the almost 400 WTO cases involving the European Union as a complainant, respondent, or third party.[1] The other half was not deemed delicate or important enough to bother Duncan, and Jasper often filled in for him. Whenever they work together, Jasper is invariably impressed by Duncan's all-round skills. Not only does he have a remarkable grasp of the big-picture strategy of each case, he also reviews every submission with the keenest eye for detail. To be Duncan-proof, a text must be perfect down to the last footnote. One day, mildly annoyed by his

---

[1] See WTO website, *Disputes by Member*, www.wto.org/english/tratop_e/dispu_e/dispu_by_country_e.htm (accessed 24 September 2020).

boss' punctiliousness, Jasper asked Duncan whether he sleeps at all. The answer was itself quite irritating: '*De minimis et maximis curat praetor*'.

Early this morning, the EU permanent mission to the WTO sent the Legal Service a copy of Indonesia's panel request in the *EU – Palm Oil* dispute. Flipping through the nine-page document, Jasper tries to anticipate the arguments Indonesia will put forward in its subsequent submissions and ponders about the possible allocation of work among the litigation team. He bets that Duncan will be involved: from the looks of it, this promises to be a mammoth case – and a rather foreseeable one at that.

A few months ago, pressured by European consumer groups and environmental activists, the Commission adopted a new regulation strengthening the existing labelling requirements for food products containing palm oil. To be lawfully marketed in the EU territory, those products must now carry a label certifying that the palm oil input has been produced according to certain criteria established by the Roundtable on Sustainable Palm Oil (RSPO), a Swiss NGO with field offices in Jakarta. The RSPO criteria concern, among others, respect for workers' rights and environmental sustainability. At the time of adoption of the EU palm oil regulation, it was expected that most palm oil products from developing countries, like Indonesia, would not qualify for access to the label, whereas most European and US products would. Given the circumstances, it was to be expected that Indonesia would challenge the regulation on grounds of discrimination.

Now, based on the panel request, it seems that Indonesia has adopted what Duncan calls the 'kitchen sink approach'. Not only is it challenging the measure under Articles I and III of the GATT (enshrining the principles of most-favoured-nation and national treatment, respectively); it is also asserting that, as a technical regulation, the measure is inconsistent with Articles 2.1 and 2.2 of the Agreement on Technical Barriers to Trade[2] (TBT Agreement) (stipulating that technical regulations may not discriminate among like products on the basis of origin and may not be more trade-restrictive than necessary to achieve their objective, respectively).

Already at this initial stage, Jasper spots a number of red flags that do not bode well for his holiday plans. In particular, the 'necessity test' under Article 2.2 of the TBT Agreement will probably require an intense assessment of whether the EU palm oil regulation contributes to the objectives of protecting the environment and ensuring fair labour standards in

---

[2] *Agreement on Technical Barriers to Trade*, Marrakesh Agreement Establishing the World Trade Organization, Annex 1 (15 April 1994), UNTS 1868, 120.

developing countries. Indonesia is likely to come forth with tons of scientific evidence, which the European Union will have to refute. More worryingly still, Jasper seems to recognize the pen behind Indonesia's panel request: if he is not mistaken, that is the job of his former colleagues at the Geneva firm. Uh-oh: the involvement of private practitioners typically means lengthier briefs,[3] more aggressive pleadings, and more work going forward.

Jasper sighs. He picks up the phone and dials Duncan's extension.
'Did you see?'
'Yes. *Quod erat demonstrandum.*'
'I'm sorry?'
'Yep, I saw. How many people do you think we need?'
'Hmm, I'd say you as lead, me and another lawyer as sidekicks, another one for the heavy lifting, and one for the liaison with scientists and the industry. Do we have three extra staff available?'
'Let's make sure we do. Is Jane involved on Indonesia's side?'

Jane Weaver was Jasper's closest colleague at the Geneva firm. The two have remained good friends since he left for Brussels.

'I don't know, but I'd be glad if she were. You know I have a soft spot for the Southern drawl. We'll know for sure when we read Indonesia's first written submission. I can recognize her drafting style from a mile away. Where do you see this case going?'

Duncan replies cordially:

'We'll nail it. We're well trained for this kind of "do-good" cases. Remember how we handled *Seals*:[4] that was a triumph! Perhaps we can rehash some of our thoughts from that dispute.'
'Yeah, but this time around we don't have any cute and fluffy seal pups to show ...'
'Ha! But we have orangutans fleeing from deforestation.'
'I dont' know, Duncan. This regulation does seem quite broken. I mean, why rely only on the RSPO criteria? What about equivalent levels of protection?'
'Yep, that's a tricky one. We'll see how to deal with it. For the time being, let's just brief the team on what's coming. And don't worry, everything will be alright. At the end of the day ... *we are only here to tell a good story.*'

---

[3] See A. Yanovich, 'Outside Looking In, after Many Years on the Inside Looking Out', in G. Marceau (ed.), *A History of Law and Lawyers in the GATT/WTO: The Development of the Rule of Law in the Multilateral Trading System* (Cambridge University Press, 2015) 342, 346–7.

[4] *European Communities – Measures Prohibiting the Importation and Marketing of Seal Products*, WT/DS400, WT/DS401.

\*

Telling a good story, or crafting a persuasive argument, is no easy feat. During the early stages of an international dispute, counsel spend most of their time trying to come up with a convincing set of claims and defences to present to the court. The junior members of the legal teams usually conduct groundwork research on the facts, any relevant issues of domestic law, and precedents that may help advance their clients' positions. The seniors focus instead on the overall litigation strategy: they review the discrete pieces of research they are given, establish meaningful connections between them, tinker with their order, and use them as building blocks to craft a cohesive whole.

One may be tempted to dismiss this initial phase as a mere appetizer for greater things to come. At this point, no brief has yet been filed, no pleading delivered. All we have is a bunch of sleep-deprived lawyers frantically typing on their keyboards, trying to decipher their bosses' track changes, sitting through interminable conference calls, sifting through piles of boring documents, and chatting over one too many cups of coffee.

Yet, these preparatory acts are of essential importance, for they *frame* the scene for further action. By taking their first steps into the case, counsel are actually effecting a first, wondrous transformation of the case itself. Thanks to their labour, the clients' vague grievances are turning into structured sets of legal assertions; the amorphous context in which those grievances arose is condensing into a detailed and purposeful narrative; the incommensurable variety of political, economic, and social life is being packaged into conveniently sized binders; in short, the 'controversy' is becoming a 'dispute'. This early process of essentialization has a deep impact on everything that follows. By the time the first written brief reaches the court's secretaries, what was once nebulous and contingent has become determinate, structured, and structuring.

Mind you, however, that 'structured' does not mean 'static'. A party's position does not remain immutable throughout the course of proceedings, but evolves in light of the other party's rebuttals and the interactions between the litigants and the court. A tricky question from the bench (or its manifest scepticism towards a certain line of argument) may cause a party to drop or modify a claim, tone up or down the salience or a fact or precedent, or even revise the overall litigation strategy on the go; a defence raised by the other party midway through the process may deviate the discussion and set it on a new course; and so on.

As will become clear, the court itself never reasons in the abstract, but instead *reacts* to, and *grapples* with, the positions taken by the parties.[5] The reactive nature of the judges' activity is particularly evident when it comes to fact-finding: a court must limit its decision on the facts that the parties have placed on record and for which they have adduced evidence. The same restrictions do not apply to legal reasoning: by virtue of the *jura novit curia* principle, adjudicators are in principle free to develop their own theory, which may radically depart from those offered by the litigants.[6] However, no court or tribunal has ever ruled without at least some consideration of the parties' legal interpretations or without some engagement with their arguments.

The mutual adaptiveness of positions, the incessant construction and deconstruction of discursive possibilities, and the iterative quest for meaning shed a new light on the unfolding of international litigation. Far from a simple elucidation of rules through logical reasoning, the judicial process is a 'developing drama'[7] whose every step entails a variation in the arguments that prosper or wither, the relative persuasiveness of the actors making them, and the poignancy of facts and precedents. At every new turn, 'a whole series of tensions, vectors, currents, pressures is slightly rearranged'.[8] Submission after submission, pleading after pleading, question after question, certain subjects gain or lose traction; lawyers and adjudicators acquire or forgo authority; stumble momentarily; overcome roadblocks; affirm or disavow precedents; and revise interpretations.

This perpetual movement imparts a sense of contingency – sometimes even randomness – to the development of proceedings. No litigator, not even the most prescient, can fully predict the exact trajectory of a case. Legal constructs that appeared highly relevant at its early stages may be

---

[5] See e.g. Wells, 'Situated Decisionmaking', 1734; Messenger, 'The Practice of Litigation'.

[6] For recent examples of reliance on the *jura novit curia* principle by international courts and tribunals, see e.g. *Maritime Dispute (Peru v. Chile)*, Judgment of 27 January 2014, ICJ Rep. 2014, 3 ('*Maritime Dispute* judgment'), Declaration of Judge Donoghue (stating that 'neither Party's pleaded case convinced the Court', such that the Court was bound to reach an outcome 'in light of the applicable law and the evidence' before it, without 'the benefit of the Parties' views' on a number of key issues); Panel Report, *Indonesia – Safeguard on Certain Iron or Steel Products*, WT/DS490/R, WT/DS496/R (18 August 2017), para. 7.10 (where, despite the parties' concurrent position that the measure at issue was a safeguard subject to specific WTO disciplines, the panel found that the measure was *not* a safeguard and that, therefore, those disciplines did not apply).

[7] Wells, 'Situated Decisionmaking', 1734.

[8] Latour, *The Making of Law*, 141.

progressively sidelined, whereas seemingly mundane elements may rise in prominence to the point of becoming the cornerstone of the final ruling. As will be discussed, these contingencies can be exploited to gradually introduce novel approaches and unorthodox views into the gears of the judicial machinery. After all, as a poet once put it, it is through cracks that the light gets in.[9]

\*

But we are getting ahead of ourselves. Let us take a step back and watch the opposed legal teams as they scramble to put together their first written submissions. At this stage, the name of the game is to provide the adjudicators with an overview of the relevant facts, a preliminary analysis of the applicable legal rules, and a series of precedents that the court should follow or overturn to arrive at the desired conclusion. The length and detail of these first submissions vary depending on the extent to which the parties will have further opportunities to refine their positions later in the proceedings.

The ICJ rules of court, for instance, typically contemplate only one round of written briefs per party (the memorial and counter-memorial), possibly followed by second round (reply and rejoinder) if the parties so agree or if the Court so decides.[10] Under these conditions, counsel are often tempted to shoot most of their ammunition early on, lest they find themselves precluded from exploring new lines of argument as the case progresses. Similarly, WTO appellate proceedings only allow for one main and one rebuttal submission per participant,[11] thereby offering limited opportunities to clarify things in writing later on. By contrast, WTO panel and ISDS proceedings usually[12] involve multiple rounds of briefs, written responses to the adjudicators' questions, cross-comments on each party's submissions, etc. There, litigators can afford to keep a few aces up their sleeves, to be played when the occasion arises.

Constructing the relevant facts and collecting the supporting evidence can be a strenuous exercise. Wait, did we just say '*constructing*' the facts? Yes, we did. Not because of any hermeneutical ambition; not because

---

[9] Leonard Cohen, *Anthem*.
[10] ICJ Rules of Court, Article 45.
[11] WTO Appellate Body, *Working Procedures of Appellate Review*, WT/AB/WP/6 (10 April 2003), last amended on 12 January 2010, Rules 21 and 22.
[12] 'Usually', because the working procedures of a WTO panel or an arbitral tribunal are negotiated between the presiding adjudicator and the parties during the first organizational meeting.

'language is ... the condition of the possibility of the facts themselves';[13] but simply because, in practice, litigants have no interest in retelling past events as they actually occurred. Instead, each party will seek to represent those events in the light most favourable to its position. Legal counsel are not historians. They are allowed, and even expected, to be selective in their depictions of empirical reality; to omit or downplay facts that would adversely impact their clients; or to recast those facts in a light that modifies their significance. To put it bluntly, litigators are not supposed to give the adjudicators the truth – only a *plausible narrative* of the truth.

Plausibility is an elusive and impalpable quality. So much so that we feel the urge to endow it with physical attributes. Facts can have a specific *weight*, which derives from the *thickness* or *density* of the evidence supporting them. A court's factual assessment is imbued with this kind of imagery. We commonly speak of '*burden* of proof';[14] we have learned that '*unsubstantiated* assertions' do not count as proper facts;[15] we know that courts *weigh* competing pieces of information against one another to determine, *on balance*, which one *preponderates*;[16] and we portray our Lady Justice as a blindfolded woman holding a *scale*.[17]

Moreover, facts can be more or less *tight* depending on the efficacy and economy with which they are presented to the court. A factual narrative 'holds water' when its components fit well together, flow from

---

[13] G. Pavlakos, *Our Knowledge of the Law: Objectivity and Practice in Legal Theory* (Hart, 2007), 122, fn 103.

[14] For recent examples, see e.g. *Pulp Mills on the River Uruguay (Argentina v. Uruguay)*, Judgment of 20 April 2010, ICJ Rep. 2010, 71 ('Pulp Mills judgment'), para. 162; *Ahmadou Sadio Diallo (Guinea v. Democratic Republic of the Congo)*, Judgment of 30 November 2010, ICJ Rep. 2010, 639, para. 53; *Metal-Tech Ltd. v. Uzbekistan*, ICSID Case No. ARB/10/3, Award (4 October 2013), paras. 228 et seq. For discussion, see e.g. M. Kazazi, *Burden of Proof and Related Issues: A Study on Evidence before International Tribunals* (Kluwer Law International, 1996), 117.

[15] Appellate Body Report, *Russian Federation – Measures on the Importation of Live Pigs, Pork and Other Pig Products from the European Union*, WT/DS475/AB/R (23 February 2017) ('*Russia – Pigs*'), para. 5.63. See also e.g. Appellate Body Report, *United States – Measures Affecting Imports of Woven Wool Shirts and Blouses from India*, WT/DS33/AB/R (25 April 1997), p. 14.

[16] See e.g. Appellate Body Reports, *European Communities – Selected Customs Matters*, WT/DS315/AB/R (13 November 2006), para. 258; *European Communities – Definitive Anti-Dumping Measures on Certain Iron or Steel Fasteners from China*, WT/DS397/AB/R (15 July 2011) ('*EC – Fasteners (China)*'), para. 582.

[17] See e.g. D. E. Curtis and J. Resnik, 'Images of Justice' (1987) 96 YaleLJ 1727; R. Jacob, *Images de la Justice: Essai sur l'Iconographie Judiciaire du Moyen Âge à l'Âge Classique* (Le Léopard d'Or, 1994).

one another in a seemingly logical fashion, and withstand questioning and criticism.[18] Conversely, it is 'loose' or 'riddled with holes' when it presents internal contradictions and *non sequiturs*. The tighter the story, the harder for the counterpart to exploit its weaknesses and for the adjudicators to draw adverse inferences against the storyteller.

Taken alone, neither weight nor tightness takes a factual narrative very far. *Both* are needed for it to stand a chance. The most eloquent exposé of the facts would hardly be persuasive if it were not supported by solid evidence. At the same time, 'evidence only counts as evidence ... in relation to a potential narrative',[19] otherwise it would be a congeries of disconnected representations. There is no magic recipe to lend weight and tightness to a party's factual assertions. The counsel's skills and personalities, the quality of support they receive, and the specific features of the case at hand are all relevant factors.

Importantly, different courts and tribunals have different preferences and sensibilities in respect of fact-finding, and competent litigators must calibrate their narratives accordingly. For instance, as we will see,[20] the ICJ does not have a very strong record of getting the facts straight. Despite the increasing technical complexity of disputes, judges in The Hague still think of themselves as umpires rather than investigators.[21] Hence, the members of the ICJ bar – who are themselves scholars rather than sleuths – think twice before bombarding the judges with overly intricate factual arguments. It is often safer to stick to straightforward statements, make abundant use of 'commonplace positions',[22] and avoid unnecessary complications.

Other judicial bodies are better equipped at handling complex fact patterns. Investment tribunals, for instance, devote a significant portion of their proceedings to establish what happened and how. When the circumstances so require, ISDS hearings involve a rigorous examination and cross-examination of witnesses. WTO panel proceedings do not

---

[18] See e.g. N. MacCormick, 'Rhetoric and the Rule of Law', in D. Dyzenhaus (ed.), *Recrafting the Rule of Law: The Limits of Legal Order* (Hart, 1999) 163, 166.

[19] L. Gossman, 'Towards a Rational Historiography' (1989) 79(3) TransAmPhilSoc 1, 26. See also J. W. Scott, 'The Evidence of Experience' (1991) 17(4) CritInq 773, 776.

[20] See *infra*, Chapter 10.

[21] N. H. Alford, Jr., 'Fact Finding by the World Court' (1958) 4(1) VillanovaLRev 38, 52.

[22] MacCormick, 'Rhetoric', 167. See also e.g. T. Viehweg, 'Some Considerations Concerning Legal Reasoning', in G. Hughes (ed.), *Law, Reason and Justice: Essays in Legal Philosophy* (New York University Press, 1969), 257, 266–8; J. Stelmach and B. Brożek, *Methods of Legal Reasoning* (Springer, 2006), 133.

contemplate testimony, but only documentary evidence. However, panelists do not shy away from asking litigants to clarify factual matters through oral and written questions. Party-appointed experts often appear in court alongside the parties' delegations. When the case involves particularly tricky scientific questions, panels can, under Article 13.2 of the DSU, 'seek information from any relevant source and … consult experts to obtain their opinion on certain aspects of the matter'. Greater fact-finding capacity opens the door to more articulate factual narratives, which in turn pave the way for more fact-intensive litigation.

These differences in the *habitus* of the various courts and tribunals have a profound impact on the type of facts that the parties produce. An ISDS counsel spends more time prepping witnesses than an ICJ litigator; a WTO attorney makes sure that their submissions contain enough scientific evidence to meet a panel's expectations; etc. Hence, the presentation of facts and evidence to an international court, which can often make the difference between winning or losing, is shaped more by *practice* and *tradition* than by 'hard' procedural rules.

Practice and tradition also affect the organization of the legal teams themselves. There exists a curious asymmetry between the importance of mastering the facts of a case[23] and the modest professional rewards that come from being a fact-master. Scouting for relevant evidence is usually a tedious, time-consuming endeavour that does little to bolster one's position as a leading counsel. Law firms often find it harder to justify the billable hours spent on groundwork factual research than those spent on the study of legal norms and precedents.

This might explain why the facts are usually delegated to the lower (and cheaper) ranks of the workforce, such as first-year associates and other junior lawyers. As part of their rite of passage, new recruits are expected to memorize the content of the record, down to the exhibit number and page where a certain piece of factual information can be found. This knowledge will then be used to assist senior counsel during the drafting of briefs, the meetings with the client, and oral hearings.

Filibert, for example, vividly remembers the sleepless nights he spent filling in the footnotes left blank by Lionel. Frequently, his mentor would include a factual assertion in the text of a memorial and then sneakily add: '[CITE]'. It fell on Filibert to find the piece of evidence needed and add

---

[23] See e.g. S. Rosenne, *Essays on International Law and Practice* (Martinus Nijhoff, 2007), 235 ('Every jurist understands that before he or she can give a worthwhile legal opinion, he or she must know the facts.')

the citation. Jasper, too, has had his fair share of factual research. When pleading before a WTO panel, Duncan would often refer to a piece of documental evidence in support of his allegations. Jasper, sitting next to him, would frantically flip through the evidence binders and pass the relevant document to his boss. One day, Duncan had a tech-savvy idea: for the next hearing, would it not be nice to replace the physical binders with tabs on his iPad? The result was catastrophic. Jasper spent the whole week prior to the hearing scanning and saving documents on his mentor's tablet, with no time to do anything else. During the pleadings, Duncan got mixed up with the tabs, and Jasper had to repeatedly grab the tablet from his boss's hands and point him in the right direction.

Despite these hardships, fact-gathering can make for a quite intriguing challenge. Finding correlations among seemingly disjoint events, establishing causality between behaviour and effects, prioritizing materials on the basis of relevance, and filling up holes in the record: none of these is a mechanistic exercise, but one that requires a certain creativity. A good fact-finder is akin to a good *bricoleur*. Unlike the 'engineer', who first comes up with an overarching plan and then selects the tools and raw materials required to carry it through, the '*bricoleur*' must be ready to use 'whatever is at hand' to get the job done.[24] You are missing a key quote from a government official? Try to infer the gist of it from second-hand accounts. An ancient map has gone lost? Try to reconstruct it through other documents from the same era. The prison guards who mistreated your client have left no official record? Try to rely on medical reports. Circumstantial evidence, indirect testimony, even hearsay: *everything* counts, provided it builds into the narrative.[25]

Duncan's experience can attest to the creative nature of fact-gathering. In a 2014 WTO case, the European Union sought to show that Argentina had adopted a range of informal, unwritten, and diffuse import requirements potentially distorting trade. Argentina denied that any such requirements existed and argued that, if they did, they would not constitute a general measure separate from the individual instances of their

---

[24] C. Lévi-Strauss, *The Savage Mind* (Weidenfeld and Nicolson, 1966), 16–17.
[25] See Latour, *The Making of Law*, 141. Except international criminal courts, international adjudicatory bodies rarely declare evidence inadmissible, even when fraudulently acquired by a party. See e.g. W. M. Reisman and E. E. Freedman, 'The Plaintiff's Dilemma: Illegally Obtained Evidence and Admissibility in International Adjudication' (1982) 76(4) AJIL 737; W. M. Reisman and C. Skinner, *Fraudulent Evidence before Public International Tribunals: The Dirty Stories of International Law* (Cambridge University Press, 2014).

application. Predictably, the words '*probatio diabolica*' attracted Duncan like a bee to honey. Through months of meticulous research, he and his team patched together dozens of press clippings, statements by public officials, newspaper articles, and agreements signed between the Argentine government and individual companies.[26] While none of these materials proved much by itself, their aggregate effect was powerful: both the panel and the Appellate Body found that the European Union had produced a critical mass of evidence sufficient to show the existence of the unwritten import requirements as a de facto general measure.[27]

Was it only about 'mass', though? Jasper had his doubts. After the end of the case, he asked Duncan how he did it. For once, the answer was not in Latin: 'It's simple. First, I made the judges *want* to decide in my favor. Then, and only then, I gave them the facts that would *justify* that decision.'[28]

\*

But good facts are not enough to secure victory in court. The persuasiveness of a factual narrative can be measured only in relation to the *legal* narrative it supports. International adjudication is not concerned with factual representations per se,[29] but rather with the normative consequences that are ascribed to those representations. Contentious cases, which account for the overwhelming majority of court dockets, each entail at least one claim of violation of an international legal norm. Advisory cases, like those contemplated under Article 65 of the ICJ Statute, require the formulation of a legal question in 'exact' enough terms to allow a court to render its opinion. In either scenario, it is the parties' legal submissions that define the adjudicators' mandate and delineate their decision horizon. A court that rules on norms other than those invoked before it acts ultra petita, or in excess of its jurisdiction.[30] This demonstrates, once again, the power of framing that the parties exercise in the preparatory stages of a dispute.

---

[26] See Appellate Body Report, *Argentina – Measures Affecting the Importation of Goods*, WT/DS438/AB/R (15 January 2015) ('*Argentina – Import Measures*'), para. 5.126.

[27] Panel Report, *Argentina – Measures Affecting the Importation of Goods*, WT/DS438/R (22 August 2014), para. 6.231; Appellate Body Report, *Argentina – Import Measures*, para. 5.184.

[28] See Frank, *Law and the Modern Mind*, 102–3.

[29] But see M. Koskenniemi, 'Between Impunity and Show Trials' (2002) 6 UNYB 1, 28.

[30] See e.g. *Soufraki* v. *United Arab Emirates*, ICSID Case No. ARB/02/07, Annulment (5 June 2007), para. 85; *Industria Nacional de Alimentos (previously Lucchetti)* v. *Peru*, ICSID Case No. ARB/03/04, Annulment (5 September 2007), para. 98.

By identifying the applicable norms, characterizing their meaning, and mapping their interplay, counsel define the essential features of the case, delineate its boundaries, and set the tone for subsequent interactions.

How do litigators go about these crucial tasks? Quite haphazardly, in fact. As we will see in a moment, different counsel have different litigation strategies. Some spell out all the legal minutiae of their clients' positions early on, and later focus on the aspects that the court deems most relevant or controversial; others prefer to start with a more impressionistic, broad-brush picture of their case, and keep the best arguments as a riposte to the opponent's assertions. Some seek to impress the court with their encyclopaedic knowledge of rules and precedents; others try to gain the court's favour by keeping their submissions brief and on point. Some stick to technical and impersonal language; others indulge in rhetorical flourishes. Be it as it may, experienced counsel often leave their personal trademark on their filings. Flipping through the pages of Indonesia's complaint, for example, Jasper and Duncan notice that it is written in Times New Roman 12, double-spaced, unjustified margins. This leaves no doubt that Jane Weaver's law firm is involved.

As with facts, the procedural rules, the *habitus*, and the ingrained preferences of the various courts and tribunals affect the content, structure, and tone of the parties' legal submissions. Despite these variations, all briefs present a number of recurring features.

The first is the identification of the 'principal norms', that is the rules on which the parties ground their demands.[31] These rules must emanate from a legal source that falls under the jurisdiction of the court or tribunal concerned. For the ECtHR, that is the European Convention on Human Rights (ECHR or 'European Convention');[32] for the IACtHR, the American Convention on Human Rights (ACHR);[33] for a WTO panel, the WTO agreements;[34] for an ISDS tribunal, the relevant investment treaty

---

[31] L. Bartels, 'Jurisdiction and Applicable Law Clauses: Where Does a Tribunal Find the Principal Norms Applicable to the Case before It?', in T. Broude and Y. Shany (eds.), *Multi-Sourced Equivalent Norms in International Law* (Hart, 2011) 115, 117.

[32] See Article 32 of the ECHR ('The jurisdiction of the Court shall extend to all matters concerning the interpretation and application of the Convention and the Protocols thereto.')

[33] See Article 62.3 of the ACHR ('The jurisdiction of the Court shall comprise all cases concerning the interpretation and application of the provisions of this Convention that are submitted to it.')

[34] See Article 7.1 of the DSU ('Panels shall ..., in light of the relevant provisions in ... the covered agreement(s) cited by the parties to the dispute ..., make such findings as will assist the DSB [Dispute Settlement Body] in making the recommendations or in giving the rulings provided for in that/those agreement(s).')

or contract;[35] and for the ICJ, any source of international law listed under Article 38 of its Statute.[36] The enunciation of the principal norms defines the irreducible core of a dispute and, in most judicial regimes, is a mandatory condition for a court to entertain the case.[37]

Once the principal norms have been properly identified, a litigator may, *in theory*, stop there and not provide any further legal arguments. The principal legal claims, together with the facts and evidence placed on record, would be enough for the court to examine the case and render its decision. However, *in practice*, this does not happen. Any respectable counsel knows that such a minimalist approach would not go very far, and that much more work is needed to justify their fees. In fact, any decent legal brief contains lengthy and articulate argumentation that details and complements the principal claims.

The exposé typically begins with the identification of the norms deemed *relevant* and *applicable* to the facts of the case. These may encompass a host of 'incidental norms', that is rules and principles that, while not strictly necessary to the solution of the case, have the potential to guide the adjudicators in making findings and reaching conclusions.[38] Unlike

---

[35] Things are actually a little more complicated here. Depending on the text of the BIT and the circumstances of each case, the governing law of an arbitral tribunal may encompass the '[t]reaty' itself, the 'rules of law specified in the pertinent investment authorization or investment agreement', 'the law of the respondent, including its rules on the conflict of laws', and any 'applicable rules of international law'. 2012 US Model BIT, Article 30. For analysis, see e.g. H. E. Kjos, *Applicable Law in Investor-State Arbitration: The Interplay between National and International Law* (Oxford University Press, 2013).

[36] See Article 38 of the ICJ Statute ('The Court, ... shall apply: (a) international conventions, whether general or particular, establishing rules expressly recognized by the contesting states; (b) international custom, as evidence of a general practice accepted as law; (c) the general principles of law recognized by civilized nations; (d) ... judicial decisions and the teachings of the most highly qualified publicists of the various nations, as subsidiary means for the determination of rules of law.')

[37] For example, Article 6.2 of the DSU requires a complainant in WTO proceedings to 'provide a brief summary of the legal basis of the complaint'. Similarly, Article 38.2 of the ICJ Rules of Court stipulate that an application 'shall specify as far as possible the legal grounds upon which the jurisdiction of the Court is said to be based; it shall also specify the precise nature of the claim, together with a succinct statement of the ... grounds on which the claim is based'.

[38] Bartels, 'Principal Norms', 117. The distinction between principal and incidental norms was well captured by the ICJ in the *Arrest Warrant* case, where it observed that '[w]hile the Court is ... not entitled to decide upon questions not asked of it, the *non ultra petita* rule nonetheless cannot preclude the Court from addressing certain legal points in its reasoning'. *Arrest Warrant of 11 April 2000 (Democratic Republic of the Congo v. Belgium)*, Judgment of 14 February 2002, ICJ Rep. 2002, 3 ('*Arrest Warrant* judgment'), para. 43.

principal norms, incidental norms may be found elsewhere than in the sources subject to the court's jurisdiction. Next comes the *interpretation* of the norms so identified. Relying on a range of codified techniques, like those listed in Articles 31 and 32 of the VCLT, each party will seek to persuade the judges to read those norms in the manner most conducive to its position. Finally, it is time to address the *application* of the relevant norms to the specific circumstances of the case. This means connecting the general to the particular, tailoring the abstract interpretation of rules to the factual situation at issue, and demonstrating how the superposition of law and fact warrants a favourable ruling.

This tripartite structure – relevance, interpretation, application – sets the tone of virtually every legal submission in international judicial proceedings, and closely mimics the order of analysis that the court will later follow in its final decision.[39] Why is that so? Could litigators not resort to more flexible and creative narrative structures?

The answer, once again, resides in the expectations and assumptions of the international judicial community. However fictional, the belief that legal reasoning should have 'all the certitude and the inelasticity of a mathematical proposition'[40] still holds sway in our field. Competent counsel know that, if they are to convince the judges as thoroughly and easily as possible, they must present their legal arguments as rational interpretations of recognized norms[41] and conform to the formal strictures of syllogism. You may want to alter the order of the building blocks, put greater weight on one or the other, or intersperse your narrative with extraneous considerations. However, if you want to stand a chance, you cannot depart too far from 'techniques, rhetoric, and traditions' provided by the 'normative universe of international law'.[42]

Within these confines, however, narrators are free to tinker with arrangements and explore variations on the theme. Crafting a story is not only an exercise in pure method – it is *also* an open-ended process that requires choices, value judgments, and imagination on the part of the storyteller. The audience to which the story is addressed is the ultimate arbiter of its persuasiveness. A good novelist is not simply one who 'knows

---

[39] See *infra*, pp. 309–15.
[40] W. J. Brown, 'Law and Evolution' (1920) 29(4) YaleLJ 394, 400.
[41] See J. McCahery and S. Picciotto, 'Creative Lawyering and the Dynamics of Business Regulation', in Y. Dezalay and D. Sugarman (eds.), *Professional Competition and Professional Power: Lawyers, Accountants and the Social Construction of Markets* (Routledge, 1995) 238.
[42] d'Aspremont, 'The Multidimensional Process of Interpretation', 112.

how to write well', but one whose novels resonate with readers. Similarly, a persuasive legal argument is neither the soundest nor the most logical, but the one that is concretely able to convince the judges in the specific circumstances of a case.[43]

Therefore, just like the construction of facts, the construction of law entails a good measure of *bricolage*. The discursive tools available to a litigator are numerous and diverse, ranging from rigid textualism to teleological interpretation, from analogical reasoning to *a contrario* and *a fortiori* arguments.[44] Experienced lawyers know how to shift tone and emphasis as the circumstances require, adapt their argumentative postures as the discussion evolves, and in general do whatever is necessary to turn the odds in their favour. Like any other artefact in this story, legal argumentation is at once structured *and* contingent, predetermined *and* creational.

•

Not convinced? Do not take our word for it – take Duncan's. A few weeks ago, Jasper invited him to deliver a lecture on effective advocacy at the University of Leuven. As Duncan took his place at the podium, Jasper sat in the back of the classroom, ready to take notes of his boss' speech. What follows is a heavily edited summary of those notes.

*Tip No. 1: If it passes the laugh test, it flies.* When you try to persuade a court, do not be shy. Your job is to come up with whatever strategy best suits your client's position. You do not need to consider the pedigree, inherent quality, or systemic viability of your arguments – but only their ability to convince the adjudicators there and then. The immediate and practical persuasiveness of an argument is not necessarily the same as its soundness. When persuasiveness and soundness come into conflict, go for the former.

Remember: your reputational stakes as a litigator are not the same as the judges'. Judges are evaluated on the quality and clarity of their reasoning, their understanding of the issues raised, their ability to set a viable precedent, etc.[45] You, instead, will be graded on your results. When you have a winning case, you are expected to win it. When you have a losing case, you are expected to lose it as painlessly as possible. Full stop.

---

[43] C. Perelman and L. Olbrechts-Tyteca, *The New Rhetoric: A Treatise on Argumentation*, trans. J. Wilkinson and P. Weaver (Notre Dame University Press, 1969), 76–86. See also MacCormick, 'Rhetoric', 168.
[44] See MacCormick, 'Rhetoric', 167; C. Perelman, 'What Is Legal Logic?' (1968), 3(1) IsLR 1.
[45] See generally Cohen et al., 'Legitimacy and International Courts'.

Systemic considerations, like the value of a certain legal interpretation in future disputes, are simply not part of your concerns: they are a mere by-product, a corollary of your contingent needs.[46]

This, however, does not mean that *anything* goes. Firstly, and obviously, you should never breach the rules of conduct or the ethical guidelines of your national bar.[47] You want to come across as skilful, not disingenuous. If your argument is perceived as a dirty trick, your reputation will suffer. Bear in mind that different courts and tribunals have different levels of tolerance for tricksters. In ISDS, for example, litigators spare no mercy to their opponents and are not afraid of getting aggressive. Allegations of bad faith or requests for recusal of arbitrators, for example, are quite common there. At the WTO, where I usually plead, the litigants are expected to maintain a modicum of decorum and diplomatic affability. So be careful before flinging accusations of bias or dishonesty.

Secondly, you should always ask yourself if your argument passes the laugh test. That is the minimum threshold below which making an argument would become counterproductive. Ridiculous legal assertions, or ones 'made in less than good faith', may be 'exposed' in the judicial opinion or even 'prejudice or embarrass' your case.[48] If you stretch the adjudicators' patience with laughable arguments, you may risk losing their attention and goodwill. Worse even, that may harm your professional standing over time.

Distinguishing what passes the laugh test from what does not can be tricky at times. This is because the standards of acceptability and unacceptability of an argument derive from the assumptions and expectations of your audience. It is only through experience that you, as legal counsel, can learn when to push boundaries and when to stick to the beaten path, when to take gambles and when to play safe. Making a daring legal claim is like telling a culturally sensitive joke at a social dinner. Carefully tailor the joke, and you will endear yourself to your tablemates. Be reckless, and you will just offend everyone at the table.

*Tip No. 2: Do not simply make your case – establish your logic.* Any decent brief requires an internally coherent narrative, whose legal and factual

---

[46] See e.g. W. B. Wendel, 'The Craft of Legal Interpretation', in Y. Morigiwa, M. Stolleis, and J. L. Halpérin (eds.), *Interpretation of Law in the Age of Enlightenment: From the Rule of the King to the Rule of Law* (Springer, 2011) 153, 166.

[47] On the issue of professional standards for international counsel, see Sthoeger and Wood, 'The International Bar', 641–7.

[48] R. B. Bilder, 'International Dispute Settlement and the Role of International Adjudication' (1987) 1(2) EmoryJIntlDispRes 131, 141.

components flow from one another in an orderly fashion. However, for an *excellent* brief, you need something more. You need to present the judges with a whole *theory* of the case: a logical progression of inquiry that moves from a fundamental premise – of course, a premise favourable to your position – and then proceeds deductively through all the steps of the analysis, down to the tiniest minutiae. Memorize every detail, master the flow, repeat the story backwards to see if its connections hold. If you manage to persuade the bench that your premise is sound, that your *way of looking at the case* is right, you will skew the playfield to your advantage. If your logic prevails, you win big.

Here are a few rules of thumb that you should follow whenever possible. When interpreting a rule under Article 31 of the VCLT, do not simply assert that 'Rule 1 means A', because this would allow the opponent to make an equally good argument that 'Rule 1 means B'. If you *really* want your Rule 1 to mean A, try to connect it to other contextual norms, show how it relates to general principles, and so on.

Various techniques can take you there. For example, you could begin with a *reductio ad absurdum*: 'Rule 1 must mean A because, otherwise, Rules 2 and 3 would be deprived of meaning, contrary to object and purpose of the treaty and the principle of effective interpretation'.[49] Next, you could draw new connections among norms or between norms and facts: 'When it comes to the specific facts of this case, Rule 1 is informed by the context provided by Rules 2 and 3; read together in light of the object and purpose of the treaty, the three rules mean A.' Or, even better: 'Contrary to what one might think, the most pertinent rule is not Rule 2, which says B, but rather Rule 1, which says A; Rule 1 best captures the facts of the case as they *really* are'. When deploying these techniques, always remember to select your entry point: 'Rule 1 means A, because, as we have explained, Rule 2 means B; in turn, this means that Rule 3 means C'. And, as a last resort: if you cannot convince them, confuse them. Write and speak confidently even if your point is weak. Judicial oversights are rare, but possible. Whatever you do, remember: *never* accede to your opponent's logic and vocabulary. At least at the beginning, the court must have the impression that you and the other party are dealing with *two different cases*.

---

[49] See e.g. *Competence of the ILO to Regulate Incidentally the Personal Work of the Employer*, Advisory Opinion of 23 July 1926, PCIJ Rep., Series B, No. 13, pp. 18–19; *Reparation for Injuries in the Service of the United Nations*, Advisory Opinion of 11 April 1949, ICJ Rep. 1949, 174, pp. 182–3; Appellate Body Report, *Canada – Certain Measures Affecting the Renewable Energy Generation Sector / Canada – Measures Relating to the Feed-in Tariff Program*, WT/DS412/AB/R, WT/DS426/AB/R (6 May 2013), para. 5.57.

*Tip No. 3: Know your judges.* This is the most important tip of all. In making your legal argument, you should always bear in mind the adjudicators' preferences and sensibilities, and avoid alienating them from your cause. Easier said than done, of course – but here are a few things to keep in mind.

First, remember that you are not addressing Gods, but mortals.[50] Their perception of your argument will largely depend on their assumptions and acquired instincts. In years of experience, I have never had the impression that a judge had come to a dispute knowing exactly who should win and who should lose. Sure, an adjudicator may develop an initial gut feeling about the case, be more sympathetic to one or the other position, and have their cards stacked for or against you. But this does not mean that they are not required to *hesitate* and to *test* their instincts before coming to conclusions.

Crucially, you are not trying to persuade *one* person, but an entire *group* – the whole bench, the court's bureaucrats, and other invisible experts you will probably never meet. The constant conversations between these actors have a mediating effect on each individual opinion, and lead to turnarounds more often than you think. The fact that judges are human also means that they dislike being put in thorny situations. Do not attempt to corner them; do not press them into making grand statements that may cause them trouble in the future. If the conversation comes to an impasse, give them a workable path out of it – a reasonable and fact-specific way to rule in your client's favour while not sounding too sweeping.

Second, do not overestimate the judges' fluency in international law – especially in matters that fall outside their area of specialization. However knowledgeable, an adjudicator has limited time and resources to spend on the study of the discipline. Their experience largely derives from situated practice: exchanges with colleagues, specialized seminars, collective learning processes, etc. Situated practice comes with epistemic limitations. Your human rights judge may be an expert in ECtHR and IACtHR jurisprudence, but may not be up to speed with ICJ case law; your investment arbitrator will know a lot about previous awards, but probably little about WTO panel reports; and so forth.

Persuading your audience means couching your argument in a vocabulary the audience is able to understand. Whenever possible, you should begin with the text of the treaty provisions you are invoking. These are

---

[50] See famously Frank, 'Are Judges Human?'.

the core materials your judges usually work with, those they know best. Next, you should turn to the jurisprudence of the court or tribunal you are addressing. If the adjudicators do not master the precedent you are citing, you can rest assured that their legal assistants will. These are all safe bets: almost every judge can grasp an argument couched in familiar language.

But what about rules, principles, and modes of analysis that originate in 'foreign' legal regimes? Does it make sense to invoke an investment law concept before a WTO panel, or a human rights norm before the ICJ? Personally, I do not have much of a problem with peppering up my footnotes with exotic references. Why, once I even cited the ICTY in a WTO submission![51] However, it would be very risky to rely on 'foreign' materials as your main tool of persuasion. Forcing the judges into unknown territory is almost invariably a recipe for failure: they will probably not understand what you are saying, and if they do, they will be inclined to dismiss it.

For example, imagine what would happen if, in trying to convince the WTO Appellate Body that a measure is unnecessarily trade-restrictive, I were to rely on the ECtHR's doctrines of 'margin of appreciation' and 'proportionality'.[52] The judges would stare at me blankly! The safer way to argue lack of necessity in *WTO* proceedings is to show that a less trade-restrictive measure exists which would contribute to the state's regulatory objective to an equivalent degree.[53] This line of argument

---

[51] European Communities' third party submission, *United States – Final Anti-Dumping Measures on Stainless Steel from Mexico*, WT/DS344 (11 April 2007), para. 107 and fn 115. thereto. See also D. Charlotin, 'The Place of Investment Awards and WTO Decisions in International Law: A Citation Analysis' (2017) 20(2) JIEL 279, 297.

[52] See e.g. *Handyside v. United Kingdom*, Judgment of 7 December 1976, No. 5493/72, ECtHR-1976, paras. 48–9; *Sunday Times v. United Kingdom*, Judgment of 26 April 1979, No. 6538/74, ECtHR-1979, paras. 58 et seq.; *Tolstoy Miloslavsky v. United Kingdom*, Judgment of 13 July 1995, No. 18139/91, ECtHR-1995, para. 71; *Evans v. United Kingdom*, Grand Chamber Judgment of 10 April 2007, No. 6339/05, ECtHR-2007, para. 77; *Dickson v. United Kingdom*, Judgment of 4 December 2007, No. 44362/04, ECtHR-2007, para. 78; *S. and Marper v. United Kingdom*, Grand Chamber Judgment of 4 December 2008, Nos. 30562/04 and 30566/04, ECtHR-2008, paras. 101–4.

[53] Appellate Body Reports, *Korea – Measures Affecting Imports of Fresh, Chilled or Frozen Beef*, WT/DS161/AB/R, WT/DS169/AB/R (11 December 2000) ('*Korea – Various Measures on Beef*'), para. 166; *United States – Measures Affecting the Cross-Border Supply of Gambling and Betting Services*, WT/DS285/AB/R (7 April 2005) ('*US – Gambling*'), para. 307; *United States – Measures Concerning the Importation, Marketing and Sale of Tuna and Tuna Products*, WT/DS381/AB/R (16 May 2012) ('*US – Tuna II (Mexico)*'), paras. 320–2; *United States – Certain Country of Origin Labelling (COOL) Requirements*, WT/DS384/AB/R, WT/DS386/AB/R (29 June 2012) ('*US – COOL*'), para. 376.

would sound much more familiar, and therefore more digestible, to WTO adjudicators. Why look far when the solution is at your fingertips? If you really cannot do without your 'foreign' arguments, try at least to shoehorn them into provisions, principles, and analytical approaches your judges can grapple with.

That being said... high risk yields high returns. Sometimes, creative lawyers do succeed in pushing the judges out of their comfort zone. In the ICJ *Whaling* case, for example, Australia's counsel invoked the WTO Appellate Body's approach to determining the policy objective behind a state regulation.[54] According to the counsel, that approach would provide 'some useful signposts' for the ICJ to follow in assessing whether Japan's measure pursued scientific goals or concealed commercial interests.[55] Ultimately, this strategy paid off: although the Court's judgment did not expressly cite the Appellate Body, it nonetheless adopted a standard that closely mirrored that proposed by Australia.[56]

Similarly, in the *Lagrand* and *Avena* cases, the complainants' counsel argued before the ICJ that Article 36(1) of the Vienna Convention on Consular Relations (VCCR)[57] established a fundamental individual right, and cited an IACtHR decision to that effect.[58] The Court did not engage expressly with those arguments, but allegedly considered them during deliberations.[59] In yet another case, this time before an ISDS tribunal, the respondent's reliance on ECtHR case law forced the arbitrators to grapple

---

[54] *Whaling in the Antarctic (Australia v. Japan: New Zealand intervening)*, Oral Pleadings (8 July 2013), CR2013/17 (verbatim record), para. 48 (quoting Appellate Body Report, *Japan – Taxes on Alcoholic Beverages*, WT/DS8/AB/R, WT/DS10/AB/R, WT/DS11/AB/R (4 October 1996) ('*Japan – Alcoholic Beverages II*'), p. 29).

[55] Ibid., para. 49.

[56] *Whaling in the Antarctic (Australia v. Japan: New Zealand intervening)*, Judgment of 21 March 2014, ICJ Rep. 2014, 226 ('*Whaling* judgment'), para. 67 ('[T]he Court will consider if the killing, taking and treating of whales is "for purposes of" scientific research by examining whether, in the use of lethal methods, the programme's design and implementation are reasonable in relation to achieving its stated objectives. This standard of review is an objective one.')

[57] United Nations, *Vienna Convention on Consular Relations* (24 April 1963), UNTS 500, 95.

[58] *LaGrand (Germany v. United States of America)*, Written Memorial of Germany (16 September 1999), para. 4.13; *Avena and Other Mexican Nationals (Mexico v. United States of America)*, Written Memorial of Mexico (20 June 2003), paras. 156–8 (both referring to *The Right to Information on Consular Assistance in the Framework of the Guarantees of the due Process of Law*, Advisory Opinion OC-16/99 of 1 October 1999, IACtHR Series A (1999), No. 16).

[59] See R. Higgins, 'A Babel of Judicial Voices? Ruminations from the Bench' (2006) 55(4) ICLQ 791, 796; Charlotin, 'Investment Awards and WTO Decisions', 298.

with human rights jurisprudence about expropriation and jurisdiction *ratione temporis*.[60]

These are the examples of successful 'cross-judicial engagement' I can think of. I am sure there are others out there, but you get the gist. If you manage to persuade your judges to engage with 'foreign' legal sources, you stand to gain a lot in terms of persuasion. Even better, you may go down in history as 'he who introduced human rights norms in the WTO', or 'she who converted the ICJ to the cause of direct foreign investment'. However, the chances of success are slim. Only by establishing yourself as a leading litigator can you ever hope to make it. After all, and let me conclude here: 'A reputation for being trustworthy can make it possible to build bridges that would otherwise be too risky.'[61]

Have a good evening, everyone.

•

'Don't make me laugh. They'll never buy it.'
'They will, trust me.'
'Why even try? It would be an embarrassment. *Alea iacta est.*'
'Stop it.'
'I mean, that boat sailed long ago.'
'No, it didn't. And if you give me ten minutes, I'll tell you why.'
'Five minutes.'

Jasper takes a deep breath and prepares to charge head down. The sound of the rain hitting the windows of Duncan's office is so loud that he can barely hear himself think. Duncan does not seem disturbed: he is more intent on listening to Jasper's argument about the WTO panel's jurisdiction.

For the last few days, the two have been discussing the litigation strategy to defend the EU palm oil regulation. The position they envisage is quite run of the mill. On the question of whether Indonesian and EU palm oil products are 'like' for purposes of Article III:4 of the GATT and Article 2.1 of the TBT Agreement, they will argue that European consumers regard the two sets of products as radically different given the environmental and labour implications of their production processes. Further, they will submit that the palm oil regulation does not entail discrimination, for it treats

---

[60] *Victor Pey Casado and President Allende Foundation v. Chile*, ICSID Case No. ARB/98/2, Award (8 May 2008), paras. 604–11 (referring to *Loizidou* judgment on the merits). For discussion, see Charlotin, 'Investment Awards and WTO Decisions', 297.
[61] R. S. Burt, *Brokerage and Closure: An Introduction to Social Capital* (Oxford University Press, 2005), 107.

similarly situated products in similar ways. Should the panel nonetheless find discrimination, they will retort that the measure is necessary to protect public morals and human and animal life or health under Articles XX(a) and XX(b) of the GATT, and that its detrimental impact stems exclusively from a legitimate regulatory distinction under Article 2.1 of the TBT Agreement. If they manage to show necessity, this will take care of Indonesia's claim under Article 2.2 of the TBT Agreement as well.

Upon discussion, Jasper and Duncan spotted a couple of major plot holes in this narrative. In particular, the EU regulation's exclusive reliance on the RSPO criteria, without regard to equivalent certification systems, seems to fly in the face of well-established Appellate Body jurisprudence, like the *Shrimp* case.[62]

Worried about these shortcomings, Jasper spent long afternoons studying the file. Thirty minutes ago, he had a *eureka* moment. In 2014, the European Union and Indonesia negotiated a free trade agreement (FTA) that stipulates, among other things, that 'either party may adopt and maintain measures relating to the protection of biodiversity and the promotion of fair labour standards in respect of the manufacture, sale, and distribution of the products listed in Annex II'. Annex II includes palm oil and palm oil products. The FTA came into force only one week before Indonesia challenged the EU palm oil regulation before the WTO. 'That's it!', thought Jasper, 'If we can't win on the merits of the regulation, we can request the panel to dismiss the whole case on grounds of lack of good faith!' Excited by this discovery, he stormed into Duncan's office. The reaction was less than enthusiastic. Jasper has now five minutes to convince his boss.

'We should say that, by bringing a WTO challenge against a measure that was expressly agreed upon in the FTA, Indonesia abused its rights under the WTO agreements. We have some hooks in *Shrimp*.'[63]

'It won't work. First, *Shrimp* is the very precedent that puts us in trouble. Drawing the panel's attention to it is suicidal. Second, you know that WTO adjudicators do not care about non-WTO agreements. Remember *Soft Drinks*,[64] remember *Peru*.[65] The Appellate Body found no ground in the DSU to examine the rights and obligations established under FTAs. We have nothing to work with.'

---

[62] Appellate Body Report, *United States – Import Prohibition of Certain Shrimp and Shrimp Products*, WT/DS58/AB/R (12 October 1998), paras. 161–76.
[63] Ibid., para. 158.
[64] Appellate Body Report, *Mexico – Tax Measures on Soft Drinks and Other Beverages*, WT/DS308/AB/R (6 March 2006) ('*Mexico – Taxes on Soft Drinks*'), para. 56.
[65] Appellate Body Report, *Peru – Additional Duty on Imports of Certain Agricultural Products*, WT/DS457/AB/R (20 July 2015) ('*Peru – Agricultural Products*'), paras. 5.91–5.117.

'I think we do! This is not about extra-WTO rules, but about good faith in WTO proceedings. The Appellate Body said that "if a WTO Member has not clearly stated that it would not take legal action with respect to a certain measure, it cannot be regarded as failing to act in good faith if it challenges that measure."[66] Now, could we not construe the FTA as a statement that Indonesia would not complain about the European Union's palm oil measure?'

'I don't think so. Where is the express acknowledgement that Indonesia would not sue?'

'It is not expressly acknowledged in the FTA because treaty language is not supposed to do that. Look, if Indonesia's behaviour is not contrary to good faith, then I don't know what is. Besides, unlike the FTA in *Peru*, this one is already in force.'

'…'

'So?'

'Fine. Let's append a little section on this good faith business. You'll be in charge of it. Please make sure we make it a subsidiary point. I don't want to spend too much time defending a losing line of argument.'

'Great, thanks! By the way, isn't this in line with what you told the Leuven students?'

'Huh?'

'High risks yielding high returns and all that jazz.'

Duncan bursts out in laughter, leaving a puzzled Jasper to figure out why.

'Oh man, you really should stop taking me so seriously.'

---

[66] Appellate Body Report, *European Communities – Regime for the Importation, Sale and Distribution of Bananas – Second Recourse to Article 21.5 of the DSU by Ecuador – Recourse to Article 21.5 of the DSU by the United States*, WT/DS27/AB/RW2/ECU and Corr. 1, WT/DS27/AB/RW/USA and Corr. 1 (26 November 2008) ('*EC – Bananas III (Article 21.5 – Ecuador II / Article 21.5 US)*'), para. 228.

# 5

## The Invisible Army

9 June 2017, 8:30 AM.[1] This morning, in a rather unusual move, Matteo entered Centre William Rappard through the main gate instead of taking the short walk through the visitor entrance. The grey concrete building that hosts the WTO headquarters stands in the middle of the Perle du Lac park, less than 100 m from the north bank of Lake Geneva and in convenient proximity to several waterside bars. A very pleasant duty station, especially in summer.

Once inside, Matteo chuckled at the sight of the frescos and paintings that adorn the ceremonial hall. Works titled 'The Dignity of Labour', 'Ploughing the Soil', or 'Work in Abundance' all portray a socialist-inspired imagery that sits strikingly at odds with the WTO's style and purpose. However, for all the mysteries that will remain unresolved in this story, this one is readily explained. The Centre, inaugurated in 1926, initially hosted the International Labour Organization (ILO). Throughout

---

[1] The mention of a date here serves more than a narrative purpose. The pages that follow describe a typical day in the secretariat of the WTO Appellate Body. As we write this footnote, both the Appellate Body and its secretariat have ceased to function. Since early 2017, the United States has vetoed the appointment of new Appellate Body members, therefore preventing the replacement of outgoing adjudicators. In December 2019, when the Appellate Body fell below the minimum complement of three judges required to hear appeals, its judicial activity ground to a halt. The ABS was disbanded and its staff was reallocated to other WTO divisions. For more detailed discussion, see Soave, 'Who Controls WTO Dispute Settlement?', 14–15. This faced us with a dilemma: should we set this part of the story at a time prior to Appellate Body's downfall, or take subsequent developments into account? After giving it some thought, we opted for the former solution. First, we thought, it may be interesting for the reader to take a peek into the life of what, not long ago, was a powerful state-to-state adjudicative mechanism. Second, many of the observations we will make about the Appellate Body could well be applicable to WTO panels, which are still functioning. Third, this story does not seek to give a full account of the institutional settings of international adjudication but, instead, to describe the socio-professional practices that occur within the international judicial community. Those practices are unlikely to change by simply replacing the Appellate Body with some other dispute settlement mechanism. We would bet the world trading system on it.

the decades, the building was home to other entities, including the GATT Secretariat, the Office of the UN High Commissioner for Refugees, and the library of the Graduate Institute of International Studies.[2] The progressive expansion of GATT staff forced the other occupants out of the premises – something that, to this day, still prompts cheap jokes about the imperialist ambitions of the world trading system. When the WTO replaced the GATT in 1995, the Centre was considered as its natural seat.

From the entrance, Matteo headed down to the atrium to grab a quick coffee with a couple of friends, one working as an animal health expert with the Agriculture Division and the other as an economist with the Trade in Services Division. This variety of professional affiliations under the same roof may sound surprising: were we not supposed to talk about international *courts*? Again, the answer is easy: unlike the other institutions where our story takes place, the WTO is not *only* a court. Its secretariat performs many other tasks, ranging from economic and policy research to supporting the organization's diplomatic bodies.

The very layout of Centre William Rappard is such that panelists, Appellate Body members, and dispute settlement staff work next door from colleagues that have nothing to do with international adjudication. Indeed, the building displays little of the insignia that make a court readily recognizable. Hearings, for example, are held in rooms otherwise used for trade negotiation meetings. This explains why participants have to sit face-to-face at long and narrow tables – a rather uncomfortable setting for collegial discussion. Besides the hearing rooms, the overall atmosphere in the secretariat's offices has little to do with, say, the grandeur of the Peace Palace. The interiors of the WTO are modest, 'almost Spartan', and staff are crammed in 'rooms with old furniture, faded carpet and no air conditioning'.[3] While this causes some discontent among the building's occupants, it is also a point of pride for the trade community: those austere rooms symbolize the pragmatic efficiency of the WTO in contrast to the pompous, outdated style of other organizations.

When, at 9:15 AM, Matteo heads to his office on the third floor, he notices an unusual bustle around the corridor. On most days, the badge-activated glass doors separating the Appellate Body's quarters from the rest of the

---

[2] See *Centre William Rappard: Home of the World Trade Organization* (WTO Secretariat, 2011), www.wto.org/english/res_e/booksp_e/cwr11-1_e.pdf, 2, 11.
[3] L. O. Baptista, 'A Country Boy Goes to Geneva', in G. Marceau (ed.), *A History of Law and Lawyers in the GATT/WTO: The Development of the Rule of Law in the Multilateral Trading System* (Cambridge University Press, 2015) 559, 560.

secretariat open to the quiet hum of printers and the occasional chatter at the coffee corner. However, things are decidedly livelier this morning. The administrative assistants are running around offices, handing out copies of a thick document to the lawyers assigned to the *EU – Palm Oil* appeal.

A group of people in business attire is slowly making its way to the Registrar's desk at the end of the corridor, pushing two trolleys full of cardboard boxes. Matteo recognizes his friend Jane Weaver among Indonesia's delegates, and returns her hasty salute. She looks a bit sleep-deprived, he thinks. But, to be fair, any counsel would look like that on the day of the filing of an appellee's submission. Matteo is tempted to ask Jane about her recent trip to Japan, but desists. Party counsel and secretariat officers are not meant to interact much in public during the course of a dispute, so they will have to leave it at that for now.

One of the admins stops Matteo mid-corridor and informs him that a copy of Indonesia's submission is waiting on his chair.

'*Merci*, Sylvie.'

'*Prego!*'

'I'm happy you are on the case.'

'Working with you is always a pleasure, Matt!'

'Matt' has almost reached his office, but must make one last stop. He heads to his director's door, knocks twice and, receiving no answer, pops his head in. Björn Kron is sitting at his large desk, perpetually cluttered with piles of old papers, a WTO-branded coffee mug in one hand and the latest issue of The Economist in the other. He does not look pleased with what he is reading.

'Come in', he says without raising his eyes. 'Have you seen?'

'morning Björn. Yep, I've seen and am ready to roll.'

'Huh? What are you talking about?'

'Well, *Palm Oil*. Indonesia's appellee's submission is in.'

'No, I meant … have you seen this interview?' Björn hands the magazine to Matt, who immediately recognizes the picture of a famous politician. 'So apparently, the Appellate Body is no longer the "crown jewel of the multilateral trading system," but a "dyfunctional body in urgent need of reform." We are "betraying the mandate given to us by WTO members" and "exceeding our authority under the DSU"… And, hear this!, the fool even points fingers at individual judges for being "judicial activists." Why is The Economist publishing this garbage?"

Matt is taken aback by his boss' agitation. Since he assumed the direction of the Appellate Body Secretariat (ABS) more than a decade ago, Björn has never been one to be easily distracted by the hubbub of trade diplomacy. As the chief legal advisor to the Appellate Body, he simply has no time for it. His working days – and, we should add, his working nights – are taken up with the study of case files, the review of legal drafts, and frequent discussions with the judges about this or that pending appeal. Björn has always performed these tasks tirelessly but discreetly, without stirring controversy or seeking publicity. His encyclopaedic knowledge of WTO jurisprudence has guided several generations of Appellate Body adjudicators, who have rarely failed to heed his advice. Björn's admirers call him the most precious resource the ABS has ever had. His detractors have simply accepted his presence as a fixture of trade adjudication. In any event, nothing happens in the Appellate Body's quarters without Björn's notice.

Matt has long wondered about Björn's agenda. Surely, he thought, such influence had to be directed at some higher goal. One morning, talking about Björn, Matt's colleague Keiko facetiously quoted *The Usual Suspects*: 'The greatest trick the devil ever pulled was to convince the world he didn't exist.' But over time, Matt has come to the conclusion that Björn has no aims other than WTO adjudication itself. His agenda, if any, is to consolidate the role of the Appellate Body as the supreme court of world trade. That this consolidation may entail an increase in Björn's own power is, of course, purely coincidental.

Then why is Björn now so upset by a random interview? Confused, Matt mutters:

'Sorry Björn, you know I don't care much about politics. It stresses me. Can we talk about *Palm Oil* instead?'

As if waking up from a bad dream, Björn stops staring at The Economist and turns his eyes to Matt. His tone goes back to its usual geniality.

'You're right. Let's talk about serious business and forget this nonsense. Thank you Matt. That's why you're one of my best lawyers. No drama, no fuss. So, you were saying, is the team ready?'

'Yes, we're on it. By our estimates, you can expect the first draft of the issues paper early July.'

'Excellent. Anything in the parties' submissions that shocks you?'

'Nothing in particular. It's a big case, but we knew that already. From the little I've read, it's pretty standard stuff. Likeness, discrimination, necessity, general exceptions, technical regulations. You know the drill. Oh, I forgot: there's this issue about the Indonesia-EU free trade agreement. That sounds quite intriguing.'

'I've seen that, yes. Funny how someone can still invoke a non-WTO defence and hope to win. I thought we had made our views clear in *Soft Drinks* and *Peru*.'

'Actually, it looks a bit more complicated this time. But I need to dig a little deeper before I can share my thoughts.'

'Your thoughts will be precious as always. Actually, I'm glad we have this defence on appeal.'

'You think this FTA business might get the European Union out of trouble?'

'No. But it's good for Appellate Body members to have a little *divertissement* every now and then. I'm sure they'll have fun playing with that.'

Three minutes later, finally at his desk, Matt lets out a sigh. He had anticipated this day with a mix of dread and excitement. Now that the European Union and Indonesia have both filed their appellate submissions, the record is almost complete. Within a few days, the third participants will file their shorter briefs. But the team can already start working on the case.

Indeed, it *must* start working, for there is no time to waste. Under Article 17.5 of the DSU, WTO appellate proceedings should, in principle, 'not exceed 60 days' from the date a party files the appeal to the date the Appellate Body circulates its judgment ('report'), and in no case shall they 'exceed 90 days'. These treaty-set deadlines make the Appellate Body one of the most expeditious international courts in existence, but also entail a crushing amount of pressure on its staff. In practice, WTO members no longer expect the court to issue its reports within the 60-day schedule. However, they do get quite antsy past the 90-day milestone.[4] This means that, within three months of the filing of the notice of appeal, the Appellate Body is supposed to prepare the case, evaluate the parties' written arguments, hold a hearing (or two in exceptionally complex disputes), deliberate, draft the report, and have it translated into Spanish and French (the two other working languages of the WTO).

At the time of discussing the Appellate Body's institutional design, these timeframes made sense to the Uruguay Round negotiators. After all, they never intended to create a proper international court, but only a review mechanism of limited jurisdiction in exchange for the loss of the political right to block a panel report.[5] In their expectations, few

---

[4] See e.g. WTO DSB, *Minutes of the DSB Meeting of 5 October 2011*, WT/DSB/M/304 (2 December 2011), para. 4; WTO DSB, *Minutes of the DSB Meeting of 26 January 2015*, WT/DSB/M/356 (6 March 2015), paras. 5.6, 5.9; WTO DSB, *Minutes of the DSB Meeting of 19 June 2015*, WT/DSB/M/364 (21 August 2015), para. 7.8.

[5] See D. P. Steger, 'The Founding of the Appellate Body', in G. Marceau (ed.), *A History of Law and Lawyers in the GATT/WTO: The Development of the Rule of Law in the Multilateral Trading System* (Cambridge University Press, 2015), 447; P. Van den Bossche, 'From Afterthought to Centrepiece: The Appellate Body and Its Rise to Prominence in the World Trading System', in G. Sacerdoti, A. Yanovich and J. Bohanes (eds.), *The WTO at Ten: The Contribution of the Dispute Settlement System* (Cambridge University Press, 2006) 289; G. Abi-Saab, 'The Appellate Body and Treaty Interpretation', in M. Fitzmaurice, O. Elias and P. Merkouris (eds.), *Treaty Interpretation and the Vienna Convention on the Law of Treaties: 30 Years on* (Martinus Nijhoff, 2010) 97, 100.

disputes would make it to the appellate stage, and even then, the appeal would be a swift and punctual remedy to egregious panel errors. Little did the negotiators know that, from the very early years, most panel reports would be challenged on appeal, and that such challenges would cover large portions of the findings. In hindsight, it is hard to believe that no one foresaw the Appellate Body's de facto transformation into a 'high court' that reviews panel judgments 'in precisely the same way that higher courts review a first instance decision in any of our municipal legal systems'.[6]

Faced with a 'tsunami'[7] of cases, in recent years the Appellate Body has sought, and begrudgingly secured, the WTO membership's consent to exceed the 90-day deadline when the circumstances so require. As a result, appellate proceedings now stretch over five or six months on average,[8] with the most complex disputes (such as the so-called *Aircraft* cases[9]) taking significantly longer.

And this *EU – Palm Oil* business promises to be one heck of a dispute, at least judging from the length of the panel report. Although the working schedule is not yet finalized, Matt already knows that his holidays will have to wait. As he told Björn, the team will have to hand in the issues paper in little over a month. The first draft of the report will be due in about three months, and the second draft a few weeks later. Meanwhile, Matt and his teammates will be asked to prepare questions for the hearing, participate in the deliberations and the exchange of views, and check the accuracy of translations. 'Let us just hope this whole thing doesn't stretch too far into the autumn.'

We share Matt's hope. Not because we like Matt (who, so far, is rather nondescript), nor because we care about his holidays; but because, if our story were to happen in summer, it would be easier for us to narrate it. During summertime, Geneva discloses the secrets of international life and

---

[6] Weiler, 'The Rule of Lawyers', 199.
[7] T. R. Graham, *Speaking Up: The State of the Appellate Body*, address by the Chairman of the Appellate Body, www.wto.org/english/news_e/news16_e/ab_22nov16_e.pdf ('Appellate Body Chairman address'); J. Pauwelyn and W. Zhang, *Busier than Ever? A Data-Driven Assessment and Forecast of WTO Caseload*, CTEI Working Paper 2018-2 (2018), 5–7.
[8] See e.g. Appellate Body, *Annual Report for 2015*, WT/AB/26 (3 June 2016), p. 6; Appellate Body, *Annual Report for 2016*, WT/AB/27 (16 May 2017), p. 6.
[9] Appellate Body Reports, *European Communities and certain member States – Measures Affecting Trade in Large Civil Aircraft*, WT/DS316/AB/R (18 May 2011) ('*EC and certain member States – Large Civil Aircraft*'); *United States – Measures Affecting Trade in Large Civil Aircraft – Second Complaint*, WT/DS353/AB/R (12 March 2012); *European Communities and Certain Member States – Measures Affecting Trade in Large Civil Aircraft – Recourse to Article 21.5 of the DSU by the United States*, WT/DS316/AB/RW (15 May 2018).

exposes them to plain view. From June to August, a casual stroller at La Terrasse or the Bains des Pâquis will inevitably bump into members of the WTO community, exchanging impressions about their work and sharing experiences from their daily routines. Matt might well be there with his friend Jane Weaver, chatting about a past case or gossiping about a common acquaintance. Listen carefully, and you will learn about the WTO's inner workings as much as you would from rigorous empirical research.

•

But we digress. Before summer comes, before we reveal the meaning of arcane terms like 'issues paper' or 'exchange of views', we must proceed to a new round of introductions.

For the last five years, Matteo Loiudice has been working as a dispute settlement lawyer at the ABS. Officially, the role of the ABS is to 'provide legal assistance and administrative support to the Appellate Body'.[10] As our story will tell, this is the very simple description of a very complex set of tasks. The secretariat comprises 16 lawyers[11] organized hierarchically according to the WTO grade structure. Six of them hold a G7 grade (roughly equivalent to a P2 grade at the UN). Another three, including Matt, are slightly more senior and hold G8 positions (a P3 equivalent). However, their assignments do not differ substantially from those of G7s. Above dispute settlement lawyers are six counsellors at the G9 or G10 (P4 or P5) grade. Reaching this position entails a significant shift in responsibilities: counsellors serve as team leaders in specific disputes and supervise the work of subordinates. The whole secretariat is coordinated by Björn, the director, who holds a G11 grade (D1 in the UN scale). Upon taking office, all staff have two-year contracts renewed automatically on expiry. After five years of service, they become permanent. In addition to permanent staff, the ABS legal team employs varying numbers of temporary lawyers who, apart from the duration of their contracts, are functionally equivalent to G7s and G8s. Finally, up to three interns assist the secretariat at any given time.

The ABS is not the only dispute settlement team within the WTO secretariat. The Legal Affairs and the Rules Division are tasked with assisting panels, the first-instance adjudicative bodies in the WTO regime. The official functions of these two divisions are as laconic as those of the ABS: they 'have the responsibility of assisting panels, especially on the legal,

---

[10] WTO website, *WTO Bodies Involved in the Dispute Settlement Process*, www.wto.org/english/tratop_e/dispu_e/disp_settlement_cbt_e/c3s4p1_e.htm.
[11] Appellate Body Chairman address.

historical and procedural aspects of the matters dealt with, and of providing secretarial and technical support'.[12] In practice, the Rules Division services panels dealing with trade remedies (anti-dumping measures, subsidies and countervailing duties, and safeguards), whereas the Legal Affairs Division supports panels addressing all other issues arising from the WTO agreements.

This odd division of labour by subject matter is a result of the piecemeal evolution from the GATT to the WTO. For some, the allocation of trade remedy work to the Rules rather than the Legal Affairs Division was due to the reluctance of key GATT states towards the excessive 'legalization' of those matters, considered to be particularly sensitive.[13] For others, the field of trade remedies requires very specific expertise that, in addition to legal matters, encompasses knowledge of economic and technical issues.[14] Whatever its causes, the repartition of tasks between the two divisions emerged as a matter of practice and lives on to the present day, despite sporadic attempts to merge the two divisions into a unified team of panel assistants.[15] Similar to the ABS, both the Legal Affairs and the Rule Division consist of lawyers (a total of 46 in 2017[16]) and administrative assistants. The hierarchy of their legal staff ranges from dispute settlement lawyers to directors, with a number of temporary staff and interns contributing to the teams.

The organization of work in all three dispute settlement divisions follows a similar pattern. Every time a new dispute or appeal is filed, a team of two to four lawyers, headed by a counsellor, is assigned to handle it.[17] For particularly 'large' disputes (whether by paper volume or by number of claims and defences) additional staff may join in. While the ABS

---

[12] Article 27 of the DSU.
[13] See e.g. F. Roessler, 'The Role of Law in International Trade Relations and the Establishment of the Legal Affairs Division of the GATT', in G. Marceau (ed.), *A History of Law and Lawyers in the GATT/WTO: The Development of the Rule of Law in the Multilateral Trading System* (Cambridge University Press, 2015) 161, 168.
[14] See e.g. M. Koulen, 'Evolving Dispute Settlement Practice with Respect to Anti-Dumping in the Late 1980s and Early 1990s', in G. Marceau (ed.), *A History of Law and Lawyers in the GATT/WTO: The Development of the Rule of Law in the Multilateral Trading System* (Cambridge University Press, 2015) 208, 209.
[15] See P. J. Kuijper, 'From Seattle to Doha: From the Surreal to the Unreal: A Personal Account', in G. Marceau (ed.), *A History of Law and Lawyers in the GATT/WTO: The Development of the Rule of Law in the Multilateral Trading System* (Cambridge University Press, 2015) 374, 387–8.
[16] Appellate Body Chairman address.
[17] See V. Hughes, 'Working in WTO Dispute Settlement: Pride without Prejudice', in G. Marceau (ed.), *A History of Law and Lawyers in the GATT/WTO: The Development of the Rule of Law in the Multilateral Trading System* (Cambridge University Press, 2015) 400, 404.

operates in 'splendid isolation' from all other divisions – hence the glass doors – Rules and Legal Affairs are more 'porous' vis-à-vis the rest of the WTO secretariat. For instance, when a dispute requires specialized scientific knowledge in areas like sanitary or phytosanitary protection or the environment, the legal team may seek the input of colleagues from non-legal divisions (e.g. Agriculture or Trade and Environment).[18] Once the dispute is over and the report is circulated, the team is disbanded and its members will be reshuffled when the next case begins. This way, each legal officer gets to work with all of their colleagues over time, thus strengthening unity and promoting 'collegiality among the members of the institution'.[19]

The structure of the WTO's judicial bureaucracy was not always meant to look like this. In the early days of the ABS, it was suggested that every Appellate Body member have a personal clerk,[20] with whom they would have a one-to-one working relationship. Ultimately, the proposal was scrapped in favour of secretariat divisions responding collectively to the whole bench. This seemingly innocuous organizational choice has, in fact, profoundly altered the practices, the professional allegiances, and the power relationships within the WTO judiciary. The structural consequences of anodyne institutional arrangements are a source of endless amazement. Every choice, even the most mundane, brings with it a host of 'discarded possibles'; every 'reconstruction of genesis' reminds us of the 'possibility that things could have been ... otherwise'.[21]

How did Matt come to be part of the WTO bureaucracy? Quite randomly, actually. During his LLB studies at the University of Milan, he developed an interest in public international law. Upon graduation, he was admitted to an LLM at Georgetown, which he undertook without a clear idea about his professional goals. He did not know that Georgetown, along with another few academic centres,[22] is a true powerhouse for the

---

[18] See Hughes, 'Working in WTO Dispute Settlement', 404.
[19] C.-D. Ehlermann, 'Revisiting the Appellate Body: The First Six Years', in G. Marceau (ed.), *A History of Law and Lawyers in the GATT/WTO: The Development of the Rule of Law in the Multilateral Trading System* (Cambridge University Press, 2015) 482, 494.
[20] See Steger, 'The Founding', 452.
[21] P. Bourdieu, L. Wacquant, and S. Farage, 'Rethinking the State: Genesis and Structure of the Bureaucratic Field' (1994) 12(1) SociolTheory 1, 4.
[22] A non-exhaustive list includes the LLM in International Economic Law and Policy in Barcelona, the World Trade Institute in Bern, and the MIDS in Geneva.

production of WTO 'oblates'[23] – the promising students whose brains and vital forces are offered in sacrifice to the international trade machinery.

Matt remembers well his first encounters with trade scholars. Until then, he had hardly considered the WTO as a 'proper' international organization like, say, the UN or the NATO. Trade law seemed impenetrably technical and parochial. Trade practitioners looked and sounded as though they belonged to a lowlier class of international lawyers. They lacked the charm of experts in the law of war, international security, and the like. Moreover, having enrolled in university around the time of the Seattle movement, Matt suspected that the WTO's purpose would not sit well with his social-democratic ethos.

These doubts gradually dissipated as Georgetown teachers initiated Matt to the virtues of the world trading system. Matt learnt about the important 'operational functions' of rules in governing economic behaviour, as well as the advantages of 'predictability' and 'stability' in multilateral trade relations.[24] He was told that the consolidation and expansion of international trade law reflect the general 'history of civilization', that is the 'gradual evolution from a power-oriented approach, in the state of nature, toward a rule-oriented approach'.[25] He even discovered that the world trading system is a means to prevent war.[26] Over time, these 'plausible folk theories'[27] seduced Matt and reassured him in his liberal leanings. He came to believe that the general exceptions under Article XX of the GATT strike an appropriate balance between trade liberalization and domestic policy autonomy. He awoke to the fact that pragmatic-minded countries can defend their national interests through repeated and principled participation in WTO dispute settlement.[28]

WTO dispute settlement… That sounded exciting. Too many times had Matt heard about the sluggishness of life in international organizations: the pointless meetings and reports, the vague policy recommendations,

---

[23] The expression is borrowed from P. Bourdieu, *Homo Academicus*, trans. Peter Collier (Stanford University Press, 1988), 49.

[24] J. H. Jackson, *The World Trading System: Law and Policy of International Economic Relations* (MIT Press, 1989), 24.

[25] Jackson, *The World Trading System*, 86–7; J. H. Jackson, *Sovereignty, The WTO, and Changing Fundamentals of International Law* (Cambridge University Press, 2006), 89.

[26] J. H. Jackson, 'The WTO "Constitution" and Proposed Reforms: Seven "Mantras" Revisited' (2001) 4(1) JIEL 67, 68.

[27] The expression is borrowed from T. Halliday, 'Plausible Folk Theories: Throwing Veils of Plausibility over Zones of Ignorance in Global Governance' (2018) 69(4) BrJSociol 936.

[28] See Santos, 'Policy Autonomy', 631.

the all-talk-and-no-action approach.[29] Joining a private law firm was not a very enticing prospect either: to Matt's mind, that would mean endless working hours, the pressure of billables, and the perpetual feeling of selling out to somebody else's interests. However imprecise, these opposed scepticisms militated in favour of a career with an international court. Perhaps, Matt thought, joining a public institution that produces a measurable outcome (judgments) with a true impact on state behaviour would be a good compromise between dullness and overkill.

He started looking for ways to make his profile more attractive for the WTO dispute settlement divisions. In the past, numerous students recommended by Georgetown faculty had interned there, so the first thing would be to get a strong reference letter from one of his professors. In addition, Matt could participate in the WTO moot court competition organized by the European Law Student Association.[30] The contestants who distinguish themselves end up pleading before real WTO adjudicators and secretariat officers, thus getting on the radar of the WTO network.

Having followed these steps carefully, Matt was able to secure an internship with the ABS, where his supervisor quickly came to appreciate the quality of his work. Matt knew that the odds of a permanent vacancy opening up in the near future were slim, given the severe budget constraints the WTO was facing at that time. However, luck was on his side. Near the end of his internship, the WTO director-general announced a reallocation of resources across the organization and provided the ABS with additional budget.[31] A G7 vacancy was advertised and Matt was shortlisted. He spent three weeks studying on Peter Van den Bossche and Werner Zdouc's tome on WTO law,[32] the go-to manual for this kind of preparation. Then, on the agreed date, he took a three-hour written test about substantive and procedural rules and sat for a one-hour interview in front of Björn, two counsellors, and two human resources staff.

Years later, Matt still remembers vividly the last bit of the interview. Björn, who had been silently stroking his beard through most of the discussion, asked the final question.

---

[29] See J. Klabbers, 'Two Concepts of International Organization' (2005) 2(2) IntlOrgLRev 277, 282–3.
[30] European Law Student Association website, https://johnhjacksonmoot.elsa.org/.
[31] WTO website, *Azevêdo Says Success of WTO Dispute Settlement Brings Urgent Challenges*, www.wto.org/english/news_e/spra_e/spra32_e.htm.
[32] P. Van den Bossche and W. Zdouc, *The Law and Policy of the World Trade Organization* (2nd edn., Cambridge University Press, 2013).

'Thank you for your answers, Matteo. Now, to conclude our little chat, let me ask you *something naïve*: what's the value of international trade, and why should we promote it?'

'Well, hmmm, thank you for your question. At a basic level, trade is a means to raise standards of living and improve everyone's economic position. As stated in the preamble to the WTO Agreement, the rules governing ...'

'Sorry for interrupting: many developing countries wouldn't agree that their economic position, as you say, has improved much since they entered the WTO. What would you tell them *in response*?'

'Well, hmmmmm ... I would say that WTO rules do not prevent states from pursuing legitimate policy objectives, including in the economic sphere. Instead, the WTO *strikes an appropriate balance* between rights and obligations, for example through Article XX of the GATT ... and provides for special and differential treatment of developing countries ...'

As Björn maintained a poker face, Matteo had a sudden epiphany:

'... Plus, I would tell developing countries that economic integration through mutual trade a powerful tool to *avoid war*. As John Jackson wrote ...'

Björn smiled, visibly satisfied.

'Thank you, Matteo. I think that's enough.'

Matt did not know what to make of his performance. When, one month later, Björn called him to confirm that he had been recruited, he mentally reviewed his answers and tried to identify his winning shots. He could not find any. But who cares? Mission accomplished! Matt's excitement was compounded by the contract conditions: the G7 net salary was almost 90,000 CHF per annum, plus another 10,000 CHF for relocation costs; health insurance was taken care of; and, in case Matt had children one day, the organization would pay for their schooling. Add 25 days of vacation per year – which, at the time, Matt did not know would remain largely unused – and the package looked almost on par with private New York lawyers spending sleepless nights on mergers and acquisitions.

*

The account provided so far may suggest that WTO dispute settlement is somewhat unique in the field of international adjudication. In fact, legal bureaucracies exist in *all* international courts and tribunals. Recent sources reveal that around 430 lawyers currently work full-time as assistants to international judges (the figure rising to well over 2,000 people if one also counts administrative and secretarial staff).[33] Considering that the number of judges on standing courts is estimated at around 300,[34] that makes a total of about 730 legal professionals working for the permanent international judiciary.

International judicial bureaucrats will take on an increasingly prominent role as our story continues. In the chapters that follow, we will explore the great many ways in which law clerks, registry and secretariat staff, and ISDS tribunal assistants contribute to the unfolding of judicial proceedings. To narrate the deeds of this invisible army is to delve past the surface of 'foreground deliberation'[35] and deep into the bowels of the system. By telling how bureaucratic power is exercised by way of technical expertise,[36] we can truly reveal the 'myriad of everyday practices'[37] by which international judgments are slowly and painstakingly woven together.

Some of the tasks of judicial bureaucrats vary from one institution to another, but many are common across the board. First, bureaucrats take care of administrative matters like the scheduling of cases, the management of case files, and the correspondence between the adjudicators and the parties. While these activities would deserve discussion, they are not determinative of legal outcomes and, therefore, will remain at the margins of our analysis. Instead, we will focus on a second set of duties, which are directly related to the *judicial* function. As we will see, bureaucrats conduct research, provide legal advice, prepare internal memoranda, attend deliberations, and draft portions of the final decisions.[38] When a legal issue is controversial, they mediate between different positions and broker compromises; when the judge's reasoning is unclear, they test its viability and offer countervailing views. Thanks to their mastery of practice and precedent, bureaucrats also serve as 'the institutional memory of

---

[33] S. Cartier and C. Hoss, 'The Role of Registries and Legal Secretariats in International Judicial Institutions', in C. P. R. Romano, K. J. Alter, and Y. Shany (eds.), *The Oxford Handbook of International Adjudication* (Oxford University Press, 2014) 712, 713.

[34] See *supra*, p. 36.

[35] Kennedy, 'Challenging Expert Rule', 3.

[36] See M. Weber, *Wirtschaft und Gesellschaft* (Mohr Siebeck, 1922), 226. See also E. B. Haas, *When Knowledge Is Power* (University of California Press, 1991); M. Barnett and M. Finnemore, *Rules for the World: International Organizations in Global Politics* (Cornell University Press, 2004).

[37] Adler and Pouliot, 'International Practices', 2.

[38] See e.g. Cartier and Hoss, 'Registries and Secretariats', 718–21; Thirlway, 'Drafting ICJ Decisions', 16–20; Hughes, 'Working in WTO Dispute Settlement', 404–7; ECtHR website, *How the Court Works*, www.echr.coe.int/Pages/home.aspx?p=court/howit works; Brussels Legal website, *Interview with Margarita Peristeraki, Référendaire at the Court of First Instance in Luxembourg*, www.brusselslegal.com/article/display/2924/ Margarita_Peristeraki_Rfrendaire_at_the_Court_of_First_Instance_in_Luxembourg.

international judicial institutions'.[39] Indeed, their contracts often outlast the judges' terms of appointment, thus making them the only cluster of truly permanent actors in the international judiciary.[40] If adjudicators are the guardians of the system, bureaucrats are its backbone. It is, therefore, not surprising that their functions are deemed so 'critically important'.[41]

The relative influence of legal assistants vis-à-vis the adjudicators they are called to serve varies across courts and over time, depending on several factors. First, the pervasiveness of bureaucratic support may be inversely proportional to the professional competence of the judges – their knowledge of the files, their familiarity with jurisprudence, and so on. Second, personalities matter: a resolute, hands-on adjudicator may be better equipped to take ownership of their work, whereas a more insecure one may be readier to delegate. Third, the seniority of a bureaucrat may affect the extent to which the adjudicators are inclined to follow their advice. Fourth, the institutional arrangements governing the judge-assistant relationship are relevant. For instance, a law clerk whose contract is tied to a single judge is less likely to overshadow their supervisor. Conversely, a collegial registry or secretariat may have a greater impact on the organization of proceedings, the structure of legal reasoning, and the language used in the judgments. In short: 'The stronger the adjudicators, the weaker the secretariat',[42] and vice versa.

Unlike judges, bureaucrats are usually recruited through standardized application procedures. Typically, the state parties to a court or tribunal do not have a say in their appointment – at least not when it comes to the rank and file. Therefore, it is not improper to speak of a career path as an assistant to international adjudicators. As Matt's experience shows, the pool of applicants comprises graduate students and young professionals. The selection criteria include expertise in the relevant body of substantive and procedural law, familiarity with the jurisprudence of the recruiting court, and some commitment to its goals. To reach the required level of competitiveness, the ideal candidate has a strong incentive to specialize in the functioning of the court at hand by attending university courses, enrolling in dedicated master programmes, participating in moot court competitions, and networking with specialists in the field.

The push towards specialization further intensifies after recruitment by virtue of socialization with colleagues and superiors. The newcomer

---

[39] Cartier and Hoss, 'Registries and Secretariats', 722.
[40] Ibid., 721–2.
[41] D. Caron, 'Towards a Political Theory of International Courts and Tribunals' (2007) 24(2) BerkeleyJIntlL 401, 416.
[42] Ibid.

gradually learns the institution's lingo and its many acronyms, penetrates the internal logics of the system, and discerns the operations that fall 'inside' and 'outside' the scope of their job. They experience the whole panoply of 'social sanctions and rewards', the 'shaming and back-patting' that take the place of direct coercion in our civilized international world.[43] In one word, they become 'acculturated' to their position.[44]

Sure enough, many bureaucrats take great pride in rising through the ranks. They experience the 'thrill of being able to manipulate an arcane language, the power of entering the secret kingdom, being someone in the know'.[45] However, powerful exclusionary mechanisms are at work throughout their careers, whereby modes of thought that once seemed compelling lose their explanatory force, to the point of becoming 'inexpert, unprofessional, irrelevant to the business at hand'.[46]

As our story will tell, international judicial bureaucrats constantly struggle to stay vigilant and resist the anesthetizing effects of acculturation. When they succeed, they enjoy plenty of opportunities to steer the judicial process in one direction or another, and even challenge the dispositions that are inculcated upon them. When they fail, they progressively relinquish the desire and ability to exercise agency and shake up the status quo, instead limiting their ambitions to carrying out tasks efficiently. Of course, most settle for the middle ground, and continuously oscillate between frequent moments of unthinking reproduction and rare exercises of 'responsible human freedom'.[47]

•

Ok, 60 lawyers at the WTO – who are the other 370?

Instead of burdening the reader with a long list of names and titles, let us introduce some of Matt's homologues in other judicial systems. To do so, we must travel from the WTO headquarters in Geneva back to the Peace Palace in The Hague. This neo-renaissance extravaganza, home to the ICJ and the PCA, is commonly thought of as the inner sanctum of international law. Already in 1902, Andrew Dickinson White, trying to convince Andrew Carnegie to donate part of his fortune to build the Palace,

---

[43] R. Goodman and D. Jinks, 'How to Influence States: Socialization and International Human Rights Law' (2004) 54(3) DukeLJ 621, 645.
[44] The concept of 'acculturation' is further explored ibid., 639–45.
[45] See C. Cohn, 'Sex and Death in the Rational World of Defense Intellectuals' (1987) 12(4) Signs 687, 704.
[46] Cohn, 'Sex and Death', 712.
[47] J.-P. Sartre, cit. in Kennedy, 'Many Legal Orders', 645.

described it as '[a] temple of peace where the doors are open, in contrast to the Janus-temple, in times of peace, and closed in cases of war'.[48]

It is here that, in the opening pages of the book, we first met Sophie Richter as she gazed around the Great Hall of Justice. Now, it is time to follow Sophie's steps as she walks back to her office. Having passed through the marble arches, the 'hodgepodge of gifts' offered by various states over the years, the 'heavy draperies', and the thick mahogany doors[49] of the foyer, we cross a bridge that leads to the Annex. This side structure, built in the 1970s, exhibits 'the most regretful features of that era's forward-looking architecture'[50] – including a copious amount of asbestos that recently forced its occupants out of the premises for decontamination.

More importantly, however, the Annex hosts the judges' quarters. Someone may find it ironic that the guardians of the temple do not reside at its very centre, but outside of its perimeter. Yet, this division between the grandeur of the Peace Palace and the muted ambiance of the Annex embodies to perfection the gap between the space where the Law (with a capital 'L') is made visible to the world and the space where the law (with a small 'l') is constructed *à l'abri des regards indiscrets*.

As we already know, Sophie is one of the law clerks assigned to assist Judge Jürgen Lehmann. More precisely, her title is 'associate legal officer', and her official duties include providing the judge 'with legal research and related assistance' with regard to pending cases.[51] Like that of the WTO secretariat, this concise description conceals a wealth of treasures, which we will try to unearth as the plot unfolds.

The very presence of law clerks at the ICJ has quite a fascinating story. Since the Court's inception in 1946, judges have been serviced by a registry of some 120 staff.[52] The recruitment of registry officers takes place through regular UN competitions (ranging from P2 to D2 positions). The selected candidates are usually offered permanent contracts and constitute, therefore, the only tenured staff at the Court.[53] Over time, the registry's Department of Legal Matters (DLM), headed by the principal legal secretary of the Court and comprising two first secretaries, four

---

[48] See H. Thirlway, 'Peace, Justice, and Provisional Measures', in G. Gaja and J. G. Stoutenburg (eds.), *Enhancing the Rule of Law through the International Court of Justice* (Martinus Nijhoff, 2014) 75.
[49] Terris, Romano, and Swigart, *The International Judge*, 49–50.
[50] Ibid., 50.
[51] ICJ website, *Vacancy Announcement: Associate Legal Officer*.
[52] Cartier and Hoss, 'Registries and Secretariats', 713 and fn 2.
[53] Ibid., 721.

secretaries, one lawyer, and one administrative assistant,[54] started carrying out various legal tasks on behalf of the bench.[55] For instance, it was common practice for the DLM to help judges without a good command of French or English draft their notes, whose relevance we will discuss later on.[56] Likewise, the DLM usually produced a written outline of the legal issues arising in each case to assist the Court's President in coordinating the deliberation process. DLM lawyers also participated in the drafting of judgments, for instance by preparing preliminary texts for the members of the Drafting Committee or liaising between the majority and the dissenters.[57] For decades, the registry was the sole body responsible for providing assistance to the judges. Acting as a collegial bureaucracy, it progressively secured great influence over the resolution of disputes.

This monopoly came to an end at the turn of the century – in circumstances that, once again, speak volumes about the importance of interpersonal relationships in the construction of legal fields. In his 2000 annual address to the UN General Assembly, the ICJ President suggested that the Court could benefit from the contribution of clerks individually assigned to the judges. He observed that the size of some recent case files ranged between 5,000 and 7,000 pages and warned that, without appropriate research assistance, the Court would be unable to deliberate on more than two or three disputes per year.[58] However, the UN budget was too tight at the time to allow for additional hirings.

The President's plea did not fall on deaf ears. Upon hearing his address, an NYU professor came up with an idea that would both lend a much needed hand *and* increase the prestige of his own law school. He proposed that NYU select outstanding graduates and send them to The Hague to work as clerks for a period of nine months. All the expenses

---

[54] See ICJ website, *Organizational Chart of the Registry*, www.icj-cij.org/en/organizational-chart.

[55] For an overview, see P. Couvreur, 'The Registrar of the International Court of Justice: Status and Functions', in C. Jimenez Piernes (ed.), *The Legal Practice in International Law and European Community Law: A Spanish Perspective* (Martinus Nijhoff, 2007) 5, 44–58; R. Kolb, *The International Court of Justice* (Hart, 2013), 157.

[56] See *infra*, pp. 169–70.

[57] See Thirlway, 'Drafting ICJ Decisions', 16–20. See also Kolb, *The ICJ*, 157.

[58] See ICJ website, *Address by H.E. Judge Gilbert Guillaume, President of the International Court of Justice, to the UN General Assembly* (26 October 2000), www.icj-cij.org/public/files/press-releases/9/2999.pdf. Legend has it that the pleadings in the *Barcelona Traction* case, comprising the annexes, weighed 25 kilograms and amounted to over 60,000 pages. See M. Bedjaoui, 'The "Manufacture" of Judgments at the International Court of Justice' (1991) 3(1) PaceYBIntlL 29, 36–7.

incurred by the selected candidates would be covered by the university, without any financial implications for the Court or the UN. Soon enough, the University Traineeship (UT) Programme was up and running[59] and the first batch of trainee clerks flew off to the Netherlands. Other universities followed NYU's example and joined the programme. As a result, every year the Court hosts 8–10 UT clerks hailing from the world's most prestigious academic centres. Each UT clerk assists two judges. The arrangements remain quite informal and largely depend on the connections between each university and the Court. Predictably, the requirement that the university of origin fund the stay of its UT clerks entails that the programme privileges wealthy law schools from the West.[60]

Meanwhile, the Court's increased workload had become a widespread concern. Upon recommendation by the UN Joint Inspection Unit,[61] the General Assembly approved the budget for full-time career clerks starting 2002–2003.[62] Those clerks would be recruited at the P2 level and would each be assigned to an individual judge.[63] The duration of their contracts would be two years, with the possibility of a one-time renewal for an additional two-year term. Although clerks are formally part of the DLM, they respond solely to the judges they work for, and sit with them in the Annex. The establishment of full-time clerks raised the question of whether the UT Programme should remain in place. Ultimately, it was decided that the Court would continue to host UT clerks, if anything because their nine-month stay in The Hague was an opportunity to train 'ambassadors' who could spread the Court's word in their home countries.

---

[59] See NYU website, *International Court of Justice Judicial Fellow Programme*, www.law.nyu.edu/publicinterestlawcenter/forstudents/icj.

[60] Rumor has it that a UT clerk sent to The Hague by a university from the developing world had to fund their stay out of their own pocket, unbeknown to the Court.

[61] UN Joint Inspection Unit, *Review of Management and Administration in the Registry of the International Court of Justice*, JIU/REP/2000/8 (2000), www.unjiu.org/sites/www.unjiu.org/files/jiu_document_files/products/en/reports-notes/JIU%20Products/JIU_REP_2000_8_English.pdf.

[62] See UN General Assembly, *Report of the International Court of Justice: 1 August 2001–31 July 2002*, Supplement No. 4 (A/57/4), 6 September 2002, www.icj-cij.org/public/files/annual-reports/2001-2002-en.pdf, p. 17. The budget for ICJ clerks was subsequently increased a number of times, most recently by UN General Assembly, *Proposed Programme Budget for 2022*, UN Doc. A/76/6 (Sect. 7), https://undocs.org/A/76/6(Sect.7) ('ICJ budget 2022'). See also e.g. Couvreur, 'Registrar', 50–1.

[63] See UN General Assembly, *Report of the International Court of Justice: 1 August 2019–31 July 2020*, Supplement No. 4 (A/75/4), 1 August 2020, www.icj-cij.org/public/files/annual-reports/2019-2020-en.pdf ('ICJ Report 2019–2020'), para. 75. ICJ budget 2022, Annex I.

As a result of these developments, today each ICJ judge is assisted by a full-time P2 clerk, a UT clerk 'shared' with another judge, and the registry lawyers. In addition, the Court's President has a P3 special assistant.[64] Far from a mere technical change, the reorganization of the legal bureaucracy has had a structural impact on the daily practices of the ICJ. For one thing, the shift from a unified registry in charge of satisfying the Court's needs to a system where each individual judge relies on the support of personal legal assistants has altered the power relationships between the time-bound adjudicators and the permanent registry. This does not mean that the Registrar has lost all power. On the contrary, his longstanding experience in the practice and jurisprudence of the World Court makes him a go-to resource whenever a judge has doubts about the meaning of a precedent or its relationship with a pending case. However, the new division of labour between the various actors is not yet settled, and occasionally gives rise to personal and professional frictions.

Like almost everyone in this book, Sophie was in the right place at the right time. Her first steps in the Palace were made possible by the combination of an excellent academic performance, a random conversation with Judge Lehmann at an NYU cocktail party, some subsequent email exchanges, and his passing mention of the UT Programme. During Sophie's UT clerkship, which she undertook under the supervision of Judge Lehmann and Belgian Judge Jacob Huyghebaert, an associate legal officer position was advertised on the website. Given her familiarity with the ICJ's inner workings, it was only natural that Sophie would make the shortlist.

The selection process was in keeping with the solemnity of the institution. One cold morning, all the shortlisted candidates convened outside the examination office. When Sophie's turn came, she entered the room and found Judge Lehmann and two registry lawyers sitting at the interview table. The judge glanced at her sternly and, without much ado, asked her about Article 31.3(c) of the VCLT. In French. Sophie was taken aback: she had never used French during her whole UT clerkship! Nervously, she started articulating a generic answer, beginning with the meaning of 'the relevant rules of international law' and …

'*Attendez, Sophie. Je voudrais que vous me parliez plutôt des "parties." Qui sont-elles? Est-ce les parties au différend ou les parties au traité qui doit être interprété?*'

'*Je crois … Je crois qu'il s'agit des parties au différend. Supposons que le traité est un traité multilatéral. Si c'était toutes les parties au traité,*

---

[64] See ICJ Report 2019–2020, para. 75.

*il y aurait très peu de règles, sauf peut-être celle de droit coutumier, qui s'appliqueraient aux relations entre tous ces états ...'*

'*Est-ce que vous avez entendu parler du rapport du panel de l'OMC concernant l'affaire* Biotech Products? *Ce panel a dit quoi par rapport aux "parties"?*'

Sophie panicked. No, she had never heard of the WTO panel report in *Biotech Products*. During her university years, she had always found WTO law excruciatingly boring, so she had made sure never to take a class on that subject. It was even a bit surprising that Judge Lehmann would know anything about trade: he had always shown a certain proclivity for human rights and humanitarian law, and had never referred to WTO jurisprudence in their daily talks. Perhaps, thought Sophie, he had come across that panel report while preparing his questions for the interview. If he mentioned that case now, perhaps it was because the panel said something different from what she was answering. Make it or break it.

'*Oui, en effet ce panel a indiqué que les "parties" au sens de l'Article 31.3(c), c'est tous les états membres des accords OMC ...*' Sophie held her breath.

'*Très bien, Sophie. Comme le panel l'a remarqué, si les "parties" n'étaient que celles au différend, certains membres de l'OMC pourraient avoir entre eux des droits et des obligations différentes de ceux qu'ils ont vis-à-vis des autres membres.*'

'*Oui, Monsieur le Juge. Mais dans ce cas, on arrive à la situation paradoxale dans laquelle* aucune *disposition de droit des traités ne s'applique aux relations entre tous les membres de l'OMC. Même les dispositions de la Charte des Nations Unies qui n'ont pas atteint le statut de droit coutumier ne s'appliquent pas à tous les membres. Pensez à Taipei!*'

'Good point, Sophie. I think we are done here.'

Sophie stood up and walked out. That afternoon, she took a three-hour written test focusing, to her great relief, on less esoteric ICJ case law and the ILC Articles on State Responsibility.[65] A few weeks later, she received confirmation that she had won the competition: a net annual salary of over 60,000 USD, coupled with the usual benefits accruing from UN status, made for a pretty sweet deal.

Had she known Matt, Sophie would have perhaps envied his higher salary and long-term appointment at the WTO. Yet, the chances of the two having met are slim. Why, may you ask? Well, certainly not the fact that they have different nationalities, or that they live and work in different cities. After all,

---

[65] ILC, *Draft Articles on Responsibility of States for Internationally Wrongful Acts*, Supplement No. 10 (A/56/10) (November 2001).

Matt and Sophie are both part of a transnational elite of highly educated lawyers envisaging a career in the small world of international adjudication. They are both prospective members of the invisible college.

No: the reason why Sophie and Matt will hardly ever meet is because they inhabit separate regions of the international judicial community, to which they came through highly particular trajectories. Throughout their studies, they made different discoveries, learnt to speak different vernaculars, and were imbued with different mythologies. Sophie's international law hinges on the peaceful resolution of conflicts between sovereign states. She has learnt to worry about war, to be deeply sceptical of international politics, and to lament the lack of a universal compulsory jurisdiction able to curb power. Matt's international law is one of mutual exchange of concessions between trading nations, akin to the contractual conditions buyers and sellers make in the marketplace. His preoccupation is to ensure that no contracting state gets more than its fair share of trade benefits, and his judicial posture aims at preventing beggar-thy-neighbour practices.

In their daily routines, they both interact with other professionals who share the same culture, speak the same language, and have a similar pattern of world sense-making. This, in turn, reinforces and sharpens their partial focus. Hence, despite their similar job descriptions and their superficial allegiance to a 'global community of courts',[66] Sophie and Matt could not be more distant from one another. Hear them talk, and you might get the impression that their only shared background is having read the *Lotus* case.[67]

•

Continuing our round of introductions, we now travel southeast, from The Hague to Strasbourg. The ECtHR complex, inaugurated in 1994, is a modernist building made of steel, concrete and glass, designed to be 'anything but intimidating or fortress-like'.[68] A visitor crossing the sliding door entrance finds themselves in wide spaces featuring 'many open bridges, like paths connecting several floors'. This architecture, vaguely reminiscent of a 'spaceship', seeks to convey the impression of an 'innovative Court'.[69] While the building's appearance differs starkly from the

---

[66] Slaughter, 'A Global Community of Courts'.
[67] See Kennedy, 'Many Legal Orders', 648.
[68] Archello website, *European Court of Human Rights*, https://archello.com/project/european-court-of-human-rights.
[69] N.-L. Arold, *The Legal Culture of the European Court of Human Rights* (Martinus Nijhoff, 2007), 42.

Peace Palace's, its layout presents the same distinction between the space where public hearings are held – the iconic cylindrical chambers in the front – and the space where the adjudicators and their supporting staff work on a daily basis – the rather drab structure in the back.

Despite its floor area of over 28,000 m², the ECtHR complex 'appears to have already exhausted its ability to provide even a modest working space to its attorneys and legal assistants'.[70] Indeed, the Court's registry is, by far, the largest bureaucracy among all international courts and tribunals. The 47 judges, whose offices are located on the top floors, are assisted by over 640 registry staff, including 270 lawyers, who work literally below them.[71]

This, in turn, is a direct result of the ECtHR's output, which dwarfs that of any other international judicial mechanism. Every year, the Court issues decisions on over 90,000 applications filed by individuals and member states. Of these, some 1,100 are 'proper' judgments containing at least a modicum of substantive reasoning, while the rest are summary dismissals of applications for lack of admissibility or manifest unfoundedness.[72] These numbers bring the ECtHR closer to high courts in civil law jurisdictions (e.g. the French *Cour de Cassation*) than to typical inter-state adjudicatory bodies. Such an impressive caseload – and the backlog that goes with it[73] – imparts a tangible weight to the Court's activity: as dossiers pile up in the registry's offices, a critical mass grows which needs to be processed, managed, and disentangled.

Indeed, the Court's recent history is essentially a continuous attempt to oil its bureaucratic machinery and streamline it adjudicative processes.[74] Protocol No. 11 to the ECHR, which came into force in 1998, abolished the European Commission of Human Rights, which was tasked with filtering

---

[70] Terris, Romano, and Swigart, *The International Judge*, 53.
[71] ECtHR website, *How the Court Works*, www.echr.coe.int/Pages/home.aspx?p=court/howitworks. See also J.-P. Costa, 'The Evolution and Current Challenges of the European Court of Human Rights' (2009) 1(1) RegentJL&PubPol 17, 33.
[72] See ECtHR website, *Statistics 2013*, www.echr.coe.int/Documents/Stats_annual_2013_ENG.pdf; Crawford, 'The International Law Bar', 343. The conditions of admissibility of individual complaints include the exhaustion of domestic remedies and the obligation to file the complaint within six months of the date of the last decision of a national court or body. See Article 35 of the ECHR.
[73] See Costa, 'Evolution and Current Challenges', 33.
[74] For a comprehensive overview, see e.g. J. Gerards, 'Judicial Deliberations in the European Court of Human Rights', in N. Huls, M. Adams and J. Bomhoff (eds.), *The Legitimacy of Highest Courts' Rulings* (Asser Press, 2009) 407, 417–18; E. Fribergh and R. Liddell, 'The Interlaken Process and the Jurisconsult', in L. Berg et al. (eds.), *Cohérence et impact de la jurisprudence de la Cour européenne des droits de l'homme: Liber amicorum Vincent Berger* (Wolf Legal Publishers, 2013) 177.

individual complaints and dismissing inadmissible ones.[75] The removal of that filter greatly expanded the jurisdictional scope of the Court but, at the same time, caused an explosion in its workload.[76] Ten years later, the members of the Council of Europe adopted Protocol No. 14 to simplify the processing of applications.[77] First, applications are now decided by different 'judicial formations' (a single judge, a three-judge committee, a seven-judge chamber, or the 17-judge Grand Chamber) depending on their novelty and complexity. Second, individual complaints are now admissible only if the applicant suffered a 'significant disadvantage' from the alleged violation. Third, the registry has been reorganized by reallocating competences between permanent lawyers and temporary lawyers.

Given the number of cases decided every year, it would be downright impossible for the judges to take care of the entire process alone. Instead, they work in close cooperation with the registry, giving rise to a 'dualism' in the judicial function that has a profound impact on 'both the process of preparation and deliberation' and 'the style in which … decisions are drafted'.[78]

Navigating the intricacies of the Court's bureaucracy would require more analysis than the reader is willing to bear. In a nutshell, the whole ECtHR registry is overseen by a Registrar and Deputy-Registrar, who respond directly to the President of the Court.[79] Below this top management level, the Court is divided into five sections, which operate like miniature versions of the whole. Each section consists of 8–10 judges, who appoint a section president and vice-president among themselves, and a dedicated section of the registry, headed by a section registrar and section

---

[75] See Council of Europe website, *Explanatory Report to Protocol No. 11 to the Convention for the Protection of Human Rights and Fundamental Freedoms, Restructuring the Control Machinery Established Thereby*, https://rm.coe.int/16800cb5e9; S. Greer, 'What's Wrong with the European Convention on Human Rights?' (2008) 30(3) HumRtsQ 680, 682–3.

[76] Between 1961 and 1998, the year of entry into force of the Protocol, the ECtHR issued 800 judgments. Between 1998 and 2008, the Court delivered over 9,000 judgments. See Costa, 'Evolution and Current Challenges', 18.

[77] See ECtHR website, *Protocol No. 14 to the Convention for the Protection of Human Rights and Fundamental Freedoms, Amending the Control System of the Convention*, www.echr.coe.int/documents/library_collection_p14_ets194e_eng.pdf.

[78] L. Garlicki, 'Judicial Deliberations: The Strasbourg Perspective', in N. Huls, M. Adams and J. Bomhoff (eds.), *The Legitimacy of Highest Courts' Rulings* (Asser Press, 2009) 389, 392.

[79] ECtHR website, *Organisation Chart*, www.echr.am/resources/echr//pdf/fa3ab5b9c072d93a4f27d4559e8ae42a.pdf. See also ECtHR, *Rules of Court* (16 April 2018), Rule 17; P. L. McKaskle, 'The European Court of Human Rights: What It Is, How It Works, and Its Future' (2005) 40(1) USFLRev 1, 26.

deputy-registrar.[80] In turn, each section of the registry comprises a number of legal divisions, for a total of 33.[81] Each division is in charge of handling applications originating in a specific country or group of countries parties to the Council of Europe. For instance, Division X will be in charge of cases from France, Division Y will be assigned to those from Turkey, and so forth.

A division is the key analytical unit in the bureaucracy. It is there that we meet Aphrodite Petrakis. Aphrodite works as a lawyer for Division 2.4, tasked with processing complaints from Greece and Cyprus. Like most of her division colleagues, Aphrodite is a Greek national. This means that, in her daily routine, she deals mostly with alleged human rights violations perpetrated by her home state. This is quite common: the registry lawyers in each division are typically of the same nationality as the member state(s) covered by that division.

This allocation of labour along national lines might sound surprising, as it does not sit well with the cosmopolitan, pan-continental vocation of the ECtHR. However, it is an inevitable consequence of the way the Court operates. Individual complaints can be filed in any of the languages of the Council of Europe, and it is only when they are declared admissible and get to the judicial phase that the official working languages of the Court (English and French) kick in.[82] Therefore, it is crucial that the staff assigned to a case be able to read the language in which the application is written.[83] Moreover, the processing of an application requires a certain familiarity with the domestic legal system of the state concerned, as this facilitates the assessment of threshold issues like the satisfaction of the admissibility conditions.

Aphrodite's official duties are slightly more articulate than the meagre descriptions we have seen at the WTO and the ICJ. She is expected, among other things, to prepare case-files for the examination by the judge-rapporteur and for submission to the Court; provide legal analysis; present cases during the Court's sessions; and draft judgments, decisions, minutes, reports, notes, and other documents. In carrying out these duties, Aphrodite and the rest of Division 2.4 operate more akin to the WTO

---

[80] ECtHR website, *Composition of the Court*, www.echr.coe.int/Pages/home.aspx?p=court/judges&c=.
[81] ECtHR website, *Organisation chart*, www.echr.am/resources/echr//pdf/fa3ab5b9c072d93a4f27d4559e8ae42a.pdf.
[82] See Arold, *ECtHR Legal Culture*, 59–60.
[83] See Garlicki, 'Judicial Deliberations', 392–4.

secretariat than to ICJ clerks: instead of being assigned to an individual judge, lawyers respond to the section registrar, and assist the whole judicial formation tasked with dealing with a particular file.[84] Again, collegiality is quite inevitable, given the Court's caseload and the managerial attitude that has come to dominate the system.

Division 2.4 is overseen by a lead lawyer who, in addition to dispute work, is in charge of administrative matters. In addition, the Division's staff comprises 8–10 lawyers, subdivided in permanent and temporary. Temporary lawyers (or simply 'temps') have fixed-term contracts of four years, non-renewable,[85] and occupy a lower position in the hierarchy. Once their term is over, they are expected to return to their home countries as 'ambassadors' of the European human rights system.[86] Some of Aphrodite's temp colleagues are quite unhappy with this prospect. Going home means a break from the game of international adjudication, with the risk of never being able to play again. Moreover, temps have seen the importance of their role decrease since the entry into force of Protocol No. 14. Previously, there was no official distinction between the duties of temps and 'perms', and both categories could work on the admissibility and the merits of disputes. Since the Protocol's adoption, temps have been relegated to the admissibility phase, whereas the merits of disputes have become the exclusive prerogative of perms.

Similar to Matt and Sophie, Aphrodite was recruited through a written exam and oral interview in Strasbourg. A graduate of the Kapodistrian University of Athens and the College of Europe, she had distinguished herself at the Concours René Cassin, the most prestigious moot court competition in European human rights law. Upon completing her studies, Aphrodite applied and was selected for a temp position. She was lucky enough to join the registry before Protocol No. 14 entered into force, and was therefore able to work on both admissibility and merits. As the end of her four-year term approached, Aphrodite started to get anxious: how could she continue working in the field of human rights adjudication? The idea of going back to Greece was not appealing. In a country hit hard by recession, law firms focusing on international litigation were few and

---

[84] McKaskle, 'The ECtHR', 27–8.
[85] See Parliamentary Assembly of the Council of Europe, Committee on Legal Affairs and Human Rights, *Reinforcement of the Independence of the European Court of Human Rights*, Doc. 13524 (5 June 2014), http://assembly.coe.int/nw/xml/XRef/Xref-XML2HTML-en.asp?fileid=20933&lang=en, para. 42.
[86] Arold, *ECtHR Legal Culture*, 43.

far between, and law firms specializing in ECtHR law virtually non-existent. Her only hope was to stick around the Council of Europe for as long as she could.

Fortunately, Aphrodite managed to secure another temporary position at the European Commission for the Efficiency of Justice, the Council's organ devoted to the improvement of the justice systems of member states. She did not particularly enjoy the research and reporting duties that her new job required. As they say, once you have tried dispute settlement, the rest of international life seems dull and ineffective. Yet, Aphrodite's continued presence in Strasbourg allowed her to maintain personal ties with her former colleagues, which she cultivated out of both affection and calculation. Eventually, Aphrodite's patience was rewarded. The moment a permanent lawyer vacancy was advertised on the ECtHR's website, she applied without hesitation. Thanks to her good performance and her professional network, she earned her way back to Division 2.4 – this time with indefinite tenure and a net salary of circa 5,000 EUR per month.[87]

It is too early for Aphrodite to plan her next moves. But if you asked her, she would have no doubts about her ultimate ambition: joining the office of the Jurisconsult.[88] Established in 2001, the Jurisconsult is de facto the ECtHR's most senior legal officer.[89] He and his elite team of registry lawyers assist the Grand Chamber, the highest judicial formation in the system.

The Jurisconsult's official mandate is to 'ensur[e] the quality and consistency of [the Court's] case-law'.[90] To achieve this goal, he reads the draft judgments and decisions produced by section judges and their staff. If he considers that any draft may give rise to discrepancies in jurisprudence, he addresses written recommendations to the competent judicial formation. For instance, he can request a chamber to stay its proceedings and wait for the Grand Chamber to rule on a similar case. Alternatively, he can highlight lacunae in judicial reasoning and

---

[87] See Council of Europe website, *Summary of Conditions of Employment: All Grades*, https://wcd.coe.int/ViewDoc.jsp?p=&id=2167659&direct=true. Permanent lawyers are hired at the A1–A2 level.
[88] ECtHR website, *Organisation Chart*, www.echr.am/resources/echr//pdf/fa3ab5b9c072d93a4f27d4559e8ae42a.pdf.
[89] See M. Voicu, 'Vincent Berger: A Master of Jurisprudence of the European Court of Human Rights', in L. Berg et al. (eds.), *Cohérence et impact de la jurisprudence de la Cour européenne des droits de l'homme: Liber amicorum Vincent Berger* (Wolf Legal Publishers, 2013) 431, 432.
[90] See ECtHR, *Rules of Court* (16 April 2018), Rule 18(b).

propose solutions. When required, he attends section deliberations on particularly delicate matters. Moreover, the Jurisconsult reviews all draft judgments and decisions of the Grand Chamber, takes part in its hearings and deliberations, and suggests ways to reconcile possible jurisprudential conflicts. Finally, he is a member of the Conflict Resolution Board together with the President of the Court and the five section presidents. During Board meetings, the Jurisconsult presents written and oral analyses of past and current case law, and makes proposals to maintain harmony and coherence.[91]

Given these broad functions, we can readily understand how the office of the Jurisconsult exerts formidable control over the content and evolution of ECtHR decisions. Therefore, as we momentarily leave Aphrodite to her duties, we can only wish her good luck with her career plans.

•

Next stop: San José. Finally a break from the heart of Europe. The IACtHR sits in a white colonial house donated by the Costa Rican government, reminiscent of a more famous building in Washington DC. The central aisle, adorned with a semi-circular portico, is now used mostly for receptions, official visits, and public speeches. Faithful to the distinction between the judicial stage and the judicial backstage, the real action unfolds in the annexes on the two sides of the house, where the seven judges and the IACtHR secretariat have their offices.

The secretariat consists of 50–60 lawyers, is headed by a Secretary and Deputy-Secretary, and is divided into eight teams. Each team comprises a senior lawyer, in charge of overseeing the team's activities, and a number of junior legal staff, including some interns. Compared to Strasbourg, this is an agile bureaucracy that suits well the IACtHR's current needs. The Court issues roughly 20 judgments per year and each secretariat team never handles more than four or five cases at a time.

This modest caseload stems from the institutional design of the Inter-American human rights system. In a nutshell, the system works similarly to the ECtHR before the adoption of Protocol No. 11. Individual applications ('petitions'[92]) are screened by the Inter-American Commission on Human Rights, which assesses their

---

[91] See the website of former Jurisconsult Vincent Berger, www.berger-avocat.eu/en/echr/jurisconsult.html.

[92] OAS website, *Rules of Procedure of the Inter-American Commission on Human Rights*, www.oas.org/en/iachr/mandate/Basics/rulesiachr.asp, Chapter II.

admissibility and prima facie soundness.[93] If a petition passes this initial scrutiny and becomes a 'proper' case, the Commission evaluates its merits and, if a human rights violation is found, issues recommendations to the responding state. If the state does not comply with the recommendations, the Commission refers the case to the Court. Given the filtering role of the Commission, one might think that IACtHR secretariat staff are less busy than their colleagues in Strasbourg. However, the small number of cases is more than compensated by their size, symbolic relevance, and visibility in the public debate of member states.

Take Soledad, for example. An Ecuadorian national who has been serving as a secretariat lawyer for about five years, Soledad Pinto has worked on roughly ten disputes during her whole career. That's nothing compared to Aphrodite, who, as a temporary lawyer in Strasbourg, processed over 400 files over the same period. Yet, while the vast majority of Aphrodite's dossiers were thin and supple, each of Soledad's dossiers consisted of 8,000–10,000 pages of submissions and evidence, with a recent one coming close to a staggering 40,000 pages.

The first case handled by Soledad concerned the operation conducted by the Colombian military in response to the M-19's takeover of the Palacio de Justicia in Bogotá.[94] The guerrilla attack and the army's reaction, which took place on 6–7 November 1985, resulted in almost 100 casualties, including half of Colombia's Supreme Court justices. The army was accused of engaging in torture and inhumane treatment of suspects, extrajudicial killings, and forced disappearances. Soledad was too young to have any first-hand recollection of the events. Yet, she still remembers the emotion of going through the thousands of pages of factual evidence. The judgment to which she was contributing would be regarded as the most authoritative historical reconstruction of an incident that deeply shook Colombia's public consciousness and indelibly marked its recent history.[95] Who was she, a 28-year-old graduate from the University of Notre Dame, to have a say in *that*?

A few months later, she worked on a case about the operation Chavín de Huántar, during which the Peruvian army killed a Túpac Amaru

---

[93] Articles 48–51, 61 of the ACHR.
[94] *Case of Rodríguez Vera et al. (The Disappeared from the Palace of Justice)* v. *Colombia*. Preliminary Objections, Merits, Reparations and Costs, Judgment of 14 November 2014, IACtHR Series C, No. 287.
[95] See e.g. N. Cosoy, '30 años de la toma del Palacio de Justicia en Colombia', BBC, 6 November 2015, www.bbc.com/mundo/noticias/2015/11/151030_colombia_30_aniversario_toma_palacio_de_justicia_entrevista_nicolas_pajaro_nc.

commando and ended a hostage crisis at the Japanese ambassador's residence.[96] To this day, Peruvian public opinion remains divided between those who recognize the unlawfulness of the extrajudicial killings and those who hail the heroic bravery of the military.[97] Once again, skimming through the file, Soledad experienced imposter syndrome. How could she ever draw bright-line distinctions, apportion good and evil, and re-establish historical truth amidst two decades of horror and dishonour by guerrilla and armed forces alike?

Despite these misgivings, Soledad carried on with her assignments. Driven by her commitment to the system, she gradually essentialized and rationalized the tragic events that had given rise to the disputes. By the time she completed her work and the files landed on the judges' desks, she was exhausted and elated. This, as we will see, is a prodigious feature of international adjudication: just like incandescent magma eventually solidifies into cold stone, so do the most dramatic circumstances and the most intractable crises eventually solidify into dry, technical, 'justiciable' matters. Reading an international judgment is, in many ways, like strolling in Pompeii.

But then again, we are anticipating too much. For now, let us say that Soledad's emotional detachment was helped by the fact that she is neither Colombian nor Peruvian. In fact, secretariat lawyers are forbidden from working on cases involving their home countries. In this regard, the organization of labour in the IACtHR secretariat is the *opposite* of that in the ECtHR registry. The inner workings of the two tribunals differ enough to allow for such a distinction. To recall, applications in Strasbourg are filed in any of the languages of the Council of Europe and require native speaking staff to be processed. By contrast, petitions in San José are filed almost exclusively in Spanish or English, thus reducing language barriers.

To be sure, Soledad was not well acquainted with either the Colombian or the Peruvian domestic legal systems when she started working on the two disputes. Therefore, she had to spend considerable time understanding the two countries' constitutional structures, relevant regulations, and juridical cultures. She found this challenge to be more an opportunity than a burden, for it allowed her to get a better grasp of Latin American

---

[96] *Case of Cruz Sánchez et al. v. Peru*. Preliminary Objections, Merits, Reparations and Costs. Judgment of 17 April 2015, IACtHR Series C, No. 292.

[97] See e.g. 'Peru: President Kuczynski Honors Chavin de Huantar Commandos', Andina News, 19 April 2017, www.andina.com.pe/ingles/noticia-president-kuczynski-honors-chavin-huantar-comandos-663504.aspx.

legal traditions. After all, she kept telling herself, what other job offers you the opportunity to engage in comparative legal analysis on a daily basis?

•

We could explain the selection process by which Soledad came to her current post: another written test, another interview, another profession of faith.

Instead, we will skip straight to our last judicial bureaucrat: Carlos Emiliano Perez Sanchez. Carlos works for a leading international arbitrator, Professor François Gal. The two first met when, as a third-year student at the University of Paris 1, Carlos enrolled in Professor Gal's course in international investment law. At that time, the venerable scholar was already a superstar in the field of ISDS – a field whose formative doctrines were, in no small part, influenced by the Professor's own writings. Every year, Professor Gal sits on some 15 arbitral tribunals, often as party-appointed arbitrator and occasionally as president. Given his reputation, it should come as no surprise that his classes were packed well beyond the normal capacity of the Sorbonne's antiquated locales.

Carlos' scored top marks in the course and repeatedly told François Gal about his interest in international dispute settlement. Upon graduation, the Professor advised him to strengthen his CV by undertaking a master's programme in the United States.

'After that,' he suggested, 'I might have something lined up for you back in Paris.'

Emboldened by this promise, Carlos applied for an LLM at Harvard Law School, to which he was admitted thanks to a solid dossier and Professor Gal's weight behind him. In Massachusetts, Carlos took almost every international law and dispute settlement course on offer. Some classes, like Commercial Arbitration, were relatively familiar, with the instructor using the jurisprudence of various tribunals as the main teaching material. Other classes, however, proved far more esoteric. The course in Global Law and Governance, for example, was unlike anything Carlos had experienced during his studies in France. What could Foucault's *Discipline and Punish*[98] possibly have to do with *jus ad bellum*? Why on Earth would international law students be asked to read Freud?[99] Carlos was perplexed: while most sessions were admittedly *interesting*, none seemed to convey anything *useful* to an aspiring

---

[98] M. Foucault, *Discipline and Punish: The Birth of the Prison* (Vintage Books, 1977).
[99] S. Freud, *Thoughts for the Times on War and Death* (The Hogarth Press, 1957).

practitioner. Worse still, the class readings suggested a certain scepticism about the virtues of the international legal order: the unsettling insinuation that, far from being a vehicle for social progress and moral advancement, international law might in fact be an 'instrument of ... poverty, ... conflicts, and ... injustice'.[100]

Carlos resisted the disruptive call of the siren. International law was a *good* thing, he kept telling himself. If the system had flaws, those could be fixed from the inside. He would be a fixer, an actor who really matters. With a bit of luck, François Gal would really have something in store for him.

That 'something' turned out to be a junior associate position with the Professor's newly established law firm, Gal Elmosnino LLP. Receiving the job offer erased in an instant all of Carlos' concerns. What better position in the constellation of international adjudication than the inner circle of one of the most influential adjudicators around?

At that time, Carlos did not suspect that his recruitment could conceal ulterior motives. In fact, since their early conversations, Professor Gal had done his homework, and had discovered Carlos' family ties with the Argentine government. Despite his fame, the Professor had been struggling to secure appointments by Argentina, the golden goose of ISDS. Therefore, he hoped that having Carlos aboard would kill two birds with one stone – getting a skilful assistant and expanding his market in Latin America. All this would become apparent to Carlos only much later. Right now, it was time to celebrate. *Adieu* Foucault, *adieu* Freud: while someone at Harvard fiddled with the dead poets society, someone else was about to make an *actual* career!

Co-founded by Professor Gal and another eminent arbitrator, Gal Elmosnino LLP does not do counsel work. Instead, the main task of the firm's legal staff is to assist the two founding partners whenever they sit on arbitral tribunals, either as co-arbitrators or as presidents. This peculiar arrangement is increasingly common in the ISDS field: given the *ad hoc*, fragmented nature of the system, there is no one set of premises where the whole process is carried out. Indeed, a major feature of this area of international dispute settlement is that adjudicators are in competition with each other – or, less flatteringly, are on the market.[101] Thus, each arbitrator seeks the most efficient allocation of administrative and legal resources to maximize gains and enhance competitiveness.

---

[100] Kennedy, 'Many Legal Orders', 852.
[101] See Dezalay and Garth, *Dealing in Virtue*, 7.

Early pioneers in the arbitration market were typically luminaries of public international law or transnational commercial practice,[102] whose social capital consisted mostly of their 'general legal and social aura'.[103] Having to decide relatively few cases, these 'Grand Old Men'[104] usually worked as solo practitioners and handled the whole files themselves, without the support of stable legal structures. Occasionally, they relied on the assistance of the secretariat of the arbitral institution under whose rules the dispute was being adjudicated (e.g. the ICSID). When that happened, the secretariat staff would carry out all the administrative and legal duties that the arbitral tribunal assigned to them.

This configuration is increasingly rare in today's market. The profound transformation of the field over the last two decades has led to a radical reorganization of how arbitrators work. On the one hand, as we have seen, the system has gradually condensed around a small club of top arbitrators, who built their reputation through intense activity and highly specialized expertise. Unlike their predecessors, these second generation arbitrators tend to sit on numerous tribunals at once.[105] On the other hand, disputes have exponentially grown in size, evolving from narrow legal issues to veritable 'mammoth arbitrations'[106] with dozens of claims for astronomical damages.[107] For instance, the PCA award in the *Yukos* case, currently under review by Dutch courts, required Russia to pay over USD 50 billion to the claimants, at the end of proceedings which saw the parties file over 4,000 pages of submissions, deliver oral pleadings for a total of 2,700 pages of transcripts, and submit over 8,800 exhibits.[108] Extreme examples aside, about one

---

[102] See *supra*, pp. 62–5.
[103] T. Schultz and R. Kovacs, 'The Rise of a Third Generation of Arbitrators? Fifteen Years after Dezalay and Garth' (2012) 28(2) ArbIntl 161, 162.
[104] Dezalay and Garth, *Dealing in Virtue*, 21.
[105] For an in-depth overview of the current state of affairs, see Puig, 'The Arbitration Market'.
[106] *Hulley Enterprises Limited (Cyprus)* v. *Russian Federation*, PCA Case No. AA 226, Final Award (18 July 2014); *Yukos Universal Limited (Isle of Man)* v. *Russian Federation*, PCA Case No. AA 227, Final Award (18 July 2014); *Veteran Petroleum Limited (Cyprus)* v. *Russian Federation*, PCA Case No. AA 228, Final Award (18 July 2014) (collectively 'Yukos arbitral award'), para. 4.
[107] See e.g. P. Tercier, 'The Role of the Secretary to the Arbitral Tribunal', in L. W. Newman and R. D. Hill (eds.), *The Leading Arbitrators' Guide to International Arbitration* (3rd edn., Juris, 2014) 531, 543–4.
[108] Yukos arbitral award, para. 4.

tenth of all arbitral disputes exceed USD 100 million in value.[109] Even in moderately complex cases, it is common for a tribunal to receive multiple rounds of submissions of some 400 pages each, coupled with 800–1,000 exhibits per party.

Faced with these new and pressing needs, leading arbitrators progressively established permanent or semi-permanent legal teams to assist them during disputes.[110] The qualifications and working arrangements of those teams vary from person to person. Some arbitrators, like François Gal, rely on lawyers working as associates in dedicated law firms. Others, mostly university professors, resort to young academics (doctoral and post-doctoral students, assistant professors, etc.) to do the job.[111] Arbitrators who are also judges at permanent judicial institutions (e.g. the United States-Iran Claims Tribunal) may ask their clerks under such institutions to help them in arbitral proceedings. Since many arbitrators have multiple concomitant affiliations, they are free to tinker with any combination available.

Carlos' assignments in each dispute change depending on whether Professor Gal sits as president of the tribunal or as party-appointed arbitrator. Unless the tribunal decides otherwise, the president usually takes care of the bulk of the work, from leading the proceedings to preparing the draft award.[112] The co-arbitrators' role is often limited to participating in deliberations, commenting on the president's draft, and making sure that the appointing parties have their views properly heard.

Another important variable is whether Carlos' assistance to a tribunal is or is not disclosed to the parties. Back in the day, the arbitrators' assistants used to operate mostly off the radar. Nowadays, however, it is increasingly common for the president to seek the parties' authorization to appoint an official tribunal secretary. This is usually done through a letter to the parties indicating the reasons for which such support is needed and what functions the designated person will fulfil. Typical tasks include 'the review of submissions and evidence', the 'preparation of summaries

---

[109] See A. Stone Sweet and F. Grisel, 'The Evolution of International Arbitration: Delegation, Judicialization, Governance', in W. Mattli and T. Dietz (eds.), *International Arbitration and Global Governance: Contending Theories and Evidence* (Oxford University Press, 2014) 22.

[110] See e.g. Z. Douglas, 'The Secretary to the Arbitral Tribunal', in B. Berger and M. E. Schneider (eds.), *Inside the Black Box: How Arbitral Tribunals Operate and Reach Their Decisions* (Juris, 2013) 87, 88–9.

[111] See e.g. Douglas, 'Secretary', 87.

[112] See Tercier, 'Secretary', 546.

and/or memoranda', some 'research on specific factual or legal issues', the preparation of the 'initial drafts of procedural orders and awards', and 'support to the Tribunal ... during hearings and deliberations'.[113]

More often than not, the parties consent to these terms: the prospect of having a fourth person do the heavy lifting on behalf of the tribunal, at a much lower hourly rate than the arbitrators, is appealing in terms of both expeditiousness and costs. In case of agreement, the secretary is involved in all the official stages of the arbitration, including the exchange of communications between the parties and the bench, the filing of submissions, hearings, and deliberations.

But what if the parties do *not* consent? One might think that, in that case, the arbitrators would conduct the proceedings without any external assistance. That would be a naïve thought: in today's market, the figure of the 'lone arbitrator'[114] is a romantic myth. How could an arbitrator as distinguished as Professor Gal, who must juggle several arbitrations at once, digest the voluminous stacks of paper, conduct the required legal and factual research, and reach a timely decision all by himself? You guessed it – he cannot. In fact, the parties' refusal to appoint a tribunal secretary means, quite often, that the legal assistant to the president will simply carry on working in the backstage, without formal investiture. The main difference is that, in that case, the assistant will not have direct access to official correspondence and the hearing and deliberation rooms, with all the logistical complications that ensue.

The final factor affecting the scope of Carlos' duties is the tribunal's relationship with the relevant arbitral institution (PCA, ICSID, etc.). When Carlos is officially appointed as tribunal secretary, his duties will 'not duplicate' those of the institution, but rather 'complement them'.[115] In practice, this means that the institution's staff will take care of the administrative aspects of proceedings (handling of documents, correspondence with the parties, editing of the award, etc.), whereas Carlos will focus on legal research, advice, and drafting. When Carlos works *incognito*, his arrangements with the institution will have to be negotiated behind the scenes.

---

[113] Model Letter from Arbitral Tribunal to Parties on the Appointment of an Arbitral Secretary or Assistant, in G. Kaufmann-Kohler and A. Rigozzi, *International Arbitration: Law and Practice in Switzerland* (3rd edn., Oxford University Press, 2015), 312 ('Model Letter').

[114] Douglas, 'Secretary', 90.

[115] Model Letter.

To be sure, the reliance of arbitral tribunals on legal assistants is quite controversial, as it raises the concern that the adjudicators may abdicate their duties in favour of a faceless 'fourth arbitrator'.[116] Similar preoccupations are emerging with respect to all the other international judicial bureaucracies we have introduced so far. Indeed, despite their different profiles and affiliations, Matt, Sophie, Aphrodite, Soledad, and Carlos are all invisible. Or, to be more precise, they are carefully, staunchly obscured from public view.

Let us take a closer look, shall we?

---

[116] See e.g. C. Partasides, 'The Fourth Arbitrator? The Role of Secretaries to Tribunals in International Arbitration' (2002) 18(2) ArbIntl 147; Tercier, 'Secretary', 536–45.

# 6

## The Three Wise Monkeys

For decades, people from all over world have been speculating about Area 51. The thick veil of secrecy surrounding the Nevada military base has given rise to all sorts of conspiracy theories. For some, the United States government would be using the site to conduct studies on captured extra-terrestrials; according to others, including the Las Vegas Tourism Bureau, the area would host laboratories for the development of teleportation and time travel technologies. Meanwhile, every year thousands of tourists take a detour from their stays in Vegas to travel State Route 375 – aptly renamed 'Extraterrestrial Highway' – and go take a peek at the base's surroundings. From sci-fi novels to Hollywood blockbusters, from cartoons to videogames, everyone talks about Area 51.

That is, everyone except the US government. Up until 2013, national authorities never officially acknowledged the site's existence. Area 51 did not appear on official geological survey maps; the Air-Force kept denying that there ever was a facility by that name; and any reference to it was redacted from official documents. The almost comical mismatch between, on the one hand, the government's cover-up efforts and, on the other hand, the fame that the base had meanwhile acquired was well captured in an article by the Los Angeles Times, which referred to Area 51 as 'the most famous military institution in the world that doesn't officially exist'.[1]

It is early to tell whether the legal bureaucracies assisting international courts and tribunals will attract the same curiosity as Area 51 (alright, they probably will not). Two things, however, are certain. First, those bureaucracies form part and parcel of the international judicial community, whose socio-professional interactions incessantly shape the interpretation and application of international law. Second, their crucial role in the adjudicative process is meticulously obscured from public view. Their

---

[1] A. Jacobsen, 'The Road to Area 51', Los Angeles Times, 16 September 2014, www.latimes.com/entertainment/la-mag-april052009-backstory-story.html.

daily tasks and duties, their relationships with the adjudicators, and their impact on the merits of decisions remain glaringly absent from official discourse, public debate, and scholarly analysis.

On the one hand, international courts are reticent to reveal their internal processes and impose strict confidentiality duties on their employees. This reluctance can be understood as an effort to preserve the secret of deliberations, whose breach may impair a court's ability to render its judgments in conformity with the appropriate procedures and may even call into question its impartiality.[2] On the other hand, academics and commentators are remarkably skittish on the subject. They carefully avoid questioning the inner workings of international courts, fret to ask uncomfortable questions, and tend to take official discourse at face value. This is particularly striking given that scholars, unlike judicial staff, are not subject to confidentiality obligations. Hence, to paraphrase the Los Angeles Times, the invisible army of judicial bureaucrats constitutes the most significant set of players in the adjudication game that doesn't officially exist.

Hopefully, the remainder of this book will help pierce the veil of secrecy. Before doing that, however, it is perhaps useful to pause for a moment and consider secrecy as an object of interest in itself. Why is the role of international judicial bureaucrats a secret in the first place? What strategies and preoccupations determine this state of affairs?

Again, you may protest: Stop digressing and tell us already! Patience, dear reader. The existence of a secret is an intriguing circumstance, irrespective of what that secret is about. What a professional community says and *does not* say about its own operations is often revealing of its self-perception as an agent in society, its tacit rules and ingrained assumptions, its ambitions, and its idiosyncrasies. The spoken and the unspoken in the international judicial community reflect the ever-evolving power relations among its participants, give prominence to certain actors while relegating others to marginality, and delineate the horizon of discursive possibilities within the field.[3]

---

[2] For instance, in 2013, an email was leaked where an ICTY judge accused the Tribunal's president of bias in a number of cases (http://a.bimg.dk/node-files/511/6/6511917-letter-english.pdf). The leak prompted many commentators to question the continued credibility of the court. See M. Simons, 'Hague judge faults acquittals of Serb and Croat commanders', New York Times, 14 June 2013, www.nytimes.com/2013/06/14/world/europe/hague-judge-faults-acquittals-of-serb-and-croat-commanders.html?pagewanted=all&_r=2&.

[3] See Bourdieu, 'The Force of Law', 827; J. Crawford and M. Koskenniemi, 'Introduction', in J. Crawford and M. Koskenniemi (eds.), *The Cambridge Companion to International Law* (Cambridge University Press, 2012) 1, 4.

So please indulge us as we move from one military base to another. During World War II, a poster placed at the entrance of the premises of the Manhattan Project depicted the traditional Japanese simian trio – the three wise monkeys who speak no evil, see no evil, and hear no evil – to invite the participants in the nuclear development programme to the utmost discretion. The caption underneath the picture read: 'What you see here, what you do here, what you hear here, when you leave here, let it stay here'.[4]

Depictions of this kind, often associated with classified activities, perfectly capture the essence of a 'conspiracy of silence', the social phenomenon whereby 'a group of people tacitly agree to outwardly ignore something of which they are all personally aware'.[5] What distinguishes a conspiracy from a mere secret is the cooperation between the conspirators, a collaborative endeavour that 'presupposes discretion on the part of the non-producer of the information as well as inattention on the part of its non-consumers'.[6] The three wise monkeys cannot be separated: the first monkey's refusal to speak would be meaningless if the other two did not equally refuse to see and to hear.

The routine activities of judicial bureaucrats, as well as their impact on judicial outcomes, are subject to a conspiracy of silence on the part of our profession – a sort of mutual denial aimed at obscuring their role from public view. Not convinced? Then try to ask an international judge whether they ever receive any assistance in conducting the relevant legal research, deciding the issues arising in a dispute, or drafting their judgments. At best, they will offer a generic response praising the 'terrific' support of their staff,[7] without providing any meaningful details. At worst, they will ask you to leave the room, outraged by your impudence. Knocking at the door of a registry or secretariat would hardly yield better results: those who try are usually met with poker faces and pre-cooked answers.

Such a dismissive attitude would probably bewilder a domestic lawyer desirous to learn more about international adjudication. In many national legal traditions, the functions and prerogatives of court assistants have long been discussed by academics and the general media alike, to the point that few would consider the topic taboo. For instance, it is well-known

---

[4] See https://en.wikipedia.org/wiki/Three_wise_monkeys#/media/File:Oak_Ridge_Wise_Monkeys.jpg.
[5] E. Zerubavel, *The Elephant in the Room: Silence and Denial in Everyday Life* (Oxford University Press, 2006), 2.
[6] Zerubavel, *Elephant*, 48.
[7] See e.g. the statement of an anonymous ECtHR judge in Terris, Romano, and Swigart, *The International Judge*, 82.

that US Supreme Court Justices rely heavily on the assistance of clerks, who, among other things, conduct legal research, summarize the parties' briefs, make recommendations, edit, cite-check, and draft portions of opinions.[8] America's most prominent lawyers proudly list their Supreme Court clerkships near the top of their CVs, and many judicial appointments have been made among the ranks of former clerks.

To be sure, the suspicion that clerks act as the judges' 'ghostwriters', without being subject to 'the usual security or loyalty checks', occasionally stirs some controversy.[9] Yet, these forms of contestation and the reactions thereto tend to take place in the open, from scholarly pieces[10] to newspaper articles,[11] without necessarily giving way to censorship as to clerks' existence and activities. Other national discourses are a bit less overt about judicial bureaucracies, but nonetheless feature specialized discussions of the topic.[12]

By contrast, in vain would our naïve domestic lawyer look for similar references to the registries, secretariats, and clerks serving international adjudicators. With some rare exceptions, which we will discuss in a moment, all they would find is a resounding, deafening silence.

*

Who, then, are the conspirators? Who are the three wise monkeys who do not speak, hear, and see international judicial bureaucrats? The part of the mute ape – the 'non-producer of information'[13] – will be played

---

[8] See e.g. R. Stern et al., *Supreme Court Practice* (6th edn., Bureau of National Affairs, 1986), 257–8, 573; S. J. Kenney, 'Beyond Principals and Agents: Seeing Courts as Organizations by Comparing Référendaires at the European Court of Justice and Law Clerks at the US Supreme Court' (2000) 33(5) CompPolStud 593, 603.

[9] C. A. Newland, 'Personal Assistants to Supreme Court Justices: The Law Clerks' (1961) 40(4) OrLRev 299, 311.

[10] In addition to the few pieces already cited, see e.g. J. B. Oakley and R. S. Thompson, *Law Clerks and the Judicial Process: Perceptions of the Qualities and Function of Law Clerks in American Courts* (University of California Press, 1980); J. D. Mahoney, 'Law Clerks: For Better or for Worse?' (1988) 54(2) BrookLRev 321; K. O'Connor and J. R. Hermann, 'The Clerk Connection: Appearances Before the Supreme Court and Former Law Clerks' (1995) 78(5) *Judicature* 247; E. P. Lazarus, *Closed Chambers: The First Eyewitness Account of the Epic Struggles inside the Supreme Court* (Times Books, 1998); T. C. Peppers, *Courtiers of the Marble Palace: The Rise and Influence of the Supreme Court Law Clerk* (Stanford University Press, 2006); R. C. Black, C. L. Boyd and A. C. Bryan, 'Revisiting the Influence of Law Clerks on the US Supreme Court's Agenda-Setting Process' (2014) 98(1) MarqueeLRev 75.

[11] See e.g. W. H. Rehnquist, 'Who Writes Decisions of the Supreme Court?', US News and World Report, 13 December 1957, 74–5; A. M. Bickel, 'The Court: An Indictment Analyzed', *New York Times Magazine*, 17 April 1958, 16.

[12] See e.g. Latour, *The Making of Law*; A. Paterson, *The Law Lords* (Macmillan, 1982).

[13] Zerubavel, *Elephant*, 48.

by international judicial institutions themselves, which maintain strict confidentiality with respect to their inner workings. All the phases of the resolution of an international dispute, from the preparation of the case to the drafting of the final decision, are classified, and none of the inputs provided by the adjudicators' assistants is disclosed to the public.[14] The prohibition to speak publicly about what happens behind closed doors applies to adjudicators and bureaucrats alike, and is strictly enforced through a series of interlocking and overlapping measures.

For instance, upon recruitment at the ABS, Matt was asked to sign a confidentiality agreement by which he committed never to disclose the full extent of his activities, not even to colleagues working for other WTO divisions. The agreement covered, first and foremost, what happened in specific proceedings and deliberation sessions. Nothing strange, Matt thought. A modicum of discretion concerning ongoing cases is the hallmark of an independent and impartial court. In fact, any governance body must balance transparency with the need to ensure that decision-makers are in a position to air their opinions freely, without undue pressures, while their governance output – the statute, the policy, and the judgment – is still in the making.[15]

Very few would argue, for example, that transparency commands a full disclosure of an individual adjudicator's views at the initial stages of a dispute or their opinions as expressed in the deliberation room. The crystallization of judicial positions is a tentative and hesitant journey that requires dialogue, contestation, and continuous testing of one's instincts. If any differences are to emerge, they ought to do so at the end of the process, for example through concurring and/or dissenting opinions. Besides, it is important that judges be able to trust their assistants, given the principal-agent character of their relationship.

However, to Matt's surprise, the notion of confidentiality proved to extend well beyond the secret of deliberations in *specific* disputes. In fact, Björn insisted that Matt refrain from discussing his *general* assignments, that is the activities he would be expected to undertake every time a new case was filed. From now on, terms like 'issues paper' or 'list of hearing questions' would be banned from Matt's vocabulary whenever he spoke in

---

[14] As a partial exception to this rule, the procedure of the Court of Justice of the European Union requires that the opinions of advocates general be published as part of a dispute's official record.

[15] See e.g. G. Guillaume, 'Some Thoughts on the Independence of International Judges vis-à-vis States' (2003) 2(1) LPICT 163, 165; Kolb, *The ICJ*, 1007.

public.[16] The cases to which he was assigned could not be named. For the outside world, Matt would simply 'assist WTO Appellate Body members with the preparation of their positions and arguments towards the deliberation of trade disputes'. Björn even took pains to go through Matt's CV to verify that the relevant job description would not to raise any eyebrows.

At no point did Björn mention the consequences of a possible breach of Matt's confidentiality agreement. However, the seriousness with which he broached the topic suggested that a violation could result in disciplinary action, possibly including the termination of Matt's contract. Subtler forms of control continued throughout Matt's service. These included a general duty to secure authorization before delivering lectures, submitting publications, or speaking to journalists.

Matt's homologues in other judicial systems are subject to similar restrictions. For instance, since the very beginning of their collaboration, Judge Lehmann forbade Sophie from disclosing her role in the preparation and drafting of notes.[17] He sternly reminded his pupil that ICJ judges are free to rely on external help in assembling materials, but 'may not delegate to anyone the drafting of their respective note'.[18] Similarly, Aphrodite was instructed always to seek her lead lawyer's approval before releasing interviews about the ECtHR registry's activities.

Carlos' position is particularly thorny. When the parties consent to his official appointment as tribunal secretary, he is barred from disclosing his work to anyone extraneous to the arbitration. If questioned by someone involved in the case, his default answer is a simple recital of the terms contained in the tribunal's appointment letter. At the end of the case, a summary of his activities is presented to the litigants as part of the final invoice. When the parties do *not* consent to the appointment, the conditions become prohibitive. Forced to work completely off the radar, Carlos simply ceases to exist: no mention that he is involved in any arbitration whatsoever; no reference to his assignments to friends and colleagues – nothing at all. At some point, the situation grew quite uncomfortable. As he worked on a string of cases in an unofficial capacity, Carlos found himself unable to justify long 'gaps' in his résumé. Should he quit his job at Gal Elmosnino LLP one day, how would he explain them to prospective recruiters?[19]

---

[16] We will discuss the meaning of these terms *infra*, pp. 165–6, 261–2.
[17] More on the note *infra*, pp. 169–70.
[18] Kolb, *The ICJ*, 1007.
[19] See Douglas, 'Secretary', 87.

Through the combined operation of these techniques, international judicial bureaucrats are made aware of their invisibility. As the temptation to speak up is always an attempt at relevance,[20] it is as though the international judicial machinery sought to distinguish between more and less significant actors among its workforce. Not only does the first monkey not speak: it also imparts an injunction to silence on others, a no-comment posture whereby there is 'nothing to say ..., nothing to see, and nothing to know'.[21] Over time, the addressees of the injunction internalize the culture of the unspoken, begin to appreciate its virtues, and eventually become its unwitting champions. Breaking the silence is not just a potential breach of contract: it is also frowned upon as an unsavoury, inelegant, and *unprofessional* act.

For instance, Sophie remembers the resentment she felt when Hugh a former senior legal secretary at the ICJ published an article detailing his role in shaping the text and content of judgments.[22] To Sophie's mind, the author did not intend to foster public awareness of the World Court's internal dynamics, but rather to carry out an unwarranted attack on the system.[23] Similarly, in 2019, a paper was circulated which criticized the extensive power of the WTO secretariat in the resolution of trade disputes.[24] Björn, Matt, and many other WTO insiders turned up their noses. It seemed inconceivable that one of the authors, a former secretariat officer, would betray his colleagues at a time of institutional turmoil.

Now, to the blind and the deaf monkeys. If international courts and tribunals act as the non-producers of information, international law scholars play along as its non-consumers.[25] To date, only a handful published works have dared to discuss the role of international judicial bureaucrats in any meaningful detail.[26] Usually, those actors are given no more than a passing mention.[27]

---

[20] Zerubavel, *Elephant*, 33.
[21] M. Foucault, *The History of Sexuality*, trans. R. Hurley (Pantheon Books, 1978), 4.
[22] Thirlway, 'Drafting ICJ Decisions'.
[23] That legal secretary himself later wished that the article be perceived as a 'slight' and 'discreet' disclosure of the Court's deliberation and drafting processes. H. Thirlway, 'The International Court of Justice: Cruising Ahead at 70' (2016) 29(4) LJIL 1103, fn 12.
[24] Pauwelyn and Pelc, *Who Writes WTO Rulings*.
[25] Zerubavel, *Elephant*, 48.
[26] In addition to the above-mentioned articles, see e.g. Cartier and Hoss, 'Registries and Secretariats'; Vauchez, 'Communities of International Litigators'; R. Howse, 'Does the Appellate Body Need a Senior Judicial Officer?', International Economic Law and Policy Blog, 26 November 2015, http://worldtradelaw.typepad.com/ielpblog/2015/11/does-the-appellate-body-need-a-senior-judicial-officer.html; Baetens, *Legitimacy of Unseen Actors*.
[27] See e.g. Caron, 'Political Theory', 416; Pauwelyn, 'Mars and Venus', 795–8; Garlicki, 'Judicial Deliberations', 391–2.

The one partial exception to this dearth of literature concerns the secretaries and assistants to arbitral tribunals, which have attracted some attention over the last few years.[28] Such an interest arose from a few incidents that allegedly tarnished the reputation of ISDS. The first incident saw a top arbitrator being forced to resign from a tribunal after one of his clerks had posted views on legal issues related to the case in an online blog.[29] The second incident, not yet resolved, relates to the already mentioned arbitral award in *Yukos*.[30] In its writ for annulment of the award before The Hague District Court, Russia alleged that, unbeknown to the parties, the arbitrators had delegated substantive responsibilities to the tribunal's assistant (an associate with the tribunal president's law firm), thereby breaching their mandate to perform their duties personally.[31] While these occurrences made enough noise to arouse some curiosity, they remained mostly confined to specialized circles and failed to open the door to a comprehensive analysis of the relationship between adjudicators and their assistants.

This obstinate inattention to the phenomenon on the part of scholars may be superficially dismissed as a mere failure to notice, as a casual analytical omission. After all, we lawyers like to talk about law, not social structures: we are not expected to have the 'sociological imagination'[32] that would enable us to see power dynamics, influence networks, and

---

[28] See e.g. Partasides, 'The Fourth Arbitrator?'; W. W. Park, 'Arbitration's Protean Nature: The Value of Rules and the Risks of Discretion' (2003) 19(3) ArbIntl 279; C. J. Restemayer, 'Secretaries Always Get a Bad Rep: Identifying the Controversy Surrounding Administrative Secretaries, Current Guidelines, and Recommendations' (2012) 4 PeenYBArb&Med 328; Tercier, 'Secretary'; M. Polkinghorne and C. B. Rosenberg, 'The Role of the Tribunal Secretary in International Arbitration: A Call for a Uniform Standard' (2014) 8(2) DispResIntl 107; T. Timlin, 'The Swiss Supreme Court on the Use of Secretaries and Consultants in the Arbitral Process' (2016) 8 PeenYBArb&Med 268.

[29] See e.g. L. Markert, 'Challenging Arbitrators in Investment Arbitration: The Challenging Search for Relevant Standards and Ethical Guidelines' (2010) 3(2) CAAJ 237, 265, fn 127.

[30] See *supra*, p. 133.

[31] See Pleading Notes of Professor A. J. Van Den Berg before the Hague District Court (9 February 2016), http://res.cloudinary.com/lbresearch/image/upload/v1455205591/rf_pleading_notes_9_february_2016_final_edited_111116_1546.pdf, paras. 94–114. For discussion, see e.g. D. Galagan and P. Živković, 'The Challenge of the Yukos Award: An Award Written by Someone Else – A Violation of the Tribunal's Mandate?', Kluwer Arbitration Blog, 27 February 2015, http://kluwerarbitrationblog.com/2015/02/27/the-challenge-of-the-yukos-award-an-award-written-by-someone-else-a-violation-of-the-tribunals-mandate/; R. Howse, 'The Fourth Man: An Intriguing Sub-Plot in the Yukos Arbitration', International Economic Law and Policy Blog, 29 March 2017, http://worldtradelaw.typepad.com/ielpblog/2017/03/the-fourth-man-an-intriguing-sub-plot-in-the-yukos-arbitration-.html.

[32] C. W. Mills, *The Sociological Imagination* (Oxford University Press, 1959), 5–11.

institutionalized rationalities. Yet, such a dismissal would be disingenuous. That international adjudicators are embedded in institutional structures tasked with assisting them in all sorts of ways is, quite simply, too important a fact for us to overlook. It is part of those 'highly conspicuous matters' we deliberately *choose* not to see.[33]

If you are not yet convinced that the three wise monkeys act in concert, consider one last element. As mentioned, the conspirators are typically aware of the truth they are outwardly ignoring. They have all seen with their own eyes that the emperor is naked, and yet no one dares to break the silence. Our object of inquiry is no exception. The role of international judicial bureaucrats, while zealously kept secret from the public, is no mystery to some insiders to the legal community – at least those who, having served as judges or assistants, have since joined national governments, private law firms, or academia.

Anyone close enough to the field can attest this. Matt, for instance, had long suspected that the deference with which counsel addressed him during hearings was due to more than politeness. His intuition found confirmation during one of his drinks with Jane Weaver at the Bains des Pâquis. Furious at an Appellate Body ruling against her client, Jane suddenly hissed: 'I am very disappointed, buddy. Normally, *you* write much better than that mumbo-jumbo!' Another day, Matt had a bitter exchange with a senior officer from Legal Affairs, who had drafted a panel report the Appellate Body reversed rather unceremoniously. 'You guys sure have guts: overruling *me*? I have been working here for twenty years, and the day has yet to come when a rookie teaches me about WTO law!'

Soledad had a similar epiphany at a conference about recent IACtHR jurisprudence. Two of the speakers, currently professors at Los Andes and Notre Dame, had both previously worked at the Court's secretariat. During the debate, each took issue with certain judgments, knowing perfectly well that the other had written them. As an insider, Soledad found the scene quite entertaining: by ostensibly criticizing the Court's case law, the two professors were secretly trading jabs.

Sitting at another conference, Carlos witnessed a surprising transformation. The keynote speaker, an eminent arbitrator and long-time competitor of Professor Gal, was delivering a lecture on the legitimate expectations of investors. As soon as the speaker recognized Carlos in the crowd, she suddenly shifted gears and focused on cases arbitrated by the Professor. Her

---

[33] Zerubavel, *Elephant*, 9.

eyes remained intently fixed on Carlos, as if to gauge his reactions. What had started as an academic lecture to the benefit of all attendees turned into a coded pleading directed at one attendee only.

These, together with many other examples, show how the role of international judicial bureaucrats in decision-making and drafting processes is a *secret de Polichinelle*. Of course, the fact that some community insiders are aware of the activities that bureaucrats indulge in does not prevent them from feigning ignorance, especially when interacting with outsiders. During hearings or public speeches, they will strictly respect the boundaries of their assigned roles and carefully avoid any express statements that would reveal their inside knowledge. At most, they will wink and nod at each other as if to say: 'I know you helped out with this: well done!' (or: 'Go back to law school!'). Some may find this double standard quite amusing. Others will retort that 'there are few aspects … that better deserve the unwelcome moniker of "hypocrisy"'.[34]

Certainly, on occasion, the obstinacy of silence borders on the surreal. Consider, for instance, the already mentioned writ for annulment in the *Yukos* arbitration. In support of its contention that the tribunal delegated too much authority to the assistant, Russia's counsel produced the expert testimony of a top forensic linguist, who attested, 'with over 95% certainty', that the assistant 'wrote approximately 70% of the [award's] three most important chapters'.[35] Ironically, Russia's counsel was himself part of the super-arbitrator elite. As such, even without hiring a presumably costly expert, he would be well aware of the drafting tasks often assigned to tribunal assistants. As someone once said: 'You sin in thinking bad about people – but, often, you guess right'.[36]

*

At this point, it is worth asking: *cui bono*? What are the reasons behind the invisibility of international judicial bureaucrats? Two sets of arguments are commonly put forward by practitioners and scholars alike.

The first argument relates to the perceived legitimacy of international adjudication. As a relatively recent phenomenon, international courts are in a fragile institutional position – certainly more so than their domestic counterparts. Indeed, even the most powerful among them

---

[34] C. Partasides, 'Secretaries to Arbitral Tribunals', in B. Hanotiau and A. Mourre (eds.), *Players' Interaction in International Arbitration* 84 (Kluwer Law International, 2015).
[35] Howse, 'The Fourth Man'.
[36] This quote, of uncertain origin, is usually attributed to Pope Pius XI.

must rely to a great extent on 'the goodwill of their constituents for both support and compliance'.[37] One way to ensure that states remain committed to international adjudication is to give them tools to exercise some measure of political oversight over the functioning of courts and tribunals. In particular, diplomats routinely engage in complex negotiations when it comes to the appointment of international judges.[38] Such carefully selected individuals are expected to remain at the helm of the judicial process. Emphasizing the routine activities of judicial assistants may convey the impression that adjudicators abdicate their responsibilities in favour of faceless bureaucrats with no direct investiture. In turn, this impression may diminish the legitimacy of courts and tribunals in the eyes of their constituent states, which may prove less inclined to comply with judicial decisions.

The problem is particularly acute in the field of ISDS, whose legitimacy has been facing severe backlash in recent years. As the parties' counsel invest considerable time and money setting up the strategy for the appointment of arbitrators, the members of the tribunal are contractually bound to discharge their duties in person, without delegating their judicial functions to third-parties. Failure to do so would amount to a breach of the principle of *intuitu personae*,[39] erode state support to the system, and exacerbate the 'lack of trust towards arbitrators'.[40]

These preoccupations have led a number of arbitral institutions to adopt rules and recommendations on the use of secretaries. According to those guidelines, only the members of an arbitral tribunal are allowed to participate in deliberations, with no other person admitted to the room unless the tribunal decides otherwise.[41] Secretaries are expected to perform mere organizational and administrative tasks.[42] Against this backdrop, it has

---

[37] J. L. Gibson, G. A. Caldeira, and V. A. Baird, 'On the Legitimacy of National High Courts' (1998) 92(2) AmPolSciRev 343.

[38] See e.g. Slaughter and Helfer, 'Why States Create International Tribunals', 946–9; E. Voeten, 'The Politics of International Judicial Appointments' (2009) 9(2) ChiJIntlL 387.

[39] See e.g. Tercier, 'Secretary', 537; C. J. Moxley, Jr., 'Selecting the Ideal Arbitrator' (2005) 60(3) DispResJ 1, 3–4; Polkinghorne and Rosenberg, 'Secretary'; T. Carbonneau, *Cases and Materials on Arbitration Law and Practice* (7th edn., Thomson/West, 2015), 14; Timlin, 'The Swiss Supreme Court', 268, 272–4.

[40] Tercier, 'Secretary', 554. See also Restemayer, 'Bad Rep', 337–8.

[41] See e.g. Article 15(2) of the ICSID Rules of Procedure for Arbitration Proceedings.

[42] See e.g. 'ICC Note on the Appointment, Duties and Remuneration of Administrative Secretaries', in L. W. Newman and M. J. Radine, *Soft Law in International Arbitration* (Juris, 2014) 235, 236–7.

been argued that revealing the extensive involvement of judicial assistants in ISDS – especially if the parties are unaware of that involvement – may unleash a 'perfect storm' able to destroy the system altogether.[43]

Albeit compelling at first glance, the legitimacy narrative proves unconvincing on closer scrutiny. For one thing, its proponents show little confidence in the ability of international adjudicators to remain in charge. In fact, issues arising from principal-agent relationships are common to most expertise-driven systems, from statutory legislation to economic policy-making, without for that reason spurring the same concerns as those associated with international judicial bureaucrats. When a client seeks the services of a legal counsel, they do not expect the firm's managing partner to perform all the required tasks personally, or to write all the briefs without the help of subordinates.[44] Similarly, our representatives in parliament seldom write – and sometimes do not even read – the bills that affect our daily lives.[45]

Yet, curiously, we seem more inclined to accept that the lawmaker we elected delegates the drafting of statutes than to concede that an international judge may rely on the help of legal assistants. At this point, someone may retort that adjudicators are in a unique position, which differs from that of all other decision-makers. But how so, exactly? When it comes to legitimacy, how can we distinguish the duty to impartially interpret and apply rules from, say, the duty to faithfully fulfil an electoral mandate? Actually, assertions about the exceptionalism of judges[46] often go hand in hand with claims about the determinate, objective, and rational nature of legal norms.[47] If international law has a preordained meaning ready to be excavated, why should we be worried about the interpreter relying on assistance in carrying out the excavation exercise? The force of law will always prevail!

---

[43] Douglas, 'Secretary', 88. Besides, let us not forget that, unlike judges in standing international courts, arbitrators are on the market for appointments, remuneration, and prestige. See Dezalay and Garth, *Dealing in Virtue*, 7 (quoting J. Werner, 'Competition within the Arbitration Industry' (1985) 2(2) JIntlArb 5, 6). Therefore, an arbitrator who is too talkative with regard to the support she receives from their assistants may run the risk of revealing precious trade secrets to competitors.

[44] Tercier, 'Secretary', 538.

[45] See e.g. S. Gailmard, 'Accountability and Principal-Agent Theory', in M. Bovens, R. E. Goodin, and T. Schillemans (eds.), *The Oxford Handbook of Public Accountability* (Oxford University Press, 2014) 90, 95–101.

[46] See e.g. E. O'Connell, 'The Natural Superiority of Courts', in U. Fastenrath et al. (eds.), *From Bilateralism to Community Interest: Essays in Honour of Judge Bruno Simma* (Oxford University Press, 2011) 1040.

[47] For discussion of this dominant view, see *infra*, pp. 226–7.

The second common argument turns, so to speak, the legitimacy narrative on its head. Instead of focusing on the perceived authority of international courts, it points the finger at the bad faith of international bureaucracies. Those bureaucracies would be part of a power struggle whereby judicial reasoning is just a rhetorical tool to confer a veneer of objectivity to the discretional expression of policy preferences. Working in the shadows like puppet masters, bureaucrats set out the courts' agendas, guide judges in the articulation of legal analysis, and keep jurisprudential departures from established case law in check. Seen from this angle, the invisibility of bureaucrats ceases to be a condemnation to irrelevance and, instead, becomes a convenient shield behind which they preserve the 'back-room discourse'[48] of judicial politics from public accountability and overt challenge.

The roots of this narrative can be traced back to Max Weber, who observed that a bureaucracy seeks to increase its superiority by keeping its intentions secret and 'hid[ing] its knowledge and action from criticism as well as it can'.[49] Critical Legal Studies built on Weber's ideas and looked more specifically at the functioning of judicial bureaucracies. In his trenchant *Critique of Adjudication*, Duncan Kennedy targeted the false-consciousness of US courts, which seek shelter from contestation by casting their decisions as the inevitable product of legal rationality. People running judicial institutions, writes Kennedy, 'operate in bad faith in the same way judges do'.[50] While they perceive their missions as technically defined, they 'constantly deploy their resources, they constantly work, just as judges do, to shape and reshape the necessity that they are supposed merely to submit to'.[51]

Others have observed that judicial bureaucrats, like any other global experts, prefer to operate beneath the surface in order to perpetuate their 'hugely unrecognized influence' and exercise 'invisible governance'.[52] Their continued relevance as players in the adjudication game rests precisely on their depiction as technical experts with no political clout. Any recognition of their discretion would expose them to controversy and therefore diminish their power.[53]

---

[48] D. Kennedy, *A Critique of Adjudication (Fin de Siècle)* (Harvard University Press, 1997), 369.
[49] Weber, *Economy and Society*, 992.
[50] Kennedy, *A Critique of Adjudication*, 369.
[51] Ibid.
[52] J. Trondal et al., *Unpacking International Organizations: The Dynamics of Compound Bureaucracies* (Manchester University Press, 2010), 97, 99.
[53] Kennedy, 'Challenging Expert Rule', 17.

For all its apparent poignancy, this 'bad faith' account inaccurately portrays the international judicial community as sharply divided into two camps: on one side, courts and tribunals concealing their shady secrets behind closed doors; on the other, the rest of the community – government officials, private counsel, civil society organizations, scholars, etc. – desperately trying to penetrate those secrets in the name of transparency and accountability. If the conspiracy of silence were that one-sided, with one camp withholding information and the other seeking access to it, it would not be much of a conspiracy. In fact, as discussed, things do not work this way. At least some participants in the community, irrespective of their roles and functions, are aware of the existence and tasks of judicial bureaucrats and acquiesce to silence. The three monkeys always act in concert.

But then – why is it so? If legitimacy concerns and institutional bad faith are not at stake, what drives our reluctance to recognize international judicial bureaucrats as relevant actors in adjudication? Probably the rituals, the *habitus*, and the self-image that the international judicial community has cultivated over the last fifty years. Like any other profession, we international lawyers are informally and contextually bound to a common 'repertoire of communal resources, words, tools, ways of doing things, stories, symbols, and discourse'.[54]

Some of the most pervasive foundational myths in our discipline derive from Anglo-Saxon legal traditions,[55] where judges enjoy great prestige and occupy an exalted position.[56] In our quest for relevance, we have meticulously constructed a fictional (or at least outdated) portrait of The Judge as a venerable sage who, from the heights of wisdom, gracefully pens the decisions that we study at law school.[57] In a world of irrational politics, this high-minded vision confers an aura of sanctity, mystery, and even beauty to our enterprise. Revealing the inner workings of international courts and tribunals may shatter the *illusio*[58] of the Herculean Judge and show the international judicial process for what it really is: a humble laboratory where very important decisions are taken collectively by very ordinary men and women.

---

[54] Adler, *Communitarian International Relations*, 15. See also Cohen, 'Finding International Law, Part II'.
[55] See e.g. M. Koskenniemi, *The Gentle Civilizer of Nations: The Rise and Fall of International Law 1870–1960* (Cambridge University Press, 2004), 353–412.
[56] See Terris, Romano, and Swigart, *The International Judge*, 87–8.
[57] Douglas, 'Secretary', 89.
[58] On the concept of *illusio* as the motivating factor to keep playing a game, see P. Bourdieu, *Practical Reason: On the Theory of Action* (Stanford University Press, 1998), 76–7.

At the same time, silence perpetuates the protection of the international judicial community from the external interference of competing social forces. As discussed,[59] the community comprises a close-knit group of individuals who gained universal recognition only in relatively recent times, after having long suffered the mockery of their domestic colleagues.[60] The relative tightness of the community stems from the connections of its members and the revolving door that exists among the bench, the bureaucracy, government departments, law firms, NGOs, and research centres. It is only natural that the inner circle of international dispute settlers would wish to maintain its capital for at least some time to come. A most effective way to secure relevance and prestige is to remain the only ones in the know, the sole initiates to the arcane mysteries of international adjudication. While the various community participants compete with each other for dominance and persuasion, they also show a striking 'closeness of interests'[61] when it comes to the external relations of their club with society at large.

The twofold structure of the community – internal struggle and external autonomy – explains why its members all acquiesce to the injunction to silence concerning the role of judicial bureaucracies. The counsel regularly appearing before international courts have an obvious interest in preserving the status quo. As we know,[62] their inside-out knowledge of the intricacies of adjudication grants them a competitive advantage over new entrants in the litigation market.

Likewise, academics devoted to the study of an international judicial system often have direct or indirect stakes in the system itself. For instance, much of the writing on investment treaty arbitration 'is done by authors who themselves are involved in [it]'[63] as either adjudicators or counsel. Similarly, European Union law scholarship is dominated by 'authors working for institutions structurally geared towards the expansion and consolidation of a genuine European legal order'.[64] Similar findings may apply to human rights, environmental, and trade law scholarship as well. The gravitation of scholars around specific courts and tribunals is strengthened by a panoply of thematic fora, ranging from traditional

---

[59] See *supra*, Chapter 2.
[60] See B. Simma, 'Fragmentation in a Positive Light' (2004) 25(4) MichJIntlL 845, 845–6; d'Aspremont, 'Professionalisation', 22–3.
[61] Bourdieu, 'The Force of Law', 842.
[62] See *supra*, pp. 69–71.
[63] Schill, 'W(h)ither Fragmentation?', 894.
[64] Schepel and Wesseling, 'The Legal Community', 171.

academic conferences to dedicated internet spaces, such as the OGEMID[65] or the International Economic Law and Policy Blog,[66] where practitioners and academics, selected on an invitation basis, exchange opinions every day. Several institutions, such as the WTO, have internal publishing houses on which they exert direct editorial control.

This contiguity between the bench and the academe poses an 'obstacle for independent and clear positioning'.[67] Any attempt to speak up could expose a scholar to the resentment of their colleagues on the court, and even undermine their continued membership in the club. Most remarkable is the continued silence of those who, for one reason or another, retire from the game. Maybe they fear that breaching the trust of one professional community today may hamper their career prospects with another community tomorrow. However, something else may be at work. Perhaps an enduring sense of gratitude, which sacrifices retrospective self-reflexivity at the altar of nostalgia. Or, perhaps, the need to believe that serving the international Rule of Law meant something more ennobling or more durable than the 'humble immanence'[68] of the judicial field.

Whatever the reasons, we hope that the remainder of this book helps shed light on the unseen and unspoken role of bureaucracies as a key actor in international adjudication. Not only to let Matt, Sophie, Aphrodite, Soledad and Carlos explain their job to outsiders without the risk of being fired. But also because such an overt recognition would re-focus our attention and let us overcome the many tensions silence carries with it. By finally acknowledging the elephant in the room, we might stop 'gingerly skirt[ing] the perimeter' of taboo topics[69] and break free from the 'labyrinthine social maze of closed doors and ever-narrower passages'.[70]

Over time, the elephant would shrink in size and become less threatening, eventually turning into another social fact with which we can grapple, and upon which we can build. When, in 2013, the CIA declassified information about Area 51, it turned out that its facilities were merely a testing site for aerial surveillance programmes. All speculation and conspiracy theories were instantly put to rest.

---

[65] Transnational Dispute Management website, www.transnational-dispute-management.com/. For a description of the social role of OGEMID, see Schill, 'W(h)ither Fragmentation?', 886–7.
[66] International Economic Law and Policy Blog, http://worldtradelaw.typepad.com/ielpblog/.
[67] Schill, 'W(h)ither Fragmentation?', 894. See also J. L. Dunoff, 'International Legal Scholarship at the Millennium' (2000) 1(1) ChiJIntlL 85, 89.
[68] Latour, *The Making of Law*, 196.
[69] R. Wajnyb, *The Silence: How Tragedy Shapes Talk* (Allen and Unwin, 2001), 246.
[70] Zerubavel, *Elephant*, 84.

# 7

## The Lyophilization of Life

Matt and Sophie have never met each other. We already know that.[1] Therefore, it must be a pure coincidence that, this morning, they are doing the exact same thing: staring at the voluminous dossiers on their desks. The binders contain the parties' briefs and supporting evidence in the respective cases. For Matt, it is the European Union's and Indonesia's submissions in *EU – Palm Oil*; for Sophie, the Philippines' and Malaysia's memorials in *Sovereignty over the Territory of Sabah, North Borneo*. Two very different disputes, which nonetheless share the fact of comprising vast amounts of paper: each legal brief largely exceeds 200 pages, and each party has produced some 150–200 exhibits.

Our two young and hopeful lawyers, all of a sudden, feel a little older and definitely less hopeful. Going through the piles of material is a slow and painful process that will take most of their time for the weeks to come. The size of the two disputes will demand special care with references and footnotes. Yet, both Matt and Sophie find the sight of the cardboard binders strangely soothing. For all their intimidating thickness, they have a certain stillness to them, as if all the noise and drama that led to their formation had crystallized into a quiet and disciplined body of paper. The covers of the folders delineate the outer boundaries of the cases, the limits beyond which neither Matt nor Sophie will have to venture.

To be sure, the records still resonate with a faint echo of the indignation and upheaval that gave rise to the proceedings. Somewhere in a distant land, people rallied in the streets to claim their ancestral right to occupy a territory in South East Asia, defiant of police repression.[2] Somewhere else, NGOs issued alarming reports about the unsustainable methods used in palm oil production, where they denounced the brutal ill treatment of workers, warned against the calamitous consequences of

---

[1] See *supra*, pp. 121–2.
[2] See *supra*, p. 73.

savage deforestation, and showed pictures of helpless orangutans being forced out of their natural habitats.[3]

Both cases saw lawmakers, diplomats, economists, lobbyists, advocacy groups, and scientific advisors make opposing assertions, voice competing concerns, and resort to all sorts of strategies to delegitimize their adversaries. Bills were passed, referenda were held, and policy debates raged. Flipping through the pages of the binders, one finds traces of that ferment. In Matt's case, the evidence includes not only 'dry' trade documents, but also government press releases, scientific reports, *amicus curiae* briefs from environmentalist organizations, and surveys about the tastes and preferences of European palm oil consumers. In Sophie's dossier, one finds yellowed colonial maps, ancient declarations of independence, and history book excerpts.

Yet, these are but inanimate signs, the ossified remains of past conflicts. At some point, someone decided to turn social and political turmoil into a *legal* claim. Maybe a Philippine official thought that a clear territorial delimitation by the ICJ could ease the international tensions with Malaysia while, at the same time, showing protesters that the government had their back. Perhaps the representatives of the Indonesian palm oil industry managed, after much insistence, to persuade the trade ministry that a WTO case against the European Union would advance Indonesia's economic and development interests. We will never know for sure.

Surely, however, recourse to international adjudication has brought about a fundamental metamorphosis of the underlying conflict. The unfathomable complexity of context has somehow been channelled into a few thousand pages of briefs and exhibits.[4] The initiators of this transformation, as we know,[5] are the parties' counsel who, after months of meticulous work, have turned amorphous sets of facts and grievances into coherent legal narratives.

Now that the parties' filings have reached the ICJ and the WTO, the transformation continues. Matt and Sophie are next in the chain of 'amanuenses'[6] who, tirelessly and discretely, *lyophilize* life into a binary legal equation – the only form in which it can be adjudicated by an international court. As lyophilization progresses, the folders of relevant materials will become thinner and thinner. The most salient information will be

---

[3] See e.g. Say No to Palm Oil website, https://saynotopalmoil.org/.
[4] See Schlag, 'Spam Jurisprudence', 816.
[5] See *supra*, pp. 82–4.
[6] Latour, *The Making of Law*, 77.

gradually selected while the rest will fall into the background. Memoranda will be prepared which summarize the parties' arguments, distil the core issues to be addressed, and suggest options for solution. Eventually, a judgment will emerge which obscures all the intricacies, inconsistencies, and hesitations that marked every step of the process. After much meandering, the law will become The Law.

This explains Matt and Sophie's ambivalent feelings about the files they have just received. On the one hand, they are relieved by the finite nature of the binders. Thanks to the parties' initial distillation of information, the two judicial assistants are free to concentrate on what really matters: legal norms to be interpreted and applied to the facts. No longer are they required to dig out the history of their cases or to Google-search the underlying crises. In fact, their impartiality duties demand that they *refrain* from looking outside the four corners of the files. Their physical removal from the places where the disputes originated enables them to carry out their duties with a measure of serenity. 'Fortunately the world is so, so far away!'[7]

On the other hand, being green on the job, Matt and Sophie have yet to learn the art of emotional detachment from the object of their cases. Sometimes, they regret not having time to fully understand the broader context. Maybe, greater awareness would help them understand the legal issues in dispute or, at least, get a better idea of where the parties are coming from. These hopes are in vain. The transmutation of social conflicts into judicial proceedings comes with profound epistemic limitations. Once raised before international courts, common-sense concepts turn into legal concepts, whose defining feature is 'precisely their (potential) divergence' from empirical reality.[8] Throughout the process, certain aspects of life gain focus and prominence, while many others become unknowable, unspeakable, and unthinkable. Sometimes, Matt and Sophie feel as though they were looking at the world through the shadows projected on the walls of Plato's cave.[9] What they see is not reality itself – but only a vaguely resembling replica of reality, made of intricate legal constructs.

If that is so, imagine the frustration experienced by Aphrodite and Soledad, who, as part of their daily jobs, are routinely faced with grievous

---

[7] Quino, *Toda Mafalda* (8th edn., Ediciones de la Flor, 1997), 332.
[8] A. Lang, 'Governing "As If": Global Subsidies Regulation and the Benchmark Problem' (2014) 67(1) CLP 135, 150. See also K. Knop, R. Michaels, and A. Riles, 'From Multiculturalism to Technique: Feminism, Culture and the Conflict of Laws Style' (2012) 64(3) StanLRev 589.
[9] Plato, *Republic* (ca. 380 BC), Book VII, 514a–520a.

claims of human rights violations. How are they supposed to remain impassive to the mourning of a mother who has lost her son, to stories of prison mistreatment, or to the discrimination of LGBT+ communities? Yet, Aphrodite and Soledad must strive to maintain some distance and avoid losing perspective. The ethics of their expertise are akin to those of a doctor: if you get too emotionally attached to your patients, you cannot be objective about their health.

There is no escaping this moment of disempowerment, this mismatch between the unknowable reality outside the court and the knowable simulacrum of reality that transpires from the papers. But perhaps it is best so. What would happen if a judicial assistant set out to fully understand the context that gave rise to a dispute? Not only would the exercise be unreasonably time-consuming – it would be paralysing. Our overzealous bureaucrat would get tangled in a web of social, political, and cultural nuances. It would turn out that every party has some plausible reason for acting the way it did. The case would become unsolvable.

And yet, the case must be solved. As a communicative system, international adjudication operates according to a strict 'binary code', revolving around dichotomies like lawful/unlawful, conformity/deviation, legitimate/illegitimate, and the like.[10] Nuance and indecision are simply not contemplated by that code. A court could never say: 'since everyone appears to have good arguments, we decline (or are unable) to reach a conclusion'. That would amount to an impermissible *non liquet*.[11] The very essence of the judges' mandate is to declare a winner and a loser, to apportion rights and wrongs – to express a *judgment*.[12] And, as Max Weber put it, whenever a man expresses a judgment on the facts, 'a complete understanding of the facts *comes to an end*'.[13]

•

Matt and Sophie's first task in the preparation of the respective cases is to summarize the parties' arguments. Given the length, complexity, and

---

[10] See N. Luhmann, *Das Recht der Gesellschaft* (Suhrkamp, 1993), 61; W. N. Hohfeld, 'Fundamental Legal Conceptions as Applied in Judicial Reasoning' (1917) 26(8) YaleLJ 710; M. Koskenniemi, 'Hierarchy in International Law: A Sketch' (1997) 8(4) EJIL 566, 568.
[11] See P. Weil, 'The Court Cannot Conclude Definitely … Non Liquet Revisited' (1997) 36(1&2) ColumJTransnatlL 109, 110.
[12] See e.g. R. S. Summers, 'Formal Legal Truth and Substantive Truth in Judicial Fact-Finding: Their Justified Divergence in Some Particular Cases' (1999) 18(5) L&Phil 497, 505.
[13] M. Weber, 'Science as a Vocation' (1919), in *The Vocation Lectures* (D. S. Owen and T. B. Strong eds., Hackett, 2004), 21 (original emphasis).

occasional fuzziness of written briefs, it is crucial that they be pre-digested and streamlined before being circulated to the judges. The goal here is to identify the most salient points made by each litigant while, at the same time, ironing out colourful language and excising non-legal considerations.

Volume reduction is of the essence. Björn, for instance, instructed Matt that the ideal ratio between the length of the original submission and that of the summaries should be circa 10:1, and in no case exceed 3:1. Judge Lehmann was less specific and did not quantify how much fat Sophie should trim from the parties' memorials. He put it eloquently:

'Just cut through the crap.'

Succinctness aside, there is little indication of how to prepare summaries. This lack of guidance might be intentional: in some courts, interns and junior lawyers are expected to go through the exercise as their first testing ground. As Matt is still waiting for his new intern, he will have to summarize himself this time. He places the briefs next to his computer, opens the pre-formatted template (Verdana size 9, line-spacing 1.5) and types in the title: 'Main claims and arguments of the participants'. Other judicial bureaucrats work on templates, too: Carlos on that developed *ad hoc* for Gal Elmosnino LLP; Aphrodite and Soledad on those available on the ECtHR and IACtHR internal servers. Because the internal practices of the ICJ are somewhat less standardized, Sophie will have to content herself with a blank Word document.

A week into the task, Matt is still scratching his head over the parties' positions. On both sides, the arguments are repetitive, convoluted, and scattered all over the texts of the submissions. To be fair, the EU palm oil regulation[14] and the panel's findings thereon are quite complicated, too.

The panel has ruled in favour of Indonesia. It found that: (i) imported and domestic palm oil products are 'like' within the meaning of Article III:4 of the GATT and Article 2.1 of the TBT Agreement; and (ii) by excluding from the EU market most Indonesian palm oil products on the ground that they do not carry the RSPO label, the EU palm oil regulation unlawfully discriminates against those products. The panel also dismissed the European Union's defences. After a lengthy examination of the evidence, it concluded that the measure at issue is 'necessary' to protect public morals and 'human, animal or plant life or health', thereby being provisionally justified under Articles XX(a) and XX(b). However, the panel

---

[14] See *supra*, p. 80.

found that, by relying exclusively on the RSPO criteria and not according market access to products carrying equivalent labels, the measure results in arbitrary and unjustifiably discrimination under the *chapeau* of Article XX. For the same reasons, the panel concluded that the measure does not stem exclusively from a legitimate regulatory distinction under Article 2.1 of the TBT Agreement. Finally, as Duncan had predicted,[15] the panel attached no significance whatsoever to the FTA that would allegedly allow the European Union to maintain the palm oil regulation in place.

In short, Jane and her law firm have scored a crushing victory at the panel stage, against which Duncan and Jasper are now appealing. The European Union's appeal challenges virtually all of the panel's findings. Unsurprisingly, Indonesia is requesting the Appellate Body to uphold them all. This 'kitchen sink approach' has its drawbacks. Had the European Union been more selective in its appeal, the Appellate Body and its supporting staff would have had more time to focus on the most salient issues at stake. Instead, they will have to rush through an avalanche of claims and dispose of them rather summarily. But then again, given the sensitivity of the case at hand, it is normal that Duncan and Jasper would spare no ammunition to prevail. Any restraint on their part could have been construed as a lack of interest or conviction.

What really strikes Matt is the difference in tone and argumentative style between the two appellate submissions. According to the European Union, the adoption of measures governing the content, packaging, and labelling of food products 'is a fundamental policy prerogative of sovereign states and a common governance tool in advanced economies'. Throughout the brief, the European public is depicted as 'citizens' concerned about the sustainability of palm oil production and as responsible 'consumers' seeking greater access to information about food processing.

As he goes through the text, Matt increasingly identifies with the image of the *citizen-consumer*.[16] This narrative seems to perfectly capture the ethos, sensibility, and modes of governance of Europe's social capitalism. The society that transpires from the submission is made of educated, self-aware individuals who carefully pick up goods from supermarket shelves while, at the same time, wishing to make a positive impact in the world. Citizen-consumer discourse enables the adoption of measures, such as

---

[15] See *supra*, pp. 99–101.
[16] For discussion, see e.g. J. Johnston, 'The Citizen-Consumer Hybrid: Ideological Tensions and the Case of Whole Foods Market' (2008) 37(3) Theory&Soc'y 229.

the EU palm oil regulation, that unilaterally impose economic burdens on domestic and foreign producers in order to induce virtuous behaviour, without interfering directly with the sovereignty of other nations. A sort of 'legislation for humanity'[17] that seeks to address global welfare concerns through sheer market force.

Indonesia's submission tells a whole different story: one where the production and exportation of palm oil are crucial for the development of a nation recovering from a dire economic recession.[18] According to Indonesia, the EU measure is 'contradictory' in its pursuit of its stated goals and, behind 'the veneer of moral righteousness', conceals a protectionist intent that effectively strips Indonesian citizens of a legitimate source of income. In a way, Indonesia is contrasting the image of the citizen-consumer with that of a *developmental citizen*, who strives for the advancement and modernization of their country's economy and 'whose highest priority is the national collective good'.[19]

Reading Indonesia's brief, Matt finds himself sympathizing with the developmental citizen, and his approval of the European Union's position begins to fade. Matt relishes this feeling of hesitation. As they often do, the opposed counsel have managed to instil a doubt in his mind – the doubt that *both* parties could be right.

Meanwhile, Sophie is going through similar motions. In their memorials, the Philippines and Malaysia both articulate complex narratives to assert their competing territorial claims over North Borneo. Here too, the tone and style of the two briefs differ wildly.

The Philippines grounds its narrative on the colonial past of South East Asia. Its story reads like an enthralling historical treatise. In 1878, the Sultan of Sulu, then a recognized international actor, signed a deed granting rights to three European adventurers over the Northern Bornean part of his domains. According to the Philippines, the deed was a private lease (albeit in perpetuity) and not a full-fledged cession of sovereignty. In 1888, an agreement between the British North Borneo Company and the British Crown created the State of North Borneo as an overseas territory under

---

[17] See E. Benvenisti, 'Legislating for Humanity: May States Compel Foreigners to Promote Global Welfare?', in R. Liivoja and J. Petman eds., *International Law-making: Essays in Honour of Jan Klabbers* (Routledge, 2014) 1.

[18] A position Indonesia already took at the end of the 1990s. See Article 21.3(c) Arbitration Report, *Indonesia – Certain Measures Affecting the Automobile Industry*, WT/DS54/15, WT/DS55/14, WT/DS59/13, WT/DS64/12 (7 December 1998), para. 24.

[19] P. Kitley, *Television, Nation, and Culture in Indonesia* (Ohio Center for International Studies, 2000), 329.

British protection. After the Japanese occupation in World War II, in 1946 Britain reinstated North Borneo as one of its colonies. In 1962, the heirs of the Sultan of Sulu announced the transfer of sovereignty over North Borneo to the Philippines, the Sultanate's successor under international law. In 1963, North Borneo achieved independence from the British and joined newly formed Malaysia. The Philippines now claims the land as its own. In its view, Britain's creation of the State of North Borneo as a territory separate from the Sultanate of Sulu is illegal, for the Sultan's deed of 1878 had never ceded sovereignty over that territory. Therefore, the Philippines concludes, the incorporation of North Borneo into Malaysia is to be considered of no legal effect.[20]

Malaysia's memorial has a completely different flavour. Instead of referring to remote historical events, it focuses on the right to self-determination of Northern Bornean residents. In particular, in 1963, UN Secretary-General U Thant held a consultation in the newly independent North Borneo. In response, a sizeable majority of the people was in favour of joining Malaysia. In light of these events, the Philippines' pre-colonial and colonial claims must be considered as devoid of merit.[21]

Sitting at her desk, the memorials open in front of her, Sophie nervously taps her foot on the floor. At first glance, the Philippines and Malaysia have both put forward convincing reasons to assert their sovereignty over the disputed territory: succession of states on one side, self-determination of peoples on the other. Sophie starts wondering how Judge Lehmann will go about it. How can the Court strike an appropriate balance between two competing principles that are both cardinal tenets of international law? Weighing them against each other, she thinks, would be 'like trying to weigh precisely a handful of feathers against a handful of grass: it can be done, but not very convincingly'.[22]

The parties' memorials, as they stand now, are *irreducibly* incompatible. Not only do they invoke different doctrines of international law, they also draw different connections between the relevant rules, attribute

---

[20] These arguments are based on real submissions submitted to the ICJ by the Philippines. See *Pulau* judgment on third-party intervention, Oral Pleadings (25 June 2001), CR 2001/1 (verbatim record). See also N. Berman, 'The Quest for Rationality: The Recent Writings of Tom Franck' (2003) 35(2) NYUJILP 339, 344–5.
[21] This, too, is based on a true story. See *Pulau* judgment on third-party intervention, Observations of Malaysia (2 May 2001), paras. 10–11.
[22] *Sovereignty over Pulau Ligitan and Pulau Sipadan (Indonesia v. Malaysia)*, Judgment of 17 December 2002, ICJ Rep. 2002, 625, Dissenting Opinion of Judge *ad hoc* Franck, para. 17. See also Berman, 'The Quest for Rationality', 343.

salience to different facts, and largely ignore the opponent's logic.[23] The Philippines and Malaysia are talking past each other. Skim through their memorials, and you will hardly believe they are talking about the same dispute. Sophie smiles: she has just realized that the expression 'to make one's case' means more than she thought.

*

By summarizing, incommensurability must somehow be reduced to commensurability. In a sense, a good summarizer is an expert Lego player. They must be able to deconstruct the parties' submissions into their basic building blocks, tinker with their order, test their interconnections, and try to reconstruct them in a less adversarial, more harmonious way. If the parties have produced a fruit salad of legal, factual, ethical, and policy arguments, one has to carefully separate its components and proverbially compare apples and apples, oranges and oranges.

Of course, any Lego player knows that there are countless ways to assemble the pieces and that no two constructions are exactly alike. Similarly, the reconstruction of the parties' logics is not an exact science, but implies a series of choices based on the reader's inclinations and sensibilities. What Matt considers as a solid argument, worth a couple of pages of summaries, might seem completely devoid of merit to Sophie; where Sophie sees two radically incompatible statements, Matt might see two different ways of saying the same thing. As discussed,[24] the scope and nature of the parties' arguments will not remain static throughout the proceedings, but gradually evolve, become more refined, and gain focus thanks to the repeated exchanges between the court and the parties. At each new interaction, the summarizers will keep selecting the legal points they deem salient, focus on certain factual elements to the exclusion of others, etc.[25]

This process of 'denial, reduction, abstraction, [and] essentialization'[26] puts a great deal of influence in the hands of judicial bureaucrats. Typically, the adjudicators do not have the time nor the patience to go through the parties' lengthy briefs, and much prefer to rely on the summaries prepared by their assistants. Therefore, deciding what gets summarized, and how, has a profound impact on the judges' perception

---

[23] Once again, Duncan was right. See *supra*, pp. 94–5.
[24] See *supra*, pp. 82–4.
[25] Umberto Eco described this hermeneutic process as one of 'abduction'. See U. Eco, *The Limits of Interpretation* (Indiana University Press, 1991), 152–62.
[26] Schlag, 'Spam Jurisprudence', 816.

of the arguments and their appraisal of the issues at stake. In turn, shaping how problems are defined is the first step towards narrowing the range of solutions considered.[27]

The drafting of summaries has other tangible effects. As they fill in the pages of their templates and patiently annotate the paragraphs of the submissions, Matt and Sophie grow increasingly *invested* in their respective cases. Vague and unrefined thoughts begin to pop up in their heads: potentially useful precedents, relevant academic articles, or simply instinctive reactions to this or that argument put forward by either party. Whether they realize or not, they have already started to *evaluate* the merits – or, at least, to develop a first impression, a gut feeling about the direction the proceedings will take. Matt and Sophie feel the thrill of being the only ones in the know. At this stage, neither the Appellate Body division assigned to the *EU – Palm Oil* case nor Judge Lehmann have probably read a single line.

At the same time, the epistemic exclusions inherent in the judicialization of conflicts are in full swing. The context has faded away, obscured by the congeries of legal claims and defences presented to the court. Indonesia and the European Union are no longer juxtaposing citizen-consumer and developmental citizens. Instead, as per Matt's summary, they are now arguing over: (i) criteria for establishing 'likeness'; (ii) the panel's 'necessity' analysis; and (iii) the relevance of bilateral FTAs in WTO proceedings. The Philippines and Malaysia are no longer trying to make sense of the history of the Northern Bornean people. As Sophie's summaries explain, they are now focusing on: (i) whether 'the Sultanate of Sulu can be considered as the Philippines' predecessor under international law'; (ii) the 'legal effects of the Sultan of Sulu's deed'; and (iii) the 'relevance of the consultation held by the UN Secretary-General in light of the principle of self-determination'.

The lyophilization of life is under way. Now we can start talking real business.

---

[27] Kennedy, 'Challenging Expert Rule', 13.

# 8

## The Memo

Choices, choices, choices...[1] The punk rock record playing in Carlos' headphones syncs almost perfectly with his frantic typing on the computer keyboard. At the end of each song, he catches his breath and checks the wall clock. It is just past 5:00 PM, so he still has a few hours to go. Before lunchtime, François Gal asked him to submit the first draft of the Memo by the end of the day. Carlos liberally interpreted the deadline as the time at which his mentor wakes up. In this line of work, 'close-of-business' is often synonymous with 'first-thing-in-the-morning'. Too bad if Professor Gal is a notoriously early riser: the silence of the office at night will help Carlos concentrate and speed up the process. By his estimate, he should complete the substantive drafting by 1:00 AM, before turning to the formatting of the references and footnotes for another three hours. At 4:00 AM, no matter what progress he has made, he will have to click 'send'. Fortunately, he thinks, this is only a rough take on the case. It does not have to be perfect – just good enough.

Carlos' night shift is not an isolated case. In fact, the 'Memo' he is now wrapping up is familiar to anyone working for Gal Elmosnino LLP. All associates at the firm are required to prepare one whenever either partner, François Gal or Jean-Pierre Elmosnino, is appointed president of an arbitral tribunal. The Memo serves to provide the president with all the information he needs to get a sense of the case and prepare the next steps of the proceedings. In addition to the summaries of the parties' arguments, discussed in Chapter 7, the document contains a thorough description of the state conduct that gave rise to the arbitration; a comprehensive review of the non-contentious facts; a preliminary assessment of the disputed

---

[1] The Buzzcocks, *Choices*.

facts and the supporting evidence; a list of the core legal issues that need to be resolved; an indication of potentially relevant case law; and a tentative analysis of the merits of the dispute.

Professor Gal, who is presiding the tribunal in *Kingsland Mining Corp. v. Turkey*, will go through Carlos' draft and submit comments in a week or so. If Carlos knows his boss, the review will take place on a long-haul business-class flight: perhaps the one that connects Vienna, where Professor Gal is delivering a lecture in the morning, to New York, where he is scheduled to meet his co-arbitrators in another proceeding. François Gal *loves* reading legal documents on planes. He finds it relaxing. Carlos does not remember him ever mentioning a novel or any other work of fiction.

Sometimes, by the time he receives the Memo, the Professor has already had the opportunity to skim through the file and the parties' submissions. In this case, he relies on the Memo simply to get a clearer picture, to know where in the record to find the relevant information, and sometimes to test his initial instincts. This time, however, Professor Gal did not go through the file. The Memo is his entry point into the current case. Carlos knows what this means: by the time the plane touches the ground, the 238 pages will be riddled with question marks, multicolour highlights, and handwritten scribbles.

If Professor Gal finds the Memo sufficiently thorough, he will circulate a redacted version to his co-arbitrators to facilitate their participation. The redacted version will retain the non-controversial portions of the document – typically, the description of the state conduct at issue, the stipulated facts, the summaries of the parties' positions, and perhaps a list of the issues to be resolved. But the juicier parts of the Memo, like the preliminary examination of the disputed facts and the initial legal assessment of the case, will *not* be circulated and will remain for the sole use of Professor Gal.

The existence of two versions of the Memo – a complete one for the arbitral president, a redacted one for the co-arbitrators – is quite common in ISDS. It would be risky for the president to share the full extent of their knowledge so early in the game, unless the three arbitrators know each other by reason of prior experience.[2] Showing one's cards too soon could prejudge the tribunal's decision at a stage where the parties have yet to present their oral arguments. It could also enable the co-arbitrators to

---

[2] See P. Bernardini, 'Organisation of Deliberations', in B. Berger and M. E. Schneider (eds.), *Inside the Black Box: How Arbitral Tribunals Operate and Reach Their Decisions* (Juris, 2013) 15, 17.

strategize in advance of the deliberations phase, thus diminishing the role and influence of the president.

One might call it distrust. François Gal simply calls it prudence. Let us not forget that arbitrators of his calibre are, first and foremost, competitors for the top positions in the ISDS field, with no other capital than their reputation and with no institutional framework to serve as a mediating agent. It is only normal that, even when they sit together on the same tribunal, arbitrators abide by an old Moroccan adage: without trust, there is no betrayal.

\*

Legal memoranda of this kind are not unique to the ISDS regime. In fact, they are arguably the second most important piece of paper in international adjudication, after the judgment itself. The preparation of these documents is often the exclusive prerogative of judicial bureaucrats, and is central to their role as *consiglieri* of the court. The memoranda discuss all the legal and factual aspects of the case at hand, and provide the adjudicators with suggestions on how to solve the issues raised by the litigants. The bureaucracies of most international courts follow standardized practices for the preparation of memoranda. While the form and content vary from one institution to another, they all tend to follow a common pattern.

For instance, whenever a WTO appeal is filed, the ABS lawyers assigned to it are expected to produce a so-called issues paper, that is, 'a background paper' containing 'a summary of the … claims and the arguments on appeal' as well as the secretariat's 'legal analyses and views on the merits of the issues appealed'.[3] The first ABS director established the practice of drafting issues papers since the Appellate Body's earliest days. Soon thereafter, the directors of Rules and Legal Affairs followed suit for panel proceedings.[4] Today, the practice is so deeply ingrained that, whenever Matt briefs new interns on their prospective duties, he invariably tells them:

'If you guys want to prove your worth, try to do two things well: the issues paper and the report.'

An ABS issues paper is a mammoth document that often exceeds 250–300 pages. According to Björn, its drafting must follow one simple rule: 'leave no stone unturned'. By contrast, the issues papers prepared by the Legal Affairs and the Rules Division tend to be more concise and

---

[3] Steger, 'The Founding', 453. See also Ehlermann, 'Revisiting the Appellate Body', 494.
[4] Hughes, 'Working in WTO Dispute Settlement', 406.

focused. The key is not to exhaust the issues at stake, but to distil the core factual and legal points on which the panel will eventually have to rule. This difference in the scope and length of issues papers might be due to the different positions that panels and the Appellate Body occupy in the hierarchy of WTO adjudicators – the latter being expected to ensure finality and thoroughness in trade dispute settlement. However, the decisive factor is probably just the distinct professional styles and sensibilities of the respective division directors.

Once the draft prepared by junior officers has been reviewed by the team leader and the division director, the issues paper is circulated to the panelists or Appellate Body members a few days before each hearing. This way, trade adjudicators can become acquainted with the dispute and start thinking about the questions they wish to ask the parties. (Spoilers alert: the secretariat will assist in the drafting of questions, too[5]). Once they have received the issues paper, panelists and Appellate Body members will carry a hard copy with them wherever they go. On a couple of occasions, the ABS administrative staff had to organize rescue missions to retrieve copies of the precious document from public transports, where they had been misplaced.

Normally, WTO adjudicators do not interfere with the preparation of issues papers, which they see as a valuable source of guidance. In recent years, however, some Appellate Body members have voiced concerns about the length of the documents and the excess of detail in the secretariat's analysis. One adjudicator once suggested that the judicial division assigned to an appeal should hold a preliminary meeting with the secretariat to decide which topics should be addressed in the issues paper and which ones should be left out. Predictably, the secretariat staunchly opposed the idea. Not only would that suggestion undermine the time-honoured 'leave no stone unturned' approach – it would also encroach on the secretariat's role as an independent provider of legal advice.

The ECtHR and the IACtHR follow slightly different practices, dictated by their own internal procedures. In Strasbourg, the in-depth examination of a case begins at the judicial phase, that is when the Court officially communicates to a responding state that a complaint has been filed against it. Usually, this official communication follows from the registry's determination that the application is not manifestly inadmissible and therefore worthy of consideration. Occasionally, however, the registry may decide to issue a communication even *without* the reasonable suspicion of a violation. For example, when a state adopts a new general regulation with

---

[5] See *infra*, pp. 261–2.

a potential impact on human rights, the registry may wish to gauge its systemic implications and elicit the views of government officials. The communication recites the complainant's description of the facts, lists the claims raised against the responding state, and normally contains some factual questions for both the complainant and the state's government.

While preparing the official communication, the registry also starts working on an *internal* draft that contains a preliminary analysis of the case and suggests options for solution.[6] Once ready, the draft is forwarded to the judge-rapporteur,[7] who signs it and presents it to the whole judicial formation for deliberation. In ECtHR lingo, this means that a case is 'Section-ripe'.[8] The breakneck pace at which the European Court churns out decisions leaves relatively little time for registry lawyers to examine each file thoroughly before presenting the results of their research to the judge-rapporteur. Indeed, it is quite common for a single registry lawyer to handle some 100 files a year.[9]

Grand Chamber cases, albeit less frequent and therefore less time-pressured, are often more complex than section cases. Hearings, which are rare in section proceedings, are routine before the Grand Chamber. Written submissions and oral pleadings are significantly more articulate. Despite its greater sophistication, the Grand Chamber process follows the same pattern as the section process: senior registry lawyers work side-by-side with the judge-rapporteur towards the preparation of the internal draft and its discussion with the other 16 judges sitting on the Grand Chamber.[10]

The IACtHR secretariat works at a more leisurely pace. Each of the eight secretariat teams handles only a few disputes at a time, most of which stretch over several years. Here too, the secretariat produces an internal draft for each case. Throughout the drafting process, the team has frequent exchanges with the judge-rapporteur, who often makes preliminary comments and requests that certain specific points be addressed or developed further. Once the draft is ready, the judge-rapporteur uses it as the basis for deliberations with their colleagues.

Aphrodite and Soledad have become quite the experts in getting their drafts ready quickly. Over time, they have learnt how best to cater for the expectations and sensibilities of judge-rapporteurs; which elements are considered informative and which anodyne; what tone to use to come

---

[6] See Arold, *ECtHR Legal Culture*, 44.
[7] The role of the judge-rapporteur will be detailed *infra*, pp. 289–92.
[8] Garlicki, 'Judicial Deliberations', 393.
[9] See Arold, *ECtHR Legal Culture*, 45.
[10] Garlicki, 'Judicial Deliberations', 394.

across as respectful and professional; and much more. Certainly, Soledad has an easier task. As the head of her secretariat team, she has no other reviewers than the judge-rapporteur. Conversely, Aphrodite's drafts must go through several layers of review, including her lead lawyer and the section registrar.[11] The ECtHR's Jurisconsult may also be involved when Aphrodite's draft raises potential conflicts with past jurisprudence.[12] Despite these differences, Soledad and Aphrodite have become so skilful that they take the preparation of drafts as a quasi-automatic exercise.

Sophie, by contrast, does not have the luxury of following standardized guidelines. For her, each new memorandum is a whole new adventure. At the ICJ, the extent of each clerk's contribution to legal research depends largely on the individual preferences of the judge to whom that clerk is assigned. This sparse approach reflects the institutional arrangements and the *habitus* of the World Court. First, as discussed,[13] judges and their clerks are bound by a one-to-one relationship, which can be easily attuned to individual needs. Indeed, the very establishment of the clerkship program in the early 2000s may be due to the judges' need for more personalized assistance than the registry alone could offer. Second, the egos on the bench may not always have patience for bureaucracy and managerialism. Their grand style and 'ritualistic' postures[14] might appear pompous, but are certainly effective in maintaining an aura of sanctity around the Peace Palace.

This being said, the World Court's practices do offer ample opportunities for clerks to get involved in the preparation of internal memoranda. All 15 judges are required to participate fully in every case – joined by one or two *ad hoc* judges when either or both parties do not have a national sitting on the bench. This requirement makes analysis and deliberation cumbersome and 'bafflingly elaborate'.[15] The ICJ's procedures, which are partially inherited from the Permanent Court of International Justice, have been explored at length elsewhere[16] and need not be restated in full here.

---

[11] See Arold, *ECtHR Legal Culture*, 44.
[12] See *supra*, pp. 127–8.
[13] See *supra*, p. 120.
[14] R. B. Lillich and G. E. White, 'The Deliberative Process of the International Court of Justice: A Preliminary Critique and Some Possible Reforms' (1976) 70(1) AJIL 28, 39.
[15] Ibid.
[16] See e.g. R. Jennings, 'The Internal Judicial Practice of the International Court of Justice' (1989) 59(1) BYBIL 31; S. Rosenne, *The Law and Practice of the International Court, 1920-2005* (Brill, 2006), 1507–610; Thirlway, 'Drafting ICJ Decisions'; Terris, Romano, and Swigart, *The International Judge*, 58–9; Kolb, *The ICJ*, 1006–18; G. I. Hernández, *The International Court of Justice and the Judicial Function* (Oxford University Press, 2014), 95–125; J. J. Quintana, *Litigation at the International Court of Justice: Practice and Procedure* (Martinus Nijhoff, 2015), 527–30.

In a nutshell, once hearings have taken place, the judges meet for a preliminary discussion of what they consider the main points in dispute. Immediately afterwards, the Court's president, aided by his special assistant and clerks, prepares an outline of 'the issues which in his opinion will require discussion and decision by the Court'.[17] At this stage, any other judge may comment or 'call attention to any other issue or question which he considers relevant'.[18]

Once the list of issues is finalized, each judge has to produce an individual note, that is a written piece where they express their 'views on the case'. The note should indicate, among other things, 'whether any questions which have been called to notice should be eliminated from further consideration'; the 'precise questions which should be answered by the Court'; the judge's 'tentative opinion as to the answers' to such questions and the 'reasons therefor'; and their 'tentative conclusion as to the correct disposal of the case'.[19] Once circulated, the notes will serve as the basis of deliberations and the subsequent formation of the Drafting Committee.[20]

The drafting of the notes is a key moment in the ICJ process. Formally, these are simple internal memoranda, ranging from a few dozen to over 100 pages, by which the judges share their opinions with their colleagues for further consideration. Substantively, however, notes often look like 'fullblown statements of a point of view and occasionally the first drafts of subsequent opinions'.[21] This practice has raised some controversy. Its enthusiasts highlight how it demands a significant effort from each judge, thereby ensuring commitment to the process and in-depth knowledge of the file.[22] Its detractors warn against the perils of writing a quasi-opinion at an early stage of the proceedings. Two former judges, for instance, have observed that once ideas have been committed to paper, it becomes 'difficult to change them'.[23] Another two have linked the practice of note drafting to the abundance of separate opinions in the Court's jurisprudence.[24]

---

[17] ICJ, *Resolution Concerning the Internal Judicial Practice of the Court*, adopted pursuant to Article 19 of the Rules of Court (12 April 1976) ('ICJ Note on Judicial Practice'), Article 3.
[18] Article 3 of the ICJ Note on Judicial Practice.
[19] Article 4 of the ICJ Note on Judicial Practice.
[20] See *infra*, pp. 281–3.
[21] Lillich and White, 'Deliberative Process', 34. See also Bedjaoui, 'The Manufacture of ICJ Judgments', 47.
[22] See Terris, Romano, and Swigart, *The International Judge*, 98.
[23] Lillich and White, 'Deliberative Process', 34, fn 49.
[24] As of October 2010, ICJ judges have expressed a total of 1,127 separate opinions. See Kolb, *The ICJ*, 1018.

After spending several weeks putting their thoughts in writing, judges loathe to make the additional effort of merging their views into the majority opinion.[25] 'Here is my decision: polish the English, fix the footnotes, and publish it!'

The extent to which clerks are involved in the preparation of the notes depends on the individual preferences of each judge. Some judges are quite jealous of their prerogatives and keep most of the work for themselves.[26] Other judges, perhaps busier on other fronts or less proficient in international law, are happy to rely on their assistants for research, analysis, and even drafting.[27] Of course, this reliance takes place under conditions of strict confidentiality, given that judges are expected to write their notes 'by their own efforts'.[28] Acknowledging that a junior lawyer contributed to a fundamental step of the process would be tantamount to admitting to a lack of authority and expertise, thereby incurring the reprobation of colleagues.

Jürgen Lehmann has taken, so to speak, the middle ground. Whenever he has to write a note, he asks Sophie to think carefully about the issues circulated by the President. 'If you see any additional questions we should consider, let me know.' Once the list of issues is finalized, the two discuss them at length – usually sipping wine at the *Restaurant des Juges*, a high-end canteen where judges and staff can enjoy three-course meals prepared by trainee cooks. Typically, Judge Lehmann identifies one or two topics where Sophie's help would be most valuable, and asks her to conduct preliminary research in the form of memos. The research may entail the examination of a set of exhibits, the collection of relevant precedents, or a more open-ended analysis of the assigned issues.

Once Sophie has submitted the results of her work, Judge Lehmann reviews them and incorporates the relevant portions into the main draft he has been preparing in the meantime. Sophie is then asked to go through the whole text to spot internal inconsistencies, challenge the factual or legal points with which she disagrees, and test the validity and persuasiveness of her mentor's reasoning. Needless to say, Sophie takes great pride in the exercise. Although Judge Lehmann seldom accepts her views, the fact he bothers to ask for her advice is a source of constant gratification.

\*

---

[25] See Terris, Romano, and Swigart, *The International Judge*, 98.
[26] Ibid., 57–8.
[27] Ibid., 58.
[28] Kolb, *The ICJ*, 1007.

To sum up: whether called an issues paper, a note, or otherwise, the Memo is an essential piece in the puzzle of international adjudication. Its importance is attested by the many iterations it has to go through before landing on the adjudicators' desks. Its editing often requires a level of care and attention comparable to those that go into the court's final decision. In the next chapters, we will examine the various elements of the Memo in greater detail.

For now, let us consider the properties of the Memo as a legal artefact. That artefact symbolizes the power of bureaucracies and their relationship with the judges. By pre-digesting all the aspects of the case at hand, judicial assistants gain a level of familiarity with the file that often surpasses the adjudicators' own knowledge. While the latter maintain a grasp of the *big picture*, it is the former who master the *minutiae* of the dispute, understand the complex connections among its components, and know where to find the relevant information. Thus, when a judge has doubts about the disputed facts, they will turn to bureaucrats for clarification; when an arbitrator intends to pursue a certain line of argument, they will turn to the Memo for supporting case law; etc.

Because it guides the adjudicators in the interpretation and application of the relevant legal norms, the Memo serves as the functional equivalent of a *pre-judgment* of the case for the benefit of the court. Ostensibly, the adjudicators are not bound by their assistants' advice, and remain free to depart from it as they please. In fact, however, the content of the Memo exerts a major influence on their decision horizon, for it nudges their attention and frames their understanding of the issues. Borrowing from behavioural psychology, we could say that the assessment conducted by the bureaucracy has an 'anchoring effect'[29] on subsequent debates. Even when they disagree with their assistants' opinions, judges will rarely redo the analysis from scratch or radically change the structure of the reasoning. More often, their disagreement will be limited to discrete portions of the analytical framework that has already been laid out for them.

These properties make the Memo something more than a piece of paper. Under the veneer of technical advice and trustful cooperation, the document embodies a silent confrontation between bureaucrats and adjudicators, each vying for control of the process. Given their subordinate position, judicial assistants must show a measure of deference, discretion, and flattery. Their drafts are replete with adulatory phrases: 'Should the

---

[29] See D. Kahneman, *Thinking, Fast and Slow* (Penguin, 2013), 119–28.

Court agree with this interpretation …'; 'The Tribunal may wish to consider …'; and the like. During meetings, bureaucrats display an impeccable demeanour, speak only when given the floor, and avoid any gestures that may betray impatience or contempt.

Yet, the bureaucracy also enjoys certain advantages that help rebalance the power dynamic. Those advantages are tenure and expertise. Unlike the adjudicators, bureaucrats are not subject to political scrutiny, and are therefore in a better position to conduct legal and factual analysis without fear of consequences. Also, thanks to their long-term contracts, registry and secretariat lawyers have the opportunity to build an encyclopaedic knowledge of the relevant law and jurisprudence, which grants them the upper hand in internal legal discussions. Indeed, when it comes to technical skill, senior court officials (e.g. the ICJ Registrar, the ABS Director, or the ECtHR's Jurisconsult) can outmatch even the most articulate and learned judges.

As we will see, the ambiguous relationship between the bench and the bureaucracy – at once cooperative and competitive – deeply affects the unfolding of the international judicial process. Amazingly, such a fundamental relationship is nowhere made explicit in the official procedural rules of courts and tribunals, but gradually develops by way of *social interaction*. In other words, the authority conferred to international adjudicative bodies by their written treaties is 'totally redefined by unwritten practice'.[30]

With these considerations in mind, we are ready to ask: How do judicial bureaucrats go about preparing the Memo? What challenges do they encounter? How does it feel to provide legal advice to the 'men and women that decide the world's cases'?[31] To answer these questions, we are about to review of the essential components of the Memo: the description of the state conduct that gave rise to the dispute (Chapter 9); the assessment of the controversial facts and the supporting evidence (Chapter 10); the identification of the international legal norms applicable to the case (Chapter 11); and the interpretation and application of those norms to the facts in dispute (Chapter 12).

Obviously, we are not the first to tackle these topics. International law scholarship offers a wide array of studies about fact-finding techniques,

---

[30] M. McDougal, H. Lasswell and M. Reisman, 'The World Constitutive Process of Authoritative Decision' (1967) 19(3) JLegEduc 253, 260.
[31] Terris, Romano, and Swigart, *The International Judge*.

theories of legal interpretation, judicial behaviour, and argumentative strategies. Yet, as discussed,[32] those studies tend to treat courts and tribunals as unified entities speaking with a single voice. They typically ask questions like: How do arbitral tribunals engage with factual evidence? What are the interpretive strategies of the WTO Appellate Body? How does the ICJ promote its legitimacy vis-à-vis member states?

By contrast, our own account will keep unravelling the *internal* socio-professional dynamics that punctuate the preparation of the Memo. From our vantage point, 'the court' looks nothing like a monolithic entity, but more like an aggregate of actors who contribute in various ways to the resolution of the case. For instance, it makes little sense to speak of 'the court's' interpretation and application of international law. Instead, these activities are carried out collectively by the judges, their assistants, the parties' counsel and, less directly, by scholars with an interest in international adjudication. At each step of the proceedings, these actors exchange views and information, take competing positions, and put forward expert claims aimed at increasing their social capital.

Alas, we are bound to distort reality to some extent. For the story to be intelligible, we have to tell it as if that each component of the Memo were independent of the others, or if the drafter could proceed orderly through each stage before turning to the next. This is but a narrative expedient. In practice, the preparation of the Memo follows tortuous paths, full of detours and bumps in the road. Along the way, fact and law get enmeshed in an inextricable bundle. The assessment of the evidence becomes inseparable from the application of legal rules; the interpretation of texts is calibrated on the precise state conduct at issue; and so on.

With this caveat, and without further ado…

---

[32] See *supra*, pp. 7–15.

# 9

## To Capture the World

The intern Matt had been waiting for is finally here. Last week, Björn appointed Michelle, a Chinese national, to assist the secretariat team in the *EU – Palm Oil* appeal. Poor Michelle had to hit the ground running. She had barely finished setting up her computer when Matt urged her to read the panel report and the parties' submissions. Fortunately, Björn has a knack for picking the right candidates. In a few days, Michelle got up to speed with the file and is now ready for her first assignment: help Matt understand the functioning of EU palm oil regime.

Easier said than done. The prescriptive content of the palm oil regime is scattered across multiple legislative and administrative instruments issued by the European Commission. The main instrument, a Commission regulation, sets out the core provisions. A series of implementing directives refine and detail those provisions through specific guidelines and recommendations. To make things more complicated, the measure refers and attributes binding force to the labelling criteria developed by the Roundtable on Sustainable Palm Oil (RSPO), a non-governmental standard-setting entity. Cherry on top, a French court has issued two separate rulings on the legality of the palm oil regime under EU law. The Court of Justice of the European Union (CJEU) has not yet had a chance to rule on the matter.

This normative labyrinth requires careful examination. In a few weeks, Matt and Michelle will have to explain to the Appellate Body members how the EU palm oil regime works, how its various elements interact with each other, and what aspects of the measure are relevant to this appeal. If Matt knows his audience, the task will be laborious. The secretariat lawyers, aided by an overcrowded PowerPoint slideshow, will go out of their way to make things intelligible, only to be met with blank stares. Hopefully, the Appellate Body members will later drop by their assistants' offices to air their doubts and ask for further clarification.

Matt and Michelle must get to work at once. Understanding how the EU palm oil regime operates is essential to all the subsequent stages of the appeal. The worst sin would be for the Appellate Body to misstate the functioning of the regime in its final report, thereby attracting the ire of the European Union, the mockery of other WTO member states, and the criticism of trade law academics.

Michelle prepares a first draft description of the measure and submits it to Matt for review.

'This looks very good. Kudos!' Matt takes a sip of coffee.

'Thank you, Sir!'

'"Matt" will do. We all call each other by first name here.'

'Oh, I see. Even Mr. Kron?'

'Even Björn, yes. And even the Appellate Body members. Basically everyone except the DG, who is "the DG." Anyways: If I understood your draft correctly, the conditions for the importation of palm oil products are set out in Article 5 of the main Commission regulation, right?'

'Yes and no. Article 5 of the regulation states that the importation and internal sale of food products containing palm oil is conditioned on the requirements set out in Article 8. Article 8 provides a long list of requirements that palm oil products must meet.' Michelle takes out a copy of the regulation and points Matt to the relevant provision. 'One of the requirements, listed under letter (g), says that palm oil products shall carry a label that conforms to the criteria issued by the relevant standard-setting bodies.'

'Huh? And what are the criteria?' asks Matt, perplexed.

'Those are indicated in the first implementing directive.' Michelle takes out another paper. 'Look: paragraph 3 of the directive says that the relevant labelling criteria "shall include, in particular," those developed and administered by the Roundtable on Sustainable Palm Oil.'

'So, basically you are telling me that the measure Indonesia is challenging stems from the combined application of Articles 5 and 8(g) of the main Commission regulation, plus paragraph 3 of the first implementing directive, plus the RSPO's privately developed criteria …'

'Basically yes.'

'What a mess. And what about these words? The labelling criteria "shall include, in particular"… Does that mean that criteria *other* than the RSPO's might be accepted as valid?'

'That's unclear to me. The French court said they might, but …'

'Right, the French court. Another headache, that one.'

'What's unclear to me is: Does the French court's interpretation determine our characterization of the measure?'

'No, it doesn't. That's an interpretation under domestic law. It's just another fact we must grapple with.'

'How can a *judicial* interpretation be ... a fact?'

'Long story, we don't have time for it. Well, I guess we'll have plenty of questions for the European Union at the hearing. For now, keep piecing the puzzle together and feel free to ask if there's something you don't understand. Good job, Michelle.'

'I will. Thank you Sir.'

'Matt.'

'Matt. Oh, there's also this issue of the free trade agreement between Indonesia and the European Union. Should I research that as well?'

'Not for now. Björn doesn't seem too interested at this stage.'

'Ok, but are *you* interested?'

'I don't know yet.'

\*

Scenes like this are common across international courts and tribunals. The identification of the state conduct that gave rise to a dispute is the first logical step that any judicial bureaucrat should undertake when compiling the factual portion of the Memo. Depending of the circumstances of each case, the conduct at issue may be relatively straightforward (as was the case with the sinking of a Turkish vessel by the Lotus steamer[1]) or very cumbersome to ascertain (e.g. when it consists a congeries of seemingly disjointed acts and omissions[2]). The EU palm oil regime that Matt and Michelle are examining falls somewhere in between.

Faithful to our image of a Lego player,[3] we could say that, to assess what constitutes the conduct at issue, a good judicial bureaucrat must be able to deconstruct the responding state's behaviour and try to isolate those aspects that are *salient* to the dispute at hand. If they have done their job properly, the complainant's counsel will have already pinpointed the elements they consider relevant. Quite often, however, the respondent's counsel will portray the conduct at issue in a completely different light.

Examples of such mismatches abound. For instance, in the WTO *US – Animals* dispute, Argentina claimed that the United States' refusal to import Argentine beef, ostensibly aimed at preventing the spread of foot-and-mouth disease (FMD) in the US territory, was actually an import ban lacking an adequate scientific basis.[4] The United States

---

[1] *The Case of the SS. Lotus*, Judgment of 7 September 1927, PCIJ Rep., Series A, No. 10.

[2] See e.g. the unwritten import requirements imposed by Argentina in a recent WTO case, discussed *supra*, pp. 88–9.

[3] See *supra*, p. 161.

[4] *Agreement on the Application of Sanitary of Phytosanitary Measures*, Marrakesh Agreement Establishing the World Trade Organization, Annex 1 (15 April 1994), UNTS 1867, 493.

retorted that its measure was not a ban at all, but merely a temporary suspension of imports from Argentina until the US veterinary authorities verified the FMD-related risks associated with the products at issue. Therefore, argued the United States, the most Argentina could get was a ruling that the verification procedure incurred undue delays.[5]

In the ECtHR case *Nada v. Switzerland*, the complainant argued that the Swiss authorities had placed undue restrictions on his freedom of movement, thereby infringing his right to respect for private and family life. Switzerland protested that the measure was a mere implementation of UN Security Council Resolutions 1267 (1999) et seq., which required UN member states to restrict the movement of individuals inscribed on the UN terrorism watch list.[6]

The ICJ proceedings in *Gabčíkovo-Nagymaros Project*[7] and *Fisheries Jurisdiction*[8] showed how 'what one party terms an overriding environmental issue, another sees as rather relating to treaty obligations, or the law of State responsibility, or the law of the sea'.[9]

The list could continue. The point is that even simple measures, like those exemplified here, can raise thorny problems as soon as one tries to delineate their legal contours and insulate them from their broader context. Faced with the parties' opposed rationalizations, the observer will often find themselves between a rock and a hard place: Is the measure a product ban or to a simple delay in allowing imports? Is the restriction on freedom of movement attributable to the will of the state's government or to the orders of the Security Council?

As you might expect, there is no clear-cut answer to these questions. In fact, the framing of the state conduct at issue is laden with *value judgments* and depends very much on the epistemic categories applied by the observer. The essence, scope, and operational boundaries of the conduct will remain elusive until the court *decides* what they are. If the parties disagree bitterly, a judicious legal assistant may draft the dedicated section of the

---

[5] See Panel Report, *United States – Measures Affecting the Importation of Animals, Meat and Other Animal Products from Argentina*, WT/DS447/R (24 July 2015) ('*US – Animals*'), paras. 7.4–7.5.

[6] See *Nada v. Switzerland*, Grand Chamber Judgment of 12 September 2012, No. 10593/08, ECtHR-2012, paras. 102–6.

[7] *Gabčíkovo-Nagymaros Project (Hungary v. Slovakia)*, Judgment of 25 September 1997, ICJ Rep. 1997, 7.

[8] *Fisheries Jurisdiction (Spain v. Canada)*, Jurisdiction, Judgment of 4 December 1998, ICJ Rep. 1998, 432.

[9] R. Higgins, 'Respecting Sovereign States and Running a Tight Courtroom' (2001) 50(1) ICLQ 121, 122.

Memo in tentative terms, or provide options for the judges' consideration: 'Depending on how one looks at it, State X's measure may be seen as Y or Z; we recommend that you see it as Z'. However, in most cases, the language used in the Memo is quite assertive, such that the judges will be unlikely to question the characterization of the measure as it is presented to them.

Albeit not purely objective, this framing is not arbitrary either. In fact, judicial bureaucrats are well trained to spot and attribute salience to certain acts or omissions while, at the same time, dismissing others as immaterial. The (ir)relevance of a given aspect is not left to the unfettered discretion of the observer, but rather reflects the sensibilities and dispositions of the court or tribunal they serve.

Consider, once again, the EU palm oil regime. This composite measure pursues a host of policy objectives, including the protection of domestic consumers, the promotion of sustainable harvesting methods, the preservation of the environment, and the advancement of labour standards. While, incidentally, certain aspects of the measure may have an impact on trade, those aspects do not exhaust the goals of European lawmakers. Like most public regulations, the palm oil regime is *pluralist* in nature and reflects the ebbs and flows of political deliberation.

Yet, it is precisely on the *trade* aspects of the measure that Indonesia has built its entire complaint; and it is precisely the mandate of WTO adjudicators to assess the consistency of the measure with *trade* agreements. As a member of the WTO community, Matt is inclined to concentrate his attention on those elements of the regulation that are capable of skewing trade flows. As the pages of the issues paper fill up, those trade elements gain prominence and become the cornerstone of the case, while non-trade considerations are increasingly relegated to the margins of the analysis. As has been written in countless issues papers before, Matt will recommend that the Appellate Body ground its analysis on the 'design, structure, and expected operation'[10] of the EU palm oil regime. What that *really* means, though, is that the Appellate Body should base its decision on discrete elements of that regime, that is those that make it susceptible to WTO dispute settlement.

Of all the assumptions that will mark the remainder of the proceedings, this one is *never* going to be challenged or discussed again: Matt's

---

[10] Appellate Body Report, *Thailand – Customs and Fiscal Measures on Cigarettes from the Philippines*, WT/DS371/AB/R (17 June 2011) ('*Thailand – Cigarettes (Philippines)*'), paras. 129–30. See also e.g. Appellate Body Reports, *United States – Tax Treatment for 'Foreign Sales Corporations' – Recourse to Article 21.5 of the DSU by the European Communities*, WT/DS108/AB/RW (14 January 2002), para. 215; *Korea – Various Measures on Beef*, fn 44 to para. 142.

description of the EU palm oil regime as a trade measure (and not as, say, an environmental or a labour-related measure) becomes instant *doxa*, something that remains 'beyond question'.[11]

This tendency to bend empirical reality to make it 'digestible' to an international court or tribunal is not unique to the WTO, nor should it be blamed only on Matt. In fact, the need to appraise 'complex lifeworld situation[s] ... in a selective manner'[12] stems from the fragmentation of the international legal order into 'special regimes of knowledge and expertise'[13] in areas like trade, human rights, investment, security, or criminal law. Fragmentation has not only produced an artificial differentiation in the types of disputes that each court or tribunal is entitled to hear. It has also sliced up international adjudicative practice into a multitude of institutional projects that speak to specific audiences, pursue particular interests, and develop their own 'categories and concepts with which to make sense of the world'.[14]

In an 'irreducibly pluralistic'[15] society, virtually every problem can be appraised through the lens of multiple overlapping legal regimes, thereby opening the door to institutional competition among the respective adjudicatory forums. Absent any 'meta-regime' able to allocate priorities, each court deploys its authority, prestige, and expertise to *capture* the problem at hand in its gravitational field.[16]

Sometimes, competition takes a mild form, with the various courts showing a certain degree of comity and deference to one another. For example, in the *Mox Plant* litigation, an arbitral tribunal established under the UN Convention on the Law of the Sea[17] suspended its proceedings to give the parties time to determine whether the European Court of Justice had exclusive jurisdiction over the dispute.[18] Relying on *Mox Plant*,

---

[11] Bourdieu, 'Structures, Habitus, Power', 164.
[12] Habermas, *Between Facts and Norms*, 199.
[13] Koskenniemi, '20 Years Later', 9.
[14] Lang, 'Rethinking Trade and Human Rights', 357–8.
[15] ILC Fragmentation Report, para. 488.
[16] See *Southern Pacific Properties (Middle East) Limited* v. *Egypt*, ICSID Case No. ARB/84/3, Decision on Jurisdiction (27 November 1985), para. 84 ('When the jurisdictions of two unrelated and independent tribunals extend to the same dispute, there is no rule of international law which prevents either tribunal from exercising its jurisdiction.')
[17] United Nations, *Convention on the Law of the Sea* (10 December 1982), UNTS 1833, 3.
[18] *MOX Plant Case (Ireland* v. *United Kingdom)*, PCA Case No. 2002-01, Order No. 3 (24 June 2003), paras. 20–30. For discussion, see e.g. N. Lavranos, 'Regulating Competing Jurisdictions among International Courts and Tribunals' (2008) 68 ZaöRV 578; Allen and Soave, 'Jurisdictional Overlap', 2.

another arbitral tribunal observed that 'international tribunals have a certain flexibility in dealing with questions of competing forums'.[19]

However, most of the times, the confrontation is fierce. Each competing court defends its turf and asserts its jurisdiction over the disputed matter, irrespective of what is happening elsewhere. For instance, in *Mexico – Taxes on Soft Drinks*, the WTO Appellate Body paid no heed to the fact that Mexico's measure was being arbitrated under NAFTA rules;[20] nor did the Appellate Body pause to consider what those rules may say.[21] Similarly, in *Eureko B.V. v. Slovak Republic*, an UNCITRAL arbitral tribunal refused to suspend its proceedings pending resolution of an infringement procedure filed by the European Commission against Slovakia.[22]

In a recent decision, the CJEU set aside the arbitral clause contained in a BIT among three EU member states. In the Court's view, that arbitral clause delegated to 'a body which is not part of the [EU] judicial system' the task of deciding disputes that may relate to the interpretation of EU law,[23] thereby 'prevent[ing] those disputes from being resolved in a manner that ensures the full effectiveness' of the European legal system.[24] With unusual candor, the Court justified its decision in light of 'the autonomy of EU law with respect both to the law of the Member States *and to international law*', the 'constitutional structure' of the European Union, and the characterization of the EU treaties as an 'independent source of law'.[25]

Even more recently, the CJEU found that the 2017 Hungarian law on higher education violated Article XVII of the WTO General Agreement on Trade in Services (GATS).[26] Throughout the proceedings, Hungary

---

[19] *SGS Société Générale de Surveillance S.A. v. Philippines*, ICSID Case No. ARB/02/06, Decision on Jurisdiction (29 January 2004), para. 171. For discussion, see Allen and Soave, 'Jurisdictional Overlap', 46.

[20] See e.g. *AdM and Tate & Lyle Ingredients Americas, Inc. v. Mexico*, ICSID Case No. ARB(AF)/04/5, Award (21 November 2007); *Corn Products International, Inc. v. Mexico*, ICSID Case No. ARB(AF)/04/1, Award (15 January 2008); *Cargill, Inc. v. Mexico*, ICSID Case No. ARB(AF)/05/2, Award (18 September 2009).

[21] Appellate Body Report, *Mexico – Taxes on Soft Drinks*, para. 56.

[22] *Eureko B.V. v. Slovak Republic*, PCA Case No. 2008-13, Award on Jurisdiction, Arbitrability and Suspension (26 October 2010), para. 292. For discussion, see Allen and Soave, 'Jurisdictional Overlap', 46–7.

[23] *Slowakische Republik v. Achmea BV* (C-284/16), Request for a Preliminary Ruling from the Bundesgerichtshof, Grand Chamber Judgment of 6 March 2018, ECLI:EU:C:2018:158, para. 58.

[24] Ibid., para. 56.

[25] Ibid., para. 33 (emphasis added).

[26] *European Commission v. Hungary* (Case C-66/18), Grand Chamber Judgment of 6 October 2020, ECLI:EU:C:2020:792, para. 244.

argued that WTO panels and the Appellate Body have exclusive jurisdiction to decide on the WTO-consistency of state regulations. It further warned that the Court's autonomous interpretation of the GATS would deprive WTO adjudication of its utility.[27] The Court rejected Hungary's argument, and held that the existence of WTO dispute settlement had no bearing on its own jurisdiction.[28] In particular, it observed, its findings on the Hungarian regulation would not affect any assessment that might be made by WTO panels or the Appellate Body.[29] At most, in examining the measure, the Court would *take account* of the interpretation of the GATS rendered by WTO adjudicatory bodies.[30]

In these examples, the various courts and tribunals *expressly* addressed the overlap of multiple forums, likely because the disputing parties raised the issue. However, such an express acknowledgement is rare. In the vast majority of cases, the adjudicators simply *feign ignorance* of the existence of competing jurisdictions and carry on with their duties like nothing happened. Why take pains to engage in sophisticated conflict-of-laws reasoning? Would it not be easier to *forget* that the same problem may be appraised through multiple normative lenses? Overt 'inter-judicial dialogue', as some like to call it,[31] is tiresome. Courts will tend to avoid it unless forced by the parties' arguments or by reasons of good neighbourliness.

In turn, the choice of the applicable legal regime is not value-neutral: framing a problem in a certain vernacular means identifying the legal categories through which that problem will be addressed, thereby largely determining the outcome of the case. Consider, for instance, the radically divergent views expressed by the ICTY and the ICJ on the attribution of individual acts to a state. The ICTY's endorsement of the loose 'overall control' test[32] resonates well with the Tribunal's ingrained aversion to impunity, whereas the stringent 'effective control' test[33] adopted

---

[27] Ibid., paras. 60–3.
[28] Ibid., para. 86.
[29] Ibid., para. 89.
[30] Ibid., para. 92.
[31] See e.g. E. Kassoti, 'Fragmentation and Inter-Judicial Dialogue: The CJEU and the ICJ at the Interface' (2015) 8(2) EurJLegStud 21; C. P. R. Romano, 'Deciphering the Grammar of the International Jurisprudential Dialogue' (2009) 41(4) NYUJILP 755.
[32] *The Prosecutor* v. *Dusko Tadić*, ICTY Judgment, Case No. IT-94-1-A (15 July 1999), para. 122.
[33] *Military and Paramilitary Activities in and against Nicaragua (Nicaragua* v. *United States of America)*, Merits, Judgment of 27 June 1986, ICJ Rep. 1986, 14, paras. 115 et seq.; *Application of the Convention on the Prevention and Punishment of the Crime of Genocide (Bosnia and Herzegovina* v. *Serbia and Montenegro)*, Judgment of 26 February 2007, ICJ Rep. 2007, 43 ('*Bosnian Genocide* judgment'), paras. 400 et seq.

by the ICJ reflects the more state-friendly attitude of the World Court. Or think about the strategies deployed by the parties' counsel to select a forum where their clients have some political clout.[34]

Hence, whether they know it or not, Matt and his fellow judicial bureaucrats are pawns in an *appropriation struggle*, colliding as they are 'with their respective institutionally ingrained problem definitions and strategies for solution'.[35] Through the recursive practice of framing, they incessantly remodel the boundaries among specialized judicial regimes, contribute to the reallocation of authority,[36] and redefine the fault lines around which strategic and cognitive expectations are organized. In this contest for epistemic hegemony, political conflict 'is waged on the description and re-description of aspects of the world so as to make them fall under the jurisdiction of particular institutions'.[37]

•

Fortunately, however, these thoughts have not crossed Matt's mind. He simply does not have time to speculate about the politics of fragmentation in international law. Right now, his most pressing concern is to work with Michelle to figure out how the EU palm oil regime (sorry: its *trade* dimension) operates and how it affects international markets.

In the days following their first meeting, the two secretariat lawyers keep parsing the various provisions, examining the RSPO criteria, and trying to understand the ruling of the French court. Matt is a bit worried by the complexity of the measure. He knows all too well that the Appellate Body is not forgiving of incomplete characterizations. Once, for example, the judges scathed a panel for conducing 'a segmented analysis that isolated consideration of each element of the measure without accounting for the manner in which the elements are interrelated', and 'without aggregating or synthesizing its analyses or findings relating to those elements'.[38]

---

[34] See *supra*, p. 76.
[35] G. Teubner and A. Fischer-Lescano, 'Cannibalizing Epistemes: Will Modern Law Protect Traditional Cultural Expressions?', in C. Graber and M. Burri-Nenova (eds.), *Intellectual Property and Traditional Cultural Expressions in a Digital Environment* (Edward Elgar, 2008) 17, 20.
[36] See Shaffer and Trachtman, 'Interpretation and Institutional Choice', 122.
[37] Koskenniemi, 'The Fate of Public International Law', 7. See also Lang, 'Legal Regimes and Professional Knowledges', 113; Soave, 'Three Ways', 172–3.
[38] Appellate Body Report, *United States – Measures Concerning the Importation, Marketing and Sale of Tuna and Tuna Products – Recourse to Article 21.5 of the DSU by Mexico*, WT/DS381/AB/RW (20 November 2015) ('*US – Tuna II (Mexico) (Article 21.5 – Mexico)*'), para. 7.21.

Matt and Michelle will not make the same mistake. Little by little, they combine the elements of the palm oil regime and test how they interact with one another. As they draw connections and identify relationships among the provisions, the picture starts to come together. Sure, there remain some rough edges, and the Appellate Body will have to ask for clarifications at the hearing. But after a week, the two lawyers feel like they have more or less understood the essentials.

At some point, Matt thinks back to Michelle's question: 'How can the French court's interpretation of the EU palm oil regime be a mere fact?' At a doctrinal level, Matt knows the answer. His professors at the University of Milan often referred to the PCIJ's statement that, '[f]rom the standpoint of International Law …, municipal laws are merely facts which express the will and constitute the activities of States.'[39] Matt never had reason to question that '*locus classicus*'.[40] It made sense to him that, when appraising the laws of a state, an international court would not be bound by the interpretation of those laws provided by that state's municipal courts. From the vantage point of international adjudication, a domestic court ruling is no different from a president's executive order, a congressional bill, or an act of war.

At a *practical* level, however, Matt is not so sure anymore. What have he and Michelle been doing for days, if not interpreting the *legal* content and architecture of the EU palm oil regime? Did they not ascertain how that *law* affects the behaviour of market actors? Is there a *differentia specifica* between their assessment 'from the standpoint of international law' and the French court's assessment 'from the standpoint of domestic law'? And what about the RSPO criteria? Do they not require a *legal* reading despite being developed by a private standard-setting body? And if so, *who* should read them? Would it be incumbent on the RSPO to provide an authoritative interpretation of its own criteria, or is it for Matt and Michelle to ascertain what they mean?

---

[39] *Certain German Interests in Polish Upper Silesia* (1926), PCIJ Rep., Series A, No. 7, p. 19. See also e.g. *Frontier Dispute (Burkina Faso v. Mali)*, Judgment of 22 December 1986, ICJ Rep. 1986, 554, para. 30; Appellate Body Report, *India – Patent Protection for Pharmaceutical and Agricultural Chemical Products*, WT/DS50/AB/R (19 December 1997), para. 65; *Ioannis Kardassopoulos v. Georgia*, ICSID Case No. ARB/05/18, Decision on Jurisdiction (6 July 2007), para. 146.

[40] M. M. Mbengue, 'National Legislation and Unilateral Acts of States', in T. Gazzini and E. De Brabandere (eds.), *International Investment Law: The Sources of Rights and Obligations* (Martinus Nijhoff, 2012) 183, 197.

These questions confound and intrigue Matt. The more he thinks about it, the more the distinctions between law and fact, domestic and international, private and public appear artificial. The more he tries to navigate the maze of doctrines, the more matters of law seem to 'grow downward into roots of fact' and matters of fact 'reach upward, without a break, into matters of law'.[41] Amid his doubts, Matt suddenly remembers the interview in The Economist that Björn showed him some time ago. The interviewee accused the Appellate Body of treating the meaning of municipal law as a matter of WTO law, in violation of its mandate under the DSU.[42] 'That guy doesn't understand', muses Matt. 'It's not as if we are overstepping our mandate *deliberately*. It's just that, in practice, we have no time for fine-grained distinctions. There's no grand scheme here: only a bunch of lawyers racing against the clock.'

---

[41] J. Dickinson, *Administrative Justice and the Supremacy of Law* (Harvard University Press, 1927), 55. See also e.g. R. J. Allen and M. S. Pardo, 'The Myth of the Law-Fact Distinction' (2003) 97(4) NWULR 1769.

[42] See e.g. USTR Report, 40–4.

# 10

# Bricolage

With a dozen of ongoing arbitrations and an academic calendar scheduled to the minute, François Gal has little time for holidays. That is why Carlos was surprised when his mentor announced his decision to take a week off and fly to the Maldives with this wife. Carlos and his fellow associates at Gal Elmosnino LLP sighted in relief. With the boss gone, they would finally have some downtime, right? Wrong. Before leaving, Professor Gal stopped by Carlos' office with a thick folder under his arm.

'I need you to get the facts straight by the time I come back.'

Carlos did his best to remain impassive.

'Yes, Professor. Would you like me to focus on anything in particular?'

'The issue of legitimate expectations. Was Claimant led to believe that the investment contract would be renewed? I'm in talks with one co-arb about this, and I want to give him the facts straight as soon as possible.'

'I'm on it. You will find the section of the Memo waiting on your chair on your return.'

'That's my boy. I have to run now, or I'll miss the flight. Imagine tomorrow's headlines: "Top international arbitrator brutally murdered by his wife."'

Carlos did not have time to contrive a laugh: the Professor was already walking away, giggling at his own joke.

\*

'Getting the facts straight' is the second fundamental step in the preparation of the Memo, right after the identification of the state conduct at issue. The exercise consists of a preliminary assessment of the facts on which the litigants disagree and an evaluation of the evidence they have produced. The scope and extent of the disagreement varies greatly depending on the circumstances of the case, the parties' litigation strategies, the personalities of the opposed counsel, and the features of the specific court concerned.

Some disputes raise little factual controversy and leave judicial bureaucrats free to concentrate on the legal aspects. For instance, in the *Wall* advisory opinion,[1] the ICJ was confronted with a relatively straightforward factual scenario. No one contested that Israel had built a barrier bordering some of the Palestinian Occupied Territories, and the main question was whether such a barrier was lawful under the applicable norms, including humanitarian and human rights law.[2]

Other cases, by contrast, see the parties bitterly disagree over what happened, who did what, and to what effect. Generally speaking, international disputes have become considerably more fact-intensive over the last few decades. For example, in the *Armed Activities* case, the ICJ had to go to great lengths to assess the factual accuracy of the Democratic Republic of the Congo's claims that Uganda had unlawfully used force, supported irregular troops, and occupied portions of its territory.[3] Similarly, in the *Genocide* case, the Court had to ascertain whether Serbia had actually committed the many atrocities of which Bosnia and Herzegovina accused it. This proved to be a monumentally complex task, not to speak of the difficulty of evaluating genocidal intent.[4]

Other courts and tribunals are no stranger to the intricacies of fact-finding. At the ECtHR, it is quite common for the responding state to object to the complainant's factual allegations. For instance, in cases involving extrajudicial killings, the parties typically disagree about whether the evidentiary record (police reports, witness testimonies, etc.) sufficiently corroborates the complainant's position.[5] In such cases, the Court is 'inevitably confronted when establishing the facts with the same difficulties as those faced by any first-instance court'.[6] The IACtHR faces even greater challenges. Many of its cases involve allegations of large-scale human rights violations, often perpetrated by paramilitary or unofficial agents. A dispute concerning the Honduran *desaparecidos*,[7] for example,

---

[1] *Legal Consequences of the Construction of a Wall in the Occupied Palestinian Territory*, Advisory Opinion of 9 July 2004, ICJ Rep. 2004, 136.

[2] Terris, Romano, and Swigart, *The International Judge*, 114.

[3] *Armed Activities on the Territory of the Congo (Democratic Republic of the Congo v. Uganda)*, Judgment of 19 December 2005, ICJ Rep. 2005, 168.

[4] *Bosnian Genocide* judgment. For discussion, see e.g. J. G. Devaney, *Fact-Finding Before the International Court of Justice* (Cambridge University Press, 2016), 1–13.

[5] See e.g. *Çakıcı v. Turkey*, Grand Chamber Judgment of 8 July 1999, No. 23657/94, ECtHR-1999, paras. 9–55; *Timurtaş v. Turkey*, Judgment of 13 June 2000, No. 23531/94, ECtHR-2000, paras. 10–47, 63–72; *Nachova and Others v. Bulgaria*, Grand Chamber Judgment of 6 July 2005, Nos. 43577/98 and 43579/98, ECtHR-2005, paras. 10–54.

[6] *Tanış and Others v. Turkey*, Judgment of 2 August 2005, No. 65899/01, ECtHR-2005, para. 160.

[7] See e.g. *Velásquez Rodríguez v. Honduras*, Merits, Judgment of 29 July 1988, IACtHR Series C, No. 4; *Godínez Cruz v. Honduras*, Merits, Judgment of 20 January 1989, IACtHR Series C, No. 5; *Fairén Garbi and Solís Corrales v. Honduras*, Merits, Judgment of 15 March 1989, IACtHR Series C, No. 6.

required the Court to engage in an extensive review of the underlying factual circumstances, including an examination of whether state officials were implicated in each victim's disappearance.

In principle, human rights adjudicators are not entitled to second-guess the factual determinations of domestic authorities.[8] They must take the findings of fact rendered by national courts at face value. However, they feel compelled to take a more proactive role when the government of the responding state has exclusive access to the evidence and does not wilfully cooperate with the Court. So, starting in the 1990s, ECtHR judges and their staff began to conduct 'fact-finding missions' to take depositions from witnesses and inspect the locations where the alleged violations had occurred. Those 'first-hand testimonies' often enabled the Court to draw decisive factual inferences.[9]

The WTO and ISDS were among the first international judicial systems to witness the rise of science-based disputes – that is disputes whose solution depended on the processing of vast amounts of scientific or technical information. Trade and investment jurisprudence is rife with cases about the health safety of hormones-cured beef or biotech food products;[10] the effects of monetary policies on domestic economic stability;[11] the animal welfare implications of certain hunting methods,[12] and the effectiveness of plain-packaging of cigarettes in reducing smoking

---

[8] See e.g. *Certain Aspects of the Laws on the Use of Languages in Education in Belgium*, v. *Belgium*, Judgment of 23 July 1968, Nos. 474/62; 1677/62; 1691/62; 1769/63; 1994/63; 2126/64, ECtHR-1968; *Observer and Guardian* v. *United Kingdom*, Judgment of 26 November 1991, No. 13585/88, ECtHR-1991, para. 30.

[9] *Imakayeva* v. *Russia*, Judgment of 9 November 2006, No. 7615/02, ECtHR-2007, para. 117. For discussion, see e.g. L. R. Helfer, 'Redesigning the European Court of Human Rights: Embeddedness as a Deep Structural Principle of the European Human Rights Regime' (2008) 19(1) EJIL 125, 142–4; M. T. Kamminga, 'Is the European Convention on Human Rights Sufficiently Equipped to Cope with Gross and Systematic Violations?' (1994) 12(2) NQHR 153; R. Harmsen, 'The European Convention on Human Rights After Enlargement' (2001) 5(4) IJHR 18.

[10] See Appellate Body Report, *European Communities – Measures Concerning Meat and Meat Products (Hormones)*, WT/DS26/AB/R, WT/DS48/AB/R (16 January 1998) ('*EC – Hormones*'); Panel Report, *European Communities – Measures Affecting the Approval and Marketing of Biotech Products*, WT/DS291/R, WT/DS292/R, WT/DS293/R (29 September 2006) ('*EC – Approval and Marketing of Biotech Products*').

[11] See e.g. *CMS Transmission Co.* v. *Argentina*, ICSID Case No. ARB/01/8, Award (12 May 2005); *Enron Creditors Recovery Corp. Ponderosa Assets, L.P.* v. *Argentina*, ICSID Case No. ARB/01/3, Decision on the Application for Annulment of Argentina (30 July 2010).

[12] See e.g. Appellate Body Report, *European Communities – Measures Prohibiting the Importation and Marketing of Seal Products*, WT/DS400/AB/R, WT/DS401/AB/R (22 May 2014) ('*EC – Seal Products*').

prevalence.[13] In recent years, the practice of submitting scientific data as evidence has spilled over into other areas of international adjudication,[14] such that most courts and tribunals are 'increasingly concerned with scientific and technological facts'.[15]

This trend towards greater factual complexity stems from various factors. As discussed,[16] the professionalization and specialization of the international bar has produced a new generation of counsel able to provide their clients with in-depth legal advice. Modern litigators are well equipped to dissect the factual minutiae of each case, gather the relevant evidence, and build persuasive factual narratives.[17] The increasing sophistication of the parties' arguments forces the adjudicators to grapple more thoroughly with the facts on record and to produce more articulate assessments in response.[18] In turn, the growing factual complexity of judgments feeds case law with precedents that require even greater sophistication of future litigants. Over time, the interplay between the bar and the bench reinforces the length and technicality of decisions. The tightening of the international judicial community has caused the system to descend from the Platonic hyperuranion of legal concepts to the Aristotelian world of materiality.

Despite these developments, judges remain strikingly *reluctant* to engage with the facts. If disentangling intricate evidence 'make[s] the paradise of lawyers and practitioners', adjudicators tend to see it an excruciating 'purgatory' they must trudge through before reaching the lofty heights of legal analysis.[19]

---

[13] See *Philip Morris Asia Limited (Hong Kong) v. The Commonwealth of Australia*, UNCITRAL Case No. 2012-12, Award on Jurisdiction and Admissibility (17 December 2015); Panel Report, *Australia – Certain Measures Concerning Trademarks, Geographical Indications and Other Plain Packaging Requirements Applicable to Tobacco Products and Packaging*, WT/DS434, WT/DS435, WT/DS441, WT/DS467/R (28 June 2018).

[14] See e.g. *Pulp Mills* judgment; *Whaling* judgment. See also M. M. Mbengue, 'Scientific Fact-Finding at the International Court of Justice: An Appraisal in the Aftermath of the *Whaling* Case' (2016) 29(2) LJIL 529.

[15] S. Rosenne, *International Law and Practice*, 237. See also e.g. L. Boisson de Chazournes, 'Introduction: Courts and Tribunals and the Treatment of Scientific Issues' (2012) 3(3) JIDS 479; M. M. Mbengue, 'Scientific Fact-Finding by International Courts and Tribunals' (2012) 3(3) JIDS 509; L. Malintoppi, 'Fact Finding and Evidence Before the International Court of Justice (Notably in Scientific-Related Disputes)' (2016) 7(2) JIDS 421; Devaney, *Fact-Finding*, 1–13.

[16] See *supra*, Chapter 3.

[17] See e.g. Malintoppi, 'Fact Finding', 424.

[18] See Wells, 'Situated Decisionmaking', 1734; Messenger, 'The Practice of Litigation', 223.

[19] *Pulp Mills* judgment, Dissenting Opinion of Judge Cançado Trindade, para. 148.

The ICJ is possibly the worst offender, with its bench being described as 'poorly equipped for handling complex facts'.[20] The Court is often accused of strategically eschewing lengthy and complicated assessments of the factual record and focusing its decisions on pure legal principles.[21] This reluctance may be due to the limited support available to ICJ judges in processing the voluminous case files. To recall,[22] the institution of clerks in the early 2000s was partly motivated by need to enhance the Court's capacity to digest thousands of pages of submissions and exhibits. In theory, the ICJ could, pursuant to Article 50 of its statute, appoint official experts to assist it in making factual determinations and appraising scientific or technological data. However, that option has rarely been used. Instead, judges have frequent recourse to *experts fantômes*,[23] that is, temporary staff members hired for the very purpose of bringing their technical competence to bear in specific disputes. The identities of these invisible experts, the nature and scope of their advice, and the weight given to it by the Court are not disclosed at any time.[24]

The WTO Appellate Body is similarly skittish when it comes to fact-finding. Its mandate is, in principle, 'limited to issues of law ... and legal interpretations developed by [a] panel'.[25] However, a party may introduce factual considerations on appeal by claiming that a panel has failed to conduct 'an objective assessment of the facts' of the case under Article 11 of the DSU. When faced with such a claim, the Appellate Body must assess whether, in handling the facts, the panel has committed 'an egregious error that calls into question [its] good faith'.[26] This requires appellate

---

[20] R. Teitelbaum, 'Recent Fact-Finding Developments at the International Court of Justice' (2007) 6(1) LPICT 119, 119–20.

[21] T. M. Franck, 'Fact-Finding in the ICJ', in R. B. Lillich (ed.), *Fact-Finding Before International Tribunals: Eleventh Sokol Colloquium* (Transnational Publishers, 1992) 21, 21–31.

[22] See *supra*, pp. 117–20.

[23] D. Peat, 'The Use of Court-Appointed Experts by the International Court of Justice' (2014) 84(1) BYBIL 271, 288. See also J. Jennings, 'International Lawyers and the Progressive Development of International Law', in J. Makarczyk (ed.), *Theory of International Law at the Threshold of the 21st Century: Essays in Honour of Krzysztof Skubiszewski* (Kluwer Law International, 1996) 413, 416.

[24] Peat, 'Court-Appointed Experts', 288.

[25] Article 17.9 of the DSU.

[26] Appellate Body Report, *EC – Hormones*, para. 133. See also e.g. Appellate Body Reports, *Korea – Taxes on Alcoholic Beverages*, WT/DS75/AB/R, WT/DS84/AB/R (18 January 1999) ('*Korea – Alcoholic Beverages*'), para. 164; *Japan – Measures Affecting Agricultural Products*, WT/DS76/AB/R (22 February 1999), para. 141; *United States – Definitive Safeguard Measures on Imports of Wheat Gluten from the European Communities*, WT/DS166/AB/R (22 December 2000), para. 151; *European Communities – Anti-Dumping Duties on Imports of Cotton-Type Bed Linen from India – Recourse to Article 21.5 of the DSU by India*, WT/DS141/AB/RW (8 April 2003), para. 177.

judges to reopen the factual record and test the resistance of the panel's analysis in light of the evidence submitted by the parties.

Not surprisingly, Appellate Body members and ABS lawyers dread being flooded with DSU Article 11 claims. Parsing through the record is a tedious and time-consuming exercise that detracts from consideration of the legal issues raised on appeal. Yet, much to Matt's chagrin, the number of fact-intensive appeals has exploded in recent years, due in no small part to the Appellate Body's own short-sightedness.

In its early decisions, the Appellate Body liberally rejected claims brought under substantive WTO provisions on the ground that they 'fit more properly under Article 11 of the DSU'.[27] Matt surmises that, by dismissing those claims based on their alleged mischaracterization, the Appellate Body thought it had found a clever way around ruling on thorny legal issues.

However, this approach backfired quickly. Counsel started advising their clients to append dozens of DSU Article 11 claims to their substantive appeals, lest they risk the summary dismissal of important issues. As a result, those claims popped up like mushrooms. In a 2014 case, the complainant requested the Appellate Body to review the panel's assessment of the facts no less than 50 times.[28]

As a reaction, the Appellate Body tried to make amends by declaring it 'unacceptable for an appellant simply to recast factual arguments that it made before the panel in the guise of an Article 11 claim',[29] and came up with standard language to quickly dispose of frivolous fact-based appeals. However, this was in vain: Humpty-Dumpty could not be put back together. Possibly by chance, and certainly without thorough consideration of consequences, the court had created a *target* that any diligent litigant felt compelled to shoot at.

In turn, the proliferation of DSU Article 11 claims hampered the Appellate Body's ability to thoroughly evaluate the legal merits of appeals: given the stringent schedule of appellate proceedings, the court found

---

[27] Appellate Body Report, *Canada – Measures Relating to Exports of Wheat and Treatment of Imported Grain*, WT/DS276/AB/R (30 August 2004), para. 176. See also Appellate Body Report, *EC and certain member States – Large Civil Aircraft*, para. 1316.

[28] Appellate Body Report, *United States – Countervailing Measures on Certain Hot-Rolled Carbon Steel Flat Products from India*, WT/DS436/AB/R (8 December 2014).

[29] Ibid., para. 4.79. See also Appellate Body Report, *EC – Fasteners (China)*, para. 442.

itself stuck in a quagmire of evidentiary issues and was sometimes unable to deliver confident and coherent reasoning on legal questions. This story testifies, once again, to the mutual observation and the adaptive dialogue between the international bench and the counsel litigating before it.[30]

By comparison, other international courts and tribunals are better positioned to review facts and evidence. WTO panels, the ECtHR, the IACtHR, and ISDS tribunals often set up dedicated procedures for witness examination, review of scientific or technical information, and the like. Yet, even there, one can sense a certain disdain for exceedingly complex fact patterns. Why is it so?

According to some, international judges are too far removed from the contexts where disputes originate, and are therefore unable to 'spot the cultural or other cues that enable local judges to assess factual assertions or the credibility of witnesses'.[31] For others, the background of adjudicators – who usually hail from the academe, the diplomatic service, and domestic high courts – makes them more inclined towards legal reasoning than factual assessment.[32] Their self-perceived role is that of 'guardians of the *law* and builders of *legal* institutions'[33] – not sleuths with magnifying glasses or scientists in white coats. Whatever the reason, 'facts lie at the periphery of judicial control'.[34]

This explains the readiness with which adjudicators delegate the bulk of fact-finding to their assistants. Throughout the proceedings, judicial bureaucrats are invested with extensive authority over the evidence presented by the parties. They have to sift through the record, establish the probative weight of each piece of information, spot possible lacunae, and present the results of their research both orally and in writing. The Memo is typically expected to identify a core set of 50–100 exhibits on which to ground subsequent analyses.

---

[30] See *supra*, pp. 82–4.
[31] J. E. Alvarez, 'Are International Judges Afraid of Science? A Comment on Mbengue' (2011) 34(1) LoyLAIntl&CompLRev 81, 84. See also B. S. Brown, 'Primacy or Complementarity: Reconciling the Jurisdiction of National Courts and International Criminal Tribunals' (1998) 23(2) YaleJIntlL 383, 416.
[32] R. B. Bilder, 'The Fact/Law Distinction in International Adjudication', in R. B. Lillich (ed.), *Fact-Finding before International Tribunals: Eleventh Sokol Colloquium* (Transnational Publishers, 1992) 95, 98.
[33] Terris, Romano, and Swigart, *The International Judge*, xix (emphasis added). See also Føllesdal, 'To Guide and Guard', 793–5.
[34] M. M. Mbengue, 'International Courts and Tribunals as Fact-Finders: The Case of Scientific Fact-Finding in International Adjudication' (2011) 34(1) LoyLAIntl&CompLRev 53, 54.

Clearly, not all pieces of evidence are of equal value, nor must a fact-finder scrutinize them all with the same level of attention. In fact, as we have seen,[35] the parties' briefs normally contain clear indications of the exhibits they consider most significant, the connections that exist among them, and the main bones of contention. Yet, the fact-finding process remains rife with peril: the slightest lapse in concentration, the most benign mishandling of the evidence might cast doom on the credibility of the court's decision.[36]

•

Carlos stares at the pile of cardboard boxes, labelled '*Kingsland Mining Corp. v. Turkey* – Exhibits', with growing despair. His downtime will have to wait. On his return from the Maldives, Professor Gal will want to know if the respondent, the government of Turkey, frustrated the legitimate expectations of the claimant, Canadian company Kingsland. The record reveals a single uncontroversial fact: that, upon coming to power, the Erdoğan administration refused to renew a contract that granted Kingsland the right to exploit Turkish goldmines. The parties vigorously disagree on almost everything else.

According to the claimant, the conduct of the Turkish authorities prior to the non-renewal gave Kingsland reason to expect that its investment would remain protected. First, it argues, the former government publicly expressed support for the exploitation of Turkish goldmines by multinational companies, which it saw as a means to promote foreign investment and create jobs. Second, government officials held at least two private meetings with Kingsland's representatives, during which they promised that the company's mining rights would continue despite possible changes in the country's politics. The respondent, for its part, maintains that, well before the non-renewal of the contract, national authorities had significantly changed their rhetoric on the foreign exploitation of goldmines, in line with the views of the new administration. Moreover, the respondent denies that any private meetings ever took place or that governmental officials made any promises, explicit or implicit, to the effect of preserving Kingsland's mining rights. In support of their respective positions, the litigants produced newspaper articles, footage of presidential speeches, and conflicting witness testimonies. This gives the tribunal a fragmentary and incomplete picture of what happened prior to the non-renewal of the contract.

---

[35] See *supra*, pp. 84–9.
[36] Franck, 'Fact-Finding', 31.

Faced with these competing factual realities, Carlos' initial reaction is one of hesitance – hence his late-night stays in the office to the sound of some old punk bands. At first, the task seems intractable. How is he supposed to ascertain the substantive truth behind the parties' factual allegations? Can he really tell beyond 'the slightest doubt'[37] whether the Turkish government is or is not lying about its private conversations with Kingsland? Of course not: Carlos was not in the room where the alleged conversations occurred.

Yet, the inflexible deadline set by Professor Gal forces him to draft the Memo section quickly. Within a few days, his initial discomfort begins to abate. If he cannot know the truth, he can at least assign rough probabilities to the different scenarios, reduce the range of uncertainty, and perhaps even 'convey security and calculability where there is none'.[38] Carlos collects the information scattered throughout the submissions and the supporting exhibits, organizes it by theme, compares its content, and identifies gaps in the stories skilfully told by the parties' counsel. Hour after hour, the pages fill up with prudent language, rich in caveats and qualifiers: 'it seems that Kingsland…'; 'allegedly, the Turkish government…'; 'we understand that the parties…'; etc.

By the end of the exercise, Carlos has somehow managed to narrow the scope of uncertainty down to two core factual issues, where he finds the evidence *truly* irreconcilable. First: did an attaché of the Ministry of Energy and Natural Resources meet Kingsland's deputy general counsel on 6 November 2002, and if so, what was said during that meeting? Second: once the Erdoğan administration took over, was Kingsland promptly put on notice that the government's policy on natural resources had changed, so as to recalibrate its mining investments accordingly? Carlos suggests that Professor Gal probe those issues with the parties and their witnesses at the hearing. To this end, the Memo specifies the elements that the hearing questions should cover and lists the relevant exhibit numbers.

This slow and painstaking quest for the facts, this series of attempts at rationalizing and absorbing the uncertainty of a discombobulated world, should not surprise the reader. As we know,[39] judicial fact-finding cannot aspire to full objectivity. The bottom line is not truth,[40]

---

[37] See *Fisheries Jurisdiction (Germany v. Iceland)*, Jurisdiction, Judgment of 2 February 1973, ICJ Rep. 1973, 49, para. 24.
[38] O. Kessler, 'Same as It Never Was? Uncertainty and the Changing Contours of International Law' (2011) 37(5) RevIntlStud 2163, 2168.
[39] See *supra*, pp. 84–5.
[40] H. Putnam, *Reason, Truth and History* (Cambridge University Press, 1981), 130.

but a plausible *construction* of truth that combines elements of both reason *and* choice.[41] Best-case scenario, this construction will approximate what actually happened,[42] or at least conform to common 'criteria of rational acceptability'.[43] But whatever the outcome, the facts are 'what the judge thinks they are'.[44]

Carlos is surprised by how tentative and disorderly the construction process is. As he reorders and reassembles the patchwork of available information, he finds himself unable to follow any discernible methodology. All of a sudden, his fancy Ivy League training, based on legal problem-solving and IRAC analysis,[45] proves woefully inadequate to the task. 'Learn how to think like a lawyer', they used to say at Harvard. 'To hell with that. Why didn't they teach me how to think like a detective?' Gradually, Carlos gives up any hope to reach unassailable factual conclusions, and surrenders to the impossibility of 'a sharp distinction between factual observations and normative judgments'.[46]

This surrender is liberating. Little by little, like other *bricoleurs* in our story,[47] Carlos starts using whatever comes at hand to achieve his goal. Almost unwittingly, he resorts to 'sometimes complementary, sometimes divergent' techniques to cobble together an acceptable reconstruction.[48] He magnifies the importance of some pieces of evidence, while reducing that of others. He discusses certain exhibits at length in the main text of the Memo, while burying others deep into the 'see also' part of some recondite footnote.[49] As a cognitive psychologist would say, he focuses on some objects in his perceptual field and excludes the rest.[50]

---

[41] See P. C. Davis, '"There Is a Book Out…": An Analysis of Judicial Absorption of Legislative Facts' (1987) 100(7) HarvLRev 1539 (original emphasis).
[42] H. Kelsen, 'The Principle of Sovereign Equality of States as a Basis for International Organization' (1994) 53(2) YaleLJ 207, 218. See also e.g. E. M. Morgan, *Some Problems of Proof under the Anglo-American System of Litigation* (Columbia University Press, 1956), 128; D. V. Sandifer, *Evidence before International Tribunals* (University Press of Virginia, 1975), 13, 198; Summers, 'Formal Legal Truth'.
[43] Putnam, *Reason, Truth and History*, 130.
[44] Frank, 'Are Judges Human?', 35–6.
[45] IRAC stands for 'Issue, Rule, Application, Conclusion'. It is the common law equivalent of demonstrative syllogism.
[46] Wells, 'Situated Decisionmaking', 1743.
[47] See *supra*, p. 88.
[48] Berman, 'The Quest for Rationality', 339.
[49] See J. Frank, *Courts on Trial: Myth and Reality in American Justice* (paperback edn., Princeton University Press, 1973), 39.
[50] S. Kassin, *Psychology* (Prentice Hall, 1998), 107. See also D. Carson, 'A Psychology and Law of Fact Finding?', in D. Carson et al. (eds.) *Applying Psychology to Criminal Justice* (Wiley and Sons, 2007) 115, 121.

One day, midway through the process, Carlos starts tinkering with the sound settings of his music player. The results are amazing: boost the low frequencies, and the song will become a lot more percussive; amp up the medium, and you will have a track led by guitar and voice; augment the treble, and the cymbals will pierce through the mix. Carlos chuckles: the same considerations could very well apply to the factual narrative he is trying to build. Put the accent on certain pieces of evidence, and you will see a ruthless multinational corporation trying to coerce a sovereign nation to let it plunder its precious natural resources; focus on other exhibits, and you will see a government acting in bad faith to shrug off an unwelcome irritant from its political landscape.

Ultimately, it will be impossible to tell if the outcomes of Carlos' assessment are dictated by mediated reason or unmediated instinct, innate proclivities or professional acculturation. His favourite punk rockers would say: 'DIY – do it yourself'. What is certain is that, from now on, Professor Gal will ground his analysis on the facts as they are described in the Memo, with little deviation therefrom. The handful of exhibits on which Carlos happened to focus his attention will come to the fore as the basis for the final award, whereas the many others that remained at the margins of his analysis will gradually slip into oblivion.

•

If Carlos' fact-finding exercise is tough, Matt's is excruciating. During the course of the WTO panel proceedings, both Indonesia and the European Union produced ample scientific and technical evidence in support of their positions. The bone of contention is whether the EU palm oil regime actually contributes to the promotion of environmentally sustainable methods of palm oil production.

Indonesia argued that, overall, the production methods of its local producers are not particularly harmful to the environment and that, therefore, the European Union's concerns about the reduction of biodiversity are grossly overstated. In support of its argument, Indonesia submitted four different studies concerning the dietary and reproductive characteristics of orangutans and other endangered species, the evolution of the national wildlife habitat over the last 20 years, and the measures put in place by Indonesian authorities to combat deforestation. The European Union countered this information with its own scientific studies, showing that the preoccupations underlying the adoption of the EU palm oil regime are anything but exaggerated.

After its defeat at the panel stage, the European Union is now appealing the panel's characterization of the scientific evidence contained in the studies under Article 11 of the DSU. Matt is disappointed. He secretly hoped that the European Union's appeal would be manifestly spurious – or, as his friend Jane would call it, 'your typical bogus eleven'. Unfortunately, this does not appear to be the case. The panel's description of the evidence does seem a bit messy. Its findings are chaotically scattered across several subsections and footnotes of the report, and they appear to neglect some important exhibits on which the European Union built its case. At least for now, Matt cannot avoid addressing the issue in a dedicated section of the issues paper. 'Leave no stone unturned'...

As he reads through the intricate scientific information, Matt finds himself at a loss. The studies on record comprise both quantitative and qualitative sections. The former are riddled with figures and formulae unintelligible to anyone without a background in statistics or data analysis. The latter engage extensively with previous academic literature, triangulate different sources, and ground every finding on a seemingly solid empirical basis.

To the untrained eye, all the studies seem thorough, methodologically sound, and moved by genuine scientific curiosity. They bear the hallmarks of 'objectivity, authority and verifiability' that make scientific knowledge a 'crucial resource' in international adjudication.[51] And yet, each study *invariably* supports the legal position of the party that produced it. Those submitted by Indonesia conclude that deforestation in Indonesia poses a 'low to moderate' threat to wildlife and the environment. Those offered by the European Union describe that threat as 'serious or extremely serious'. The conclusions on both sides are presented as a pure application of technical and scientific competence.

Matt is amazed. How can science, the objective discipline *par excellence*, yield such partisan results? Is it because, as some have noted, 'much of the relevant information and technical expertise resides with the industrial interests' or with 'scientists and researchers with strong industry affiliations'?[52] Are Indonesia and the European Union producing *fake* science, skewed by seedy compromises and tainted by intellectual corruption?

---

[51] A. Orford, 'Scientific Reason and the Discipline of International Law', in J. d'Aspremont et al. (eds.), *International Law as a Profession* (Cambridge University Press, 2017) 93, 109.

[52] R. Howse and P. C. Mavroidis, 'Europe's Evolving Regulatory Strategy for GMOs: The Issue of Consistency with WTO Law: Of Kine and Brine' (2000) 24(1&2) FordhamIntlLJ 317, 351.

No, Matt ponders, something else must be at play here. Perhaps, there is no such a thing as pure and disinterested scientific research, independent of the 'social conditions that produce scientific expertise and priorities'.[53] Perhaps, rather than reflecting the *'communis doctorum opinio'*,[54] scientific production is a contest for authority, where the contestants deploy the vernacular of expertise to bolster their prestige and increase their capital.[55] If this is true, then 'natural' science is not so different from 'legal' science after all. Both rest on 'an interested fiction' that enables its authors to present a version of the dominant representation, 'neutralised and euphemised into a particularly misrecognisable and symbolically, therefore, particularly effective form'.[56]

Ok, maybe Matt does not think *exactly* in Bourdieusian terms. The socially constructed character of science may be new to him, but is not new to those who have explored the politics of knowledge production. However, something else intrigues Matt. It is not so much the effect of science on the judicial process, but rather... the effect of the judicial process on science.

Apparently, during the panel hearing, the parties' environmental experts came at loggerheads and accused each other of bias, sloppiness, and deviance from mainstream consensus. At some point, one expert snorted that another had a poor publication record and was very junior in the academic ranks. For a precious brief moment, the WTO courtroom became the physical site of a confrontation for scientific dominance.[57] Suddenly, the invisible social conflicts of the scientific field became apparent. Dragged into an unfamiliar environment, the opposed experts broke with the internal 'norms' and 'protocols'[58] of their usual game and let themselves go to otherwise unacceptable insults.

More strikingly still, the WTO panel and the Appellate Body *have a say* in this confrontation. By siding with Indonesia or the European Union, the adjudicators will validate one scientific truth over the other, thus sanctifying one vision of reality and protecting it from contestation. To borrow from the Appellate Body's own language, one set of studies will be

---

[53] Orford, 'Scientific Reason', 110.
[54] P. Bourdieu, 'The Specificity of the Scientific Field and the Social Conditions of the Progress of Reason' (1975) 14(6) SocSciInf 17, 24.
[55] Ibid., 19.
[56] Ibid., 36.
[57] Ibid., 22.
[58] Orford, 'Scientific Reason', 111.

celebrated as 'a respected and qualified source', while the other will be dismissed as lacking 'the necessary scientific and methodological rigour'.[59] Much to Matt's amusement, a court of law will turn into a court of science.

These idle thoughts, of course, are not helping Matt with the task at hand. 'If Indonesia and the European Union cannot be both right, then who is?', he keeps asking. But this is mere shorthand for the real, more troubling question: 'How am *I* supposed to tell who is right?'

Matt's unease is understandable. He is hardly 'knowledgeable enough about science to recognize the uncertainty and hypothetical qualities that make up the very essence of scientific research'.[60] Why, he chose to study law because he was scared of numbers! Today, he could not solve a second degree equation – much less gauge the accuracy of complex calculations and datasets. Moreover, Matt has never *seen* Indonesian wildlife; never witnessed the effects of deforestation; and never observed whether Indonesia's plans to protect the environment are effectively implemented or remain dead letter. Hence, even if Matt could read the scientific data on record, he would not be able to tell if those data correspond to the empirical reality on the ground.

What a conundrum! Matt anticipates Jane's anger next time they meet for a drink at the Bains des Pâquis. 'What is wrong with you, man? We gave you all the evidence you needed, and you still could not get those damn facts straight!'

The only practical solution is to cheat. Or, more benignly, to use *proxies* to work around the impossibility of a conclusive scientific assessment. Instead of reviewing each piece of information submitted by the parties, Matt turns his attention to *the panel's evaluation* of that information. First, he carefully reads the relevant portions of the panel report in light of the arguments raised on appeal. Second, he gauges the tightness of the panel's reasoning, writing down possible lacunae and inconsistencies at the margins of each page. Seen this way, the exercise is less daunting: a *second-hand* review of the panel's own assessment should be feasible, even for a non-scientist. Besides, Michelle, the new intern, is eager to help.

Matt feels a bit guilty, for he knows that Keiko, his secretariat colleague who assisted the panel, worked very hard to dissect the scientific evidence on record. Keiko is not better versed than Matt in environmental science,

---

[59] Appellate Body Report, *Australia – Measures Affecting the Importation of Apples from New Zealand*, WT/DS367/AB/R (29 November 2010), para. 214. See also e.g. Appellate Body Report, *United States/Canada – Continued Suspension of Obligations in the EC – Hormones Dispute*, WT/DS320/AB/R, WT/DS321/AB/R (16 October 2008) ('*US/Canada – Continued Suspension*'), para. 591.

[60] A. Eliason, 'Science versus Law in WTO: The (Mis)Interpretation of the Scientific Process and (In)Sufficiency of Scientific Evidence in *EC – Biotech*' (2009) 41(2) NYUJILP 341, 401.

and her examination is no more rigorous than his. But Matt is no longer after scientific rigour. All he needs now is to verify that the panel's discursive *description* of the scientific record is clear and coherent enough to reasonably withstand the appellants' criticism.

Despite the initial impressions, Keiko somehow did a decent job. Her conclusions on the scientific evidence, however imperfect, are solid enough to obscure the doubts and uncertainties inherent in the fact-finding process. Thankfully, she has also cited each of the most relevant exhibits in at least one footnote of the panel report, thus refuting the European Union's claim that the panel has disregarded material information.

Matt is relieved: this should be enough to salvage the panel. After all, the Appellate Body could manage to dismiss the European Union's DSU Article 11 claim. Maybe it will strategically exercise judicial economy.[61] Or maybe it will resort to one of its standard phrases: 'a panel's mandate under Article 11 of the DSU does not require it to accord to factual evidence of the parties the same meaning and weight as do the parties'; or 'the mere fact that a panel does not explicitly refer to each and every piece of evidence in its reasoning is insufficient to establish a claim of violation under Article 11'.[62] Let us wait and see.

This shift from *facts* to *language* has profound implications on judicial outcomes. By the time it reaches the Appellate Body, the amorphous world of scientific data has already been filtered twice – once by the parties' counsel and once by the panel's assistants. The lyophilization of life causes some data to rise in prominence and others to disappear from view, thereby delineating the horizon of the knowable, the speakable, and the thinkable. At each stage of the proceedings, certain doors for assertion and contestation are kept open, while others are shut forever. If a party fails to convince a panel that a certain scientific fact is relevant to the case, it will have a hard time persuading the Appellate Body to reopen that line of inquiry. Amid the maelstrom of reduction and essentialization, discarded elements can hardly be retrieved. There is something deeply contingent and unpredictable about the international judicial process, dependent as it is on the vagaries of the human episteme.

By filling up the pages of the issues paper, Matt has become the *master of the facts* in the *EU – Palm Oil* appeal. He is now the only person on the team

---

[61] See M. L. Busch and K. Pelc, 'The Politics of Judicial Economy at the World Trade Organization', 64(2) IntlOrg 257 (2010).
[62] Appellate Body Report, *European Communities – Definitive Anti-Dumping Measures on Certain Iron or Steel Fasteners from China – Recourse to Article 21.5 of the DSU by China*, WT/DS397/AB/RW (18 January 2016), para. 5.61.

who can handle the scientific information on record. If he treads carefully enough, he will enjoy broad discretion to convey that information as he sees fit. More discretion, we would add, than he will enjoy in his *legal* analysis. In fact, as we are about to see, the disposition of the legal claims on appeal will require the collective effort of several people, including Matt's secretariat colleagues, his director Björn and, of course, the judges themselves. By contrast, no one will dare to question his assessment of the disputed science. The adjudicators, who share Matt's lack of scientific background, will probably defer to his understanding, and so will Björn.

This double standard is common in the world of international adjudication. The interpretation and application of norms needs to conform to the expectations and dispositions shared by the judicial community. Conversely, not many expectations and dispositions exist as to the proper way to assess facts, ascribe weight to evidence, or decipher scientific information. Besides the commonsensical view that factual allegations ought to be supported by evidence, judicial professionals remain largely free to *select* their own fact-finding techniques.

So, here is an interesting plot twist. If you naïvely thought that facts, as natural phenomena, are objective and that laws, as social phenomena, are open to interpretation,[63] you might be surprised to discover that, in the judicial field, these propositions work the other way around. Legal interpretation wrestles with stringent social constraints, whereas facts can be purposefully construed to make one's legal narrative 'seem natural' and empirically grounded to those subject to it.[64] At close scrutiny, a judicial fact does not pre-exist the law: '*sa structure est définie par le droit [et] sa pertinence est liée au choix de la règle applicable*'.[65]

As he prepares to leave the office, Matt feels reinvigorated. His fears are gone. He walks out of Centre William Rappard through the West gate, exchanges a few words with the security guards, and cheerfully heads home. Who knows, maybe he will bump into a friend or two at the Bains des Pâquis.

---

[63] See generally K. R. Popper, *Objective Knowledge: A Realist View of Logic, Physics, and History* (Clarendon Press, 1972).

[64] S. L. Winter, 'The Cognitive Dimension of the Agon between Legal Power and Narrative Meaning' (1989) 87(8) MichLRev 2225, 2270.

[65] N. Burniat and G. Delforge, 'Le Syllogisme Dialectique: Modèle pour une Analyse Structurelle des Rapports entre Fait et Droit dans le Cadre du Raisonnement Juridique en Droit International Public – Étude de Cas: L'Arrêt *Gabcikovo-Nagymaros* Rendu le 25 Septembre 1997 par la CIJ' (1999) 32 RBDI 435, 440.

# 11

## The Explorer

Aphrodite was on a roll. Over the last few months, she sent out a dozen drafts to her lead lawyer, who was extremely pleased with the quality of her work.

The winning streak, however, came to a sudden halt when Aphrodite turned her attention to *Esquivel and Dimitriou v. France, Spain, and Greece*. The case is woefully complicated. In a nutshell, France has adopted an anti-terrorism decree enabling the police to carry out house searches without a warrant. To implement the decree extraterritorially, France has stipulated protocols of cooperation with certain partner countries, including Spain and Greece, but not with others, such as Germany and Belgium. Under these protocols, French police officers can operate in the territories of the partner countries by previously notifying their authorities. The complainants, Messrs. Esquivel and Dimitriou, challenged their home searches before the Spanish and the Greek authorities, respectively, but both governments dismissed their requests on the ground that the searches had been performed by French officials.

Aphrodite has tried to make sense of these facts for weeks. Now that she has a clearer picture, she is about to turn to her next task: the identification of the legal norms applicable to the case.

Yes, dear reader. After much ado, we are finally approaching the core duty of international judicial bureaucrats: legal interpretation. The bulk of their Memos is devoted to a detailed evaluation of the issues of law raised by the parties, the compilation of relevant precedents, and the articulation of options for solution. Essentially, bureaucrats *pre-interpret* the law and submit that pre-interpretation to the consideration of judges.

According to a recently proposed taxonomy, the process of legal interpretation consists of two distinct but interrelated steps. The first step, called *law-ascertainment*, requires the interpreter to identify the international legal norms that are relevant to the case at hand. The second step, called *content-determination*, requires the interpreter to attribute meaning to the norms so identified.[1] As we are about to see, both steps reflect a wealth of socio-professional practices. However, those practices are not necessarily the same for both. In fact, law-ascertainment and content-determination rest on different standards, are subject to different constraints, and raise different questions of power and authority.[2] They are two different games.

Law-ascertainment, which we discuss in this chapter, is a contest to define *what* constitutes international law. The normative ground of the contest is Article 38 of the ICJ statute, which codifies the formal sources of international law. As any player knows, Article 38 calls upon courts to apply the relevant 'conventions', 'custom[s]', and 'general principles of law', while also considering the 'judicial decisions and the teachings of the most highly qualified publicists'.[3] Drawing from this basic rule, the goal of the game is to divide legal materials between those that fall inside and those that fall outside of the scope of judicial practice. Certain materials are sanctified as unquestionably *legal* in nature, thereby acquiring cogency and normative force, whereas others are dismissed as aspirational, hortatory, or 'soft-law'.[4]

In a fragmented legal system, law-ascertainment is also the site of a struggle for the definition of the operational boundaries of each specialized judicial regime, that is its degree of openness or closure towards external influences. As a result of ever-evolving practices, some adjudicatory bodies are inclined to consider legal materials located outside their areas of expertise, while others are more inward-looking and act like 'separate little empires'.[5]

By contrast, the game of content-determination, which we discuss in the next chapter, sees its players compete for the authority to define

---

[1] The dichotomy is borrowed from d'Aspremont, 'The Multidimensional Process of Interpretation', 116–22.
[2] Ibid., 112.
[3] It has become 'almost a ritual presentation among commentators to make Article 38 … the central focus' of any exposition of the sources of international law. M. McDougal and M. Reismann, 'The Prescribing Function in World Constitutive Process: How International Law Is Made' (1980) 6(2) YaleStudWorldPubOrd 249, 259, 260. See also A. Pellet, 'Article 38', in A. Zimmermann et al. (eds.), *The Statute of the International Court of Justice: A Commentary* (Oxford University Press, 2006), 731.
[4] As an early attempt to distinguish between 'hard' and 'soft' sources of international law, see e.g. Weil, 'Relative Normativity'.
[5] C. Greenwood, 'Jurisdiction, NATO and the Kosovo Conflict', in P. Capps, M. Evans, and S. Konstadinidis (eds.), *Asserting Jurisdiction: International and European Legal Perspectives* (Hart, 2007) 145, 166–7.

what the law *means*.[6] The playground is Articles 31 and 32 of the VCLT, which codify the formal rules of treaty interpretation. Given the fluidity and indeterminacy of international norms, their meaning is incessantly asserted and contested by the myriad actors involved in the judicial process. Winning the game means securing dominance over the norms at stake, determining acceptable standards of argument, and shaping the range of admissibility of future interpretations.[7]

As we approach this part of our story, we must admit to a certain trepidation. Legal interpretation, which many see as *the* essential feature of adjudication,[8] has attracted so much scholarly attention that any attempt to add something meaningful seems bound to fail.

Yet, we feel compelled to try. As lamented in the opening pages of this book,[9] most theories of interpretation conceive of the 'interpreter' – the court – as 'one over-riding single consciousness',[10] which 'communicates' with an audience through judgments. Depending on the theorist, 'communication' may take several forms: a technical and objective elucidation of international law; a veiled expression of the interpreter's policy preferences; an attempt at strengthening the interpreter's legitimacy; and so forth. This focus on the *output* of judicial interpretation tells us little about the practices and interactions – the *inputs* – by which interpretation comes about.

By contrast, we will *deconstruct* the 'interpreter' and reveal it for what it is: a heterogeneous *group* of professionals who, in the 'empirical conditions'[11] of existing social structures, cooperate and compete with one another for the monopoly of the right to determine the law.[12] This entails a deconstruction of 'interpretation' itself. Rather than the harmonious voice of the court, we will hear a cacophony of arguments and counter-arguments, narratives and counter-narratives, assertions and contestations that reverberate across the international judicial community.

•

---

[6] See e.g. Bianchi, 'Textual Interpretation', 36–9; d'Aspremont, 'The Multidimensional Process of Interpretation', 121.
[7] See Venzke, *How Interpretation Makes International Law*, 58.
[8] As Roscoe Pound famously stated, 'the three steps in the decisions of causes' are the 'finding of rules, interpretation of rules, and application to particular controversies of the rules when found and interpreted'. R. Pound (cit. in Frank, 'Are Judges Human?', 19).
[9] See *supra*, pp. 7–15.
[10] Hernández, *The ICJ*, 108. See also E. Hambro, 'The Reasons behind the Decisions of the International Court of Justice' (1954) 7(1) CLP 212, 222.
[11] Fish, *What Comes Naturally*, 153.
[12] Bourdieu, 'The Force of Law', 817.

For starters, let us go back to Strasbourg and watch as Aphrodite ascertains the applicable law in *Esquivel and Dimitriou*. Luckily, she never had much patience for legal theory, otherwise she would find the task quite intimidating. From her point of view, this is an eminently *practical* business.

Unlike statutes in civil law traditions, the legal materials listed in Article 38 of the ICJ Statute (treaties, custom, general principles of law, judicial decisions, and the teachings of qualified publicists) are not neatly systematized or codified anywhere. Therefore, if interpretation was a purely deductive exercise, Aphrodite would have to 'look at dozens of sources without ever being certain of having found them all',[13] similar to a computer searching files in a folder.

But in reality, things do not work that way. Intuition plays a major role in guiding the search for the relevant law. When a man is accused of killing another, a judge does not read the criminal code from the first to the last article, trying to find the offence that best fits the act. Instead, the judge immediately jumps to the provisions that deal with homicide. The legal issues boil down to, say, whether the killing was intentional or negligent, whether the circumstances excluded culpability, etc. All potentially difficult questions, but much more limited in scope than the deductive method would have us believe.

The same holds true for Aphrodite. Despite the complex fact pattern in *Esquivel and Dimitriou*, she has a loose idea of where to find the law she seeks. Rather than reading the ECHR from cover to cover, she follows her instincts. Before she even realizes, she is already focusing on a tiny slice of all international legal sources in existence: Articles 6 and 8 of the Convention (devoted to the right to a fair trial and the right to respect of private and family life, respectively), Article 14 (prohibiting discrimination in the application of the enjoyment of the rights enshrined in the Convention), and the ECtHR's rich jurisprudence concerning those provisions. Some additional research might be warranted at a later stage – but for the time being, Aphrodite needs no more than this.

How is this possible? How did she come to *those* sources and not others? The answer lies in Aphrodite's position in the social world of international adjudication. Like any other member of the community, she 'can only see a certain distance'.[14] The limits of her visual field are dictated by the *habitus* and the collective practices of the ECtHR registry. Every day,

---

[13] Terris, Romano, and Swigart, *The International Judge*, 112.
[14] A. Bianchi, 'Reflexive Butterfly Catching: Insights from a Situated Catcher', in J. Pauwelyn, R. A. Wessel, and J. Wouters (eds.), *Informal International Lawmaking* (Oxford University Press, 2012) 200, 204.

she speaks with colleagues who share the same sensibilities and work with the same repertoire of materials. Through repeated interactions – and long coffee sessions – each colleagues points Aphrodite to bits of legal information that may come in handy, from recondite precedents to general principles of law.

Take this example:

'Knock knock!'

'Oh, hey Juan, long time no see!'

'Good to see you, Aphro! How's it going with the case? Looks like a tricky one.'

'Tell me about it. The claims per se are fairly easy, but this business of discrimination and extraterritorial application is quite a headache. It's bizarre, really. I've never seen a state regulation work this way.'

'Indeed. Our friend on the top floor is probably on cloud nine right now.'

'That sounds ominous. I hope Adam doesn't get too excited this time.' Adam is the Jurisconsult. 'My last case are his fetish. All these recent problems with the EU and welfare, you know.'

'I was stopping by precisely for that reason. I'm working on a file about discrimination in police controls, even though it does not involve extraterritorial application. I thought that perhaps you might want to have a quick chat.'

'Wow, yeah, that would be great. Article 14 involved?'

'Yes. The applicant was stopped for a search by the Spanish police because he's Pakistani.'

'Hmmm, so in your case it's discrimination on the basis of ethnicity?'

'Correct. That's what the guy alleges, at least.'

'But here I'm dealing with discrimination on a national basis: only Spaniards and Greeks, no matter their ethnicity, are subject to the enhanced police controls set up by France.'

'I know, it's a bit different. But perhaps there are common elements. We could work together on the jurisprudence section. Perhaps also on the description of the applicable provisions. We don't have to *reinvent the wheel* every time!'

'Sounds good. Any suggestions on case law?'

'Nothing special yet. At this stage, we're reading the *usual suspects*. For example, take a look at … 'Juan takes a piece of paper out of his pocket.'… *Gaygusuz v. Austria*,[15] *Koua Poirrez v. France*,[16] *Luczak v.*

---

[15] *Gaygusuz v. Austria*, Judgment of 16 September 1996, No. 17371/90, ECtHR-1996.
[16] *Koua Poirrez v. France*, Judgment of 30 September 2003, No. 40892/98, ECtHR-2003.

*Poland*,[17] *Dhahbi v. Italy*.[18] All cases of discrimination on the basis of nationality, in conjunction with the right to property or the right to a fair trial. Again, not exactly your case, but see if there's something useful in there.'

'Thank you! I've read *Dhahbi*, not the others. What else?'

'Well, I was also thinking about Protocol 12: discrimination not only in the enjoyment of Convention rights, but in any dealings with public authorities. Did your applicants invoke it?'

'No they didn't. How could they miss it? How could *I* miss it? That's a good one, thank you. Wow, this is a productive conversation. Give me more!' Aphrodite laughs.

'Nothing else for now, sorry. But let's keep each other in the loop. Meanwhile, I can email you what I have.'

'You are an angel, Juan. Coffee?'

'Coffee.'

Conversations of this kind will continue to punctuate Aphrodite's weeks to come. Her direct supervisor, the lead lawyer of Division 2.4, will review the thoroughness of Aphrodite's draft, verify that she has spotted all necessary sources, and eventually green-light the circulation of the document to the judge-rapporteur. But Aphrodite will also consult with other colleagues, from her officemates to lawyers from other divisions who might have worked on similar cases, in order to elicit their views about the salience of this or that material, its connections with other sources, etc. Meanwhile, Aphrodite will read a few academic treatises to make sure she is not missing anything useful.

In the background looms Adam, the Jurisconsult, who might intervene at any moment if he sees a potential inconsistency between Aphrodite's draft and past ECtHR jurisprudence. Usually occupied with more important business (Grand Chamber cases), Adam keeps quiet and seldom interferes with Aphrodite's drafts. However, on the rare occasions when the Jurisconsult does intervene, the research and drafting become more complex and require in-depth examination of a lot more case law. Hence Aphrodite's hope that Adam does not get too excited.

\*

What do these interactions tell us? Basically, that there exists a fundamental mismatch between the formal doctrines and the practical realities of law-ascertainment. The former insist that, with the exception of *jus cogens*, there is no hierarchy among the different sources of international

---

[17] *Luczak v. Poland*, Judgment of 27 March 2007, No. 77782/01, ECtHR-2007.
[18] *Dhahbi v. Italy*, Judgment of 8 April 2014, No. 117120/09, ECtHR-2014.

law,[19] such that they all form part of the same, indistinct body of rules and principles. By contrast, the latter show that the quest for the applicable law does, indeed, follow an order of priority, with certain sources being examined first, others second, and yet others being virtually ignored. The absence of a formal and absolute hierarchy of norms does not preclude the existence of many *informal and situated hierarchies* – as many as the international courts and tribunals in existence.

Viewed through the lens of practice, the law-ascertainer is essentially an *explorer*, whose search for the applicable norms radiates *horizontally*, in concentric circles. The exploration starts from the base camp – that is from the legal materials closest to the centre of gravity of the court concerned – and gradually ventures into less familiar territory – that is the legal materials located at the periphery of the court's jurisdiction. In turn, what constitutes the 'centre' and the 'periphery' depends on the position that each court, and the professional sub-community that orbits around it, occupies in the constellation of international adjudication. Legal materials that are well known to one sub-community of interpreters may be *terra incognita* to another, and vice versa. One court might be more inclined to parse through treaty text, while another might rely chiefly on jurisprudence. Some interpreters may take into account the decisions of other judicial mechanisms, while others may be oblivious to what happens outside their own tribunal.

Despite these variations, the practice of law-ascertainment presents certain regularities. Most explorers tend to follow a certain order in their search for the applicable law. To trace this order is to understand the centre-to-periphery hierarchy of sources in international law.

The first set of sources, that closest to the base camp, consists of what we have called the *principal norms*.[20] These are, quite simply, the norms on which the parties base their claims and defences, and which they expressly ask the court to apply. If the parties' counsel have done their work diligently, they will have properly identified the principal norms and discussed their applicability to the facts at hand. Irrespective of the parties' characterizations, the interpreter will be naturally inclined to use the principal norms as the starting point of the exploration.

On rare occasions, law-ascertainment ends there: the principal norms identified by the litigants exhaust the scope of the relevant law. However, most of the times, this is just the beginning. According to the *jura novit curia* principle, the interpreter is free to consider norms *other* than those

---

[19] See e.g. P.-M. Dupuy, *Droit International Public* (3rd edn., Dalloz, 1995), 14–16.
[20] Bartels, 'Principal Norms'. See *supra*, pp. 90–1.

invoked by the parties. The extent to which each court departs from the parties' claims varies. Some courts liberally develop their own independent analyses to ensure finality and thoroughness in their judgments. For instance, in recent years, the ICJ has adopted a rather flexible approach to the selection of the relevant legal sources, and has sometimes reached its conclusions on different legal grounds from those indicated by either litigant.[21] Similarly, some arbitral tribunals have asserted their freedom to provide the legal qualifications they deem appropriate, even when the parties have not expressly invoked them.[22] Other courts show greater restraint. For example, the WTO Appellate Body tends to defer to the parties' positions and, on occasion, has declined to complete the analysis on novel legal issues in the absence of their 'full exploration' in the litigants' submissions.[23]

Whichever approach one prefers, the fact remains that the interpreter is often forced to expand the scope of law-ascertainment beyond the legal materials identified by the parties. After all, an explorer who never sets foot outside the base camp could be accused of laziness.

This brings us to the second set of legal sources: the *contextual norms*. These are found in the immediate proximity of the principal norms – typically, in other provisions of the same treaty or in other legal instruments falling under the jurisdiction of the court. For Aphrodite, that would be the ECHR and its protocols; for Soledad, the ACHR and its protocols; for Matt, the WTO agreements; and for Carlos, the arbitral clause or the substantive content of the BIT. Because the jurisdiction of the ICJ is not formally limited to any specific treaty, Sophie's search for contextual norms is more open-ended.

The purpose of contextual norms is to provide the interpreter with a better understanding of how the principal norms operate, how they relate to one another, and on what overarching principles they rest.[24] Imagine, for instance, that a WTO complainant challenges a quantitative restriction under

---

[21] See e.g. *Maritime Dispute* judgment, Declaration of Judge Donoghue; *Arrest Warrant* judgment, para. 43. For discussion, see e.g. T. Sugihara, 'The Principle of Jura Novit Curia in the International Court of Justice: With Reference to Recent Decisions' (2012) 55 JapanYBIL 77.

[22] See also e.g. *Patrick Mitchell* v. *Democratic Republic of Congo*, ICSID Case No. ARB/99/7, Decision on the Application for Annulment of the Award (1 November 2006), para. 57. For discussion, see e.g. I. Kalniņa, '*Iura Novit Curia*: Scylla and Charybdis of International Arbitration?', 8 BaltYIL 89 (2008).

[23] Appellate Body Report, *EC – Seal Products*, para. 5.69.

[24] T. Broude and Y. Shany, 'The International Law and Policy of Multi-Sourced Equivalent Norms', in T. Broude and Y. Shany (eds.), *Multi-Sourced Equivalent Norms in International Law* (Hart, 2011) 1, 7.

Article XI of the GATT. In that case, Matt may wish to have a look at Articles II or III to understand what distinguishes a quantitative restriction from an import duty or a discriminatory trade measure. Or suppose that the responding state in a ECtHR case invokes public morals to justify an intrusion into private life under Article 8 of the ECHR. Here, Aphrodite may want to check Articles 9–11 of the Convention to get a sense of which other protected rights incorporate a public morals exception. Finally, think about two ICJ litigants arguing over the meaning of a treaty provision. Sophie could examine the preamble of the treaty to discern its object and purpose, compare the treaty with other instruments bearing on a similar subject matter, etc.

As you might expect, there is no fixed recipe for the identification of contextual norms. Their scope varies with the normative density of each judicial regime. The ACHR, for example, comprises a few dozen articles and a couple of additional protocols, whereas the WTO agreements span 600 pages of thick text. Therefore, Soledad has less treaty context to work with than Matt, and may therefore privilege other legal sources. More fundamentally, the (ir)relevance of a given contextual norm rests with the discretion of the interpreter and their interactions with colleagues. The act of drawing connections among various rules and principles is neither objective nor scientific. Those connections emerge by choice, perseverance, or happenstance. What is relevant context for one interpreter may be irrelevant for another. Had Aphrodite not shared a cup of coffee with Juan, she would have not thought about Protocol 12 to the ECHR. Her exploration of the relevant law would have taken a whole other path.

Our more traditional readers may retort that Article 31 of the Vienna Convention on the Law of Treaties (VCLT) sets forth detailed rules for the identification of the context relevant to treaty interpretation. They would, of course, be right. Yet, as we will see,[25] the VCLT rules are flexible enough to accommodate 'practically all approaches'[26] and accord the interpreter almost unfettered discretion to focus on certain contextual elements and disregard others. At most, the ubiquitous references to the VCLT in judicial reasoning serve as a rhetorical device to present law-ascertainment as rational and dispel 'the suspicion of deciding cases on subjective or arbitrary grounds'.[27]

Having identified the principal and the contextual norms, the interpreter will invariably turn to a third set of legal sources: the relevant *jurisprudence* of their court of allegiance. Here, the exploration begins with precedents

---

[25] See *infra*, Chapter 12.
[26] Bianchi, 'The Game of Interpretation', 44.
[27] J. Stone, 'Fictional Elements in Treaty Interpretation: A Study in the International Judicial Process' (1954) 1(3) SydLRev 344, 346.

that touch directly upon the legal and factual issues at stake, and gradually expands to include more indirect or circumstantial rulings.

Similar to treaty context, the density of available case law varies from one institution to another. As the ICJ has rendered just over 120 judgments since its establishment in 1946, Sophie will usually focus only on a handful of relevant decisions. Conversely, in the span of 20–30 years, the IACtHR has rendered over 300 rulings, the WTO adjudicatory bodies almost 400, and investment tribunals more than 600, thus providing Soledad, Matt, and Carlos with a much broader pool of jurisprudence to pick from.

As discussed,[28] the ECtHR stands out as the most prolific international court, having issued tens of thousands of judgments since its creation. Managing this massive output requires an extraordinary coordination effort. First, the Jurisconsult and his team provide a weekly brief to judges and registry lawyers detailing the most recent developments in case law. Second, the Jurisconsult assists in the compilation of a digest of leading judgments, decisions, and advisory opinions that filters out minor or photocopy cases.[29] Third, in 2011, the Court adopted the so-called pilot judgment procedure (PJP), a device that enables the joint examination of large numbers of cases arising from the same underlying problems.[30] One of the implications of the PJP is that the Court's assessment in a 'pilot' case 'necessarily extends beyond the sole interests of the individual applicant and requires it to examine that case also from the perspective of the general measures'.[31] The increasing popularity of the PJP facilitates the navigation of ECtHR case law, thus relieving registry lawyers of some of their burden.

---

[28] See *supra*, pp. 123–4.
[29] ECtHR website, www.echr.coe.int/Pages/home.aspx?p=caselaw/reports&c=.
[30] See e.g. D. Harris, M. O'Boyle, and C. Warbrick, *Law of the European Convention on Human Rights* (2nd edn., Oxford University Press, 2009), 851; P. Leach, H. Hardman, and S. Stephenson, 'Can the European Court's Pilot Judgment Procedure Help Resolve Systemic Human Rights Violations? *Burdov* and the Failure to Implement Domestic Court Decisions in Russia' (2010) 10(2) HRLRev 346; P. Leach et al., *Responding to Systemic Human Rights Violations: An Analysis of Pilot Judgments of the European Court of Human Rights and Their Impact at National Level* (Intersentia, 2010).
[31] Hutten-Czapska v. Poland, Grand Chamber Judgment of 19 June 2006, No. 35014/97, ECtHR-2007, para. 238. The adoption of the PJP is yet another example of the mutually constitutive relationship between judicial and academic fields. Indeed, its introduction was advocated in a series of strategically timed scholarly articles written by the incumbents in the European human rights regime. See e.g. L. Wildhaber, 'Pilot Judgments in Cases of Structural or Systemic Problems on the National Level', in U. Deutsch and R. Wolfrum (eds.), *The European Court of Human Rights Overwhelmed by Applications: Problems and Possible Solutions* (Springer, 2010) 69.

To collect the relevant precedents, law-ascertainers can use the search engines available to most courts and tribunals. The ICJ's engine is for internal use only. The public, by contrast, has to use the cumbersome official website of the Court,[32] which does not allow for theme-based searches. (Yet another sign of the jealousy with which insiders protect their prerogatives?) Similarly, ISDS lawyers rely mostly on internal servers, although in recent years the UNCTAD and other organizations have started to collect arbitral awards and make them searchable according to a number of criteria.[33] The ECtHR and the WTO are more transparent when it comes to disseminating their jurisprudence. The Human Rights Documentation (HUDOC) portal provides comprehensive search tools for the entire body of ECtHR case law, for the great benefit of the registry and the public alike.[34] Registry lawyers also use internal databases, which can be coded to semi-automatically fill in the dedicated sections of drafts. Similarly, the WTO Analytical Index[35] and a number of subscription-based websites[36] provide full, searchable access to the case law of panels and the Appellate Body.

The importance of jurisprudence cannot be overstated. Here too, we see a major discrepancy between doctrine and practice. Article 38 of the ICJ Statute relegates international judgments to a 'subsidiary means for the determination of rules of law'. No principle of *stare decisis* officially exists in international adjudication, such that a court decision binds only the parties to the dispute at hand.[37] Thus, in theory, adjudicators could refrain from relying on past case law and focus exclusively on the issues presently pending before them.

However, these formal considerations are 'at severe odds with large chunks of legal practice'.[38] In fact, international courts do regularly cite their past jurisprudence.[39] For example, 26 per cent of all ICJ cases decided

---

[32] ICJ website, www.icj-cij.org/en/list-of-all-cases.
[33] UNCTAD website, http://investmentpolicyhub.unctad.org/ISDS. Other databases are available, e.g., on the Italaw website, www.italaw.com/.
[34] HUDOC website, https://hudoc.echr.coe.int/eng.
[35] WTO website, www.wto.org/english/res_e/booksp_e/analytic_index_e/analytic_index_e.htm.
[36] See e.g. World Trade Law website, www.worldtradelaw.net/; Trade Law Guide website, www.tradelawguide.com/.
[37] See Article 59 of the ICJ Statute.
[38] Venzke, *How Interpretation Makes International Law*, 161.
[39] See generally N. Ridi, 'The Shape and Structure of the "Usable Past": An Empirical Analysis of the Use of Precedent in International Adjudication' (2019) 10(2) JIDS 200.

between 1948 and 2002 referred to the Court's past rulings.[40] Virtually all ECtHR and WTO decisions rely extensively on prior case law.[41] ISDS resembles 'a house of cards built largely by reference to other tribunal awards', with 'little consideration of the view and practices of states in general or the treaty parties in particular'.[42]

At a strategic level, reliance on precedent serves to convey an impression of coherence, predictability, and rationality in judicial reasoning. An erratic court, one that pays no heed to its prior case law, may lose credibility in the eyes of its audience.[43] At a professional level, the ethos and culture of international judges make them particularly sensitive to the weight of precedent. To respect the authority of past decisions is to confirm one's allegiance to the judicial field.[44] Those decisions constrain discretion, allow courts to 'imbu[e] treaties with meaning',[45] and establish 'authoritative reference points for later legal practice'.[46]

A precedent may be viewed as the 'burden' that prior interpretations of a rule place on 'future arguments' about the content of that rule.[47] Once an interpretation has been rendered, prospective litigants will be forced to engage with it and adapt their arguments accordingly. The opposed counsel will 'fight about the meaning' of that interpretation just like they fight about the meaning of any other legal sources.[48] Some will insist that the precedent confirms their client's legal position. Others will ask the court to depart from that precedent and provide reasons for

---

[40] See K. J. Pelc, 'The Politics of Precedent in International Law: A Social Network Application' (2014) 108(3) AmPolSciRev 547, 549.

[41] See Y. Lupu and E. Voeten, 'Precedent in International Courts: A Network Analysis of Case Citations by the European Court of Human Rights' (2012) 42(2) BrJPolSci 413, 416.

[42] A. Roberts, 'Power and Persuasion in Investment Treaty Interpretation: The Dual Role of States' (2010) 104(2) AJIL 179.

[43] F. Schauer, 'Precedent' (1987) 39(3) StanLRev 571, 600. See also A. von Bodgandy and I. Venzke, 'The Spell of Precedents: Lawmaking by International Courts and Tribunals', in C. P. R. Romano, K. J. Alter, and Y. Shany (eds.), *The Oxford Handbook of International Adjudication* (Oxford University Press, 2014) 504, 508.

[44] See e.g. D. Kennedy, 'Freedom and Constraint in Adjudication: A Critical Phenomenology' (1986) 36(4) JLegEduc 518, 550–1 (describing judges' *desire* to agree with past enunciations of the relevant rules).

[45] von Bodgandy and Venzke, 'The Spell of Precedents', 504.

[46] Ibid., 508.

[47] H. G. Cohen, 'Theorizing Precedent in International Law', in A. Bianchi, D. Peat, and M. Windsor (eds.), *Interpretation in International Law* (Oxford University Press, 2015) 268, 275.

[48] von Bodgandy and Venzke, 'The Spell of Precedents', 507; Venzke, *How Interpretation Makes International Law*, 161.

doing so.[49] Hence, case law connects the past, the present, and the future of interpretation, as it anchors the inherent indeterminacy of norms to the expectations and dispositions of the international judicial community.

In light of the above, we can readily understand why an exploration of relevant jurisprudence is a core component of the Memos prepared by judicial assistants. As discussed,[50] this is one area where judicial bureaucrats possess particularly strong capital. The lengthy terms of their contracts enable them to witness the progressive accumulation and evolution of case law to a degree that is normally precluded to other actors.[51] The ICJ's Registrar, the ECtHR's Jurisconsult, or the ABS Director have seen more disputes in their careers than even the most experienced judges.

Of course, it would be naïve to think that the Memos contain purely descriptive and neutral digests of past decisions. In fact, the *choice* of relevant precedents is as discretional and value-laden as the identification of contextual norms. Any stipulation of (ir)relevance depends on the inclinations of bureaucrats, their knowledge and experience, the time at their disposal, and their mutual interactions.

An old decision is *never* imported wholesale into the context of a new dispute. Instead, judicial bureaucrats meticulously break that decision down to its essential components, separate the main holdings from *dicta*, and ascertain which portions of the decision are most suitable to the present case. Precedents can be 'brushed aside, distinguished, narrowed, ... or extended'[52] depending on the contingent needs of the interpreter. An uncomfortable precedent – for example one at odds with the interpreter's position – can be quietly culled by paraphrasing or selectively quoting its content.[53] Conversely, an insignificant *dictum* buried in a forgotten footnote can be brought to the

---

[49] von Bodgandy and Venzke, 'The Spell of Precedents', 507; Cohen, 'Theorizing Precedent', 282–3.
[50] See *supra*, pp. 171–2.
[51] See e.g. C. A. Rogers, 'Apparent Dichotomies, Covert Similarities: A Response to Joost Pauwelyn' (2016) 109 AJIL Unbound 294, 297.
[52] Cohen, 'Theorizing Precedent', 282.
[53] A good example of the culling of a precedent is the Appellate Body report in *Dominican Republic – Import and Sale of Cigarettes*. In assessing the meaning of discrimination against imported products under Article III:4 of the GATT, the Appellate Body stated that 'the existence of a detrimental effect on a given imported product ... does not necessarily imply that this measure accords less favourable treatment to imports if the detrimental effect is explained by factors or circumstances unrelated to the foreign origin of the product, such as the market share of the importer in this case'. (Appellate Body Report, *Dominican Republic – Measures Affecting the Importation and Internal Sale of Cigarettes*, WT/DS302/AB/R (25 April 2005), para. 96.) The Appellate Body soon realized that, with this ruling, it had opened the door to defendants' arguments attempting to separate the market

fore and turned into the cornerstone of a new line of jurisprudence. In short, one does not *find* relevant precedents so much as one *constructs* them, amid the web of social relations that make up judicial activity.

\*

The path of law-ascertainment is becoming clearer. So far, we have mentioned three steps of the exploration: the principal norms identified by the parties, the contextual norms derived from adjacent treaty provisions, and the jurisprudence of the court for which a judicial bureaucrat works. These are relatively familiar materials, close enough to the base camp to be accepted as authoritative. But what else is out there? What about norms and judicial decisions pertaining to *other* international regimes? What about *general* principles of international law?

This is where things get really tricky. The farther one moves away from the centre of their system, the less one is aware of potentially relevant sources. Remember Sophie's interview for the ICJ clerkship?[54] When Judge Lehmann asked her about the WTO panel report in *EC – Biotech Products*, she did not quite know how to answer. Sophie can comfortably quote ICJ judgments, but knows very little about WTO law and jurisprudence. Similar epistemic limitations apply to all judicial bureaucrats. Aphrodite and Soledad are well acquainted with the decisions of human rights courts, but are not particularly conversant in investment law. Carlos masters ISDS jurisprudence and can recite the main ICJ cases, but is unlikely to follow the latest developments in human rights litigation. Given the insularity of WTO adjudication,[55] Matt is probably unaware of whatever goes on outside Centre William Rappard.

We should not blame our protagonists for not studying hard enough. After all, they were top students at their respective universities. Rather, it

---

conditions in which importers operate from the design and operation of the measures at issue. Therefore, in later jurisprudence, the Appellate Body dropped almost all references to the *Cigarettes* report. Instead, it took the view that, in assessing discrimination against imports, one 'ought to take into account *both* the design and structure of the measure at issue *and* the way in which the measure operates (or can be expected to operate) in the light of the relevant features of the market concerned'. Appellate Body Report, *US – Tuna II (Mexico) (Article 21.5 – Mexico)*, para. 7.59 (emphasis added). See also e.g. Appellate Body Report, *US – COOL*, para. 269. The Appellate Body never felt a need to state whether, in light of these subsequent developments, its decision in *Cigarettes* was still good law: it simply let that precedent slip out of view.

[54] See *supra*, pp. 120–1.
[55] See e.g. A. Lang, 'Twenty Years of the WTO Appellate Body's "Fragmentation Jurisprudence"' (2015) 14(3) JITLP 116.

is the international legal order that has become too vast, too pluralistic and, too complex for any one individual to master it all.[56] As a result of this increased density, 'interpreters of international law are necessarily partial and selective in their reading of the sources'.[57] The average working day at court, coupled with stringent deadlines, simply does not leave enough time for bureaucrats to explore legal materials located too far from their vantage point. Even if our protagonists spent every waking hour reading international judgments, they would merely scratch the surface. Indeed, they would still miss the myriad interpretations of international law expressed *outside* the courtrooms – in diplomatic statements, advocacy papers, and scholarly treatises.[58]

Venturing too far into unknown territory may actually *diminish* the value of the Memo to the adjudicators. If the document were to contain too lengthy a review of unfamiliar legal materials, the judges would probably not understand it and refuse to engage with the argument. At any rate, the materials in the vicinity of the centre are usually sufficient for a thorough legal examination of the case at hand. As Duncan Doyle quipped during his Leuven lecture,[59] why explore uncharted territory when the solution is at your fingertips?

Seen through the lens of social practices, the emergence of 'self-contained regimes'[60] in international law acquires a new meaning. Over time, the professional sub-community orbiting around each international

---

[56] See J. Crawford, *Chance, Order, Change: The Course of International Law* (Brill, 2014), 153.
[57] Ibid. See also Waibel, 'Interpretive Communities', 147–8. This phenomenon is certainly not unique to the field international adjudication. Every facet of modern social life seems to contradict Vico's statement that we humans are, by logical necessity, able to understand and control the institutions we have created. See 'Giambattista Vico', *Routledge Encyclopedia of Philosophy* (Routledge, 1998), vol. X, 603–4. As Simone Weil observed in the 1930s, nothing in today's world 'is made to man's measure', as the scale of social affairs vastly outsizes 'the human body, human life, the year, the day, the average quickness of human thought'. S. Weil, *Oppression and Liberty*, trans. A. Wills and J. Petrie (Taylor and Francis, 2004), 102.
[58] See e.g. Bianchi, 'The Game of Interpretation', 39–40; d'Aspremont, 'The Multidimensional Process of Interpretation', 115; Waibel, 'Interpretive Communities', 156.
[59] See *supra*, p. 98.
[60] See, among many others, B. Simma, 'Self-Contained Regimes' (1986) 16 NYIL 111; Simma and Pulkowkski, 'Of Planets and the Universe'; J. Crawford, 'The ILC's Articles on Responsibility of States for Internationally Wrongful Acts: A Retrospect' (2002) 96(4) AJIL 874, 879–80; A. Lindroos and M. Mehling, 'Dispelling the Chimera of "Self-Contained Regimes": International Law and the WTO' (2005) 16(5) EJIL 857; M. Noortmann, *Enforcing International Law: From Self-Help to Self-Contained Regimes* (Routledge, 2016), 127–72.

court develops a *habitus* as to what legal sources are trustworthy and what others are not, based on its specialized expertise and its 'shared outlook' on the world.[61] The operational closure of each sub-community fosters trust among its participants[62] and, at the same time, reinforces its epistemic bias.[63] Through patterned repetition, each participant becomes 'a fully instrumentalised cog in the respective machine'[64] and learns to separate the norms that are 'in line with [its] philosophy' from those that should be kept 'at bay'.[65] Thus, the various sub-communities are reluctant to engage with materials that originate too far away from their spheres of competence, and work instead 'to sustain insulation from seemingly disturbing outside perspectives'.[66] Any attempt to transfer expertise, practices, or modes of thinking from one sub-community to another is seen as a trespass that might shake the 'context-preserving routine'.[67]

Consider, for instance, the two arbitral awards rendered against Argentina in the *CMS* and *Continental* cases. In both disputes, Argentina sought to justify its measures based on the state of necessity under customary international law and specific treaty provisions.[68] The *CMS* tribunal, for the most part, addressed Argentina's defence through the 'traditional' prism of the customary rules of state responsibility.[69] By contrast, the *Continental* tribunal observed that similarities existed between the defence raised by Argentina and the general exceptions enshrined in Article XX of the GATT. It therefore found it 'more appropriate to refer to the GATT and WTO case law ... than to refer to the requirement of necessity under customary international law'.[70]

---

[61] Waibel, 'Interpretive Communities', 160.
[62] See Burt, *Brokerage and Closure*, 93–7.
[63] Ibid., 168.
[64] Koskenniemi, 'The Fate of Public International Law', 26.
[65] Waibel, 'Interpretive Communities', 163.
[66] Venzke, *How Interpretation Makes International Law*, 157. For instance, it has been suggested that it would be 'unrealistic to request from trade delegates (the typical panelists) ... to move outside the (illusory) comfort of the [WTO] covered agreements', and that the current design of panels 'is probably the main reason why trading nations generally abstain from submitting claims that would demand that panels step outside the four corners of the covered agreements'. P. Mavroidis, 'No Outsourcing of Law? WTO Law as Practiced by WTO Courts' (2008) 102(3) AJIL 1, 53–4.
[67] R. M. Unger, *False Necessity: Anti-Necessitarian Social Theory in the Service of Radical Democracy* (2nd edn., Verso, 2001), 32.
[68] *CMS Gas Transmission Company* v. *Argentina*, ICSID Case No. ARB/01/8, Award (12 May 2005) ('*CMS* v. *Argentina*'), para. 309; *Continental Casualty Company* v. *Argentina*, ICSID Case No. ARB/03/9, Award (5 September 2008) ('*Continental* v. *Argentina*'), para. 160.
[69] *CMS* v. *Argentina*, para. 315.
[70] *Continental* v. *Argentina*, para. 192.

The different approaches adopted by the two tribunals could be due to many factors, including the ways in which the parties presented their arguments. However, a plausible explanation is that the president of the *CMS* tribunal was a practitioner with extensive experience in general international law,[71] whereas the president of the *Continental* tribunal was a sitting member of the WTO Appellate Body.[72] The former was an insider to the ISDS field, while the latter came from another sub-community carrying a baggage of 'foreign' expertise. Unsurprisingly, the 'unorthodox' approach of the *Continental* tribunal was lambasted by some incumbents in the ISDS regime, who found the tribunal's reasoning 'inadequate and flawed', making 'unsupported leaps to trade or other international law', and threatening to 'undermine the legitimacy of investor-State arbitration'.[73]

Besides avoiding invasions of turf, operational closure helps 'defuse the stakes of inter-regime conflicts'.[74] By largely ignoring one another, the various sub-communities avoid addressing normative tensions and leave thorny questions 'as open as possible, for as long as reasonable'.[75] Take, for example, the already cited ECtHR case *Nada* v. *Switzerland*.[76] The complainant claimed that the Swiss authorities had placed undue restrictions on his freedom of movement, in breach of Article 8 of the Convention. The government retorted that those restrictions were necessary to ensure Switzerland's compliance with UN Security Council Resolution 1390(2002), which required UN members to limit the movement of persons inscribed in the terrorism watch list. Many observers awaited the ECtHR's judgment with trepidation: a decision in favour of the responding state would imply that UN resolutions trump the European human rights regime; a decision in favour of the complainant would suggest the opposite.

However, the Grand Chamber avoided ruling on this delicate normative conflict. The judges went out of their way to solve the dispute on the basis of European human rights law alone. In particular, they opined that Switzerland 'enjoyed some latitude, which was admittedly limited but

---

[71] See curriculum vitae of Francisco Orrego Vicuña, www.heidelberg-center.uni-hd.de/down/cv_orrego.pdf.
[72] See WTO website, Giorgio Sacerdoti, www.wto.org/english/tratop_e/dispu_e/popup_giorgio_sacerdoti_e.htm.
[73] J. E. Alvarez and T. Brink, 'Revisiting the Necessity Defense: Continental Casualty v. Argentina', in K. P. Sauvant (ed.), *Yearbook of International Investment Law and Policy 2010–2011* (Oxford University Press, 2012) 315, 358.
[74] Lang, 'Fragmentation Jurisprudence', 121.
[75] Ibid.
[76] See *supra*, p. 177.

nevertheless real',[77] in implementing the Security Council resolution. Therefore, the restrictions imposed on the complainant were attributable to Switzerland alone. The Court's convoluted legal narrative subtly criticized the Security Council[78] without openly defying its authority.

All that being said, closure is not an ineluctable state of affairs. The centre and the periphery of a judicial regime are constantly renegotiated by the participants in each sub-community, who put forward competing claims to promote, resist, or reshape the incorporation or the exclusion of different kinds of knowledge.[79] As part of this endless turmoil, sometimes foreign and unfamiliar materials *do* enter the decision horizon of international adjudicators. Often, these 'openings' originate from the Memos prepared by judicial bureaucrats. Perhaps the drafter of the Memo took inspiration from a chat with someone working in another area of international law; or perhaps an old university reading suddenly came to mind. Usually, it is the parties' arguments that draw the drafter's attention to exotic legal sources.[80] As discussed,[81] counsel usually have an interest in sticking to safe arguments that resonate with the judges' preferences and expertise. However, at times, creative lawyering requires a deviation from the beaten path and the invocation of legal standards and modes of thinking typical of other areas of international law.

Let us see how this works in practice.

•

Remember the European Union's submission in the *EU - Palm Oil* WTO appeal? Jasper had to insist to convince Duncan to include a jurisdictional argument in the brief.[82] Now, the last section of the submission talks about the free trade agreement (FTA) between Indonesia and the European Union, according to which the latter is entitled to maintain its palm oil regime in place. The European Union maintains that, by filing a WTO complaint against the palm oil regime shortly after the entry into force of the FTA, Indonesia acted contrary to the general principle of good faith. On this basis, the European Union asks the WTO adjudicators to declare

---

[77] *Nada v. Switzerland*, ECtHR Judgment (Grand Chamber), No. 10593/08 (12 September 2012), paras. 175–98.
[78] See E. de Wet, 'From *Kadi* to *Nada*: Judicial Techniques Favouring Human Rights over United Nations Security Council Sanctions' (2013) 12(4) CJIL 787, 807.
[79] See Lang, 'Legal Regimes and Professional Knowledges', 132.
[80] Charlotin, 'Investment Awards and WTO Decisions', 297–8.
[81] See *supra*, pp. 96–9.
[82] See *supra*, pp. 99–101.

the complaint inadmissible. When he suggested this argument, Jasper was fully aware that its odds of success were slim. But he also foresaw that, were the European Union to prevail, it would score a landmark ruling changing the course of WTO jurisprudence. 'High risk yields high returns.'[83]

Jasper will probably never know, but his gambit paid off. Upon reviewing the European Union's brief, Matt finds the FTA argument quite compelling, and is now trying to figure out how best to present it in the issues paper.

The problem is that the FTA is a legal source located outside the four corners of traditional WTO expertise. Perhaps not far outside, as it deals with trade matters and not, say, with human rights or environmental protection – but still unmistakably 'foreign'. Appellate Body members are not well acquainted with the potential frictions between WTO and non-WTO obligations. To many judges, especially those lacking a solid background in international law, mastering the complex disciplines of the WTO must look intimidating enough, without a need to embark on delicate conflict-of-norms analyses, discussions of general principles, and the like. Moreover, WTO case law is adamant that neither panels nor the Appellate Body have the authority to 'determine rights and obligations outside the [WTO] agreements'.[84]

Given the circumstances, Matt expects that persuading the judges will be an uphill battle. In discussing the matter, he cannot fall back on the familiar assumptions of WTO vernacular. Instead, he must build up his argumentation from scratch. What are overlapping treaty obligations? When does a normative conflict arise, and what standards exist to assess it? What is the legal value of general principles of international law in WTO dispute settlement? And what about Article 31.3(c) of the VCLT? For a moment, Matt is tempted to give up. It would be so much easier to draft a short and dry section of the issues paper dismissing this whole FTA business altogether! The judges would surely like it, and it would take less work and fewer coffee cups.

Yet, something keeps Matt from copping out. Is he worried about judicial fragmentation? Not necessarily. As a member of the WTO community, Matt does not have a strong allegiance to general international law, and certainly does not spend his nights thinking about the cohesiveness of the system. His doubts are more of an *ethical* nature. For some reason, Indonesia's course of action bothers Matt. Probably, during the FTA

---

[83] See *supra*, p. 98.
[84] Appellate Body Report, *Mexico – Taxes on Soft Drinks*, para. 56.

negotiations, the parties made mutual trade concessions, some of which are now being surreptitiously impaired by Indonesia's WTO complaint. If that is true, then the obstinate reluctance of WTO adjudicators to engage with non-WTO agreements enables and legitimizes morally questionable behaviour on the part of litigants.

'There is something *unfair* about this', Matt thinks. But again, substantive fairness is not the goal of international adjudication. Although often invoked,[85] our Lady Justice seldom sets foot in the courtroom.[86] And when she does, she enters in the garb of specific rules and principles that seek to operationalize the fuzzy notion of fairness: due process guarantees, special and differential treatment in favour of developing countries, legitimate expectations, etc. It is to *those* rules and principles that Matt must turn if he wishes to get the judges' attention. Simply shouting 'unfair!' would be useless. Worse, it would be *unprofessional*.

Where to begin? After some thought, Matt identifies two possible hooks.

The first hook is to portray the FTA as a 'relevant rule[] of international law applicable in the relations between the parties' under Article 31.3(c) of the VCLT. This would make the FTA a source pertinent to the interpretation of Indonesia's and the European Union's obligations under the WTO agreements. In support of his narrative, Matt could refer to the principle of systemic integration, according to which an international legal instrument must be always interpreted 'in its relationship to its normative environment'.[87]

However, Matt quickly realizes that this is a non-starter. Article 31.3(c) of the VCLT does not have much traction in the WTO regime. The panel in *EC – Biotech Products* ruled that the 'parties' mentioned in that provision are *all* WTO Members, and not just those involved in a specific dispute.[88] The Appellate Body has never disavowed that ruling. Instead, it doubled down by holding that non-WTO rules are not 'relevant' under Article 31.3(c) unless they expressly bear on the interpretation of a specific term contained in the WTO agreements.[89] Reversing this trend would be a titanic task. If Matt were to insist too much

---

[85] See e.g. Article 38(2) of the ICJ Statutes, according to which the ICJ may decide cases *ex aequo et bono*.
[86] See e.g. G. Guillaume, 'The Use of Precedent by International Judges and Arbitrators' (2011) 2(1) JIDS 5.
[87] ILC Fragmentation Report, para. 423.
[88] Panel Report, *EC – Approval and Marketing of Biotech Products*, para. 7.68.
[89] Appellate Body Report, *Peru – Agricultural Products*, paras. 5.101–5.104.

on the intricacies of systemic integration, the Appellate Body members would meet the issues paper with scepticism. During deliberations, Björn could simply recommend that this whole VCLT business be dismissed as abstruse, and the judges would be all too happy to oblige.

The second hook seems to hold more promise. Matt can follow Jasper's theory and argue that the existence of the FTA makes Indonesia's WTO complaint an act of bad faith. Inspired by this idea, he opens an academic textbook that was taking dust on his shelf and starts reading about the general principle of good faith in international law.

However, after perusing the relevant WTO jurisprudence, Matt is disheartened to discover that good faith will not take him very far, either. In a recent case, the Appellate Body dismissed a very similar allegation of foul play. The complainant, Guatemala, had challenged a measure adopted by the respondent, Peru, right after the two countries had entered an FTA permitting the existence of that measure. The Appellate Body did not consider the principle of good faith under general international law, but rather *reconstructed* that principle according to the internal logics of the WTO system. In particular, the Appellate Body took the view that, pursuant to Article 3.7 of the DSU, 'Members should have recourse to WTO dispute settlement in good faith, and not frivolously set [the system] in motions'.[90] At the same time, the Appellate Body cautioned that 'the relinquishment of rights granted by the DSU cannot be lightly assumed', and that 'if a WTO Member has not clearly stated that it would not take legal action with respect to a certain measure, it cannot be regarded as failing to act in good faith if it challenges that measure'.[91] In absence of such a clear statement by Guatemala, the Appellate Body dismissed Peru's allegations of bad faith.

Reading the judgment, Matt is utterly impressed by the craftmanship of its drafters. With one swift legerdemain, the Appellate Body appropriated good faith as a principle *internal* to the WTO regime and, therefore, addressed it exclusively in light of its own jurisprudence. By doing so, the Appellate Body achieved multiple goals. First, it reaffirmed the primacy of the WTO agreements over any non-WTO rules that might stand in their way. Second, it insulated its decision from the vagaries of good faith under general international law – a principle whose fuzzy and

---

[90] Appellate Body Report, *Peru – Agricultural Products*, para. 5.18 (quoting Appellate Body Report, *Mexico – Corn Syrup (Article 21.5 – US)*, para. 73.).
[91] Appellate Body Report, *Peru – Agricultural Products*, para. 5.18 (quoting Appellate Body Report, para. 5.25 (quoting Appellate Body Report, *EC – Bananas III (Article 21.5 – Ecuador II / Article 21.5 – US)*, paras. 217 and 228).

context-dependent character causes so many headaches to other courts and tribunals.[92] And all of this in six short paragraphs!

'This isn't good,' mutters Matt. 'If the general principle of good faith doesn't help, then I'm out of options. What else could I use? Think, Matt, think …'

The epiphany comes in the form of Michelle, the intern, whom Matt had instructed to research the issue. She points Matt to the old panel report in *Argentina – Poultry*, which discusses the estoppel principle. The litigants in that dispute, Brazil and Argentina, were both signatories to the Protocol of Olivos, a legal instrument adopted in the framework of MERCOSUR. The Protocol contained a fork-in-the-road clause, whereby 'once a party decides to bring a case under either the MERCOSUR or WTO dispute settlement forums, that party may not bring a subsequent case regarding the same subject-matter in the other forum'.[93] Before the initiation of the WTO case, a MERCOSUR court had sustained the legality of Argentina's measure, which Brazil then challenged before the WTO panel.

During the panel proceedings, Argentina argued that a state is estopped from acting inconsistently with a prior 'statement of fact' that is 'clear and unambiguous', 'voluntary, unconditional', and 'relied on in good faith' by another state.[94] Argentina maintained that, by opting for the MERCOSUR forum, Brazil had implicitly stated that it would not later challenge Argentina's measure at the WTO. In turn, Argentina had relied on Brazil's statement in good faith and made negotiating concessions in exchange for it.[95] The panel seemed to agree with Argentina's abstract definition of estoppel, but ultimately rejected Argentina's argument on the ground that the Protocol of Olivos was not yet in force at the time of the initiation of the WTO proceedings.[96]

---

[92] Some scholars, for instance, lament that ISDS tribunals do not fully understand the principle of good faith and do not know how to use it. See generally B. M. Cremades, 'Good Faith in International Arbitration' (2012) 27(4) AmUIntlLRev 761. Others argue that, by circumventing the text of BIT clauses, this principle allows for the erosion of legal guarantees protecting the host state and opens the door to excessive discretion on the part of tribunals. For this reason, good faith has been labeled the 'terrorist' of international investment law. See F. De Trazegnies Granda, 'Desacralizando la Buena Fe en el Derecho', in M. M. Córdoba (ed.), *Tratado de la Buena Fe en el Derecho* (La Ley, 2004) vol. II, 2, 19, 43, 45.
[93] Panel Report, *Argentina – Definitive Anti-Dumping Duties on Poultry from Brazil*, WT/DS241/R (22 April 2003) ('*Argentina – Poultry Anti-Dumping Duties*'), para. 7.38.
[94] Ibid., para. 7.36.
[95] Ibid., para. 7.37.
[96] Ibid., para. 7.38.

*Eureka*! Matt thanks Michelle profusely. He has finally found a decent way to present the FTA in the issues paper. Unlike the Protocol of Olivos, the FTA between Indonesia and the European Union *has* entered into force prior to the initiation of the *EU – Palm Oil* case. With some imagination, one could argue that, by entering into the FTA, Indonesia recognized the legality of the palm oil regime and implicitly promised not to challenge it in WTO proceedings.

Admittedly, this narrative does not remove all difficulties. Lengthy explanations will be required to convince the adjudicators to go for Matt's proposed solution. Moreover, the proposal is almost certain to meet the resistance of Björn and other senior secretariat colleagues, who may hold more conservative views. However, the choice to resurrect a long-forgotten panel report presents the advantage of maintaining the scope of the inquiry *within* the realm of WTO jurisprudence, without straying too far into unknown territory.

All of a sudden, Matt feels very excited. He could really make it this time. For once, the Appellate Body could break with its 'splendid isolation'[97] and decide in favour of dialogue among overlapping legal regimes. This would certainly strengthen the court's 'external legitimacy' in the eyes of general international lawyers, at the cost of undermining its 'internal legitimacy' with hard-line trade insiders.[98]

If this comes to pass, it will not be because of Matt alone. It will be because of the discrete, disorderly, and sometimes contradictory positions taken by a whole chain of amanuenses who, through the practice of law-ascertainment, continuously renegotiate the boundaries of the WTO regime in a perpetual 'context-transforming struggle'.[99] History books will not remember Jasper, Duncan, Matt, Michelle, or even the Appellate Body members as the co-agents of this little revolution. Yet, if the WTO system opens up to the outer legal world, it will also be thanks to them.

Would greater openness be a good idea? Hard to tell. The macro-consequences of micro practices are difficult to predict. Certainly, however, such a paradigm shift would deeply alter the discursive possibilities in the trade field, opening the door to new argumentative avenues while making others sound outmoded and 'wrong'.

---

[97] Allen and Soave, 'Jurisdictional Overlap', 33.
[98] Howse, 'Governance by Judiciary', 37.
[99] Unger, *False Necessity*, 32.

# 12

## A Four-Letter Word

•

> The products of the territory of any contracting party imported into the territory of any other contracting party shall be accorded treatment no less favourable than that accorded to like products of national origin.[1]

Pretty straightforward: under Article III:4 of the GATT, a state must grant equal treatment to imported and domestic like products. Simple, right? Not quite. As he opens the Word file containing his draft issues paper, Matt estimates that a legal evaluation of those two-and-a-half lines of treaty text will take about a week of work. As a data analyst will surely tell you, that is roughly three days per line.

Indonesia and the European Union disagree, among other things, about whether imported and domestic palm oil products are 'like' within the meaning of Article III:4. In Indonesia's view, they are. For the European Union, they are not. Each party has provided extensive arguments in support of its position. Indonesia insists that imported and domestic palm oil products are physically indistinguishable, serve the same purposes, and are targeted at the same consumer audience. Were it not for the measure at issue, they would be perfectly substitutable. The European Union retorts that the two sets of palm oil products differ in one major respect: the domestic ones are manufactured using sustainable methods, while the imported ones are derived from deforestation and inhumane labour conditions. This difference alone is sufficient to exclude a finding of 'likeness'.

Guess who has to solve this question? Yes, you guessed right.

After the phase of law-ascertainment, which we have discussed in the previous chapter, Matt has now reached the second step of legal interpretation: content-determination. He must now *assess the meaning* of the norms it has identified as applicable to the *EU – Palm Oil* dispute. While, as we have just seen,[2] the relevance of the Indonesia-European Union FTA is highly

---

[1] Article III:4 of the GATT.
[2] See *supra*, pp. 218–23.

contentious, there is no doubt that Article III:4 of the GATT applies to the case. Non-discrimination against imported products is a 'cornerstone principle of the multilateral trading system',[3] and litigants routinely invoke it as a principal norm in WTO disputes. In other words, this portion of the dispute is rather *traditional*. The interpretation of 'likeness' is something that students learn on day one of their trade law classes. Not convinced? Then take a look at the physical state of Matt's hard copy of the WTO agreements. His 'green bible', as Björn calls it, is worn out by years of use. 'Classic' provisions like Article III:4 are almost illegible, buried under layers of pencil scribbles.

Yet, even a norm as basic as Article III:4 must be given meaning 'in accordance with customary rules of interpretation of public international law'.[4] And even a seemingly straightforward exercise is rife with conceptual difficulties. If 'hard cases make bad law',[5] easy cases best exemplify the implicit assumptions and the unthought reflexes inherent in the practice of content-determination.

Matt gazes at the text of the treaty for a few seconds, as if expecting the word 'like' to spontaneously disclose its secrets. Yet, of course, these are but four letters on a piece of paper,[6] inert marks with no life of their own. Matt has grown so used to the question 'What does the law say?' that he has almost forgotten one basic truth: the law has no voice, no arms, no legs, and no brains. Its existence resides entirely in the minds of its interpreters and enforcers. The law walks, works, and speaks only through people. A legal rule is a bit like Roland Barthes' Eiffel Tower. It is simply *there*, lying silently on the page of a tattered book. A 'pure – virtually empty – sign' upon which the reader must 'unceasingly put meaning'.[7]

In the coming days, Matt will have to climb the Tower to get a clearer view of the terrain on which the *EU – Palm Oil* dispute plays out. More prosaically, he will have to determine the meaning of the word 'like' and assess how it applies to the products at issue. How will he do this? It depends on who you ask. As should be clear by now, there is a fundamental mismatch between the formal doctrines and the practical realities of legal interpretation.

---

[3] Appellate Body Report, *Canada – Renewable Energy/Canada – Feed-in Tariff Program*, para. 5.55. See also e.g. Appellate Body Report, *Japan – Alcoholic Beverages II*, p. 18.
[4] Article 3.2 of the DSU.
[5] *Northern Securities Co. v. United States*, 193 US 197 (1904), dissenting opinion of Justice Holmes.
[6] See E. S. Tsai, '"Like" is a Four-Letter Word: GATT Article III's "Like Product" Conundrum' (1999) 17(1) BerkeleyJIntlL 26.
[7] R. Barthes, 'The Eiffel Tower', in R. Barthes, *A Barthes Reader* (S. Sontag ed., Hill and Wang, 1983) 236, 237–8 (emphasis omitted).

The former depict the interpretative process as a scientific exercise, where the preordained and unequivocal meaning of the law is extracted from its sources and mechanistically applied to the facts in dispute.[8] Under this view, the task of international courts is simply to 'clarify' and elucidate the content of norms.[9] In official discourse, adjudicators have largely embraced their role as *la bouche de la loi*.[10] So, for instance, the ICJ has stressed that 'its task is to engage in its normal judicial function of ascertaining the existence of legal principles and rules'.[11] Similarly, '[t]he dispute settlement system of the WTO ... serves ... to clarify the existing provisions of [the WTO] agreements in accordance with customary rules of public international law.'[12]

This insistence on clarity intimates that all international adjudicators, irrespective of their institutional affiliations, must resort to uniform interpretative techniques to ensure coherence in their rulings.[13] Those techniques are, of course,[14] found in Articles 31 and 32 of the VCLT, which set out the 'general rule' and the 'supplementary means' of treaty interpretation. Since the explosion of international adjudication in the early 1990s, countless

---

[8] See Klabbers, 'Virtuous Interpretation', 23; Johnstone, *The Power of Deliberation*, 35; Venzke, 'The Role of International Courts', 99–100; Latour, *The Making of Law*, 142.

[9] Lauterpacht, *The Development of International Law*, 66.

[10] See e.g. C. Greenwood, 'The Development of International Law by the International Criminal Tribunal for the Former Yugoslavia' (1998) 2 UNYB 97, 111; ICJ website, *Speech by H. E. Judge Shi Jiuyong, President of the International Court of Justice, to the General Assembly of the United Nations* (5 November 2004), www.icj-cij.org/public/files/press-releases/1/2981.pdf.

[11] *Legality of the Threat or Use of Nuclear Weapons*, Advisory Opinion of 8 July 1996, ICJ Rep. 1996, 226, para 18. See also *Fisheries Jurisdiction (Great Britain and Northern Ireland v. Iceland)*, Judgment of 25 July 1974, ICJ. Rep. 1974, 3, para. 53. See also e.g. *Jurisdictional Immunities of the State (Germany v. Italy: Greece intervening)*, Judgment of 3 February 2012, ICJ Rep. 2012, 99, Dissenting Opinion of Judge Yusuf, para. 58 ('the Court has an important role to play to provide guidance on rules of international law and to clarify them.')

[12] Article 3.2 of the DSU.

[13] Klabbers, 'Virtuous Interpretation', 33.

[14] This 'of course' must be qualified. The VCLT rules of interpretation have been overtly challenged by a number of international courts and tribunals, who saw them as ill-suited to deal with their specific subject matters. For instance, according to the ECtHR, the European Convention differs from treaties 'of the classic kind', in that it 'creates, over and above a network of mutual, bilateral undertakings, objective obligations which ... benefit from a "collective enforcement"'. *Ireland v. United Kingdom*, Judgment of 18 January 1978, ECtHR Series A (1978) No. 25, 90, para. 239. See also e.g. *Loizidou v. Turkey*, Preliminary Objections, Judgment of 23 March 1995, No. 15318/89, ECtHR-1995, para. 70. Similarly, the IACtHR has held that human rights treaties 'are not multilateral treaties of the traditional type concluded to accomplish the reciprocal exchange of rights for the mutual benefit of the contracting States', but aim at 'the protection of the basic rights of individual

treatises have appeared which dissect the VCLT doctrines and call upon judges to apply them as rigorously as possible.[15] Interpretation as an exact science does tolerate polite disagreements over the meaning of a given norm. However, those mild forms of dissent are little more than 'theological error'[16] – a failure to properly apply the heuristics offered by the legal system and to correctly extract content from the relevant texts.

To be sure, such rigid formalism is increasingly *passé*. In recent decades, a number of critics have radically challenged the objective nature of interpretation, and have instead depicted the process as a subjective and purposeful exercise. The roots of this critique can be traced back to the linguistic turn in hermeneutics, which posits that words do not have an intrinsic meaning other than that given to them by their use.[17] Under this view, the meaning of a text is inherently indeterminate.[18] Its content 'depends not so much on what the authors[] put into it, but rather what the reader takes out'.[19] As applied to legal interpretation, this entails that the meaning of a norm 'cannot be *discovered*, but only *created*'.[20] The way the interpreter creates the norm inevitably reflects their categories of thought, their implicit assumptions, and their 'stream of tendency'.[21] By postulating the primacy of the interpreting subject over the interpreted object, critics tend to portray adjudicators as political actors, who inevitably bend rules consistently with their own ideological preferences.[22]

---

human beings ... both against the State of their nationality and all other contracting States'. See e.g. *Effect of Reservations on the Entry into Force of the American Convention on Human Rights (Articles 74 and 75)*, Advisory Opinion OC-2/82 of 24 September 1982, IACtHR Series A, No. 2, para. 29; *Blake v. Guatemala (Reparations)*, Judgment of 22 January 1999, IACtHR Series C, No. 48, Separate Opinion of Judge Cançado Trindade, para. 33. For discussion, see e.g. Koskenniemi, 'The Fate of Public International Law', 4–5; J. M. Pasqualucci, *The Practice and Procedure of the Inter-American Court of Human Rights* (Cambridge University Press, 2001), 327–9.

[15] As a recent example, see E.-U. Petersmann, 'Need for a New Philosophy of International Economic Law and Adjudication' (2014) 17(3) JIEL 639, 649–61.
[16] Fish, *Is There a Text*, 338. See also Burniat and Delforge, 'Le Syllogisme Dialectique', 436.
[17] Wittgenstein, *Philosophical Investigations*, para. 43. See also Venzke, 'The Role of International Courts', 115.
[18] See e.g. J. Derrida, *De la grammatologie* (Éditions de Minuit, 1967).
[19] Klabbers, 'Virtuous Interpretation', 23. See also Shaffer and Trachtman, 'Interpretation and Institutional Choice', 120.
[20] von Bogdandy and Venzke, 'In Whose Name?', 505 (original emphasis).
[21] B. Cardozo, *The Nature of the Judicial Process* (Yale University Press, 1921), 12.
[22] See e.g. R. M. Unger, *What Should Legal Analysis Become?* (Verso, 1996); Kennedy, *A Critique of Adjudication*; Jouannet, 'La Motivation', 252; B. Leiter, 'Legal Formalism and Legal Realism: What Is the Issue?' (2010) 16(2) LegTheory 111, 115.

Despite their opposite conclusions, both formalist and critical narratives seek to provide 'large, controlling image[s]' and impart 'philosophical meaning' to the interpretive process.[23] And both neglect the infinite nuances and mundane steps that make up the interpretive process. Philosophers have never heard of Matt, a foot soldier in the invisible army that constructs international law every day. Nor, for that matter, has Matt ever spent much time exploring the theoretical underpinnings of his interpretive *practice*. Perhaps it is best so. Were he to indulge in philosophical thinking, Matt would probably end up like Captain Haddock, who becomes an insomniac the day someone asks him if he sleeps with his beard under or over the sheet.[24]

Indeed, without ado, Matt is already preparing for the interpretation of the word 'like'. Sipping coffee from his WTO-branded mug, he jots down some scribbles. On the left side of a notebook page, he writes: 'ordinary meaning; context; negotiating history'. On the right side: '*Border Tax Adjustment* criteria; jurisprudence; talk to Björn'. The two lists neatly capture the dual nature of Matt's task. The one on the left tells us what content-determination *purports* to be; the one on the right what it *really* is.

The ostensible story is one of strict obedience to the interpretive techniques prescribed by the VCLT. If used properly, these techniques are supposed to lead Matt to objective and unambiguous conclusions as to the meaning of 'likeness' under Article III:4.[25] Once one looks at them 'correctly', a rose is a rose is a rose, and like products are like products are like products. The true story, by contrast, reveals that a rose and a pair of like products are, at most, *bundles of attributes* that interpreters ceaselessly bestow upon them, depending on what 'glasses' they are wearing.[26] In turn, the choice of the 'glasses' does not depend on Matt's individual preferences, but on the expectations, the dispositions, and the standards of acceptability of the community to which he belongs.

In the pages that follow, we will unravel the dual nature of Matt's interpretive exercise. Let us be clear, though: while we take Matt as an example, similar considerations could apply to all the other characters of our story. The roots of *any* act of content-determination, irrespective of the particular area of law in which it occurs, ultimately reside in professional practice. Why Matt, then? First because, as said, 'likeness' is an 'easy' notion with which anyone in the trade field would be familiar. Second, because the WTO agreements are among the most detailed international

---

[23] M. Schorer, 'The Necessity of Myth' (1959) 88(2) *Daedalus* 359, 360.
[24] Hergé, *The Adventures of Tintin: The Red Sea Sharks* (Methuen, 1960), 42.
[25] See e.g. Orakhelashvili, *Interpretation*, 286.
[26] Waibel, 'Interpretive Communities', 148.

treaties in existence, and are therefore particularly apt at conveying the illusion of legal determinacy. Third, because the Appellate Body is famous for the 'plodding manner' in which it relies on the VCLT doctrines to support its legal interpretation.[27] And finally, because the WTO judicial community is particularly tight and exerts strict control over the interpretation of its legal concepts.

•

Let us begin with the ostensible story. Let us wrestle with the VCLT on its own terrain. The Convention requires Matt to analyze the word 'like' in light of the rules of interpretation listed in Articles 31 and 32. This is nothing but an 'outward show',[28] a lip service to the 'methods, style, and aesthetics' of international law.[29] By putting on that show, Matt seeks to bolster the credibility of his issues paper in the eyes of the adjudicators assigned to the appeal.[30] In truth, he may not even be fully aware of these theatrics. His performative act could be 'so embedded in the situation ... that it doesn't seem to be an act at all'.[31] Be that as it may, *none* of the techniques prescribed by the VCLT can provide a conclusive basis for Matt's content-determination exercise.

Let us take a closer look.

The starting point of any VCLT assessment is the *'ordinary meaning'* of the treaty term to be interpreted.[32] Different international courts rely on this basic interpretive tool in different ways. Some, like the ICJ, refer to dictionary definitions only sparingly.[33] By contrast, WTO adjudicators are so obsessed with definitions that the Oxford English Dictionary has de facto become one of the WTO agreements.[34] The practice of literal

---

[27] Howse, 'Governance by Judiciary', 33.
[28] Venzke, *How Interpretation Makes International Law*, 49.
[29] d'Aspremont, 'The Multidimensional Process of Interpretation', 119 (quoting M. Prost, *The Concept of Unity in Public International Law* (Hart, 2012), 149).
[30] Strict adherence to the VCLT has become 'reassuring to panels and litigators, who made sure to arm themselves amply with dictionaries and to structure their pleadings around textual readings under all of the elements of the VCLT'. Howse, 'Governance by Judiciary', 45.
[31] Fish, *Is There a Text*, 276. See also Bianchi, 'Textual Interpretation', 42.
[32] Article 31.1 of the VCLT (emphasis added).
[33] See e.g. *Oil Platforms (Islamic Republic of Iran* v. *United States of America)*, Preliminary Exception, Judgment of 12 December 1996, ICJ Rep. 1996, 818, para. 45. See also Bianchi, 'Textual Interpretation', 36.
[34] C.-D. Ehlermann, 'Six Years on the Bench of the "World Trade Court": Some Personal Experiences as Member of the Appellate Body of the World Trade Organization' (2002) 36(4) JWT 605, 616. See also I. van Damme, *Treaty Interpretation by the WTO Appellate Body* (Oxford University Press, 2009), 222–35; Abi-Saab, 'The Appellate Body and Treaty Interpretation', 106.

interpretation has been defended by eminent specialists, like the late Umberto Eco. In his view, the 'literal meaning of lexical items ... listed first by dictionaries' constitutes a 'constraint' on interpretation that cannot be avoided, and '[a]ny act of freedom on the part of the reader can come *after*, not *before*, the acceptance of that constraint.'[35]

Here is the catch though: dictionary definitions are themselves the result of a selection – an act of *interpretation* – by compilers and readers alike. A definition is not semantically self-contained, but invariably refers to other definitions. The word 'house' means 'building for habitation'.[36] One can understand that definition only if one knows the meaning of both 'building' and 'habitation'. Otherwise, one will have to look up the definitions of those terms, which in turn refer to other terms, which in turn... you get the point. To interpret a word based on its dictionary definition alone is to get lost in an infinite regress.[37] Moreover, when relying on a dictionary, international courts seldom list all the definitions of the relevant term. Instead, they usually *choose* the definition that best serves their purposes – to the point of switching to *another* dictionary whenever they cannot find what they are looking for.[38]

The problem of textual indeterminacy is not confined to dictionaries. Even the plainest word, one that presents little lexical ambiguity, can be easily understood or remain obscure depending on the context in which it is uttered by a speaker and received by a listener.[39] Wittgenstein would say that 'the meaning of a word is its use in language'.[40] Derrida would add that even the purest language 'cannot be reduced down to one sense that is the proper meaning'.[41] Carlos' favourite punk band would conclude that a bird is a word.[42]

In international adjudication, the best evidence of the ambivalence of words can perhaps be found in so-called 'multi-sourced equivalent norms'

---

[35] Eco, *The Limits of Interpretation*, 5–6 (emphasis added).
[36] Online *Oxford English Dictionary*, 'House', www.oed.com/view/Entry/88886?rskey=3Nvb mJ&result=1&isAdvanced=false#eid.
[37] See L. Nelson, *A Theory of Philosophical Fallacies*, trans. F. Leal and D. Carus (Springer, 2016), 131.
[38] See e.g. the unusual changes from the Oxford to the Merriam-Webster dictionary in Appellate Body Reports, *Thailand – Cigarettes (Philippines)*, fns 290 and 291 to para. 192; *US – Tuna II (Mexico)*, fn 396 to para. 185; *EC – Seal Products*, fn 1505 to para. 5.299.
[39] Bianchi, 'Textual Interpretation', 41–2.
[40] Wittgenstein, *Philosophical Investigations*, para. 43.
[41] *Stanford Encyclopedia of Philosophy*, 'Jacques Derrida', https://plato.stanford.edu/entries/derrida/.
[42] Ramones, *Surfin' Bird*.

(MSENs), that is identically or similarly termed provisions contained in separate and independent legal instruments.[43] If lexical identity or similarity were dispositive of meaning, those provisions should be interpreted in the same manner across the board. However, in reality, MSENs are often read in wildly divergent ways by different courts or tribunals, due to 'the specific legal contexts' in which they are embedded and the 'different background principles' that inform the respective treaty regimes.[44]

So, what is the ordinary meaning of the word 'like'? The dictionary that Matt has just consulted defines it as '[s]imilar, resembling, alike'.[45] 'Thanks very much', snorts Matt. 'I did not expect "like" to mean "different"'. He continues reading. '[O]f similar or identical shape, size, colour, character, etc., to something else; having the same or comparable characteristics or qualities as some other person or thing; similar; resembling; analogous.'[46] Ok, so two things are 'like' when they share comparable characteristics or qualities. Again, this does not offer much help. *What* characteristics are relevant for the purposes of *WTO* 'likeness'? A pineapple has a similar shape to a hand-grenade, a similar size to an ostrich egg, and similar colours to the flag of Brazil. Yet, something tells Matt that a pineapple is not 'like' any of the above under Article III:4.

The problem is that the characteristics that would allow him to establish 'likeness' are not univocal, but rather depend on the context in which the comparison is made. James Bond is like Tarzan and the Pope in that they are all unmarried white men. Yet, because of the different contexts in which one usually talks about them, they are seldom associated on the basis of their marital status, their ethnicity, or their gender.[47] All these considerations lead Matt to one simple conclusion. The ordinary meaning of the word 'like' remains elusive when one looks at it in the abstract. The context in which the term is used is of the essence.

To obviate this problem, the VCLT stipulates that the relevant '*context*' informs the meaning of the treaty term to be interpreted.[48] But make no mistake. In VCLT parlance, the context is *not* the communicative environment in which the term is used. Instead, the interpreter is required to locate

---

[43] Broude and Shany, 'Multi-Sourced Equivalent Norms'.
[44] Allen and Soave, 'Jurisdictional Overlap', 16. See also Broude and Shany, 'Multi-Sourced Equivalent Norms', 7–9.
[45] Online *Oxford English Dictionary*, 'Like', www.oed.com/view/Entry/108302?rskey=qJRp7f&result=3#eid.
[46] Ibid.
[47] See Bianchi, 'Textual Interpretation', 43.
[48] Article 31.1 of the VCLT (emphasis added).

the context *within the legal instruments themselves* – either in the treaty's own 'text, including its preamble and annexes', or in any related agreement between the parties in connection with the conclusion of the treaty.[49] Context is out there, ready to be discovered.

But again, 'out-there-ness'[50] does nothing to solve the problem of textual indeterminacy. How are the object and purpose of the GATT supposed to inform Matt's interpretation of the word 'like'? Do the objectives of 'raising standards of living, ensuring full employment and a large and steadily growing volume of real income and effective demand, developing the full use of the resources of the world and expanding the production and exchange of goods'[51] really provide any guidance? What meaning can Matt derive from the drafters' desire to ensure 'the elimination of discriminatory treatment in international commerce'?[52]

The truth is that context provides even broader discretion than dictionary definitions. As discussed in the previous chapter,[53] the identification of contextual norms is laden with value-judgments and strategic considerations. Interpreters are largely free to select whatever norms support their contingent needs. Some will focus on provisions located in the immediate proximity of the term to be interpreted. Others will draw inferences from materials located far away.[54] In all cases, contextual interpretation enables skilful lawyers to draw certain connections among norms while obscuring others, tinker with the object and purpose of treaties, and resort to a whole repertory of Latin dicta such as *a fortiori*, *a contrario*, etc.

Sometimes, the connections established via contextual interpretation are rather intuitive and merely confirm the interpreter's inclinations. Consider, for example, the ICJ's reading of Article 36 of the Vienna Convention on Consular Relations (VCCR) in *Avena*.[55] Pursuant to Article 36.1(b), state authorities must inform an arrested foreigner of their

---

[49] Article 31.2 of the VCLT.
[50] The expression is borrowed from d'Aspremont, 'The Multidimensional Process of Interpretation', 115.
[51] Second preambular recital of the GATT.
[52] Third preambular recital of the GATT.
[53] See *supra*, pp. 208–9.
[54] See e.g. O. K. Fauchald, 'The Legal Reasoning of ICSID Tribunals: An Empirical Analysis' (2008) 19(2) EJIL 301, 321 (noting how ISDS tribunals enjoy broad latitude in using contextual arguments as the 'starting point' for subsequent reasoning, as 'essential' interpretive elements, or as 'non-essential' interpretive elements (emphasis omitted)).
[55] *Avena and Other Mexican Nationals (Mexico v. United States of America)*, Judgment of 31 March 2004, ICJ Rep. 2004, 12 ('*Avena* judgment').

consular rights 'without delay'. Common sense would suggest that the phrase 'without delay' is quite flexible. For instance, the authorities may provide the required information either immediately upon arrest, or as soon as they have reason to believe that the arrested person may indeed be a foreign national.

The ICJ could have simply stated as much. Instead, it felt compelled to shoehorn its interpretation into the logic of the VCLT. It began by noting that the phrase 'without delay' is expressed in different terms in the various language versions of the VCCR.[56] It further observed that dictionary definitions in those various languages offer 'diverse meanings' of the phrase, such that one must 'look elsewhere' to understand it.[57] On this basis, the Court went on to consider the 'object and purpose' of the Convention, the provisions adjacent to Article 36.1(b), and the *travaux préparatoires*,[58] and concluded that '"without delay" is not necessarily to be interpreted as "immediately" upon arrest'.[59]

Other times, contextual interpretation enables surprising forms of judicial creativity.[60] The WTO Appellate Body's reading of Article 2.1 of the TBT Agreement is a good case in point. Article 2.1 requires that, when applying technical regulations, states accord products imported from any country 'treatment no less favourable than that accorded to like products of national origin and to like products originating in any other country'. On its face, the provision does not offer any justification for treating like products differently. Nor does, the TBT Agreement provide any general exceptions equivalent to those in Article XX of the GATT.

Faced with these textual constraints, the Appellate Body used contextual interpretation to introduce a measure of flexibility in Article 2.1. It began by referring to the preamble to the TBT Agreement, which states that 'no country should be prevented from taking measures necessary to ensure the quality of its exports, or for the protection of human, animal or plant life or health, of the environment, or for the prevention of deceptive practices, at the levels it considers appropriate'.[61] Based on that context, the

---

[56] Ibid., para. 84.
[57] Ibid.
[58] Ibid., paras. 85–6.
[59] Ibid., para. 87.
[60] See generally F. Zarbiyev, 'Judicial Activism in International Law: A Conceptual Framework for Analysis' (2012) 3(2) JIDS 247.
[61] Appellate Body Report, *United States – Measures Affecting the Production and Sale of Clove Cigarettes*, WT/DS406/AB/R (4 April 2012) ('*US – Clove Cigarettes*'), paras. 94–6.

Appellate Body stated that the TBT Agreement strikes a balance between the need to avoid unnecessary trade obstacles and the recognition of members' right to regulate.[62] Therefore, it held, a technical regulation that treats like products differently may nonetheless be justified when the differential treatment '*stems exclusively from a legitimate regulatory distinction*'.[63]

Matt does not know who, among his ABS colleagues, pulled this formula out of the hat. How did he or she persuade the judges to add a whole new prong to the Article 2.1 test out of thin air? How many iterations did this phrasing undergo before ending up in the judgment? Was it part of a deliberate judicial strategy[64] or did it reflect contingent preoccupations about the outcomes of that single case? Hard to tell. What is certain is that the test was reaffirmed in subsequent reports.[65] Today, the existence of a 'legitimate regulatory distinction' – or, as Jane Weaver would call it, an 'el-ar-dee' – has become a default step in any discussion of Article 2.1.

Such is the creational power of context.

The remaining VCLT techniques are, if possible, even more open-ended. Together with the context, the interpreter must take into account any '*subsequent agreements*' or '*subsequent practice*' of the parties concerning the interpretation or application of the treaty.[66] Unsurprisingly, neither of these elements is clearly defined. Their existence, scope, and content can be construed in countless ways depending on the interpreter's needs. It is quite rare to find an express agreement of the parties concerning the meaning of a specific treaty term. Most of the times, the interpreter enjoys broad discretion to *infer* – or refuse to infer – that agreement from circumstantial evidence. Similarly, the contours of subsequent practice are highly debatable and present the same heuristic difficulties as customary international law.[67] Do UN General Assembly resolutions constitute proof of subsequent practice? What about the guidelines or decisions issued by WTO committees? Reasonable minds may differ on these questions and, indeed, international jurisprudence swings both ways.[68]

---

[62] Appellate Body Report, *US – Clove Cigarettes*, para. 96.
[63] Ibid., paras. 174, 175, 181, 215 (emphasis added).
[64] In this sense, see e.g. Howse, 'Governance by Judiciary', 54–5 (arguing that the Appellate Body sought to recognize member states' right to regulate as an act of defiance against the 'deep integration' agenda of the Uruguay Round).
[65] See e.g. Appellate Body Reports, *US – Tuna II (Mexico)*, para. 215; *US – COOL*, para. 271.
[66] Articles 31.3(a) and 31.3(b) of the VCLT (emphasis added).
[67] For a comprehensive overview of these difficulties, see I. Buga, *Modification of Treaties by Subsequent Practice* (Oxford University Press, 2018).
[68] See e.g. *Certain expenses of the United Nations (Article 17, paragraph 2, of the Charter)*, Advisory Opinion of 20 July 1962, ICJ Rep. 1962, 151, p. 162; *Legal Consequences for States of the*

The next interpretive element, '*any relevant rules of international law applicable in the relations between the parties*',[69] raises intractable questions. *Which* rules are relevant? *How* does one determine their applicability to the parties? And *what* should be done to properly take those rules into account? As discussed at length in the previous chapter,[70] the identification of applicable rules does not rest on exact science, but depends on each interpreter's vantage point in the constellation of international courts, their epistemic limitations, and the assumptions in force in their community of allegiance. Hence, as with all others VCLT techniques, the value of so-called systemic integration is largely left to the discretion and the 'present calculation'[71] of the interpreter.

Matt witnessed the extent of this discretion on two separate instances. The first was when he read the WTO panel report in *EC – Seal Products*, which his colleague Keiko had helped draft. At some point, the panel referred to the UN Declaration on the Rights of Indigenous Peoples and the International Labour Organization (ILO) Convention concerning Indigenous and Tribal Peoples in Independent Countries, and examined the content of those two instruments at some length.[72] Intrigued, Matt asked Keiko about this unusual foray into extra-WTO sources. Why did the panel talk about UN and ILO rules? Was it trying to make a systemic point about their interpretive value? Keiko shrugged her shoulders:

'Nah. We simply wanted to underline the importance of protecting the interests of Inuit and other indigenous communities. The parties just so happened to cite the Declaration and the Convention in their submissions. We thought that referring to them might make the panel's narrative more credible. That's it. No grand scheme here.'

The second instance occurred when Matt was assigned to the appeal in *China – Raw Materials*. A central issue in that case was whether the trade

---

*Continued Presence of South Africa in Namibia (South West Africa) Notwithstanding Security Council Resolution 276 (1970)*, Advisory Opinion of 21 June 1971, ICJ Rep. 1971, 16, para. 52. Appellate Body Reports, *US – Gambling*, para. 174; *EC – Bananas III (Article 21.5 – Ecuador II) / EC – Bananas III (Article 21.5 – US)*, para. 390; *US – Clove Cigarettes*, paras. 260–2.

[69] Article 31.3(c) of the VCLT (emphasis added).
[70] See *supra*, pp. 206–18.
[71] Koskenniemi, 'The Fate of Public International Law', 26.
[72] Panel Report, *European Communities – Measures Prohibiting the Importation and Marketing of Seal Products*, WT/DS400/R, WT/DS401/R (25 November 2013), paras. 7.292–7.296 (referring to UN General Assembly, *United Nations Declaration on the Rights of Indigenous Peoples*, A/RES/61/295 (2 October 2007); International Labour Organization, *Indigenous and Tribal Peoples Convention*, C169 (27 June 1989)).

commitments set forth in China's WTO accession protocol are subject to the general exceptions of Article XX of the GATT, including the exception relating to the 'conservation of exhaustible natural resources'.[73] Reading the panel report, Matt noticed some remarkable variations in tone. When defining 'conservation', the panel indulged in a contextually rich analysis that generously cited extra-WTO legal sources and the precedents of other international courts.[74] However, when it came to the question of whether Article XX applied to China's accession protocol, the panel suddenly retreated to rigid textualism.[75] It found that, since the relevant paragraph of the accession protocol paragraph did not contain any explicit language linking it to Article XX, China could not invoke the conservation exception in that case.[76] To use a metaphor dear to the WTO community, the scope of the panel's reasoning was like an 'accordion':[77] broad and open-ended where the stakes were lower, narrow and dismissive where they were higher.

See how easy it is?

Finally, let us not forget the *'preparatory work of the treaty and the circumstances of its conclusion'*.[78] According to the VCLT, these supplemental means of interpretation may be examined only insofar as all prior techniques leave the meaning of the treaty 'ambiguous or obscure' or lead to a 'manifestly absurd or unreasonable' result.[79] For decades, commentators have debated whether the *travaux préparatoires* deserve their ancillary

---

[73] Article XX(g) of the GATT.
[74] Panel Report, *China – Measures Related to the Exportation of Various Raw Materials*, WT/DS394/R, WT/DS395/R, WT/DS398/R (5 July 2011) ('*China – Raw Materials*'), paras. 7.378–7.381 (referring to *S. S. Wimbledon*, Judgment of 17 August 1923, PCIJ Rep., Series A, No. 1; *Exchange of Greek and Turkish Populations*, Advisory Opinion of 21 February 1925, PCIJ Rep., Series B, No. 10; PCIJ, *Jurisdiction of the European Commission of the Danube*, Advisory Opinion of 8 December 1927, PCIJ Rep., Series B, No. 14; UN General Assembly Resolution 1803 (XVII), *Permanent Sovereignty Over Natural Resources* (14 December 1962); UNGA Resolution 626 (VII), *Right to Exploit Freely Natural Wealth and Resources* (21 December 1952); *Convention on Biological Diversity* (5 June 1992), UNTS 1760, 79).
[75] Ibid., paras. 7.121–7.160. For discussion, see e.g. J. Y. Qin, 'The Predicament of China's "WTO-Plus" Obligation to Eliminate Export Duties: A Commentary on the *China-Raw Materials* Case', 11(2) CJIL 237 (2012).
[76] Panel Report, *China – Raw Materials*, para. 7.129.
[77] This expression, which comes from Appellate Body Report in *Japan – Alcoholic Beverages II*, has entered WTO lingo like few others. These figures of speech constitute yet another tool by which a professional community differentiates itself from its broader social environment. Crack a joke about the accordion to any international lawyer and, judging from their reaction, you will be able to gauge their expertise in WTO law.
[78] Article 32 of the VCLT (emphasis added).
[79] Articles 32(a) and 32(b) of the VCLT.

role,[80] should acquire more prominence,[81] or are simply another step in the routine practice of treaty interpretation.[82] But the point remains that a determination of whether a treaty term remains 'ambiguous or obscure' is left to the interpreter. The distinction between clarity and obscurity is, once again, an interpretive *choice*. In practice, a court can always 'scrutinize the negotiating history whether the text seems clear or not'.[83] If the negotiating history supports the court's interpretation, the court can cite it as an additional source of support.[84] If the negotiating history disconfirms the court's interpretation, the court can label the text as clear and ignore the negotiating history altogether.[85]

By now, the point should be clear. The VCLT rules of treaty interpretation can be 'twisted and bent, turned upside down', and 'prioritized to one's liking'.[86] No meta-principle exists which can univocally reconstruct the 'patchwork quilt'[87] of doctrines at play. Sometimes, interpreters will simply state what they *think*, and then append some vague justificatory language: 'We find support to our interpretation in rule X, declaration Y, guideline Z'. Under *which* VCLT heading they found that 'support' is anyone's guess.[88] Narrow textualism, broad contextualism, systemic integration, interpretive isolationism – the possible '*ruses*'[89] are infinite, as are the outcomes they enable. That is why, for all his obedience to the VCLT, Matt is not getting any closer to determining the meaning of the word 'like' in Article III:4 of the GATT.

At this point, you might conclude that Matt is left free to take 'any conceivable position',[90] that he can say whatever he wants about the meaning of 'likeness'. If this were true, you would probably expect to see our

---

[80] See e.g. K. J. Vandevelde, 'Treaty Interpretation from a Negotiator's Perspective' (1988) 21(2) VandJTransnatlL 281, 296; D. J. Bederman, *Classical Canons: Rhetoric, Classicism and Treaty Interpretation* (Ashgate, 2001), 315; Abi-Saab, 'The Appellate Body and Treaty Interpretation', 104–5.
[81] See e.g. J. D. Mortenson, 'The *Travaux* of *Travaux*: Is the Vienna Convention Hostile to Drafting History?' (2013) 107(4) AJIL 780, 820–2.
[82] See e.g. J. Klabbers, 'The Declining Importance of *Travaux Préparatoires* in Treaty Interpretation' (2003) 50(3) NILR 267, 268, 285; Vandevelde, 'Treaty Interpretation', 296.
[83] Vandevelde, 'Treaty Interpretation', 296–7.
[84] See again *Avena* judgment, para. 86.
[85] Vandevelde, 'Treaty Interpretation', 296–7.
[86] Bianchi, 'The Game of Interpretation', 44.
[87] The expression is borrowed from A. Altman, 'Legal Realism, Critical Legal Studies, and Dworkin' (1986) 15(3) Phil&PubAff 205, 222.
[88] See e.g. Appellate Body Report, *Russia – Pigs*, fn 197 to para. 5.65.
[89] A. Papaux, 'Aux Sources du Droit: L'Autorité et la Ruse' (2013) 70 RIEJ 207.
[90] Koskenniemi, *From Apology to Utopia*, 565.

poor ABS lawyer lost in doubt, frantically 'jumping from one signifier to another'.[91] No. That would be a hasty conclusion. In fact, as we write, Matt is wrapping up his 'likeness' analysis with a satisfied grin on his face. A few more paragraphs to draft, a couple of references to check, and *voilà!* he is closing the issues paper and bidding goodnight to his colleagues. How did this happen? How did Matt make sense of the word 'like' when that word is textually and contextually indeterminate? Or, as some would put it, how did Matt avoid contracting the 'Derrida virus'?[92]

•

This is where the true story begins: a story firmly rooted in the interpretive practices of the WTO. Similar to law-ascertainment,[93] content-determination does not take place in a vacuum, but is 'deeply embedded in a societal context' where different actors routinely interact and communicate with one another.[94]

It simply makes no sense to say that textual indeterminacy leaves the interpreter with unfettered discretion. In fact, interpretation is constrained by the most powerful of forces: the shared dispositions and expectations of the international judicial community. These 'pressures, tendencies and orientations' shape 'reality and possibilities'[95] and determine what is 'legitimately assertable'.[96] An interpretation that meets community expectations will be recognized as competent and authoritative, and might be tolerated even if it slightly departs from established canon. Conversely, an interpretation that radically breaks from accepted standards is unlikely to 'find acceptance'[97] and could be dismissed as incompetent or aberrant. Hence, the community takes the ground between 'the pitfalls of objectivity (the plain meaning of the text)' and 'pure subjectivity (the unconstrained reading of the text)'.[98]

But community expectations are not only a source of constraint. They also *enable* action and make interpretation possible in the first place. Were it not for them, the interpreter would be caught in an infinite regress and get lost in 'all manners of metaphysical and epistemological questions'.[99]

---

[91] Bianchi, 'Textual Interpretation', 48.
[92] See e.g. N. A. Salingaros, 'The Derrida Virus' (2003) 2003(126) Telos 66.
[93] See *supra*, Chapter 11.
[94] Bianchi, 'Textual Interpretation', 35.
[95] Marks, 'False Contingency', 10.
[96] S. Kripke, *Wittgenstein on Rules and Private Language* (Blackwell, 1982), 78.
[97] Venzke, *How Interpretation Makes International Law*, 5. See also ibid., 58–9.
[98] Ibid., 48.
[99] Tsai, 'A Four-Letter Word', 27.

It is only by conforming to expectations that the interpreter can finally 'block the road of inquiry' and 'get something done'.[100]

So, back to the point: how did Matt *actually* go about interpreting 'like' products? Whence did he derive the meaning of that four-letter word?

As we know,[101] Matt has been socialized to the WTO community since his Georgetown days. Throughout the years, he has incessantly refined his ability to play the game of WTO dispute settlement. This acculturation shows through every page of his issues paper. Without hesitation, Matt jumped straight to the 1970 Report of the Working Party in *Border Tax Adjustments*, which set out certain criteria for assessing 'likeness': the physical properties of the products at issue, their end-uses, and consumer tastes and habits in the markets concerned.[102] Albeit expressed in hortatory terms, those criteria were endorsed by some GATT panels. When the WTO came into existence, the Appellate Body was quick to confirm this approach as the 'correct' interpretation of the word 'like'.[103] Case after case, the standard was slightly tinkered with, for example by adding the subsidiary element of product tariff classification.[104] Yet, by and large, the *Border Tax Adjustment* criteria remain the way in which the WTO community has made sense of the concept of 'likeness'. This is evidenced by the plethora of forums in which that concept is debated. To this day, trade law journals and conferences unfailingly sport a paper or two devoted to the topic, where the same old spiel is regurgitated over and over in light of 'new' jurisprudence.

The consistent repetition of the standard has generated a reverberating echo across the community. Its participants have first discovered an acceptable position, then espoused that position, and now 'ostentatiously reject non-believers'.[105] If Matt were to ask any of his colleagues to define 'likeness', he would get identical responses. If his issues paper were to depart from the *Border Tax Adjustment* criteria, Björn would reinstate them in the draft. And if, somehow, Matt were to persuade the Appellate Body to disavow those criteria, the final judgment

---

[100] R. Rorty, *Consequences of Pragmatism (Essays: 1972–1980)* (University of Minnesota Press, 1986), xii. See also Bianchi, 'Textual Interpretation', 49.
[101] See *supra*, pp. 110–13.
[102] Report of the Working Party on *Border Tax Adjustments*, BISD 18S/97, para. 18.
[103] Appellate Body Report, *Japan – Alcoholic Beverages II*, pp. 20 et seq.
[104] Appellate Body Report, *European Communities – Measures Affecting Asbestos and Asbestos-Containing Products*, WT/DS135/AB/R (12 March 2001) ('*EC – Asbestos*'), para. 102.
[105] Burt, *Brokerage and Closure*, 219.

would be bashed by the parties' counsel, the delegates of other WTO member states, and trade law academics across the globe.

The force of echo is twofold: on the one hand, it stabilizes cognitive expectations about the meaning to be attributed to a legal notion, thereby providing some certainty as to its application across time;[106] on the other hand, it reproduces, in fine detail, the 'clusters and holes'[107] of the WTO community. This, no more and no less, is what we mean by *precedent* in international trade law. The authority of an interpretation stems solely from its consistent use. Judicial decisions have no other force than patterned reproduction. Yet, no serious trade practitioner would ignore those decisions: the community backs their fragile existence and consolidates them into *jurisprudence*.

And so there you have it. Upon examining EU and Indonesian palm oil products in light of their physical characteristics, their end-uses, their tariff classification, and consumer tastes and habits, Matt concluded that those products are, indeed, 'like' within the meaning of Article III:4 of the GATT.

In reaching this conclusion, Matt briefly considered the European Union's argument that, given the different environmental and labour impacts of EU and Indonesian palm oil, the products at issue one cannot be considered similar. With a couple of decisive sentences, Matt recommended that the adjudicators dismiss the European Union's position. In particular, Matt wrote, the Appellate Body has consistently stated that 'likeness' is based on the *competitive relationship* among goods in the marketplace.[108] Two products are 'like' because they are substitutable for consumers, with no regard to environmental or labour factors.

This reference to competitive conditions came to Matt naturally, almost unthinkingly. He has never *questioned* the fundamental assumption that 'likeness' is about competition. Not once has he paused to consider the struggles and the confrontations that are embodied in that assumption.

Had he thought more about it, Matt would have realized that there may be *other* ways to appraise 'likeness', *other* factors that may define the essence of product discrimination. A human rights judge, for instance,

---

[106] On the relationship between law and certainty, see e.g. Kessler, 'Same as It Never Was?', 2180.

[107] Burt, *Brokerage and Closure*, 222.

[108] Appellate Body Reports, *Japan – Alcoholic Beverages II*, pp. 16–17. See also e.g. Appellate Body Reports, *EC – Asbestos*, para. 99; *Korea – Alcoholic Beverages*, paras. 120, 127; *Thailand – Cigarettes (Philippines)*, para. 117; Panel Report, *China – Certain Measures Affecting Electronic Payment Services*, WT/DS413/R (16 July 2012), paras. 7.701–7.705.

may conclude that two goods in a close competitive relationship are nonetheless 'unlike' because one is the result of child labour and the other is not; another judge, moved by environmental concerns, may ground the assessment on the greenhouse gas emissions stemming from the production of the goods in question; and so forth. In fact, different readings of the word 'like' may emerge even *within* the field of international economic law. In assessing whether foreign and domestic investments are in 'like circumstances',[109] some ISDS tribunals have focused not on whether such investments compete with one another,[110] but rather on whether they raise similar public policy concerns. A modification of competitive conditions to the detriment of foreign investors is not sufficient to show discrimination. Instead, the measure at issue must have an actual impact on a specific investor or investment.[111] Finally, what would *economists* think of the WTO's approach? They would probably be perplexed at the idea of reducing the spectrum of competitive relationships in the marketplace to a mechanistic 'likeness/unlikeness' dichotomy.[112]

Yet, all these outside perspectives have been carefully sidelined in WTO jurisprudence. By developing and continuously refurbishing its own interpretive practices, the trade community has managed to insulate its legal standards from competing epistemes. At the same time, the Appellate Body's appraisal of 'likeness' as a competition-based concept sought to pacify an *internal* conflict among the members of the trade community, who disagreed over 'the appropriate interpretation of the non-discrimination "package"'.[113]

---

[109] See e.g. Article 1102 of the NAFTA; Article 3 of the 2012 US Model BIT.
[110] See *Methanex Corp. v. United States*, NAFTA Chapter 11 Arbitral Tribunal, Final Award on Jurisdiction and Merits (3 August 2005), Part IV, Chapter B, paras. 33–7 (where the tribunal expressly distinguishes its 'likeness' approach from the WTO's competition-based test).
[111] See e.g. *D. Myers v. Canada*, UNCITRAL, Partial Award (13 November 2000), para. 248; *Pope and Talbot v. Canada*, NAFTA Chapter 11 Arbitral Tribunal, Award on Merits Phase 2 (10 April 2001), paras. 87–8, *Gami Inv. v. Mexico*, UNCITRAL, Award (15 November 2004), para. 114. For discussion, see N. DiMascio and J. Pauwelyn, 'Nondiscrimination in Trade and Investment Treaties: Worlds Apart or Two Sides of the Same Coin?' (2008) 102(1) AJIL 48, 70–2; Allen and Soave, 'Jurisdictional Overlap', 17–18.
[112] See e.g. J. Pauwelyn, 'The Use, Non-use and Abuse of Economics in WTO and Investor-State Dispute Settlement', in J. A. Huerta-Goldman, A. Romanetti Franz and X. Stirnimann (eds.), *WTO Litigation, Investment Arbitration, and Commercial Arbitration* (Kluwer Law International, 2013) 169, 173–4.
[113] A. Lang, 'The Judicial Sensibility of the WTO Appellate Body' (2016) 27(4) EJIL 1095, 1097.

Back in the GATT years, many viewed the primary purpose of multilateral trade rules as the prevention of beggar-thy-neighbour policies. Under this view, non-discrimination should be narrowly construed as a simple remedy against disguised trade protectionism. Some GATT panels adhered to this approach, and focused their inquiry on the protectionist 'aims and effect' of state regulations.[114] Their assessment of 'likeness' was typically conducted in light of the policy objectives that the relevant measures sought to achieve.

However, during the formative years of the WTO, an alternative narrative emerged which viewed non-discrimination as 'a much broader project of disciplining regulatory design more generally, by ensuring that all competitive disadvantages suffered by imports as a result of regulatory measures are carefully scrutinized and strictly justified'.[115] According to the new ethos, a 'likeness' analysis ought to be based on 'objective criteria'[116] concerning the state of goods in the marketplace, without regard to the regulatory 'aims' of member states. Such regulatory aims would, at most, enter the analysis through the backdoor of the general exceptions under Article XX of the GATT.

Some key actors in the trade community helped popularize this competition-based vision. Robert Hudec, a distinguished trade law scholar and occasional panellist, penned a widely cited 'requiem' for the 'aims and effect' test.[117] The parties' counsel started pleading along these lines, and some senior ABS lawyers followed suit. Hence, when in 1996 the Appellate Body stated that 'likeness' is about competition,[118] it did little more than ratifying and lending ultimate authority to the emerging trend.

The struggle, however, was not over, and the defeated faction kept resurfacing in later years. In 1998, a dissenting Appellate Body member broke ranks with the majority. He noted that the 'appropriateness of adopting a "fundamentally" economic interpretation of the "likeness" of products ... does not appear ... to be free from substantial doubt', and

---

[114] See e.g. GATT Panel Reports, *US – Malt Beverages*, DS23/R-39S/206 (16 March 1992), para. 5.25; *US – Taxes on Automobiles*, DS31/R (11 October 1994), paras. 5.6–5.10. For discussion, see e.g. H. Horn and P. C. Mavroidis, 'Still Hazy after All These Years: The Interpretation of National Treatment in the GATT/WTO Case Law on Tax Discrimination' (2004) 15(1) EJIL 39, 44; Howse, 'Governance by Judiciary', 47.
[115] Lang, 'Judicial Sensibility', 1097.
[116] Howse, 'Governance by Judiciary', 46.
[117] R. E. Hudec, 'GATT/WTO Constraints on National Regulation: Requiem for an "Aim and Effects" Test' (1998) 32(3) IntlLawyer 619.
[118] Appellate Body Reports, *Japan – Alcoholic Beverages II*, pp. 16–17.

that it might be better 'to reserve one's opinion on such an important, indeed, philosophical matter'.[119] Some panels have revolted against a pure competition-based approach to 'likeness' until as recently as 2011.[120] A number of scholars have cautioned against the dangers of 'impugning as "discrimination" legitimate public policies simply based upon market disadvantage'.[121] And some litigators have tried to resurrect the 'aims and effect' test under other names.

Faced with these attempts at sedition, and despite a few hiccups in its jurisprudence, the Appellate Body is still holding its ground thanks to a host of 'different and sometimes opposing' interpretive techniques.[122] Yet, the possibility of new plot twists cannot be ruled out. One day, the defeated faction may muster enough strength and accumulate enough capital to tilt the balance of power and make its views of 'likeness' and discrimination hegemonic again.

But today is not that day. The issues paper that Matt has just completed sticks to the beaten path and says nothing new or revolutionary about 'likeness'. That is understandable. Matt is thrice removed from any desire to break with established practice. First, he is not fully aware of the socially conflictive nature of that practice. Second, even if he were aware, he would probably not want to question a fundamental tenet of WTO jurisprudence in the circumstances of the present appeal. And third, even if he wanted to do so, he would still have to pick his battles. Persuading the Appellate Body members to consider the Indonesia-European Union bilateral FTA[123] will be difficult enough. One revolution a day is sufficient. Go, Matt, get out of that office. You deserve a break after your obedient service.

With this, dear reader, we have almost concluded our exploration of the practice of legal interpretation. That practice is never carried out in the abstract, but takes place amid the clashes among competing socio-professional actors. The point of view of the interpreter can never be objective and impartial, but is always shaped by the structures in which he

---

[119] Appellate Body Reports, *EC – Asbestos*, para. 154.
[120] See e.g. Panel Reports, *European Communities – Regime for the Importation, Sale and Distribution of Bananas*, WT/DS27/R/USA (22 May 1997), paras. 7.181, 7.249; *European Communities – Measures Concerning Meat and Meat Products (Hormones) – Complaint by the United States*, WT/DS26/R/USA (18 August 1997), paras. 8.183, 8.184, 8.202; *United States – Measures Affecting the Production and Sale of Clove Cigarettes*, WT/DS406/R (2 September 2011), para. 7.109.
[121] Howse, 'Governance by Judiciary', 47.
[122] Lang, 'Judicial Sensibility', 1101.
[123] See *supra*, pp. 218–23.

or she is embedded. At the same time, interpretation holds extraordinary creational power, as it enables the contestation and reconfiguration of existing structures. In short, like all other international judicial practices, interpretation is simultaneously *'context shaped'* and *'context renewing'*.[124]

What else is there to say? One last thing, actually. We must talk about emotions. Let us travel back to The Hague. Let us check on Sophie.

---

[124] C. Goodwin and J. Heritage, 'Conversation Analysis' (1990) 19 AnnuRevAnthropol 283 (original emphasis).

# 13

## What Does It Mean…

Sophie nervously taps her foot on the office floor. At regular intervals, she opens her Facebook account, only to close it in guilt and frustration a few seconds later. She is procrastinating. Her desk is a mess. Scattered copies of submissions and exhibits cover every inch of available surface, and a second layer of papers is starting to crop up on top of the first. Untidy. Stuck. Damn it. Sophie stands up angrily and opens the window. The crisp breeze of early spring ruffles her red curls. Her Annex office, located right next to Judge Lehmann's, offers a nice view of the south walls of the Peace Palace. As Sophie gazes at the temple of international law, her mind keeps wandering back to the question Norma asked her at the end of last summer:

'What does it mean for you to do what you do?'

Much has happened since their coffee at Grote Markt.[1] The Philippines' legal team, coordinated by Lionel and Filibert, filed its complaint in the *North Borneo* dispute. Some time thereafter, the parties submitted their written memorials, counter-memorials, replies, and rejoinders. The 15 regular and two *ad hoc* judges are hard at work to produce their individual notes. Over the last several weeks, Sophie spent most of her waking hours parsing through the submissions and making sense of The Philippines' and Malaysia's arguments. She has had countless conversations with Judge Lehmann at the *Restaurant des Juges*, discussing the issues arising in the case. In short, the proceedings are well under way.

Why, then, is Sophie so dejected? Because of the legal question that, two days ago, Judge Lehmann asked her to research. As the reader might remember,[2] the dispute involves an 1878 deed by the Sultan of Sulu, by which three European explorers were accorded perpetual rights over the territory of North Borneo. The Philippines' position is that the deed

---

[1] See *supra*, Chapter 2.
[2] See *supra*, pp. 159–60.

cannot be construed as a cession of sovereignty and that, therefore, the chain of sovereign title over North Borneo remains in the Sultan's successor, the Philippines itself. Malaysia, naturally, argues the opposite.

Judge Lehmann's question to Sophie was straightforward. Does the Sultan's deed amount to a *private* act between a local ruler and three foreigners, as such incapable of producing a change in sovereign title? Or should the deed instead be construed as a *public* international legal act creating a legally separate territorial entity, whose subsequent vicissitudes would see the British Empire and then Malaysia prevail in asserting sovereignty? As they parted, the Judge gave his clerk a stern look:

'It's not an easy issue, young lady, but I'm sure you can crack it. You have one week. Good luck.'

Then, Sophie revelled in excitement. Now, just two days later, those words sound like a bad omen. Her current research assignment gives us the opportunity to complete our review of interpretive practices. In the two previous chapters, we have focused on how the *habitus*, the assumptions, and the expectations of the international judicial community shape law-ascertainment and content-determination. Here, we will describe how it *feels* to conduct legal research and interpret a norm on behalf of an international judge.

The preparation of an international dispute is not only an effort at rationalization. It is also an *experience* that comes with emotions. Elation, fear, and occasional identity crises are all inherent features of our business – and all other businesses, for that matter. Our minds are not capable of 'separating reason from emotion' to derive 'clear and distinct truths'. Emotion is not only relevant to our rational functioning – 'it is *necessary* to it'.[3] One can 'fantasize' about international law, 'pursue' international law… but happens when one '*gets* it?'.[4]

•

Sophie anxiously stares at the blank page on the computer screen. She has read the Sultan's deed a hundred times and checked it against contextual materials. Still, she cannot make up her mind. The archaic text

---

[3] D. Z. Epstein, 'Rationality, Legitimacy, and the Law' (2014) 7(1) WashUJurRev 1, 15 (emphasis added). See also A. R. Damasio, *Descartes' Error: Emotion, Reason, and the Human Brain* (Putnam, 1994), 200.

[4] Kennedy, 'The Disciplines of International Law and Policy', 108 (emphasis added). See also A. Bianchi, *International Law Theories: An Inquiry into Different Ways of Thinking* (Oxford University Press, 2016), 115.

of the document comes in two official transliterations from Malay, each relied upon by one of the litigants. According to the version offered by the Philippines, the Sultan of Sulu desired to *'lease'* out of his own 'freewill and satisfaction' all 'rights and powers' which he possessed over 'all territories and lands tributary to [him] on the ... Island of Borneo'.[5] In the version submitted by Malaysia, the Sultan decided instead to *'grant and cede'* his rights and powers over the contested territory.[6]

One of the *experts fantômes* assigned to the case[7] told Sophie that the words 'lease', 'grant', and 'cede' are all reasonable translations of the Malay term *'padjak'*, which does not have an exact correspondent in Western legal traditions. Therefore, both litigants may be right in their interpretations of the Sultan's intent. Yet, both litigants cannot win. *Non liquet* is not a valid outcome of international adjudication. Sophie must somehow determine what *'padjak' truly* means in English (or French). Only that determination will allow her to conclusively tell Judge Lehmann: 'The Sultan merely leased the disputed territory to private parties, while retaining dormant sovereignty over it'; or: 'The Sultan relinquished his sovereign rights over the disputed territory, such that sovereignty accrued to whoever subsequently conquered North Borneo or ceded it by treaty.'

If this sounds like an intractable task, that is because it is. Actually, this is an inherent problem in the work of an international judicial bureaucrat. When an issue is 'easy' – or, should we say, when there is sufficient agreement about how it should be resolved[8] – articulating a tight and cohesive draft is aesthetically pleasing and soothing to the mind. However, quite often, issues are not easy at all. In virtually every dispute, there is at least one legal question about which both parties have presented compelling arguments and the court could reasonably swing one way or the

---

[5] Philippine government website, www.officialgazette.gov.ph/1878/01/22/grant-by-the-sultan-of-sulu-of-a-permanent-lease-covering-his-lands-and-territories-on-the-island-of-borneo/ (emphasis added).

[6] Sabah State government website, https://sagc.sabah.gov.my/?q=en/content/grant-sultan-sulu-territories-and-lands-mainland-island-borneo-dated-22nd-january-1878 (emphasis added).

[7] See *supra*, p. 189.

[8] As Duncan Kennedy observed, all that we mean by an easy case 'is that there is a rule that obviously applies to the facts, given some explicit or implicit combination of deductive and policy arguments'. A case is 'easy' only for those actors 'whose ideological preference is for the obvious rule'. For those who 'think[] the rule unjust, this is a hard case in the sense that it will be difficult, it may take a lot of work, and it may be impossible to displace the obvious solution'. Kennedy, *A Critique of Adjudication*, 166.

other: perhaps a point on which the relevant sources are silent; a logical mismatch between two sets of rules; a wrinkle on the smooth surface of the law. There is always a '*dilemma*' in the proper sense of the term.[9] How could it be otherwise? If all questions were self-evident, if they could be answered through a simple syllogism, the parties would have figured them out for themselves and there would probably be no dispute to begin with.

But these philosophical considerations are meagre consolation now. The 'true' meaning of the Sultan's deed does seem to present an unsolvable problem. No matter from which angle Sophie looks at it, no matter how many times she changes her draft, she cannot come up with a credible, or at least internally coherent, analysis. Sophie's initial enthusiasm gives way to frustration. Can anyone possibly reconstruct the real intent of a long dead monarch who wrote in a foreign language, did not know Western legal concepts, and most certainly was not familiar with the categories of modern international law? Deep down, Sophie is aware that the interpretations of the Philippines and Malaysia are both viable, and that both parties have high stakes in the outcomes of the case.

As days go by, Sophie's brains get closer to a shutdown. The spectre of moral and professional responsibility starts looming over her head. Hence her social media procrastination. Nevertheless, Sophie cannot desist. In one way or another, she must complete her assignment. One day, tired of her hesitations, she wraps the proverbial towel around her head and powers through the ordeal.

Her emotional process goes through five distinct phases.

The first phase is what we would call the *unreasonable retreat to formalism*. Sophie convinces herself that the solution to her problem is out there, hidden in plain sight. If only she checks the record more thoroughly, she will find the answer she is so desperately looking for. Perhaps she overlooked a critical piece of evidence, for example a historical testimony that will prove the Sultan's real intent. Or perhaps the contextual terms of the deed, such as 'territories', 'lands', or even 'tributary', will clarify the meaning of the word '*padjak*' beyond reasonable doubt. Encouraged by these thoughts, Sophie meticulously sifts through the whole file once again. Along the way, she takes accurate notes of whatever interesting materials she encounters. She even breaks her promise to limit her inquiry to what is on record, and makes several trips to the ICJ library to peruse the available treatises on the history of the *North Borneo* dispute.

---

[9] See V. Jeutner, *Irresolvable Norm Conflicts in International Law: The Concept of a Legal Dilemma* (Oxford University Press, 2017), 17–18.

When, at the end, she pulls all the strings together, her hopes are shattered. Her search was in vain. The meaning of '*padjak*' remains mockingly elusive. A 'slight vertigo' overtakes her, as the 'flexibility of solutions' and the 'sources of uncertainty' reveal themselves in all their ineluctability.[10] Sophie does not take it well. She feels she is not living up to the standards that were inculcated in her at law school – the enlightened idea that a good lawyer should commit to neutral rules, without imbuing them with personal leanings.[11]

In the second phase, Sophie comes to admit the obvious. Since the text of the deed has no preordained or objectively ascertainable meaning, she *must make a choice*. She can decide to go with the Philippines' reading of the term '*padjak*' and conclude that the Sultan of Sulu and his heirs retained sovereignty over North Borneo, or to side with Malaysia and achieve the opposite result. Both interpretative avenues are wide open in front of her. She just needs the courage to take one.

Panic. How can she make such an important choice? Or, to be more precise: who on Earth is she to make such an important choice? While experiencing this vertigo, Sophie suddenly remembers an article she read at university. The author gleefully celebrated the moment of doubt – the sudden exposure to the irreducible pluralism of possible solutions – as one of supreme 'professional freedom', where we are 'open to persuasion' and 'have lost control', precisely 'because *we do not know* what the law determines'.[12] Doubt provides us with a precious opportunity to unlearn our 'methodological predilections', transcend the 'widely shared commitments' of our profession, and bravely leap forward into the unknown.[13] Hence, argued the author, we ought not to dread the indeterminacy of the law, for it opens the door to the exercise of responsible human freedom.

Sophie finds some solace in these thoughts. At least, she is not alone in her struggle. The inherent indeterminacy of law has taunted countless other interpreters before. Wait, there was something else… Yes! Sophie recalls another reading for the same class, which invited legal professionals to exploit the indeterminacy of existing law to express

---

[10] Latour, *The Making of Law*, 98.
[11] Peter Sloterdijk has decried this 'enlightened false consciousness' as a cause of deep unhappiness. Modern humans have 'learned [their] lessons in enlightenment, but [they have] not, and probably [were] not able to, put them into practice'. P. Sloterdijk, *Critique of Cynical Reason*, trans. M. Eldred (University of Minnesota Press, 1988), 5. See also M. Koskenniemi, *The Politics of International Law* (Hart, 2011), 286.
[12] Kennedy, 'Many Legal Orders', 644 (original emphasis).
[13] Ibid., 645.

their '"political" objection'[14] and promote their own visions of justice. If Sophie is not mistaken, the article told the fictional story of a left-wing Boston judge deciding a case about union bus drivers on strike. As the company hired non-union drivers and set out to resume service, union members stood in front of the buses to stop their course. The imaginary judge wished to rule in favour of the strikers despite a line of adverse precedent.[15] The rest of the piece chronicled the judge's struggle to honour his ideological commitments and achieve the intended result.

Wow. It feels as if, in this moment of discomfort, these authors were speaking directly to Sophie! The more she recollects their arguments, the more empowered she feels. Ok then, she will be brave. Being the assistant to an influent ICJ judge puts Sophie in the enviable position to decide '*what* world among the many possible ones' she wants to create through her contribution to judicial rulership.[16] For a moment, Sophie ceases to be a frightened junior lawyer dealing with something bigger than her, and turns into someone else – someone akin to Weber's political man or Kierkegaard's man of faith. For a moment, she can break free from the shackles of her technical expertise and responsibly exercise agency for the construction of the reality she wants to live in.

Except that Sophie *does not know* what reality she wants to live in. At least, not when it comes to the specifics of the issue at hand. Which interpretation of the word '*padjak*' is politically better? Which one resonates more with Sophie's sense of justice or moral preferences? She cannot tell. The bitter truth is that she would need a much deeper understanding of the relationship between means and ends, a much fuller awareness of the consequences of her choice, to connect her interpretation of the Sultan's deed to a desirable outcome in the world.

Thus, if the second phase of the interpretative exercise had seen her ascent to heroism, the third phase entails a swift and brutal *plunge back into hesitance and indecision*. Once again, Sophie feels that she is falling short of what theorists expect of her. When the author of her class reading imagined his liberal Boston judge, he expediently equipped him with a coherent set of personal convictions, political beliefs, and ideas about progress. That judge, for instance, strongly disagrees with established precedent because he does not think that 'management should be allowed

---

[14] Kennedy, 'Freedom and Constraint', 519.
[15] Ibid., 519–20.
[16] Kennedy, 'Many Legal Orders', 644 (original emphasis). See also F. Johns, *Non-legality in International Law: Unruly Law* (Cambridge University Press, 2011), 1 (speaking of lawyers as co-agents in the 'making and remaking of global political possibilities').

to operate the means of production ... with substitute during a strike'.[17] In turn, this position rests on the judge's 'general preference for transforming the current modes of American economic life in a direction of greater worker self-activity, worker control and management of enterprise, in a decentralized setting that blurs the lines between "owner" and "worker," and "public" and "private" enterprise'.[18]

Now, if you asked Sophie what she thinks about the relationship between The Philippines and Malaysia, you would probably get a blank stare. Her vision boils down to a generic commitment to social democratic ideals, a vague propensity for the protection of human rights, an ill-defined support for economic development, a 'broad renunciation of power politics, militarism, and the aspiration to empire'.[19] These, in turn, are but reflexes Sophie has acquired through her experience as a member of the international judicial community. Throughout her university years, she did not have much time to develop particularized views as to the virtues and pitfalls of international policy-making. She was too busy studying techniques of interpretation, memorizing loads of international jurisprudence, and exploring general principles whose 'generality' rests precisely on the *neutralization* of their political and distributive significance.

Indeed, Sophie doubts that any of her colleagues – not even Judge Lehmann – has a better mental map of the end-goals of global governance. They were simply not trained for it, for they belong to a community that sees the advancement of international law as its own self-explanatory goal.[20] And even outside our profession, few people experience life as 'a swirl of vivid odds and ends'.[21] How can Sophie please her enlightened teachers? How can she translate her fuzzy feelings into concrete legal advice on the meaning of the word '*padjak*'?

On day four, Sophie decides it is time to start writing. She does not know exactly what. Neither her technical prowess nor her moral compass can fill the legal indeterminacy of the Sultan's deed. But she must begin somewhere. Time is tight and her nerves are wracked. In the fourth phase, Sophie relinquishes her grand ambitions and seeks shelter in the *standard practices* of the ICJ registry. Similar to Achilles chasing the tortoise, she breaks down her interpretive assessment into a series of tiny, discrete steps.

---

[17] Kennedy, 'Freedom and Constraint', 520.
[18] Ibid.
[19] Kennedy, 'Many Legal Orders', 645.
[20] See D. W. Kennedy, 'A New World Order: Yesterday, Today, and Tomorrow' (1994) 4(2) TransnatlL&ContempProbs 329, 335.
[21] T. Eagleton, *The English Novel* (Blackwell, 2005), 311. See also Marks, 'False Contingency', 14.

Firstly, Sophie refines and expands her summaries of the parties' positions on the issue. Then, she describes at length the undisputed facts and the uncontroversial legal arguments concerning the conclusion of the deed. Once this is done, Sophie fills in a few pages with a typical VCLT analysis of the term '*padjak*' (dictionary definitions, context found in other provisions of the deed and adjacent materials, preparatory works, etc.) while citing excerpts of relevant ICJ jurisprudence. Given the conflicting translations offered by the litigants, she throws in a paragraph about Article 33 of the VCLT for good measure. Finally, Sophie highlights the persistent ambiguity of the text and articulates two interpretative options. On the one hand, she asserts, reading the term '*padjak*' as 'lease' would entail that the Philippines maintained sovereignty over North Borneo. On the other hand, interpreting the term as 'grant' or 'cession' would mean that North Borneo came to be a separate territorial entity, whose sovereignty depended on its subsequent vicissitudes.

Sophie carries out these tasks in a mechanical, mindless fashion, as if adherence to familiar procedures could, by some odd prodigy, substitute itself for the interpretative choice. It would be easy to mock this as a delaying tactic, for none of these steps will bring Sophie any closer to the truth. Yet, along the process, something clicks. As she painstakingly advances, Sophie feels relieved that, despite all difficulties, she is actually churning out page after page – she is producing something *tangible*. The blank sheet, whose cruel emptiness signalled the unsolvable nature of the issue, is slowly turning into a semi-structured piece of writing that, without providing any conclusive answer, at least circumscribes indecision to a few paragraphs. Such is the magic of practice. The established *modus operandi*, the everyday procedures, the well-trodden techniques available to the community are all geared to de-potentiate and de-romanticize the exercise of freedom. They make important choices look like a matter of routine, thereby unlocking action and avoiding paralysis.

Sophie's relief has measurable physical effects. The amount of yellow highlights in her draft decreases over time, progressively giving way to clean text. Her desk gets less and less cluttered, while the trash bin quickly fills up. The illusion that the solution is round the corner emboldens Sophie. By adding layer upon layer of corollary information, by slowly drawing the picture from the edges to the centre, the unsolvable issue shrinks in size. Hopefully, by the end of the process, a glance at the whole mosaic will allow Sophie to add the missing tile.

•

Instead, the missing tile is added by Judge Lehmann himself. The morning before submitting the draft, Sophie knocks on his door and asks for a quick chat. The Judge's spacious office is unusually messy, with pens and markers scattered all over his mahogany desk. A stack of paper in the right-hand side is riddled with highlights of different colours, question marks, and unintelligible scribbles. Another stack on the opposite side awaits the same fate. The Judge's Twitter page is open on his computer screen. As she contemplates the scene, Sophie is amused to realize that a legendary reputation does not make her mentor any tidier than her. Law, she ponders, does possess an equalizing quality. Then she notices a cigarette butt still burning on a makeshift ashtray. It seems that the occupant of the office does not care much for the Peace Palace's non-smoking policy.

Just like his clerk a few days before, Judge Lehmann is staring out of the window, immersed in thoughts. Sophie has to clear her throat to draw his attention.

'Oh! Good morning, young lady.'

'Good morning, Sir.'

'You wanted to see me.'

'Yes Sir, it's about the memo on the Sultan's deed due tomorrow.'

'Oh, that.' Pause. 'It's a nasty one, isn't it?' Smile.

'Nothing impossible … but I would like to pick your brains for a minute.'

'Oh, let's see if there's anything in my old brains worth picking …'

Sophie notices how often the Judge has been indulging in false modesty lately. Perhaps a sign that he is finally relaxing in her presence? Or perhaps an assertion of power? Whatever.

'It's this term "*padjak.*" It's a Malay word and the parties dispute its legal meaning. I have run the usual VCLT analysis and checked case law. The word can translate either as "lease" or as "grant, cession." Which, of course, would lead to radically different outcomes.'

'Would it?'

'I think so. The first interpretation would mean that the Sultan did not cede sovereignty over North Borneo and that his heirs remain entitled to it, while the second …'

'But do you *need* to make that determination?'

'Well, I do, don't I?' Sophie simpers.

'Perhaps you don't. You know, right before you came in, I was having a chat with Marcos and Mary about our notes.'

It takes Sophie a couple of seconds to realize that Judge Lehmann is referring to Marcos Quintana and Mary Stephenson, the newly-appointed Mexican and New Zealand judges.

'... And what do they ...'

'We all seem to agree that the 1963 consultation by the Secretary-General is the key element in the case. Since the people of North Borneo have expressed their intent to be part of Malaysia, we think that should constitute a legitimate exercise of self-determination. Who cares what happened 150 years ago, right?'

'Hmm, right. But what if the deed explicitly says the contrary?'

'But does it *explicitly* say the contrary?'

'No. As I was telling you, it is rather ambiguous ...'

'Great. So, given the ambiguity, we can *retrospectively construe it* as if it had left the door open. Here's the idea: you finish your draft about the Vienna Convention, case law, etc., and conclude that, while the Sultan's intent was unclear, one could *reasonably read* the deed as a cession of sovereignty. I slap all that into the note, and then move on to highlight the importance of the 1963 consultation.'

'I will. But were the North Borneans really so vituperated at the time of the consultation?'

'Not really. The consultation alone might not be enough. Actually, probably nothing is enough taken in isolation. There's no *smoking gun* in this case. But if we put enough weight on one arm of the scale, we might be able to *tilt it* in our favour.'

'Sounds good. What else do we ... What else do *you* have to strengthen your case?'

'Well, Tom took a similar view in the 2002 *Pulau* third-party intervention judgment.'

Again, it takes Sophie a few moments to get the reference to the late Thomas Franck, Jürgen Lehmann's lifelong mentor and friend. 'Tom' spoke to the North Borneans' 'exercise of self-determination conducted in accordance with the requisites of international law', against which 'historic claims and feudal pre-colonial titles are merely relics of another international legal era, one that ended with the setting of the sun on the age of colonial imperium'.[22]

'Very convincing. And how are the other judges leaning?'

'I'm not sure yet, but I suspect we might bring a few to our side. We'll see during deliberations. I'm going to speak to the President this afternoon. I'd really like to be on the Drafting Committee this time. For now, let's focus on the note.'

---

[22] *Pulau* judgment on third-party intervention, Separate Opinion of Judge *ad hoc* Franck, para. 15.

'Good. I'll wrap up and send you something by tomorrow COB.'
'Excellent. Thank you, young lady.'
'Have a good afternoon, Sir.'
'Oh, one more thing.'
'Sir?'
'What was that word you used about the North Borneans being oppressed in 1963?'
'…"Vituperated"?'
'Exactly! Nice word. I'll remember that.'

This conversation brings Sophie to the fifth and final phase of her emotional ride: *abdication*. Having done everything she could to solve the issue herself, she relinquished control and passed the ball to her mentor. Her doubts have given way to deference. Her tentative search for truth has turned into a purposeful effort to support Judge Lehmann's position. After so much meandering, Sophie finds great comfort in realizing that, at the end of the day, she does not 'carry the responsibility for making … highly controversial decisions with significant impact on national economies or policies'.[23]

From that point onwards, Sophie will stick to Judge Lehmann's decision with relentless commitment. In drafting her portion of the note, she will use apodictic expressions indicating that the deed's meaning could not have been reasonably interpreted otherwise. Sophie's experience of content-determination as an exercise in denial will fade in the distance, reabsorbed into the *doxa* from whence it came. Sophie will soon forget about the abyss she has been gazing at for a week, as it had been some sort of bad dream standing in the way of the Rule of Law.

Everything will go back to awake, reassuring routine.

---

[23] Hughes, 'Working in WTO Dispute Settlement', 405.

# 14

## The Stage

'The Tribunal now asks Respondent if it wishes to make any conclusive remarks concerning Claimant's allegations in respect of legitimate expectations. Turkey, you have the floor.'

'Mr. President, Turkey believes that all the substantive issues arising in this case, as well as the evidence pertaining thereto, have been thoroughly explored during the oral proceedings. Turkey seizes this opportunity to thank you, Mr. President, the other distinguished members of the Tribunal, and the Secretary for the thoughtful consideration of its arguments and all the hard work on this case. We will submit the post-hearing brief by the date you have indicated.'

'Thank you, Turkey. On behalf of my esteemed co-arbitrators, I declare these oral proceedings closed.'

As the slam of the gavel resounds through the room, the attendees breathe a sigh of relief. Turkey's chief counsel plops back on his chair, straightens up his tie, and nods at the law firm associates sitting at his sides. The two young lawyers are visibly exhausted. They spent the last eight hours frantically flipping through piles of folders to find the exhibits their boss needed to support his pleadings. Neither of them has spoken a single word, as if they were communicating telepathically. The hallmark of a job well done.

It takes only a glance for Carlos to realize that François Gal is equally tired. Sitting at the centre of the tribunal's podium, the venerable Professor is making scribbles on a piece of scrap paper. A clear sign that his mind is drifting off. Who could blame him, though? For several days in a row, he presided over a very intense set of hearings, during which the parties spared no ammunition against one another. Carlos has always admired his mentor's ability to make the litigants feel at home, defuse inflammatory statements, dodge curveballs, and find ways out of deadlocks. This time, too, he managed to be an effective umpire among unruly players.

This, Carlos surmises, is what makes a good adjudicator: not legal analysis skills (a department in which Professor Gal does not excel); not high-minded ideals about justice (which the Professor invariably invokes in academic settings, but never mentions at the law firm); but, rather, a certain even-handedness in the treatment of the parties, a sort of elegant equidistance from their positions. It is all about perceived authority, concludes Carlos. And, indeed, François Gal exudes authority from every pore.

With Turkey's closing statement, the hearings are finally coming to an end. Sitting at the left end of the podium, Carlos stops the chess-clock that measures the hearing time allotted to each litigant.[1] Such an apparently innocuous gesture would actually make paradise for anthropologists, as it captures a whole host of symbols. Since its invention, the clock has revolutionized the temporality of human life. It has replaced circular conceptions of time with 'uniform and universal linearity'.[2] It has enabled the commodification of labour power into labour time, paving the way to industrial capitalism.[3] And, less ambitiously, it has come to signify procedural fairness in the judicial treatment of litigants. A curious form of fairness, to be sure. On the one hand, time limits force the parties to present 'only material and relevant evidence' and avoid 'cumulative and unnecessary testimony'.[4] On the other hand, those limits prove thoroughly inadequate when the case is 'unbalanced' in terms of the merits, the eloquence of the parties' counsel, and the amount of evidence each party has produced.[5] Like any other technology, the clock is not neutral. Its implacable automaticity cuts the Gordian knot between formal and substantive equality, obscuring all the tensions that exist between the two.

After collecting their belongings, the parties' representatives stand up and head to the podium to shake the arbitrators' hands. Professor Gal puts on his best smile as he greets the two chief counsel who have pleaded before him. 'Claimant' and 'Respondent', the litigants' formal appellatives during the hearings, are but proxy terms for Henry Bellinger QC and Maître Jacques Renault, two long-time friends of Professor Gal and prominent arbitrators in their own right. In a few months, when the dispute is over, the three amigos will meet again in their personal capacities,

---

[1] N. Ulmer, 'The Cost Conundrum' (2010) 26(2) ArbIntl 221, 243.
[2] R. Hassan, *Empires of Speed: Time and the Acceleration of Politics and Society* (Brill, 2009), 91. See also D. Engel, 'Law, Time and Community' (1987) 21(4) L&SocRev 605, 607–8.
[3] See e.g. A. Giddens, *Central Problems in Social Theory: Action, Structure and Contradiction in Social Analysis* (University of California Press, 1979), 201.
[4] D. W. Rivkin, 'Towards a New Paradigm in International Arbitration: The Town Elder Model Revisited' (2008) 24(3) ArbIntl 375, 378.
[5] Ulmer, 'The Cost Conundrum', 243–4.

catch up on each other's lives, and reaffirm their commitment to work together in future cases.

Such is the duality of our discipline. When we look at it through the lens of 'orthodox' accounts, we see abstract entities seeking justice before equally abstract courts or tribunals.[6] When, conversely, we observe it as a nexus of socio-professional practices, we come to appreciate the comedy of a pale blond-haired Briton being addressed as 'Turkey', a former classmate as 'Kingsland Mining Corp.', etc. More importantly, we observe how a well-established counsel, one who is sufficiently familiar with the bench, manages to send their message across with greater ease than most state agents or company lawyers. We could go as far as to use familiarity with the court as the benchmark of effectiveness in litigation. Rather than the raw power of the parties', success is due to their relative access to the inner circles of the profession. Yet, since we have already explored this form of *dédoublement fonctionnel*,[7] we will now rest our case and let the weary representatives of Turkey and Kingsland trudge towards the exit.

Once the room is empty, Carlos helps the tribunal members pick up the papers stacked on the podium. He carefully places all documents in a cardboard box, making sure he is not missing anything. He then inspects the garbage bin and shreds whatever scrap paper he finds into tiny pieces. Finally, he checks the computer used to beam quotes and statements up on the screen, deletes all sensitive files, and switches everything off.

Such scrupulous precaution is well justified. It would be a disaster if anyone affiliated with a party somehow managed to take a peek at the arbitrators' personal files. By the time hearings take place, the adjudicators have already devoted considerable time and effort to evaluating the merits of the case. Some of them might even have a rough idea about the content of the final award.[8]

The advanced stage of the arbitrators' thoughts is reflected in the numerous documents they carried with them into the hearing room.

First, the three arbitrators in *Kingsland Mining Corp.* v. *Turkey* are all supposed to have read Carlos' Memo, whose contents we have described at length in Chapters 8 through 13. To recall, Professor Gal got the complete version of the Memo, which includes summaries of the arguments, a list of the core issues, the identification of the relevant state conduct, a

---

[6] Messenger, 'The Practice of Litigation'. See also G. Messenger, *The Development of World Trade Organization Law* (Oxford University Press, 2016), 31–4.
[7] See *supra*, 67–9.
[8] See e.g. D. W. Rivkin, 'Form of Deliberations', in B. Berger and M. E. Schneider (eds.), *Inside the Black Box: How Arbitral Tribunals Operate and Reach Their Decisions* (Juris, 2013) 21, 22.

preliminary assessment of the contested facts, and an initial examination of the legal merits of the case. The co-arbitrators, by contrast, received a redacted version, containing only the argument summaries and the list of issues.

As we know, the Memo delineates the boundaries of the dispute, the outer limits beyond which the arbitrators will be reluctant to venture. As he picks up the three copies of the Memo from the podium, Carlos notices that both Professor Gal and one co-arbitrator have filled theirs with handwritten annotations. The other co-arbitrator's copy, by contrast, shows no trace of human interaction, as if it had just come out of the printer. Carlos wonders if the density of each arbitrator's scribbles is proportional to his engagement with the case. To find an answer, he will have to wait for deliberations. But we can already spoil the plot: yes, it is proportional indeed.

Second, in addition to the Memo, each arbitrator carries with him a copy of the hearing script. No, not the transcript – the *script*: a 30-page document prepared by Carlos, which details most of what the tribunal members said and did during the hearing. The first few pages contain, word by word, the statements that Professor Gal made at the beginning and at the end of each session. Next to each statement are annotated the relevant procedural rules governing the session, and even a couple of pre-cooked jokes to capture the goodwill of the audience. Professor Gal's standard opening line is:

'Welcome to [name of the city], everybody. I know you'd rather be at [name of a famous restaurant nearby], but I'm afraid you'll have to bear with us for a few days.'[9]

The remainder of the script consists of a detailed list of the factual and legal issues that the tribunal sought to probe with the parties and witnesses. For each issue, Carlos drafted two or three questions to be read out loud whenever the discussion turned to the relevant topic. Below each question, he annexed the most salient exhibits[10] and suggested possible follow-ups to the litigants' answers.

---

[9] The first rule of the influential lawyer's book: always make your audience chuckle, but never laugh out loud. Anglo-Saxon legal practitioners and professors have perfected this technique to an admirable degree, while the rest of our profession is still catching up. An entire book could be written about the ways in which actors in the international judicial community use self-deprecating humour to increase their social capital. See e.g. M. Galanter, *Lowering the Bar: Lawyer Jokes and Legal Culture* (University of Wisconsin Press, 2005), 196–209.

[10] Singling out a 'core collection' of exhibits among the congeries of evidence on record enhances the portability of the folder and its ease of use in the hearing room. See J. J. Coe, Jr., 'Pre-Hearing Techniques to Promote Speed and Cost-Effectiveness: Some Thoughts Concerning Arbitral Process Design' (2002) 2(1) PeppDispResLJ 53, 68.

The list of hearing questions reflects a delicate balance between thoroughness and succinctness. On the one hand, Carlos had to make sure that the litigants' answers would provide all the missing information that would later enable him to assist the tribunal during deliberations and the drafting of the award. There is nothing worse than realizing, midway through the drafting process, that a line of reasoning is unavailable because it is not properly substantiated by the record. On the other hand, Carlos was aware of Professor Gal's aversion to bombarding the litigants with too many questions. Arbitrators usually prefer to listen as the parties interact with one another and cross-examine the witnesses. An arbitrator who is too proactive may overstep the boundaries of their 'Town Elder' role[11] and possibly tank their chances at reappointment. Thus, the final list of questions had to be stripped to the bare minimum, and all unnecessary inquiries struck out.

Clearly, no one but Carlos could have achieved such a balance. At the time of putting the list together, he was the only person with sufficient knowledge of the file to identify gaps and the possible inconsistencies in the litigants' positions. Professor Gal had only a rough idea of the disputed issues, and the co-arbitrators were probably even less prepared.

To make matters more complicated, the contents of the script were not carved in stone, but kept changing as the hearing progressed. Whenever a litigant or witness anticipated the response to a specific question, Carlos promptly crossed it off the list. Conversely, if a given answer begged a follow-up question, he promptly handwrote the text of that question on a piece of paper and passed it to the arbitrators. This on-the-go adaptation, coupled with timekeeping and notetaking duties, strained Carlos' concentration to an extreme, as evidenced by his copious ingurgitation of coffee during every break.

Fortunately, in a few weeks, both parties will submit their post-hearing briefs, that is written comments on what happened during the oral proceedings. Each litigant will, among other things, summarize its views on the credibility of this or that witness testimony; support or debunk a given expert statement; clarify the connections between its arguments and the evidence on record; and articulate its theory of the case one last time before deliberations begin.[12]

While some practitioners dismiss post-hearing briefs as duplicative of oral arguments,[13] Carlos is actually relieved to get his hands on them.

---

[11] Rivkin, 'The Town Elder Model'.
[12] See Coe, 'Pre-Hearing Techniques', 63–4.
[13] See e.g. S. V. Goekjian, 'ICC Arbitration from a Practitioner's Perspective' (1980) 14(3) JIntlL&Econ 407, 425, fn 45.

These *ex post* rationalisations, however conflictive they may be, help him put some order into the freewheeling flow of the oral discussion, structure its analysis of the voluminous transcripts, and mull over the merits of the case more considerately. This is why, whenever feasible, Carlos advises the tribunal to circulate a list of additional issues which the parties should address in their post-hearing briefs.[14] As we will see,[15] Carlos' ability to pull the strings will be of paramount importance in the final phases of the dispute.

\*

For now, let us take a break from what is happening in this particular courtroom and discuss the functions of hearings more generally. The first function, as any orthodox scholar will tell you, is to collect additional information that may help the adjudicators decide the case. In principle, hearings offer each party an opportunity to refine the arguments presented in its written briefs, address the other party's counterarguments, and colour the judges' impressions. Discussions of evidence, witness and expert testimonies, exchanges among the litigants, and interactions with the bench are all part and parcel of the process. In practice, however, the extent to which hearings *actually* contribute to the goal of gathering information varies wildly from one international court to another.

As we have just seen, oral proceedings in ISDS can be quite fruitful, as they leave ample room for debate and provide the tribunal with appropriate means to elicit the parties' views.

WTO Appellate Body hearings are similarly dynamic, and equally scripted. Typically, Matt and his fellow ABS lawyers start working on hearing script right after the submission of the issues paper. As part of the script, the team prepares a detailed list of 50–100 questions, which undergoes three rounds of scrutiny by the Appellate Body members assigned to the case.[16] Each question is so carefully worded that one could mistake the list for an official court document and not a simple *aide-mémoire*.

The hearing, which may range from a one-day session to a 'forensic marathon'[17] depending on the complexity of the dispute, begins with the

---

[14] Rivkin, 'Form of Deliberations', 24.
[15] See *infra*, pp. 294–302.
[16] See Hughes, 'Working in WTO Dispute Settlement', 406; Ehlermann, 'Revisiting the Appellate Body', 494–5.
[17] D. Unterhalter, 'The Authority of an Institution: The Appellate Body Under Review', G. Marceau (ed.), *A History of Law and the Multilateral Trading System* (Cambridge University Press, 2015) 466, 470.

parties' opening statements, usually limited to 30 minutes each. After that, each Appellate Body member reads out one or more questions to the parties and offers them the time needed to respond. The beginning is typically quite relaxed. The adjudicators ask about the features of the measures at issue and the parties' specific claims concerning those measures. Then, things start to get spicy, with questions turning to the interpretation of the relevant treaty provisions, the proper reading of precedents, and the reasons underlying each party's position.[18]

Similar to ISDS, the secretariat updates the script on the go by deleting and adding new questions as the discussion unfolds. While certain Appellate Body members occasionally depart from the script, most of them stick to it meticulously: too much improvisation may have catastrophic consequences. Once, Matt aired his misgivings about the practice of question drafting with Björn. If Appellate Body members do not even come up with their own lines of inquiry, how can they get fully invested in an appeal? Björn shrugged his shoulders:

'Our job is to *spoon-feed* the judges, not to make their life harder.'

As 'spoon-fed' as they may be, WTO adjudicators enjoy Q&A a fair bit. Hearings provide Appellate Body members with the 'one opportunity to engage with the appellant(s), appellee(s) and third parties in order to get to the root of the legal issues'.[19] Back in the early days, such an emphasis on oral argument was met with some resistance by the WTO community, which was more used to the dry and bureaucratic tone of trade exchanges than to the flair of courtroom pleadings. Indeed, to this day, opening statements 'are simply read out by senior officials or counsel'.[20] However, the practice of testing the litigants' positions through questions eventually picked up, to the point that, nowadays 'no other court or tribunal subjects the parties to such intensive questioning'.[21] While experienced counsel have learnt how to cope with it, newbies still find Q&A quite gruelling.[22] The inquisitorial style of Appellate Body hearings sits in stark contrast with the adversarial, 'Town-Elder' ethos of ISDS oral proceedings, where arbitrators tend to sit quietly as the litigants exchange fire.

---

[18] A. V. Ganesan, 'The Appellate Body in Its Formative Years: A Personal Perspective', in G. Marceau (ed.), *A History of Law and Lawyers in the GATT/WTO: The Development of the Rule of Law in the Multilateral Trading System* (Cambridge University Press, 2015) 517, 532–3.
[19] Steger, 'The Founding', 455.
[20] Ibid., 456.
[21] Ganesan, 'The Appellate Body in Its Formative Years', 532.
[22] Ehlermann, 'Revisiting the Appellate Body', 496.

Another major difference between the WTO and ISDS concerns the kind of evidence presented and discussed at hearings. While witness examination and cross-examination are the bread and butter of arbitration practitioners, the Appellate Body's review is usually limited to documental exhibits, coupled with the occasional affidavit or written expert statement. This difference is often explained by the subject matter of the disputes adjudicated in the two systems. Investment cases often require oral testimony to ascertain what happened between the investor and the host state. For instance, François Gal and his co-arbitrators will rely on witnesses to determine whether Turkey government officials made representations to Kingsland about the continued viability of its investment. By contrast, the trade regulations at issue in WTO disputes are often set out in the official texts adopted by the responding state and, therefore, can usually be examined on the basis of their paper trail.

However, this distinction is not always convincing. Some ISDS cases are about state regulations of general and prospective application, such that witness testimonies may not add much to the record. Conversely, some WTO disputes concern unwritten trade practices,[23] to identify which witnesses may prove valuable. Yet, even in those cases, the kind of evidence discussed in ISDS and WTO hearings remains the same. Matt has often wondered why that is so. Why not adapt the content of oral proceedings to the specific object of the dispute at hand?

The answer, as so often in our story, lies in *habitus* and path dependence. Adherence to ingrained practices has no other justification than perpetuating the traditions of the judicial regimes concerned. Quite simply, the participants in the trade and investment communities (adjudicators, counsel, bureaucrats, etc.) have mastered the art of judicial argument in different ways. Changing the tacit rules of the game would require a steep learning curve, which incumbents would find difficult to accept.

Finally, it is worth mentioning the scientific experts that WTO panels occasionally appoint to assist in the deliberation of science-intensive disputes.[24] The consultation of experts does not take the form of

---

[23] See e.g. the case against Argentina in which Duncan was involved, described *supra*, pp. 88–9. In another case, measure at issue was a dumping calculation method 'not expressed in the form of a written document' and ascertainable only by examining 'the concrete instrumentalities', such as computer algorithms, that evidenced its existence. Appellate Body Report, *United States – Laws, Regulations and Methodology for Calculating Dumping Margins (Zeroing)*, WT/DS294/AB/R (18 April 2006), paras. 192, 198.

[24] See e.g. Appellate Body Reports, *EC – Hormones*; *US/Canada – Continued Suspension*; Panel Report, *US – Animals*.

examination and cross-examination. Instead, panels convene special meetings during which the panellists and the parties' counsel are given an opportunity to ask questions of the experts and state their views on the scientific evidence at hand.[25] The practice of holding expert meetings has occasionally raised the concern that panels may be delegating their authority to scientists who have no business ascertaining the law.[26]

However, that concern is misplaced – not because it is inaccurate, but because it ascribes too much value to science in judicial proceedings. As discussed,[27] all the scientific expertise in the world does not – and cannot – solve the unsolvable, or decide a case based on objective reason. At most, panellists and the secretariat can use scientific opinions to support – and thus enhance the legitimacy of – guesses, instincts, and choices that arise *outside* the realm of science. To put it bluntly, scientists do not appear at hearings to guide the adjudicators. They appear at hearings to make the adjudicators' conclusions 'appear legally valid' where rules alone do not provide the solution.[28]

*

Human rights courts also rely on hearings to acquire additional information and engage with the parties' positions. However, in her current capacity as an ECtHR registry division lawyer, Aphrodite does not take part in oral proceedings. As mentioned,[29] ECtHR section cases do not contemplate hearings unless strictly necessary. Holding oral proceedings on a regular basis would compound the already crushing deadlines set for deliberations and drafting.

This is one of the reasons why Aphrodite cannot wait to apply for a job with the Jurisconsult's office. At the Grand Chamber, hearings are the norm,[30] perhaps in recognition of the high profile of disputes that reach that stage. Once the 17 Grand Chamber judges, dressed in black robes and white jabots, have taken their seats at the semi-circular bench, the president recites the procedural history of the case, introduces the parties' and third

---

[25] See e.g. J. Pauwelyn, 'The Use of Experts in WTO Dispute Settlement' (2002) 51(2) ICLQ 325.
[26] See e.g. Peat, 'Court-Appointed Experts', 289.
[27] See *supra*, pp. 195–200.
[28] Epstein, 'Rationality, Legitimacy, and the Law', 19.
[29] See *supra*, p. 167.
[30] See e.g. Garlicki, 'Judicial Deliberations', 393–4; J. Hedigan, 'The European Convention on Human Rights and Counter-Terrorism' (2005) 28(2) FordhamIntlLJ 392, 401.

parties' counsel, and welcomes any external observers (usually groups of judges or prosecutors from member states of the Council of Europe). Then, the litigants, beginning with the complainant, are each given 30–45 minutes to make their case in chief, followed by third-party interventions. It is then the turn of the judges to question the litigants. Unlike the real-time Q&A of the WTO Appellate Body, Grand Chamber questions are collected all in one go, after which the president calls for a convenient 20-minute break to allow the parties to prepare their responses. The questions themselves are relatively easy to answer, and seldom challenge the parties' views on the facts or the law. Overall, Grand Chamber hearings rarely exceed three hours in length.

Aphrodite dreams of a time when she will hear prestigious counsel eloquently plead their cases in court. If she ever joins the Jurisconsult's team, though, she might be disappointed. While Grand Chamber hearings do occasionally involve sophisticated pleadings, this is not always true. Quite often, hearings follow a dry and scripted structure, with few surprises on either side of the bench. But for now, let Aphrodite cultivate her career ambitions. One needs motivation to keep going in a bureaucracy.

Soledad, by contrast, has unrestricted access to the IACtHR hearing room. In principle, the IACtHR hears the parties orally whenever 'there is a question of fact that can be clarified by witnesses or experts'.[31] The nature of the cases entertained by the IACtHR – often involving widespread state violence, repression, or persecution against entire communities – might suggest that the examination and cross-examination of witnesses are a crucial phase of the proceedings, brimming with pathos and excitement.

In fact, Soledad is no big fan of oral proceedings. Barring the most complex cases, hearings take no longer than a few hours or days – way too short a time for anyone to get a full grasp of the gruesome experiences endured by the alleged victims. While Soledad understands the need for conciseness and rigour – the sole conditions under which a court can oppose detached *objectivity* to the passions of *context* – she finds the atmosphere in the courtroom too aseptic and stale for her taste. How can one listen to the victims' stories without showing a shred of emotion? How can one reduce pain and ordeal to a few pre-cooked questions and a couple of paragraphs in a transcript? And how can one handle these

---

[31] Pasqualucci, *IACtHR Practice and Procedure*, 194.

cases in the same way one would deal with packaging requirements or the expropriation of a power plant?[32]

These questions echo in Soledad's head every time the participants deliver their oral statements. Typically, the first to testify are the alleged victims, followed immediately by the witnesses and experts appointed by the parties or by the bench. Individual victims are allowed to represent themselves before the IACtHR at all stages of the proceedings. However, when there is more than one alleged victim, they must 'designate a common intervenor' to speak on their behalf.[33] The Commission appears as a 'procedural party'[34] at each hearing, usually represented by senior staff members. Witnesses may include, say, the family members of a *desaparecido*, domestic lawyers with first-hand knowledge of their clients' detention conditions, etc. Experts range from psychiatrists to forensic analysts, from ethnographers to pathologists. After this congeries of actors makes its sorrowful parade, the poker-faced judges and the parties' counsel may proceed to ask questions and clarifications. Then, *muchas gracias*, the Court adjourns. Everyone back to their offices.

One element that makes IACtHR hearings slightly more exciting is also a unique feature of the Inter-American system. Both the parties and the bench can ask *legal experts* to intervene. Those experts differ from the parties' counsel. They are not there to defend a particular position, but rather to provide independent expertise on matters of domestic or human rights law. For instance, in a 2001 case concerning the screening of an allegedly blasphemous movie, the Court received the oral declarations of several Chilean jurists concerning national censorship laws, freedom of expression, constitutional provisions, and the legal status of IACtHR judgments in Chile's legal system.[35]

When she first joined the secretariat, Soledad found the role of legal experts a bit puzzling. According to the *jura novit curia* principle,

---

[32] Along similar lines, see C. Carpenter, '"You Talk of Terrible Things So Matter-of-Factly in This Language of Science": Constructing Human Rights in the Academy' (2012) 10(2) PerspPolitics 363.

[33] Article 23(2) of the 2001 Rules of Procedure of the IACtHR.

[34] Article 2(23) of the 2001 Rules of Procedure of the IACtHR.

[35] See *Olmedo Bustos et al. v. Chile* (Merits), 5 February 2001, Ser. C, No. 73, paras. 45(c)–(g). Other cases involving party-appointed legal experts include, e.g., *Blanco-Romero et al. v. Venezuela* (Merits, Reparations and Costs), 28 November 2005, Ser. C, No. 138, paras. 41(a)(2) and 41(b)(3)–(4); *Anzualdo Castro v. Peru* (Preliminary Objection, Merits, Reparations and Costs), 22 September 2009, Ser. C, No. 202, para. 22(f); *Dacosta Cadogan v. Barbados* (Preliminary Objections, Merits, Reparations, and Costs), 24 September 2009, Ser. C, No. 204, paras. 33(c), (e) and (f).

international courts are the 'master[s] of the characterization to be given in law to the facts of the case'.[36] Why, then, should IACtHR judges pay heed to external legal expertise? Over the years, however, Soledad has grown more comfortable with this peculiar aspect of IACtHR litigation. Firstly, independent legal experts can ease the work of the judges and the secretariat by pointing to norms and jurisprudence that they may otherwise overlook. Secondly, and more importantly, the presence of those experts imparts a cozy feeling of 'clubiness' to the whole enterprise. Allowing well-recognized jurists from different member states to appear regularly in the courtroom strengthens the professional bonds among them, establishes an interface between the Court and the local *intelligentsia*, and ultimately fosters the emergence of a Pan-American 'human rights elite' able to champion the cause across the continent.

\*

Finally, what about Sophie? You might expect her to be euphoric at the prospect of attending ICJ hearings. Given the exclusivity of the ICJ bar, the counsel appearing before the World Court are supposed to rank among the most eloquent international lawyers.[37] What better treat than listening to prominent jurists as they draw parallels with Magritte's paintings,[38] Molière's plays,[39] or Cartesian logics[40] in their flawless Oxbridge English or Metropolitan French?

Well, you might be surprised to learn that, after her initial enthusiasm, Sophie has actually *stopped* attending hearings, unless expressly requested by Judge Lehmann. She made one minor exception in the *North Borneo* dispute, but only because she was curious to see Filibert address the Court. She left the Great Hall of Justice as soon as her friend concluded his pleading. Who knows, perhaps they will bump into each other at the cafeteria later.

The reason for Sophie's lack of interest in the World Court's oral proceedings is simple. Those proceedings have little or no value in acquiring

---

[36] *Guerra and Others* v. *Italy*, Grand Chamber Judgment of 19 February 1998, No. 14967/89, ECtHR-1998, para. 44.
[37] See Terris, Romano, and Swigart, *The International Judge*, 84.
[38] See *Territorial Dispute (Libyan Arab Jamahiriya* v. *Chad)*, Oral Pleadings (13 July 1993), CR 93/31 (verbatim record), para. 19.
[39] See *East Timor (Portugal* v. *Australia)*, Oral Pleadings (16 February 1995), CR95/15 (verbatim record), para. 8.
[40] See *Maritime Dispute* judgment, Oral Pleadings (14 December 2012), CR2012/35 (verbatim record), para. 3.6.

additional information from the litigants.[41] After the President opens each sitting, the parties' representatives deliver their oral pleadings, 'virtually uninterrupted for several hours',[42] before an impassive bench. Usually, the pleadings themselves consist of prepared texts distributed in advance to the judges, where the parties largely rehash arguments previously expressed in their written memorials.[43] After each sitting, the registry prepares a transcript, typically exceeding 50 pages, which serves de facto as an additional set of written submissions.[44]

Although judges are, in principle, free to ask questions of the parties at the end of each sitting, in practice they seldom do so. Typically, they intervene no more than twice or thrice over three or four weeks of oral proceedings. And even when they do, they 'almost never expect an immediate answer', but instead 'ask the parties either to prepare an oral answer for a future sitting, or to submit an answer in writing by a later date'.[45]

Admittedly, things got slightly more interesting in recent years. For example, in the *Whaling* case, the judges engaged in the examination of the parties' witnesses and asked them a number of factual questions.[46] Still, these rare exceptions do little to break the general monotony of ICJ hearings, and have not convinced Sophie to increase her presence in the Great Hall of Justice. Soon enough, she will be spending long days assisting Judge Lehmann in deliberations. So why rush now?

*

In light of the above, it is safe to conclude that, in general, oral proceedings bring less information to the table than the parties' written briefs. Why then are international courts and tribunals so obstinate about holding hearings? Could they not request an extra round of written submissions and save time and money? Could they not make life easier for those litigants who lack the means to travel to The Hague, Strasbourg, San José, or Geneva?

---

[41] See e.g. Alford, 'Fact Finding', 60; C. Rose, 'Questioning the Silence of the Bench: Reflections on Oral Proceedings at the International Court of Justice' (2008) 18(1) JTransnatLawPol 47, 54.
[42] Rose, 'The Silence of the Bench', 49. See also Bedjaoui, 'The Manufacture of ICJ Judgments', 42.
[43] See e.g. Bedjaoui, 'The Manufacture of ICJ Judgments', 42; M. N. Shaw, 'The International Court of Justice', 857; Rose, 'The Silence of the Bench', 49.
[44] See Rose, 'The Silence of the Bench', 54.
[45] Ibid., 50.
[46] See *Whaling* judgment, paras. 20–1. See also Mbengue, 'Scientific Fact-Finding after *Whaling*', 538–9.

To find an answer, we must focus on the second and most essential function of hearings: *the show*. As already mentioned,[47] adjudication is no less of a performative act than music or theatre.[48] Just as an orchestra director interprets and gives life to the signs contained in a music sheet, so does an adjudicator interpret and operationalize the abstract provisions set out in a treaty. Both a maestro and a judge are expected to master the techniques necessary to perform their arts at the highest levels of skill. Both strive to secure authority and recognition within the respective fields. And both have ample opportunity to leave their personal mark on the performance.[49]

Every performer needs a stage. The judge's is the courtroom.

Only in the courtroom can the whole apparatus of technologies and ritual representations be in full display. The splendour of the robes, the magnificence of the premises, the central position of the podium, the archaic and pompous language are not ancillary, but 'constitutive' of the judicial process.[50] They confer an aura of universality[51] to an otherwise mundane and dreary set of activities.[52] As Sir Robert Jennings put it, the 'sight of governments arguing important disputes in public is a moving and a salutary experience', as is that of the judges operating 'in public and before the media'.[53] Hearings do not simply provide an opportunity to gather

---

[47] See *supra*, pp. 45–6.

[48] See e.g. S. Levinson and J. M. Balkin, 'Law, Music, and Other Performing Arts' (1991) 139(6) UPaLRev 1597, 1609; A. M. Jacobs, 'God Save This Postmodern Court: The Death of Necessity and the Transformation of the Supreme Court's Overruling Rhetoric' (1995) 63(3) UCinLRev 1119, 1122–3.

[49] The parallels between the musical and the legal worlds are indeed quite striking. Listen to the debates about the original intent of the composer vs. the interpretative freedom of the conductor, and you will hear echoes of the squabbles among originalist, textualist, and evolutionary readers of a constitution. See e.g. Levinson and Balkin, 'Law, Music, and Other Performing Arts', 1598–605. Savour the balanced dialogue between violin and keyboards in Mozart's and Beethoven's sonatas, and you will taste a bit of the CJEU's *Solange* jurisprudence. See F. Marisi, 'From Preeminence to Balance: A Comparative View between Court Decisions and Violin Keyboard Sonatas' (2015) 9 RAE 83.

[50] P. Bourdieu, *On the State: Lectures at the College de France, 1989–1992*, P. Champagne et al. (eds.), trans. D. Fernbach (Polity Press, 2014), 64.

[51] Legal precepts 'derive much of their force from the perception that they represent an expression of the social interest, one that is fundamentally superior to the expression of interests of one person or just a few people'. A. Stone Sweet, *Governing with Judges: Constitutional Politics in Europe* (Oxford University Press, 2000), 11.

[52] As a former Appellate Body member once noted, WTO dispute settlement 'is a tedious, boring, exhausting process, and if the world saw it, they would be bored'. J. Bacchus, cit. in G. Marceau and M. Hurley, 'Transparency and Public Participation in the WTO: A Report Card on WTO Transparency Mechanisms' (2012) 4(1) TL&D 19, 38.

[53] R. Jennings, 'The United Nations at Fifty: The International Court of Justice after Fifty Years' (1995) 89(3) AJIL 493, 498.

information. They are also the highest instance of 'theatricalization – in the sense of magical evocation, sorcery – of the united group consenting to the discourse that unites it'.[54]

In turn, the theatrics of the hearing serve a legitimizing function. Since the bulk of judicial practice takes place behind closed doors, there needs to be at least *one* moment in the proceedings where the court is *seen* in action by its audience. That moment is particularly important for those courts and tribunals that deliver their judgments only in writing and without a formal gathering. Without setting foot in the courtroom, the litigants in an investment case could not witness with their own eyes that the arbitrators they appointed are doing their work *comme il faut*; the victims of human rights violations would hardly believe that their grievances are being given full consideration; etc. Very few would enjoy music simply by reading notes on a music sheet. And fewer still would find the judicial process authoritative were they not given the opportunity to visualize it.[55]

The size and nature of the audience varies depending on the judicial institution concerned and the degree to which oral proceedings are open to the public. At the one end of the spectrum we find ISDS tribunals, whose hearings are usually confidential. The possibility to solve a case discreetly and with little external meddling has long been touted as one of the perks of arbitration as compared to state courts. Nevertheless, the rise in prominence and gradual consolidation of ISDS into a 'proper' judicial regime[56] has revealed its wider public policy implications and prompted calls for greater transparency. Today, for instance, virtually all investment cases involving the United States or Canada provide for public hearings,[57] and other countries are following suit.[58] At the opposite end of the spectrum are the ICJ, the ECtHR Grand Chamber, and the IACtHR, whose oral proceedings are regularly broadcast on the courts' websites and form part of the public record.

---

[54] Bourdieu, *On the State*, 63.
[55] On the visualizations of judges in pop culture, see e.g. D. A. Black, 'Narrative Determination and the Figure of the Judge', in M. Freeman (ed.), *Law and Popular Culture* (Oxford University Press, 2005), 677; K. Å. Modéer and M. Sunnqvist (eds.), *Legal Stagings: The Visualization, Medialization and Ritualization of Law in Language, Literature, Media, Art and Architecture* (Museum Tusculanum Press, 2012).
[56] See generally Schill, *Multilateralization*.
[57] See Marceau and Hurley, 'Transparency and Public Participation', 39.
[58] See e.g. *Pac Rim Cayman LLC v. El Salvador*, ICSID Case No. ARB/09/12; *Railroad Development Corporation v. Guatemala*, ICSID Case No. ARB/07/23.

WTO dispute settlement takes the middle ground. After years of strict closed-door policy, inherited from the club of GATT diplomats, the organization was pressured by NGOs and scholars to make its hearings more accessible.[59] A handful of WTO member states, spearheaded by the United States, internalized these pressures and advocated for opening oral proceedings to public view. Despite the resistance of other states, which feared that an honoured tradition could turn into a 'media circus',[60] the practice of holding open hearings slowly picked up. Whenever a party requested it, and provided that no one objected, panels started to allow for oral proceedings to be televised in an adjacent room for the benefit of registered attendees. The Appellate Body adapted to the new ethos shortly thereafter. While full transparency is yet to come, WTO hearings are rapidly shifting from a family business to a more overt display of judicial prowess.

But the audience does not only stand at the receiving end of a performance. Indeed, it shapes the performative act. The closure or openness of hearings to public view affects the adjudicators' demeanour in the hearing room. In confidential proceedings, judges feel less compelled to stick to protocol and are readier to air their opinions freely. By contrast, they are more risk-averse when a larger audience is watching.[61]

The dialectic between the performer and the audience is tricky to master, as some adjudicators learnt the hard way. Matt vividly recalls one incident where, it seemed to him, transparency in WTO dispute settlement went a little too far. During the widely publicized *EC – Seal Products* hearings, the panel's chairman imprudently went off the script and asked the complainants a rather naïve question about the sufficiency of their panel requests. In the public viewing room was a NYU law professor, who promptly lambasted the chairman's gaffe via Twitter: '*jura non novit curia*'. Matt doubts that the chairman ever read the professor's tweet. But, he remembers how upset he was that an 'intruder', a 'foreigner', could bash a well-respected trade adjudicator simply for raising

---

[59] See, among many others, K. Van der Borght, 'The Review of the WTO Understanding on Dispute Settlement: Some Reflections on the Current Debate' (1999) 14(4) AmUIntlLRev 1223, 1227–9; B. M. Hoekman and P. C. Mavroidis, 'WTO Dispute Settlement, Transparency and Surveillance' (2000) 23(4) WorldEcon 527, 538–40; L. Ehring, 'Public Access to Dispute Settlement Hearings in the World Trade Organization' (2008) 11(4) JIEL 1021.

[60] See Marceau and Hurley, 'Transparency and Public Participation', 38.

[61] Actually, some ICJ judges do not miss the opportunity to take a nap even when on worldwide broadcast. But we will explore the sleeping habits of international adjudicators in the following chapter.

an innocent doubt. If transparency meant *this*, Matt thought, perhaps it would be better to go back to the good old days of closed-doors meetings and protesters outside the building!

Of course, the show is not only the judges' business. All the actors involved in the process have some stakes in the theatricalization of hearings. As discussed, international judicial bureaucrats often act as invisible prompters, who cue the actors onstage and provide them with carefully crafted scripts. Interpreters, court reporters, and civil society organizations (to the extent of their access to hearings) each have a chance to shine in their respective roles. Participation can also be indirect: some advocacy and research institutions, for instance, gain publicity by submitting *amicus curiae* briefs or intervening in favour of either party.

However, it is unquestionably the parties' counsel who are there to steal the show. Hearings offer them the perfect opportunity to be watched in action by their clients, the other parties, the judges, the bureaucracy and, where possible, the public. It is one thing to write a good brief, and another to impress the court with a persuasive oral pleading. The written phase of proceedings rewards thoroughness and analytical clarity. Success in the oral phase hinges on the wit and humour of the speakers, their ability to think on their feet, and their deftness at parrying attacks: surely a more gripping spectacle than the dry technicality of legal documents. Most litigators revel in the spotlight. Through their elaborate performances, they seek not only to advance their clients' positions, but also to corroborate their reputation and capital within the community.

The first component of counsel's performance is their attire, which varies depending on the court concerned. At the ICJ, counsel are not required to follow any particular dress code, and are free to wear whichever garments best symbolize their countries of origin or their professional affiliations. For example, a British barrister will usually appear in traditional gown, short wig, and bands; a US attorney in a lounge suit; and a continental European professor in academic robe.[62] In other judicial systems, like the WTO or ISDS, counsel wear business attire as do adjudicators and other participants. As we have seen,[63] this relative informality is a point of pride for international economic lawyers, who mock – and perhaps secretly envy – '*la noblesse de robe*'.[64] By carefully choosing their wardrobe, litigators impose their presence as worthy of attention, thus making implicit statements about their socio-professional status.

---

[62] Messenger, 'The Practice of Litigation', 222.
[63] See *supra*, p. 103.
[64] Bourdieu, *On the State*, 266.

The second component of the performance is, of course, language. Lawyers work hard to perfect the art of oral argument, which involves a delicate balance of assertiveness, tact, staged deference to the court, and the ability to shift tone and register when the circumstances so require. In making their case in chief, a litigator may opt for colloquial terms, grandiloquent metaphors, or technical jargon depending on what best resonates with the expectations of the bench. Arguments made 'on the grounds of natural justice' may be more favoured by some judges than by others;[65] certain courts may privilege textual rigour over policy reasoning; and so on.

The most consummate advocates go as far as to develop a series of gestures, expressions, and figures of speech that are universally recognized as their personal brand. If you ask Sophie, she will point to one counsel who invariably begins his pleadings by sensitizing the judges of the World Court on the tragic circumstances that gave rise to the case:

'While we comfortably sit here, in this beautiful palace at the heart of Europe, people in [name of the state] are enduring unimaginable suffering.'

Another counsel may privilege dry and sarcastic humour, while yet another may revel in turning rhetorical flourishes against their user.[66] Likewise, Matt would recognize Duncan Doyle's voice from a mile away. In a perfectly rounded British accent, rarely betraying his native Irish inflexion, Duncan articulates his words slowly, often leaving unnaturally long gaps between sentences. When the pleading reaches its climax, he leans towards the microphone, lowers his glasses, sternly looks at the podium, and drops the punchline:

'If you were to accept [the opposed party]'s argument, that would mean that [description of an absurd scenario]. That. Cannot. Be. Right.'

Pause.

Not everything goes according to plan every time. Carlos still chuckles when he thinks back to one lawyer's fiasco years ago. Wishing to show that the challenged state regulation was riddled with loopholes and internal inconsistencies, the cunning litigator kept repeating that it 'looked like a Swiss cheese'. A powerful image, no doubt, were it not for the fact that, suddenly, the Swiss president of the tribunal interrupted him:

'You know, Sir ... Our traditional cheese doesn't have holes.'

Ouch.

---

[65] Messenger, 'The Practice of Litigation', 227.
[66] Ibid., 226.

The way counsel address their counterparts on the opposing side deserves a final mention. Throughout the hearing, the competing litigation teams are aware of and responsive to each other. As one might expect, each team tries to anticipate what the other will say, and adapt its 'style, forms of argumentation, and structure of legal reasoning'[67] accordingly. The dialectic between opposed counsels can be read in two ways. Under orthodox accounts of international adjudication, lawyers pleading before a court are indistinguishable from the parties they represent. The interests of counsel and clients coincide, and are both opposed to those of the counterpart.

But as soon as we focus on socio-professional practices, we realize that this is more than a simple adversarial confrontation. The WTO dispute between Indonesia and the European Union is *also* a professional contest between Ms. Jane Weaver and Mr. Duncan Doyle; the disagreements between Kingsland and Turkey *also* reflect the tactics of Henry Bellinger QC and Maître Jacques Renault; and so on. These opposed counsel are often colleagues who have known each other for a long time, and who simply *happen* to be on different sides of the fence. However unequal in terms of power or ideology, the parties are almost invariably represented by members of the club of international litigators, thereby having equal access to the inner circles of our profession. This, and this alone, means equality of arms in international law.

•

'So good to see you, man!'

As Sophie hoped, she and Filibert did manage to meet at the ICJ cafeteria during a hearing break. After queuing, trays in hand, behind state dignitaries and court officials, the two sat at a small corner table, not to raise any eyebrows. They have about one hour before the afternoon session begins.

'How've you been, Fil? How's Leonard treating you?'

'It's "Lionel," but well, thanks! What about the old German Lion? Still kicking?'

'A hundred per cent, as usual. You look good, you know.'

'A wreck, you mean. I've barely had any time to spend with the family lately. The team's exhausted. And we must survive for another week. But once we're done with hearings, our job's over ... "Filibert smirks." ... and the ball passes to you.'

---

[67] Messenger, 'The Practice of Litigation', 223.

'Yep. Now it's my turn for the night shifts.'
Both giggle. Then, after a moment of silence, Filibert whispers:
'It's an interesting case, isn't it?'
'Indeed. And quite important, too.'
'The Sultan's deed ... That was a head scratch.'
'...'
'I look forward to seeing what you guys make of it.'
'Are you on a spying mission, Fil?' Sophie recoils in her chair and nervously gazes around the cafeteria. She prays nobody heard. Filibert is quick to make amends:
'Sorry, didn't mean to be inappropriate. This case has taken up so much of my time that it's all I can talk about. Forget I said anything.'
Sophie relaxes a bit.
'It's fine, no need to apologize. And don't worry... "Sophie flicks Filibert an intent glance." ... *the Court will decide the dispute in accordance with The Law.*'

# 15

## The Moment of (Constructed) Truth

'Good morning, everyone. I hope you had a great night's sleep. Thank you for being here so early. I know you would rather be having breakfast *au bord du Lac*, but I'm afraid you'll have to bear with me instead. Our friend Guillermo has a flight to catch in exactly three days from now, so I suggest we make the most of the time we have. You have all received the list of issues, the summaries of the parties' submissions, and the post-hearing briefs. I am genuinely excited to hear your views on this important dispute. Carlos, is there anything you would like to add? Are we ready to roll?'

Carlos is struggling to stay awake. He flew in last night, had a quick dinner with Professor Gal at the hotel's restaurant, went to bed at midnight and woke up at 5:30 AM. It will take another couple of coffees before his brain starts working properly. A long-awaited day has arrived, and with it the most important part of the proceedings. Today, the arbitral tribunal in *Kingsland Mining Corp.* v. *Turkey* meets for deliberations. Carlos takes a quick look around the small room on the fourth floor of the Mandarin Oriental. It is still dark outside. Geneva is still sleeping.

François Gal, sitting at the opposite end of the table, is wearing bright yellow suspenders on a dark blue shirt. No tie, no jacket. Carlos knows that his mentor's informal attire, which contrasts with the impeccable suits of the other attendees, conveys a twofold message. First, that he is in an excellent mood. Second, that he is asserting his dominance over the co-arbitrators. It is curious how the dress-code of powerful people works in reverse. The more influential you are, the greater an effort you will make to look casual and unassuming.

On the left of the President sits Guillermo Richler-Benitez, a 65-year-old Colombian law professor and former *ad hoc* judge at the ICJ, whose experience rivals that of his lifelong friend François Gal. A staunch defender of the sovereign prerogatives of the host state, Professor Richler has built his professional reputation as a thorough and articulate pro-state co-arbitrator. Thus, despite his countless appointments, he has almost never presided a tribunal. Who knows what position Professor Richler will take this time around. Carlos is aware that Professor Gal is already leaning in favour of the claimant, so he expects to see some action.

On the right of Professor Gal sits the claimant-appointed co-arbitrator. Evgeny Mamatov is a relative newbie in the ISDS game. A 39-year-old graduate of Columbia University, he spent 10 years with a New York firm, where he dealt with corporate matters. He entered the arbitration field to try something new. Carlos notices with relief that Mr. Mamatov is as sleepy as he is. He has no idea whatsoever about that co-arbitrator's views in the case. After all, the copy of the Memo that Mr Mamatov carried with him at the hearing was almost immaculate …[1]

'Ahem. Carlos?'

Carlos awakens from his torpor. Ready to roll.

'Good morning Mr. President, good morning distinguished Members of the Tribunal. I have nothing to add to the list of issues. I have a few spare copies of the document in case you don't have yours with you. Also, I have sketched a decision tree that connects the various issues at hand. First, of course, comes the overarching question of whether Respondent failed to accord fair and equitable treatment to Claimant. Here, the Tribunal will want to decide whether Claimant had legitimate expectations about the protection of the investment. This is the first fork in the road. If you decide that those expectations exist, you will have then to assess whether Respondent's conduct frustrated them. If it did, then you may find a violation of fair and equitable treatment, and you may exercise judicial economy on the other claims. If it didn't, you may still find that Respondent has breached fair and equitable treatment and on other grounds, such as …'

'… Thank you, Carlos. One thing at a time. I will begin by asking my esteemed colleagues if they agree on addressing the existence of legitimate expectations upfront.'

Professor Richler answers with an affable nod. Mr. Mamatov yawns.

'Well, if there are no objections, I would like to ask the Secretary to present the issue of legitimate expectations for about five-to-ten minutes before we begin our discussion. Carlos, the floor is yours.'

And so it begins. For the next three days, eight hours a day, François Gal will orchestrate a debate among the three tribunal members, ably assisted by Carlos. First will speak the co-arbitrators, each stating his initial views on the issues at stake; then it will be the President's turn. While this *ordre*

---

[1] See *supra*, p. 259.

*de parole* is not mandatory, Professor Gal scrupulously adheres to it when he presides a tribunal. A consummate adjudicator, he has developed an innate distrust of co-arbitrators and seeks to avoid prejudging the merits by intervening first. If he were to state his position too early, either co-arbitrator could strategically join him to quickly form a majority, thus frustrating the purpose and spoiling the fun of the debate.[2]

The unfolding of the discussion will be anything but orderly. It will take unforeseeable turns, often reverting back to the start. It will branch out in unexpected directions, before rejoining the main path. It will stumble on major or minor problems, only to resume its course a moment later. The tone of the discussants will be sometimes cordial, sometimes acrimonious. Assertions will be made, doubts will be expressed, confrontations will occur, possibilities will emerge and others be discarded. By the end of the three days, the members of the tribunals will each have expressed his position on the merits of the case. On the basis of the instructions received, Carlos will draft the majority award, which Professor Gal will then review and circulate to the co-arbitrators for comments and edits.

This, no more and no less, is what happens inside a deliberation room. One might be tempted to describe judicial deliberations as the iconic 'moment of truth':[3] the moment when external forces cease to exert their pressures and leave the judges alone with their wisdom; the moment when, at last, the hubbub of the international judicial community subsides and gives way to the crystalline voice of The Law. But that would be a romanticized fiction. If any truth exists in international adjudication, it does not reveal itself at one magical instant. Rather, it is slowly and painstakingly *constructed* through an infinite series of choices, exchanges, and hesitations.

How could it be otherwise? First, pinpointing the exact point in time at which an adjudicator forms a definite opinion on a case is simply impossible. None of us can tell for sure when a certain idea came to mind; nor can we confidently trace its roots to any specific moment. For years, literary critics have wondered why Umberto Eco had chosen Aristotle's *Poetics* as the central plot device in *The Name of the Rose*. Shortly before passing away, Professor Eco giddily confessed that he himself did not know why.

---

[2] Bernardini, 'Organisation of Deliberations', 18.
[3] F. M. Coffin, 'Judicial Balancing: The Protean Scales of Justice' (1988) 63(1) NYULRev 16, 25. See also Bernardini, 'Organisation of Deliberations', 16.

Second, the elusiveness of mental processes is compounded by the collective nature of the adjudicative process and the myriad interactions that occur along the way. By the time a case is ripe for deliberation, the file has undergone a series of profound transformations that have shaped its contours, altered its core tenets, and excluded a universe of possibilities from the judges' decision horizon. Amorphous context has been lyophilized into justiciable facts, political and social grievances have turned into legal claims and arguments, indeterminate law and unknowable historical truth have somehow condensed into a finite range of acceptable options for solution, and so forth. A multitude of actors has left a mark on each step of the process, such that it would now be impossible to recognize a lead melody among so many dissonant voices.

Third, even if a superhuman individual could mentally reconstruct every shift and turn, the reconstruction would nonetheless remain incomplete, for the simple reason that the judgment has not yet been written. No matter how articulate one's thoughts are, it is only by putting them in writing that one can truly test their viability, spot their internal inconsistencies, and see whether they hold together as a coherent whole.[4] Law is 'a matter of words', such that 'the choice of words to convey a legal point is in itself the decision'.[5] The 'language of court opinions can be as important as the disposition of cases'.[6] Or, to put it differently, adjudication is a *craft* directed at the production of a tangible object (the judgment) through sustained and recursive labour. Like any other craftsmen, adjudicators think with their hands as much as with their brains.[7]

Being immersed in a web of social relations, it is rare for a judge to come to deliberations without a preferred outcome in mind. That preference may arise out of moral instincts, ideological inclinations, prior experience, or simple gut feelings. Personal subjectivities 'inevitably come to bear and affect the balance'.[8] To think otherwise, we should imagine the judge as a recluse who speaks to no one, interacts with no one, thinks nothing, and feels nothing. Moreover, as discussed throughout the book, a judge's vantage point in the constellation of international courts inevitably influences their sensibilities, worldviews, and

---

[4] See e.g. Bernardini, 'Organisation of Deliberations', 18.
[5] Thirlway, 'Drafting ICJ Decisions', 21.
[6] R. J. Hume, 'The Use of Rhetorical Sources by the US Supreme Court' (2006) 40(4) L&SocRev 817.
[7] Terris, Romano, and Swigart, *The International Judge*, 59. More on this *infra*, Chapter 16.
[8] Coffin, 'Judicial Balancing', 25.

epistemic categories. A trade, an investment, and a human rights adjudicator engage in deliberations in different institutional settings, moved by different ideals, and equipped with different analytical tools. Finally, a judge's preference reflects their strategic positioning in the international judicial community and the desire to increase or consolidate their capital. The pressures of the field push each adjudicator to take a cautious or risky, conservative or subversive, moderate or radical stance as the case may be.[9] In short: Lady Justice may be blindfolded,[10] but no adjudicative act is ever truly blind.

However, it is equally rare for a judge to hold an *a priori* bias in favour of either party, or to know from the outset how they will decide the case. Instead, most adjudicators will gradually form their opinions through recursive interactions with other community members. Reading the section of a memo may give pause to an otherwise set position; a quick chat at the cafeteria may challenge or cement one's impressions; and so on. In turn, these doubts, swings, and detours are informed by the social structures and the distribution of capital across the community. The views of a court's president will carry more authority than the timid suggestions of a new intern, a widely-publicized scholarly article will hold more sway than the slapdash *amicus curiae* of a small NGO, etc.

Hence, we can tentatively say that, as they enter the deliberation room, international judges are neither totally clueless nor completely fixated on a particular outcome. On the one hand, the socio-professional dynamics of the field nudge them in a given direction and guide their behaviour. On the other hand, their openness to doubt and willingness to question their initial instincts leave room for contingency in the deliberative process.[11] Indeed, 'this slowness, this heaviness and these continuous hesitations

---

[9] For example, Judge Cançado Trindade has made of lengthy and academically styled dissenting opinions his trademark contribution to IACtHR and ICJ jurisprudence. Some observers have praised the Judge's attempts to 'acculturate the international judicial bodies in which he seats', even at the cost of being relegated to the minority. A. Bianchi, 'On Certainty', EJIL Talk!, 16 February 2012, www.ejiltalk.org/on-certainty/. Others have retorted that 'while challenging orthodoxy is a good thing, a judge who allows himself to become isolated within his court is perhaps not pursuing the wisest or the most effective course of action'. M. Milanovic, 'Judging Judges: A Statistical Exercise', EJIL Talk!, 12 March 2012, www.ejiltalk.org/judging-judges-a-statistical-exercise/. Irrespective of who is right, the point remains that Judge Cançado Trindade has carefully carved out a recognizable professional role among the international judiciary.

[10] See e.g. Curtis and Resnik, 'Images of Justice'; Jacob, *Images de la Justice*.

[11] Wells, 'Situated Decisionmaking', 1736.

precisely form the primary material of justice'[12] – the material that protects us from prejudice and arbitrariness.

\*

The deliberative practices of international courts are designed to ensure that adjudicators come to their decisions at a methodical – sometimes 'glacial'[13] – pace. The ICJ stands out as a prime example. As we have seen,[14] the World Court's deliberations involve the whole bench and, where applicable, the *ad hoc* judges. This *en banc* composition means that it often takes an 'inordinate amount of time'[15] for the Court to come to an agreeable outcome.

After a preliminary round of discussion and the circulation of the individual notes, the judges convene for deliberations. As with every internal act of the Court, deliberations do not take place in the lofty locales of the Peace Palace but in a drab, grey-walled room in the Annex. Once all the judges have taken their seats around the horseshoe table, the President invites each of them, in reverse role of seniority, to declare their views, address comments to their peers, circulate additional questions, or reformulate existing ones.[16] The President speaks last. A debate then ensues where the members of the Court seek to persuade each other of the merits of their opinions, resist countervailing arguments, make and unmake alliances to send their points across. Given the judge-driven nature of the ICJ process, clerks take the backseat during deliberations: only the special assistant to the President and a handful of registry lawyers are admitted to the room.

As the discussion unfolds, fault lines emerge between an indicative majority and a number of dissenting judges. At this stage, the notion of 'majority' should be taken with a grain of salt, as further disagreements may surface later on. It is unlikely that all majority judges are in complete accord on every issue or on the overall tenor of the Court's analysis. Some may insist on a thorough and detailed analysis of all the legal questions at stake; others may prefer a shorter and more elliptical judgment. Also, majority judges may take different stances towards their colleagues in the minority. Some hardliners may stick to their guns at the risk of seeing their

---

[12] Latour, *The Making of Law*, 91.
[13] Terris, Romano, and Swigart, *The International Judge*, 79.
[14] See *supra*, pp. 168–9.
[15] Hernández, *The ICJ*, 107.
[16] Article 5 of the ICJ Note on Judicial Practice.

judgment countered by a barrage of dissenting opinions; others may be more amenable to compromise in the hope of achieving a more collegial result. Given these variables and uncertainties, it simply makes no sense to say that deliberations are the moment in which the ICJ 'decides' a case.

In fact, the most tangible result of deliberations is the formation of the Drafting Committee, a sub-group of three judges tasked with writing the actual text of the judgment. If the President agrees with the majority view, he sits on the Committee by default. If he disagrees, the Committee is presided by the most senior judge in the majority. In the latter case, the President is consulted by the Committee prior to submitting the text to the Court.[17] The other two members of the Committee are appointed among the judges 'whose oral statements and written notes have most closely and effectively reflected the opinion of the majority'.[18] Their appointment takes place 'by secret ballot and by an absolute majority of the votes of the judges present'.[19]

The reader will not fail to notice here another similarity between international adjudication and religious ritual. The dynamics that lead to the appointment of the Drafting Committee resemble those of a papal conclave. In both cases, a 'timeless abstraction'[20] – The Law of God, The Law of Men – is supposed to guide the identification of the individuals who are best able to serve its purposes; in both cases, the anointed ones become *ipso facto* the quasi-infallible heralds of that abstraction; and, in both cases, any material traces like ballots and scraps of paper are carefully hidden or destroyed at the end of the process. One can only guess the amount of negotiations, tactical positioning, and *quid pro quos* that must occur before white smoke emerges from the chimney.

Ostensibly, appointment to the Drafting Committee depends on a candidate's ability to draft in 'authoritative language', their 'inclination' and 'state of health', and the 'availability of their time for intensive work'.[21] Yet, the suspicion remains that other factors might be at play. In fact, some judges sit on the Committee regularly, whereas others rarely do. This disparity might not be due solely to eloquence or experience, but also to the struggle among 'ideological factions' at the World Court.[22] Again, the

---

[17] Article 6 of the ICJ Note on Judicial Practice.
[18] Ibid.
[19] Ibid.
[20] Terris, Romano, and Swigart, *The International Judge*, 147.
[21] Kolb, *The ICJ*, 1008.
[22] M. K. Lewis, 'The Lack of Dissent in WTO Dispute Settlement' (2006) 9(4) JIEL 895, 901.

term 'ideology' is a slippery one. The point of our story is that international adjudication is guided neither by abstract legal norms *nor* by preconceived political inclinations, but rather by the ambition to persuade 'the legal community' of the merits of one's position.[23] Thus, it would be simplistic to assume that a judge's nationality[24] or 'philosophical leanings'[25] inexorably dictate their allegiance to one faction or another. The socio-professional dynamics of the community are never that immutable, but are continuously renegotiated.

Luckily for our narrative purposes, Jürgen Lehmann has been quite in demand as of late. His experience and seniority are highly prized by the rest of the Court. The quality of his note in the *North Borneo* dispute – quality which, we should remind, depends in no small part on Sophie's contribution – immediately made him a potential candidate to the Drafting Committee. His friendly relations with President José Ignacio Rosas did the rest. The secret ballot turned out overwhelmingly in his favour. After congratulating his fellow Committee members, President Rosas and Judge Marcos Quintana, the German Lion winks at Sophie.

'Well done, young lady. Now let's nail this judgment, shall we?'

*

The deliberative practice of the WTO Appellate Body is less unwieldy than the ICJ's, but places a similar emphasis on collegiality. The deliberation room, located in the South corner of the Appellate Body corridor, used to contain a round mahogany table where the judges and their supporting staff 'all sat as equals' and 'amicably fought for room' to spread their papers.[26] In 2011, the round table was replaced by a less characteristic but more spacious oval one.

Immediately after the hearing, the three Appellate Body members assigned to the case (collectively referred to as the 'Division') meet with the secretariat for a so-called *post mortem* discussion. First, the ABS lawyers summarize and explain the issues at stake, relying on the analysis already contained in their issues paper. Then, it is

---

[23] K. J. Alter, 'Agents or Trustees? International Courts in their Political Context' (2008) 14(1) EurJIntlRel 33, 46.
[24] See e.g. A. M. Smith, '"Judicial Nationalism" in International Law: National Identity and Judicial Autonomy at the ICJ' (2005) 40(2) TexIntlLJ 197.
[25] Alter, 'Agents or Trustees?', 46.
[26] Baptista, 'A Country Boy', 567.

for the Division members to state their provisional views. As with the ICJ, 'views' does not mean 'definitive opinions'. Division members often begin by asking questions to the secretariat, expressing doubts, and consulting with their colleagues about the significance of a given argument or piece of evidence.

This tentative attitude is understandable. Up until that point, the preparation of the case and the preliminary assessment of its merits have been mostly in the hands of the secretariat. It is only during the *post mortem* that the adjudicators, so to speak, awaken to the dispute. Some Division members will have done their homework and carry densely annotated copies of the issues paper into the room. Others, by contrast, will have only a scant idea of the disputed issues and expect the secretariat to enlighten – 'spoon-feed' – them.

Matt finds the whole exercise somewhat frustrating. The intentions of the Division members are often hard to decipher, as if they were keeping their cards close to their chests and waiting for someone else to make the first move. At best, Matt can try to read between the lines of their exchanges, hoping to grasp a hidden meaning in what they are saying or withholding.

The *post mortem* is followed by the so-called exchange of views,[27] during which the four Appellate Body members who are not part of the Division join the three Division members to discuss the merits of the case. Unlike the *post mortem*, the secretariat tends not to intervene too much in the debate, leaving it to the judges to figure out how best to structure their discussion. As Björn once said, the exchange of views is when 'the kids play unattended'.

The practice of holding this collegial discussion is a rather unique feature of WTO appellate proceedings. Its purpose is to foster cooperation across the bench and uniformity in decision-making, while at the same time avoiding the burden of having each case heard *en banc*.[28] Yet, as Matt recently realized, the parties' counsel are sometimes uncomfortable with the exchange of views. As usual, the reveal came to Matt in the form of one of Jane's sermons, a beer in one hand and a cigarette in the other:

---

[27] See *Working Procedures for Appellate Review*, WT/AB/WP/W/10 (12 January 2010), Rule 4(3).

[28] See e.g. A. Alvarez-Jimenez, 'The WTO Appellate Body's Decision-Making Process: A Perfect Model for International Adjudication?' (2009) 12(2) JIEL 289; C.-D. Ehlermann, 'Experiences from the WTO Appellate Body' (2003) 38(3) TexIntlLJ 469, 476–8.

'You know, man, I'm fed up with this exchange of views thing. I mean, we work like dogs to please our three judges, bend over backwards to make ourselves understood, and ta-dah!, there comes *Monsieur le Professeur* and tells everybody what they should think. I'm fed up, I tell you.'

Matt could not guess who '*Monsieur le Professeur*' might be, given that at the time the Appellate Body counted three academics among its ranks. But he got Jane's point. While the final decision lies in the hands of the Division members, their non-Division colleagues may use the exchange of views as an opportunity to influence the reasoning, without giving the parties an opportunity to intervene. But what is worse? To partially constrain the litigants' role in the proceedings, or to forgo the possibility of every case being discussed by the brightest and most articulate Appellate Body members?

Following the exchange of views, the Division members and their ABS assistants meet again – this time for the instructions session. Here, the three adjudicators explain the core tenets of their decision and direct the secretariat lawyers through the steps of their reasoning. Based on the input received, the ABS lawyers will later draft the final report for the Division's review.

The structure, content, and tone of the instructions session vary from case to case and from judge to judge. The discussion unfolds along two main axes: firstly among the adjudicators, who react to each other's positions and try to come up with a common understanding; and secondly between the whole Division and the secretariat lawyers, who seek to persuade the judges of their own legal views. This two-level game entails a delicate interplay among the people in the room and occasionally gives rise to tensions. Suppose, for instance, Matt is asked to offer his opinion on a certain issue. As he formulates his answer, he has to carefully consider the positions taken by Björn (who has already reviewed the issues paper), the other members of the secretariat team (who may hold different opinions), and each of the Division members.

Over the years, Matt has learnt what to expect from the instructions session. He has even come up with his own mental spectrum of scenarios, scoring them from best to worst.

*10-point scenario*: the Division wholeheartedly agrees with the secretariat's advice and readily selects the desired outcome among the options provided in the issues paper. Needless to say, Matt is relieved when this scenario materializes. First, there will be no need to reconcile conflicting positions in drafting the Appellate Body's final report. Second, Matt will be able to copy and paste extensive portions of the issue paper into the text of the judgment.

Of course, the shift from an internal memo to an official judgment will require some tinkering with the language. A phrase like: 'We advise the Division to find that ...' will be replaced by a more assertive: '*We find that ...*'. Some policy considerations (e.g. 'an additional advantage of this interpretation of Article X is that it will prevent future litigants from arguing Y') will give way to apodictic and self-explanatory statements (e.g. 'based on our VCLT analysis, we conclude that Article X requires ...'). And the Division members may want certain points to be expanded and others to be shortened, thus requiring some alterations to the flow of the reasoning. Still, general accord across the table makes for very smooth sailing.

*7-point scenario*: the Division disagrees with the secretariat and rejects its advice *en bloc*. When this happens, the Division members require significant modifications to the reasoning contained in the issues paper or direct the secretariat to explore new lines of inquiry.

Why seven points? Should this not be a tragedy? Not at all, provided that the points of dissent are articulated clearly. In his early days, when Matt took his work quite personally, he would be crushed by the judges' dismissal of his analysis. Over time, however, he has perfected the art of *disagreeing with himself*: the remarkable ability to accommodate external legal views even when these clash directly with his own ideas. When the discussion comes to a deadlock, Matt typically makes one last attempt to persuade the Division of the validity of the secretariat's position and single out any flaws in the Division's preferred approach. If, at that point, the judges decide to stick to their guns, so be it. Matt will not take a bullet for them. When drafting the report, he will meticulously follow the adjudicators' instructions and try to make their analysis read as sound and convincing as possible.

Actually, the challenge intrigues Matt. He finds it uncannily *easy* to disagree with himself. Do the judges want to find trade discrimination where none exists? Sure, it is sufficient to cherry-pick the right precedents. Do they wish to exclude general international law from the scope of their decision? Matt can think of a million ways to get there. Given the inherent indeterminacy of law, nothing stands in the way of creativity. Someone might talk of apology and utopia. Matt simply heeds the words of his compatriot Ennio Flaiano: '*A volte mi vengono pensieri che non condivido*'.

*4-point scenario*: the Division members disagree with one another and take irreconcilable views on a given issue. This is a thorny situation, for the WTO dispute settlement system prizes unanimity more than any other international court. The architects of the system considered the court's ability to speak with one voice as necessary for 'the reputation, acceptability, and the ensuing legitimacy' of WTO decisions.[29] To this end, the DSU stipulates that the opinions expressed in an Appellate Body report 'shall be anonymous',[30] while the Working Procedures of Appellate Review provide that Appellate Body Divisions 'shall make every effort to take their decisions by consensus'.[31]

Dissenting opinions, albeit technically possible, are actively discouraged, lest they increase 'the appearance of judicial discretion'.[32] This ethos was particularly strong during the early years of the system. Throughout its first decade of activity, the Appellate Body saw 'only a single opinion styled as a dissent and one other separate opinion labelled a concurrence'.[33] Both were couched in 'apologetic' terms.[34] Things have started to change in recent times, perhaps due to the increasing polarization in trade debates or simply because the system has reached its maturity. Dissents have become more frequent and more assertive.[35] In a highly controversial dispute, one Appellate Body member went as far as to append a separate judgment at the end of the main report, where he vigorously took issue with the majority on every single issue.[36]

Despite these developments, unanimity remains the overarching goal of the instructions session. This is why the slightest threat of a dissent changes the flow of the debate, with the secretariat's role suddenly shifting from legal advice to mediation. Faced with conflicting positions, Matt and his ABS colleagues make every effort to flesh them out and broker

---

[29] C.-D. Ehlermann, 'Reflections on the Appellate Body of the WTO' (2003) 6(3) JIEL 695. See also e.g. J. Bacchus, 'Lone Star: The Historic Role of the WTO' (2004) 39(3) TexIntlLJ 401, 409; Soave, 'European Legal Culture', 114 16.

[30] Article 17.11 of the DSU.

[31] *Working Procedures for Appellate Review*, WT/AB/WP/W/10 (12 January 2010), Rule 3(2).

[32] Dothan, *Reputation and Judicial Tactics*, 39. See also e.g. F. Murphy, *Elements of Judicial Strategy* (University of Chicago Press, 1964), 66.

[33] Lewis, 'Lack of Dissent', 896 (referring to Appellate Body Reports, US – Upland Cotton, WT/DS267/AB/R (21 March 2005), paras. 631–41; EC – Asbestos, paras. 152–4). See also J. A. Ragosta et al., 'WTO Dispute Settlement: The System is Flawed and Must be Fixed' (2003) 37(3) IntlLawyer 697, 740–2.

[34] Lewis, 'Lack of Dissent', 903.

[35] See e.g. Appellate Body Reports, *United States – Anti-Dumping and Countervailing Measures on Large Residential Washers from Korea*, WT/DS464/AB/R (7 September 2016), paras. 5.191–5.203; *India – Certain Measures Relating to Solar Cells and Solar Modules*, WT/DS456/AB/R (16 September 2016), paras. 5.156–5.163.

[36] Appellate Body Report, *United States – Countervailing Duty Measures on Certain Products from China (Recourse to Article 21.5 of the DSU by China)*, WT/DS437/AB/RW (19 July 2019), paras. 5.242–5.281.

a compromise. The discussion becomes punctuated by long silences, moments of intense lateral thinking, and 'what if …' inquiries. The secretariat's familiarity with the inclinations and idiosyncrasies of each judge helps a great deal. Its mediation efforts are usually quite fruitful, especially when the bone of contention is more a matter of nuance than one of substance.

Sometimes, however, the gap is so wide and the discord so deep-seated that a stark choice arises. Should one strive for the 'lowest common denominator of agreement',[37] at the risk of issuing a cursory and 'cryptic'[38] judgment? Or is it better to let the dissenter go their way and salvage the cohesion and quality of the majority opinion? Matt tends to favour the latter option. He finds it easier to produce two opposite but clear-cut drafts than a unanimous but poorly explained one. Björn, however, invariably prefers the former option. Whenever the risk of a dissent becomes imminent, he clears his throat and reassures:

'Don't worry. The secretariat will come up with a draft flexible enough to capture your concerns.'

At which point, Matt rolls his eyes. The instructions session will end up with a mishmash of suggestions too heterogeneous, too vague, and too inconsistent to be reconciled within one tidy report. The draft will be mired in circular reasoning, *non sequiturs*, and loose ends, like a dish prepared by too many cooks. But it is what it is. Matt will not despair. Back to his office, he will rewatch that YouTube comedy sketch where an indecisive client asks a graphic designer to draw seven red lines, all of them perpendicular, some with green ink, and some with transparent ink.[39]

*1-point scenario*: the Division members have no clue. No matter how hard the ABS lawyers try to explain the issues at stake and elicit constructive views, they are met with nothing but blank stares. In this (rare) scenario, the adjudicators try to save face by saying the magic words:

'Hmmm, let's see a draft first.'

---

[37] C. G. Weeramantry, 'Some Practical Problems of International Adjudication' (1996) 17(1) AustYBIL 1, 3. See also e.g. I. Scobbie, '"Une Hérésie en Matière Judiciaire"? The Role of the Judge *Ad Hoc* in the International Court' (2005) 4(3) LPICT 421, 445; Hernández, *The ICJ*, 108.
[38] Scobbie, 'Une Hérésie', 445.
[39] L. Beinerts, *The Expert (Short Comedy Sketch)*, 23 May 2013, YouTube, www.youtube.com/watch?v=BKorP55Aqvg.

What a curious utterance. If it is true that craftsmen think with *their* hands, it must be tough to think with *someone else's*. Matt screams internally every time: '*What* draft? How are we supposed to write anything if you don't tell us what you want? Aren't you supposed to *do* something?' Of course, the words that come out of his mouth sounds more like:

'Yes, we will happily provide you with a first draft. Could you please give us some general pointers so that we can fine-tune the reasoning to your liking?'

The instructions session then turns into a protracted and gruelling attempt to extract as much information as possible from the three sphinx-like judges. The secretariat's discontent with this situation may sound surprising; after all, an indecisive Division leaves ample room to manoeuvre. However, Matt quivers at the idea of having the last say: his self-perception as a technical expert does not sit well with feelings of discretion and responsibility.

Moreover, indecision during the instructions session may actually result in a mere *postponement* of the decision. There is no guarantee that, when the secretariat presents the draft report to the Division, the adjudicators will rubberstamp it without raising any objections. Indeed, the first reading of the draft report often prompts the Division members to finally state the views they should have expressed beforehand. By that time, the secretariat will be hostile to last-minute overhauls of the draft. To avoid surprises, Matt and his colleagues will word the judgment in bland and generic terms, or provide two or more drafts for the Division's consideration.

\*

If the collegial nature of ICJ and WTO deliberations makes decision-making quite burdensome, then the practice of human rights courts throws another ingredient into the mix: the *judge-rapporteur*.

Whenever an ECtHR dispute is assigned to a section, the judge-rapporteur is appointed to serve as the main person of reference for the case.[40] This is usually the 'national judge', that is the judge of the same nationality as the responding state. However, if the case raises particularly delicate issues, the section president may choose a different judge.[41] The judge-rapporteur

---

[40] Cases heard by single-judge formations do not contemplate the appointment of a judge-rapporteur. Rather, in those cases, the Court is 'assisted by non-judicial rapporteurs who ... form part of the Court's Registry'. See ECtHR, *Rules of Court* (16 April 2018), Rule 18(a).
[41] See Garlicki, 'Judicial Deliberations', 393; L. L. Guerra, 'The National Judge and Judicial Independence: The Case of the Strasbourg Court' (2017) 24(4) MJECL 552.

is the first recipient of the registry's output. To recall,[42] that output consists of an internal draft that lists the issues at stake, summarizes the parties' positions, states the uncontroversial facts, and provides a preliminary analysis of the relevant legal questions. On the basis of the internal draft, the registry team works side-by-side with the judge-rapporteur (and with the national judge when the two do not coincide) to prepare a draft *decision*, which is then submitted to the whole section for deliberation.[43]

At the outset of the deliberation session, the section president asks the judge-rapporteur to state their views and walk their colleagues through the draft decision. The registry lawyers sit in the back, ready to clarify points of the reasoning or flesh out factual issues upon request. Where applicable, the exposé of the judge-rapporteur is followed by that of the national judge. After that, all the other section judges are given an opportunity to discuss, make comments, and suggest edits. At the end of the first round of deliberations, a preliminary vote is cast, based on which the registry and the judge-rapporteur will revise the text of the decision.[44]

As with every other international court, individual personalities play an important role in the discussion. Some judges are very proactive and seek to assert themselves as authoritative legal voices; others pick their battles and insist only on a few selected issues; yet others may not be very invested in the case at all. The position of each adjudicator may depend on the specifics of the dispute at hand or reflect deeper inclinations, convictions, and strategies. The experience of the judges sitting on the ECtHR is notoriously uneven. Some are leading authorities in human rights law; others lack in quality.[45]

Overall, the atmosphere is quite relaxed and tensions are kept in check. That is, except when the Jurisconsult descends from the lofty heights of the Grand Chamber and steps into the room. On those rare occasions, the guardian of ECtHR jurisprudence is welcomed with a mixture of reverence and suspicion. All of a sudden, speakers become more circumspect,

---

[42] See *supra*, p. 167.
[43] See Arold, *ECtHR Legal Culture*, 62.
[44] Ibid., 63.
[45] See e.g. K. Dzehtsiarou and D. K. Coffey, 'Legitimacy and Independence of International Tribunals: An Analysis of the European Court of Human Rights' (2014) 37(2) HastingsIntl&CompLRev 271, 308. According to many, the roots of the problem lie in the national nomination of candidates, which are seen as 'unclear, apparently politicised and unaccountable'. J. Limbach et al., *Judicial Independence: Law and Practice of Appointments to the European Court of Human Rights* (Interights, 2003), 21.

their interventions more guarded, as if talking too much could expose them to scorn and derision. Only the most experienced judges attempt to stand their ground. The others tend to surrender to a higher power.

The description above reveals important differences between the deliberative practices of the ECtHR and those of other international courts. In those other courts, judgments are drafted *after* deliberations, based on the instructions that adjudicators give to their legal assistants. By contrast, ECtHR decisions are drafted jointly by the registry and the judge-rapporteur *before* collegial deliberations take place. Such a peculiar arrangement stems from the crushing caseload of the Court. The sheer number of judgments that must be churned out every year simply does not leave time for lengthy back-and-forths between the section judges, the judge-rapporteur, and the registry. In turn, this gives rise to a specific set of socio-professional dynamics, which present both advantages and disadvantages.

On the bright side, the close cooperation between the judge-rapporteur and the registry lawyers in the preparation of the draft decision strengthens the bonds between them. The various members of this 'reporting team' are free to develop their text in a relatively informal setting, without external meddling, before presenting the results of their collective efforts to the section. Aphrodite thoroughly enjoys her interactions with the judge-rapporteur. After years of familiarization with her section judges, she can now read them like an open book and adapt her legal advice accordingly. A certain judge has a distaste for lengthy factual assessments? No problem, Aphrodite will make sure not to delve too deep into the evidence on record. Another judge appreciates citations to the jurisprudence of other international courts? Sure, Aphrodite will put more effort in reviewing the case law of the IACtHR, the CJEU, and other relevant dispute settlement mechanisms. This versatility makes our skilful registry lawyer 'crucially influen[t]' and often 'decisive' in shaping the content of the draft judgment.[46]

However, the intense cooperation among the members of the reporting team is also likely to entrench their views and make them averse to criticism by the other section judges. Aphrodite, for instance, remembers one instance when the team had produced a persuasive, elegant, and politically progressive draft on the right to respect of private life against Greece's religious sensitivities. Despite the judge-rapporteur's enthused presentation, the section's reaction to the draft was lukewarm. One particular judge,

---

[46] Dzehtsiarou and Coffey, 'Legitimacy and Independence', 309.

perhaps concerned by the controversy surrounding France's ban on burkinis, convinced the section to tone down the text and make it more deferential to the responding state. Later that afternoon, the judge-rapporteur commented in private to Aphrodite:

'That bunch of bigots destroyed *our* decision. I hope the Grand Chamber rips them apart.'

\*

Being partly modelled after the Strasbourg Court, the IACtHR works in similar ways. There are, however, some significant differences. Firstly, all seven IACtHR judges simultaneously participate in deliberations instead of being divided in sections. Secondly, the Court has no Grand Chamber, such that the judges' opinions are final and cannot be appealed. Thirdly, and most importantly, the IACtHR and its registry are less strapped for time than their counterparts in Strasbourg, and can therefore come to their decisions at a more deliberate pace.

Here, too, the secretariat and the judge-rapporteur play a pivotal role in the deliberative process. As mentioned,[47] the secretariat team assigned to each case prepares an internal file with a preliminary assessment of the factual and legal issues at stake, and sends it to the judge-rapporteur. The latter offers some preliminary views as to what the draft decision should contain, which points should be given most salience, and so on. Based on these instructions, the secretariat team prepares a first draft decision, which it shares with other secretariat teams for comments. Allowing the whole secretariat to have a say on the draft ensures a certain level of coherence and consistency in the Court's jurisprudence. Another team might have worked on a similar issue in the past, or harbour concerns about the legal reasoning adopted.

After this exchange of views among secretariat officers, the draft decision is sent back to the judge-rapporteur, who spends roughly one month reviewing it. Depending on the circumstances and personal preferences, the judge-rapporteur might revert to the secretariat for modifications or decide to implement them personally. In either case, frequent interactions occur between the judge-rapporteur and the secretariat team throughout the review period. Like Aphrodite, Soledad is adept at playing along her judges' expectations, such that her input often undergoes little change.

---

[47] See *supra*, p. 167.

Upon completing the review, the judge-rapporteur introduces the draft decision to the other judges for discussion, comments, and suggested edits. The secretariat team attends the deliberations and intervenes upon request. Based on the judges' input, the secretariat lawyers will then edit the decision together with the judge-rapporteur. Given the high profile of the cases being discussed, the members of the Court all engage extensively in the exploration of the issues at stake and often express strong opinions on the draft. Here too, certain individuals shine more than others. Indeed, some judges have left such a mark in the Court's 40-year history that one may speak of a 'Buergenthal era', a 'Cançado Trindade era', and so forth.[48] As in other systems, coping with disagreements among the judges entails a trade-off between collegiality and coherence in the reasoning. Given the political importance of IACtHR judgments across Latin America, Soledad tends to prefer unanimous, if a little abridged, decisions.

Once, for example, the Court was asked to order provisional measures to allow Beatriz, a 22-year-old Salvadoran woman who was suffering from severe pregnancy complications, to abort her anencephalic foetus. El Salvador's laws prohibits abortion in all circumstances, including when the mother's life or health are at risk. During deliberations, the judges were fiercely divided. Some were squarely in favour of saving Beatriz's life, while others feared that setting a precedent on this matter would unduly invade the religious and ethical prerogatives of states.

The judge-rapporteur, who sided with the pro-abortion camp, estimated that he could snatch a 4-3 majority in favour of the provisional measures. Soledad advised him that such a sensitive decision should be upheld by the whole Court, and offered to take a first crack at revising the draft order. She remained in her office 48 hours straight, producing the on-paper equivalent of walking on eggshells. Instead of making sweeping statements about abortion rights, the draft simply recited the facts, underscored the gravity of the situation, and required El Salvador to 'adopt and guarantee, urgently, all the necessary and effective measures' to 'avoid any damage that could be irreparable to the rights to the life, personal integrity and health'.[49] The text suggested that one such measure could be to induce 'an immature birth by caesarean section',[50] thereby introducing a subtle distinction between immature birth and abortion.

---

[48] See e.g. M.-B. Dembour, *When Humans Become Migrants: Study of the European Court of Human Rights with an Inter-American Counterpoint* (Oxford University Press, 2015), 312.
[49] *Matter of B. regarding El Salvador*, Order on Provisional Measures (29 May 2013), p. 14.
[50] Ibid., p. 13.

On the third day of deliberations, the judge-rapporteur forcefully pleaded in favour of Soledad's draft. On the fourth day, when the order was finally issued, it bore the signatures of all seven judges. Doctors performed the caesarean section on Beatriz and saved her life. The Salvadoran health minister boasted that 'the procedure was not an abortion' because the anencephalic foetus had been placed in an incubator, provided fluids, and lived for another five hours.[51] For weeks afterwards, Soledad kept reading the news coverage of the Court's order. Some praised the judges for stepping in, whereas others criticized them for squandering the opportunity to say more about abortion rights. 'If you only knew what it took to get here,' Soledad thought, 'you'd just shut up and thank us'.

•

Having reviewed the deliberative practices of different international courts, it is time to fly back to the room on the fourth floor of the Mandarin Oriental. During our absence, Carlos delivered his presentation about Kingsland's legitimate expectations in front of Professor Gal and his co-arbitrators. Aided by a PowerPoint presentation, Carlos began by summarizing the parties' conflicting factual statements on the alleged private meetings between Turkish officials and the company's representatives. Then, he briefly reviewed the relevant evidence on record. On this basis, he invited the tribunal to find, as a matter of fact, that Turkey's government officials did make representations that Kingsland's mining rights would survive the change of administration.

Next, Carlos discussed the legal significance of government representations to investors, and provided an overview of relevant ISDS case law. He acknowledged that most BITs, including that between Canada and Turkey, do not contain any express clause protecting legitimate expectations. However, he added, the jurisprudence of prior tribunals may help shed light on the issue. Carlos then showed a slide dividing precedents into two columns: on the left, those that upheld investor claims about legitimate expectations; on the right, those that dismissed them.

Beginning with the left column, the tribunal in *SPP* v. *Egypt* took the view that acts 'cloaked with the mantle of Government authority and communicated as such to foreign investors who relied on them in making their investments' create 'expectations protected by established principles

---

[51] K. Zabludovsky, 'A High-Risk Pregnancy Is Terminated. But Was It an Abortion?', New York Times, 4 June 2013, www.nytimes.com/2013/06/05/world/americas/woman-who-sought-abortion-in-el-salvador-delivers-baby.html.

of international law' even if the domestic legal system of the host state does not attach legal value to those acts.[52] Several other tribunals followed this lead and insisted on the investor's reliance on promises made by the government.[53] Some awards pushed the boundaries even further and accorded legal protection to *implicit* expectations arising from the conclusion of the agreement to invest.[54] At the bottom of the column, Carlos cited the ICJ's famous statement that oral declarations made 'by way of unilateral acts, concerning legal or factual situations' may 'have the effect of creating legal obligations' if 'given publicly, and with an intent to be bound'.[55]

Moving to the right column, a number of tribunals rejected the notion that *any* representation by a government would be sufficient to raise legitimate expectations in the investor. For instance, the arbitrators in *Thunderbird* v. *Mexico* denied legal significance to an opinion expressed by Mexican authorities about the legitimacy of the investor's gambling operations.[56] Similarly, the tribunal in *Feldman* v. *Mexico* considered that 'ambiguous and largely informal' assurances by a government do not meet the test.[57] Finally, the tribunal in *El Paso* v. *Argentina* took the view that 'political and commercial incitements cannot be equated with commitments capable of creating reasonable expectations'.[58] For the sake of symmetry, the right column includes a reference to ICJ decisions involving the *rebus sic stantibus* clause.[59]

As we enter the room, Carlos is wrapping up.

---

[52] *Southern Pacific Properties (Middle East) Limited* v. *Egypt*, ICSID Case No. ARB/84/3, Award and Dissenting Opinion (20 May 1992), paras. 82–3.

[53] See e.g. *Metalclad Corp.* v. *Mexico*, ICSID Case No. ARB(AF)/97/1, Award (30 August 2000), para. 89; *Waste Management, Inc.* v. *Mexico*, ICSID Case No. ARB(AF)/00/3, Award (30 April 2004), para. 98; *Sempra Energy International* v. *Argentina*, ICSID Case No. ARB/02/16, Award (28 September 2007), para. 298; *EDF (Services) Limited* v. *Romania*, ICSID Case No. ARB/05/13, Award (8 October 2009), para. 216.

[54] *Parkerings-Compagniet AS* v. *Lithuania*, ICSID Case No. ARB/05/8, Award (11 September 2007), para. 331. See also e.g. *Saluka Investments BV* v. *Czech Republic*, UNCITRAL-PCA, Partial Award (17 March 2006), para. 329.

[55] *Nuclear Tests (New Zealand* v. *France)*, Judgment of 20 December 1974, ICJ Rep. 1974, 457 ('*Nuclear Tests* judgment'), para. 46.

[56] *International Thunderbird Gaming Corporation* v. *Mexico*, NAFTA/UNCITRAL, Award (26 January 2006), paras. 145–66.

[57] *Feldman* v. *Mexico*, ICSID Case No. ARB(AF)/99/1, Award (16 December 2002), para. 149.

[58] *El Paso Energy International Company* v. *Argentina*, ICSID Case No. ARB/03/15, Award (31 October 2011), para. 392 ('*El Paso*').

[59] *Fisheries Jurisdiction (Germany* v. *Iceland)*, Judgment on Jurisdiction of 2 February 1973, ICJ Rep. 1973, 49, para. 36.

'To conclude, here are two strands of jurisprudence pointing in different directions. Should you find that, as a matter of fact, respondent made representations to claimant, you will have to decide whether, as a matter of law, such representations fall more under an *SPP-* or an *El Paso*-type scenario. Thank you for your attention.'

President Gal is visibly satisfied by the clarity and concision of his protégé's presentation. He keeps fidgeting with his yellow suspenders while the co-arbitrators state their views. The first to speak is Professor Richler, who has been squinting at Carlos with his glacial blue eyes.

'Thank you for the interesting lecture, Carlos, but I don't see how this case law is of any assistance to this tribunal.'

'I beg your pardon?'

'The notion of legitimate expectations is not in the BIT. So, claimant has no claim. End of story. Let's move on to the next issue.'

Such an aggressive start prompts Professor Gal to jump to Carlos' aid.

'But Guillermo, the obligation to ensure fair and equitable treatment *is* included in the BIT, and we all know that the obligation requires the host state to be consistent and predictable in its behaviour …'

'Ha! *You* know that, François. You and all the arbitrators who, with all due respect, use good faith and legitimate expectations as a way around treaty commitments. Where *I* come from, the ICJ, sovereign states are still allowed to design policies as they see fit, without being straightjacketed by greedy multinationals and activist judges.'

Carlos was prepared for that line of argument, but did not expect it to come up this soon. Oh well, let us play this card up front.

'Actually, Professor, some of your esteemed colleagues have argued in favour of protecting legitimate expectations. Take Michael Reisman: he writes, and I quote, that '[w]here a host State which seeks foreign investment acts intentionally, so as to create expectations in potential investors with respect to particular treatment or comportment', that state should be 'bound by the commitments and the investor is entitled to rely upon them in instances of decision'.[60] The ICJ itself stated, in the *Nuclear Tests* cases, that …'

'… That the unilateral commitments of a state can instil confidence in other states and create an expectation that those commitments will be respected.[61] I know that, thanks. But again, it is one thing to make

---

[60] W. M. Reisman and M. H. Arsanjani, 'The Question of Unilateral Governmental Statements as Applicable Law in Investment Disputes', in P. M. Dupuy at al. (eds.), *Common Values in International Law: Essays in Honour of Christian Tomuschat* (Norbert Paul Engel Verlag, 2006) 409, 422.

[61] *Nuclear Tests* judgment, para. 49.

unilateral representations to another state by way of official communications, and another to resort to a bit of *dolus bonus* to encourage a private company to make an investment. You quoted *El Paso*, Carlos. Here is the full quote: 'Professor Richler checks the screen of his tablet.' '[W]hat is involved here are two totally different types of unilateral declarations – one made before the highest judicial body in the world, the other in commercial meetings – and ... no lesson can be drawn from the *Nuclear Tests* cases to give legal weight to investment-promoting road shows.'[62]

'But here we are not talking about road sh ...'

'... Let me finish, please. I respect Mike Reisman as a friend and as a scholar. But he'll never convince me that a sovereign government is bound by its predecessor's decision to have an informal chat with some foreign CEO. Besides, other public international law scholars have taken a diametrically opposite stance. The truth is, political priorities change with the contingent needs of society. Therefore, barring an explicit treaty provision to the contrary, a state should remain free to amend and revise its policies as the circumstances evolve. Sorry, François, but if you have in mind a broad interpretation of legitimate expectations, I will have to dissent.'

Carlos and Professor Gal exchange a nervous look. They had anticipated that Professor Richler would side in favour of Turkey, but did not expect him to be this decisive and articulate. Most of the co-arbitrators they worked with in the past were relatively hands-off and limited their input to a few suggested edits to the president's draft. Their questions typically touched on minor points, like the interpretation of a given treaty term, the reading of a precedent, and so on. 'Is our decision in line with jurisprudence or are we breaking new grounds?', 'Can we avoid sounding too harsh on the investor/the state?', 'How will this decision be perceived?', 'Will they accuse us of being activist/too cautious?', etc. Professor Gal could easily assert his authority over matters like these. Yet, since his very first words, Professor Richler has shown he is different. Not only has he studied the file carefully, he is introducing systemic policy reasoning from the get-go. This will be one tough cookie to crack.

Professor Gal smiles, inhales deeply, and launches his counteroffensive.

'Perhaps we started with the wrong foot. Guillermo, your concerns deserve our full consideration. However, I would still like to discuss the case law Carlos has presented to us before jumping to conclusions. Let's at least hear what Evgeny has to say!'

---

[62] *El Paso*, para. 392.

Upon hearing his name called out, Mr. Mamatov resurfaces from deep thoughts. Carlos could swear he heard him snore once or twice.

'I think Claimant was unfairly treated. Let's stick to the jurisprudence.'

Carlos glances at Professor Gal again, this time out of amusement. This one will be an *easy* cookie to crack.

'Well, Mr. Mamatov, *which* jurisprudence should we stick to? As I said during the presentation, tribunals are divided as to the types of state conducts that may give rise to legitimate expectations.'

'Well, let's go with the more protective. Investors need certainty.'

'But Professor Richler has just …'

François Gal raises a finger and stops Carlos mid-sentence.

'I suggest that we proceed in an orderly fashion. First, do we all agree that, *as a matter of fact*, Turkish officials held two meetings with Claimant's representatives, during which they discussed the continued protection of Claimant's mining rights?'

Both co-arbitrators nod in agreement.

'Excellent, duly noted. Second, do we agree that, during those two meetings, the government's agents repeatedly reassured Claimant that the upcoming change in government would not affect Claimant's mining rights?'

Mr. Mamatov agrees. Professor Richler less so.

'We can say something along the following lines: "Turkey's representatives informally suggested to Claimant that their mining rights could continue under the new administration."'

'I wouldn't put the accent on the informality of the meeting, but rather on the suggestion made by state officials. This does not preclude our findings on the legal relevance of the suggestion later on. Would this be agreeable to you, Guillermo?'

'Ok, fine.'

'Alright. So: "Turkey's representatives suggested to Claimant that its mining rights would continue." Carlos, are you taking notes?'

Carlos nods. He sees what his mentor is doing. By securing Professor Richler's agreement on one point after another, Professor Gal is flanking his opponent and preparing for the lunge.

'Now, to the *legal* findings. Guillermo, would you agree to begin by saying that the BIT does not expressly contemplate the protection of legitimate expectations, but that this notion has been clarified and developed in jurisprudence as part of the concept of fair and equitable treatment?'

'I would certainly begin by noting the absence of an express clause in the text. But as I just said, I believe that ends the discussion. You won't convince me that …'

A sudden thud prevents Professor Richler from finishing his sentence. The three arbitrators turn to the window. A crow, perched on the sill, is tapping its beak against the glass. Carlos titters, relieved at the break in the tension. Professor Gal remains impassive. This is exactly what he needed.

'It seems we have company. Should we take a technical break of five minutes and resume when our avian guest leaves?'

The arbitral president stays seated at the table while the co-arbitrators head to the restroom. Five minutes later, the room quiet again, Professor Gal smiles cordially at his colleagues.

'Sorry about the interruption. Guillermo, you were saying?'

'I don't remember.'

'We were discussing the jurisprudence on fair and equitable treatment. As we discuss it in the award, should we add a mention to the general principle of good faith?'

Professor Richler fumbles to retrieve his train of thought.

'Yeah, as I was saying … You must qualify the principle of good faith by specifying that not every government act or representation is capable of creating legitimate expectations. Oh, and include a reference to the sovereign prerogatives of states over their natural resources.'

'Yes, will do. So, the incipit of the reasoning would read more or less like this …' Professor Gal clears his throat. 'The Tribunal notes that Article 5 of the BIT requires each Party to accord to covered investments fair and equitable treatment in accordance with customary international law. On its face, this provision does not list the acts or omissions of a Party that would be inconsistent with the fair and equitable treatment standard. In the Tribunal's view, it is clear that not every act or omission would amount to a breach of that standard. The Tribunal further notes that, under customary international law, states are sovereign over their natural resources. *At the same time*, prior investment tribunals have clarified that certain unilateral representations communicated by a state to an investor, on which the investor relied in making its investment, may create expectations protected by established principles of international law, in particular the principle of good faith.' Here we insert the references to the ICJ, *SPP*, etc. What do you think, Guillermo?'

'Not bad, but I don't like the sequence. Referring to sovereignty over national resources in the middle of the reasoning on legitimate expectations sounds like a *non sequitur*. Also, why would we start with concessions to the state and *then* juxtapose the principle of good faith? It would be better to reverse the terms.'

'Ok for the sentence on natural resources, but I'm not sure I follow you on the rest.'

'If you say: "States have sovereignty over national resources, *but* also good faith obligations," you are placing the emphasis on good faith. If you say: "States have good faith obligations, *but* are sovereign over their natural resources," you are emphasizing sovereignty. Get it?'

'Yes, I get it. Evgeny?'

'...'

'Alright, Carlos will help me phrase the reasoning in a way that addresses all the comments made so far. Next, and I believe finally, comes the question of the legal value of the representations made by Turkey to Claimant, and whether Claimant reasonably relied on those representations in deciding to make the investment. To me, the appropriate standard hinges on the degree of *specificity* and *precision* of the representations being made. The more specific the assurance, the more legitimate the investor's expectations.'

'Yes. I believe ...'

'Hear me out before you comment, Guillermo. First, I would review the former government's public declarations in support of foreign exploitation of goldmines, and come to the interim finding that those declarations are not specific enough to give Kingsland legitimate expectations ...'

Professor Richler looks pleased at Professor Gal's apparent concession. Carlos grins, for he knows that the concession is actually in line with case law.[63] His mentor is packing the final punch.

'... Then, I would move on to the degree of specificity of the representations made by Turkey to Claimant *during the two meetings*. I would reason very matter-of-factually, without any explicit departure from existing standards. Based on the facts before us, I would conclude that Turkey's representations were sufficiently specific and precise to raise Kingsland's legitimate expectations.'

Professor Richler tries to retort, but with less conviction than before. Professor Gal pre-empts him.

---

[63] See e.g. *PSEG v. Turkey*, ICSID Case No. ARB/02/5, Award (19 January 2007), para. 241; *BG Group Plc. v. Argentina*, UNCITRAL, Final Award (24 December 2007), paras. 171, 172, 300, 305; *Continental Casualty Company v. Argentina*, ICSID Case No. ARB/03/9, Award (5 September 2008), para. 261.

'Of course, the fact that these expectations are not based on the terms of a contract, but rather on unilateral promises, will be duly taken into account in determining the *quantum* of reparation. Moreover, this ruling would allow us to exercise judicial economy on the other claims, thereby saving the Tribunal a lot of time and Turkey a lot of potentially unfavourable findings.'

François Gal pauses and gives his friend a reassuring smile. 'Would this work for you, Guillermo?'

After an interminable silence, Professor Richler finally caves.

'... Perhaps that could work. If we are clear enough about the default setting being state freedom to set the political agenda, sovereignty over natural resources, and so on, maybe we can give Turkey a little slap on the wrist. And yes, of course, this means that we should calculate the *quantum* more leniently and exercise judicial economy on the rest of the case. If all these conditions are met, perhaps we can find a common ground. However, François, – curiously, Professor Richler stares at Carlos instead – 'I expect you to phrase the reasoning *very carefully*, not overstepping the boundaries of what we have just agreed. I will comment more once I see the draft.'

'Of course, Guillermo. Thank you.'

Carlos is in utter awe. With a few well-aimed jabs, his mentor turned an apparent stalemate into a swift and brutal knockout. Honour to you, Guillermo. You wrestled well, but not well enough to derail the triumphant march towards state accountability and legal consistency. As The Clash would put it, you fought the law and the law won.[64]

François Gal and Evgeny Mamatov are equally jubilant. Mission accomplished.

'Well, I would like to thank my distinguished colleagues for their thorough engagement so far. Now, what about a proper coffee break before we turn to the remaining issues?'

Relieved, Carlos stands up and opens the window to refresh the air in the room. No sign of the crow. He has thirty minutes to type up his handwritten notes before deliberations resume. The arbitrators stretch their legs, grab their cups of coffee, and start chatting amicably. Suddenly, all the tension that marked the morning session is gone, vanished into thin air, as though it was part of a strange theatrical performance. Carlos gets distracted by the tittle-tattle and gazes around the table. Professor Gal

---

[64] The Clash, *I Fought the Law*.

is commenting on the unseasonably cold weather in Geneva. Professor Richler retorts that at least Europeans have proper seasons – in Colombia the climate remains the same all year round! The conversation then turns to the award of the Nobel Peace Prize to the Colombian president.

'Now, he's a *serious* recipient,' observes Professor Gal. 'Not like Bob Dylan, who did not even show up for the ceremony!'

Professor Richler is not quite familiar with Bob Dylan, but politely guesses that the prospect of traveling to Scandinavia in December would discourage most people.

As he hears this remarkable collection of platitudes, Carlos stares out of the window, steam coming out of his mug. For no apparent reason, his mind wanders back to his law school days. People then tried oh so hard to sound interesting. Students wanted to look clever in class, professors wanted to be professors, political associations issued manifestos and calls for action. Everyone had something to say, or so they pretended. Carlos remembers the evenings spent debating the dichotomy between natural and positive law, the colonial origins of the international legal system, and the conservative and progressive aspects of law enforcement. He finds himself wondering if debates of that sort are still happening out there. Has the tenor of global conversations really sunk to the level of weather talk?

A sudden epiphany jolts Carlos back to the room. Professor Gal is not doing small talk: once more, he is asserting authority over his interlocutors. His artful banality, his proud vapidity, his cordial tone serve as reminders that he is in a position of power. That he *need not try* to sound clever. Every word he speaks gains force and momentum for the sole reason that it is coming out of his mouth. He may utter such horrors as 'the rule of law is important for democracy', or 'a judge must be impartial', whatever. That would not be very different from saying that 'Colombia has no real seasons'. What matters is that those utterances are quotable enough to take on a life of their own, acquire a specific weight – become *true*. One thing is for sure: François Gal will never, under any circumstance, stoop to sounding interesting. Otherwise, people may think that he has something left to prove, someone left to impress.

As the arbitrators sit down for the next session, Carlos stares at his mentor and concludes, for the millionth time, that he is a very smart man.

# 16

# Truth Woven Together

Since time immemorial, philosophers have debated the relationship between a statue and the marble from which it is sculpted. According to some, the image of the statue is already in the marble, and needs to only be freed by chipping away superfluous material. Replace one sculptor with another and the result will not change. For others, the marble is nothing but inert matter, and it is rather the sculptor's craftsmanship that shapes it into whatever image the sculptor has in mind. Replace one marble block with another and the result will not change.

Rarely have philosophers paused to consider the empirical conditions in which the craft of the sculptor takes place. Had they done so, perhaps they would have concluded that the image of the statue is neither inherent in the marble nor fully formed in the sculptor's mind. What we see in the museum is actually the product of strenuous labour, careful studies of the properties of the input material, continuous revisions to the original plan, harrowing uncertainty, and failed attempts. Quite probably, Michelangelo only had a rough idea of what the *Pietà* would look like when the chisel first hit the stone. Also, the *Pietà* was not only the fruit of the Maestro's individual genius. We can picture him conversing with the marble dealers of Carrara, the commissioners of the work, intermediaries, and fellow artists; carefully studying religious iconography; and comparing his creative process to that of his predecessors. Each of these encounters informed Michelangelo's vision and, directly or indirectly, contributed to the timeless perfection we admire today.

Now, dear reader, think about another – far less timeless – artefact: the text of an international judgment. The orderly series of words, sentences, and paragraphs through which an international court *resolves* a case, *apportions* rights and wrongs, *develops* legal standards for future litigation, and *speaks* the true language of Law. The ultimate object of reverence in our profession.

Just like a statue, this artefact has been the object of intense philosophical scrutiny. If you substitute the law for the marble, the judge for the sculptor, and the content of the judgment for the statue, you will hear the echoes of old debates. Traditionalists will say that the content of the judgment depends on predetermined law, which must simply be discovered, organized, and turned into a logically coherent decision. Replace the judge and the result will not change.[1] Critics will retort that the content of the judgment depends on the unbridled creativity of the judge, who can bend the law at whim, tweak the source materials to fit a desired outcome, and reduce formal legal reasoning to a smokescreen for the exercise of discretion.[2] Replace the law and the result will not change.

This entire book has been devoted to deconstructing this stale dichotomy and revealing the international judgment for what it really is: the humble fruit of collective *practices* marked by epistemic uncertainty, social interactions, and professional struggles. If you have had the patience to read this far, you will have learnt quite a bit about these dynamics. Now it is time to wrap up. It is time to discuss how, at last, the endless series of choices that marked every step of the adjudicative process turns into a text.

The drafting of the judgment is the final selection point in the process. The point where all 'hesitations, compromises and obscure negotiations'[3] are eclipsed behind seemingly logical and coherent reasoning. The point where the lyophilization of life completes its course and reality is reduced to signs on paper. The point where the statue is given the final polish. The text of the ruling will remain as the only tangible result of all the efforts described so far. It will bind the conduct of the disputing parties, which will have to abide by the *dispositif*. It will be out there to be appraised, systematized, and critiqued by a legion of commentators eager to discern the court's intent. All the practices that slowly led to the formation of that text will fall into oblivion.

If, at this point, we were to look back at where it all started – the grievances that gave rise to the dispute, the parties' early submissions, the court's initial understanding of the matter – we would be overtaken by vertigo. Too many metamorphoses have occurred, too much inertia has built up, too many possibles have been erased from the horizon for any

---

[1] See *supra*, pp. 7–11.
[2] See *supra*, pp. 11–13.
[3] Latour, *The Making of Law*, 142.

one person to retrace them all. International adjudication is a 'gigantic slaughterhouse of discarded possibilities'.[4]

Nor, for that matter, will the drafter of a judgment attempt to unravel Ariadne's thread. At this late stage, the goal is not to reopen the complexities of the case, but to *craft a finished product*. The judgment is no longer a medium for legal analysis, but has become an end in itself. The facts that gained salience at some point in the process will remain salient until the end, while the rest will be doomed to irrelevance. The legal opinions expressed during deliberations will dominate the final phases of the debate, while others will be lost in time, like tears in the rain. In short, the content of the judgment will be largely determined by the layers of interactions accumulated during the prior stages of the dispute.

However, the drafting process is not a simple crystallization of everything that came before. It is itself an indeterminate, open-ended, and creational exercise. Writing is 'experimental and unpredictable'.[5] No writer, not even the most meticulous, can confidently tell how their thoughts will read on paper. Judicial drafting is no exception. As discussed,[6] it is impossible to separate the Court's mind – its 'decision' on a given point – from the Court's hand – the 'choice of words' through which to express that decision.[7] The persuasiveness of the reasoning can be tested only once it is written down in a semi-final form. Only then do its wrinkles come to the fore, and only then can they be ironed out.

The dual nature of drafting – determinate and creational, structured and open-ended, constrained and free – is intimately linked to the forms and aesthetics of judicial performance. In a seminal book, Annelise Riles likened the production of a legal text to the weaving of ceremonial mats in Fijian tradition. Both artefacts are the result of 'collective, anonymous, and highly labor intensive exercises' that require great care and attention to detail. And both exercises see discrete components – words, threads – being 'strung together' into a proper sequence that adheres to a 'predetermined format' while producing 'its own variations of the standard form'.[8]

---

[4] The expression is borrowed from F. Moretti, *Distant Reading* (Verso, 2013), 30, fn 34. See also e.g. Burniat and Delforge, 'Le Syllogisme Dialectique', 445 (referring to '*l'occultation de toute une partie du 'réel' pour la suite du raisonnement juridique*').
[5] A. Orford, 'In Praise of Description' (2012) 25(3) LJIL 609.
[6] See *supra*, p. 279.
[7] Thirlway, 'Drafting ICJ Decisions', 21.
[8] A. Riles, *The Network Inside Out* (University of Michigan Press, 2000), 72–3.

Guided by these analogies, we must now describe the last set of international judicial practices: those pertaining to the drafting of the judgment itself. What are the pains and pleasures of producing 'a good specimen of a particular genre'?[9] What does it take to *weave* legal truths together?

Let us start with the collective and labour-intensive character of the exercise. Both a Fijian ceremonial mat and the text of an international judgment result from the superposition of multiple layers. Just like a weaver repeatedly draws the weft through the warp, so does a judicial decision undergo numerous revisions before finalization. The number, scope, and nature of those revisions vary from one court to another. As we know,[10] the first draft is prepared by the legal bureaucrats assisting the court – sometimes in cooperation with one or more judges, sometimes on their own – on the basis of the instructions that emerged from deliberations. That draft is then scrutinized, discussed, and amended multiple times by the bench, the bureaucracy, and sometimes editors and translators.

Each new revision tinkers with the pre-existing text, rearranges the order of its components, adds or deletes portions of the reasoning, and shifts the emphasis onto new elements. Every member of the drafting team, from the most junior legal assistant to the highest ranking judge, takes part in this collective process of quality control. The iterative nature of the exercise has measurable physical connotations. Step by step, the amount of track changes and comment bubbles decreases giving way to clean text, office phones stop ringing every two minutes, and mailboxes become less clogged with requests for change and clarification.

A casual observer may think that the drafting and revision process proceeds in an orderly fashion, leaving adequate time for the actors involved to carefully read, think, and (re)write. Nothing could be farther from the truth. In fact, the drafting phase often entails a maelstrom of social interactions, hasty conversations, and frantic scrambles both inside and outside deliberation rooms. Judges may hold private meetings to overcome disagreements over the use of a certain word or phrase. Bureaucrats may coordinate to ensure consistent terminology or broker compromises between conflicting views. Emergency review sessions may be called if unexpected problems arise. The final edits to the text can come as late

---

[9] Ibid., 72.
[10] See *Supra,* Chapter 15.

as the day before the issuance of the judgment – much to the chagrin of translators and proofreaders. Nothing is done until it is done.

Next, let us turn to the fundamental question of form. The number of patterns available to a Fijian weaver is vast but finite, thereby imposing a certain structure to the creative process and delimitating the range of possible outcomes. Likewise, the drafters of an international judgment are bound by certain traditions, techniques, and argumentative standards that constrain creativity and guide the pen (well, the keyboard). The text of a judgment is as performative as the narratives crafted by the parties' counsel.[11] Both are specimen of a particular *literary genre* – legal writing – and must follow its rules. Few readers would enjoy a crime novel if the author revealed the killer's identity on page one. Even fewer would appreciate comic relief at the climax of a Shakespearean tragedy. And most would expect international judgments to adhere to a given style and structure.

Literary analysis of court decisions has a long and noble lineage. A century ago, Benjamin Cardozo famously drew the attention to the various styles used in judicial writings, which may range from the 'magisterial' and 'sententious' to the 'conversational' and 'homely', from the 'demonstrative' and 'persuasive' to the 'tonsorial' and 'agglutinative'.[12] Later, the Law and Literature movement looked at legal production as 'a linguistic and cultural practice' that generates 'shared community values'.[13] Recently, scholars have appraised the argumentative structure of international courts in light of various principles of effective storytelling.[14] These and other works[15] offer precious insights into the mindset of the judicial writer, who constructs 'some sort of plot, including the facts, the people involved and the applicable law',[16] to persuade the audience and achieve compliance.

However, those insights should be taken with a grain of caution. A writing style, an argumentative structure, a narrative strategy all require

---

[11] See *supra*, pp. 89–93.
[12] B. Cardozo, 'Law and Literature' (1925) 14 YaleRev 699.
[13] A. Bianchi, 'International Adjudication, Rhetoric and Storytelling' (2018) 9(1) JIDS 28, 31–2.
[14] See e.g. L. Gasbarri, 'Courtspeak: A Method to Read the Argumentative Structure Employed by the International Court of Justice in its Judgments and Advisory Opinions', in J. Klabbers, M. Varaki and G. Vasconcelos Vilaca (eds.) *Towards Responsible Global Governance? An Exploration* (University of Helsinki, 2018) 91.
[15] See e.g. Perelman and Olbrechts-Tyteca, *The New Rhetoric*.
[16] Bianchi, 'Rhetoric and Storytelling', 33.

*intentionality*,[17] which in turn presupposes the existence of an *author* or *mind* behind the judicial text. Yet, it is hard to pinpoint exactly *who* writes for an international court or tribunal. Since most adjudicators do not draft their own decisions, one cannot readily attribute them a specific writing style.[18] An arbitrator has as many styles as the legal secretaries that assist them. The seven WTO Appellate Body members have only one style – that of the secretariat. Moreover, as we have just discussed, the text of a judgment is not the work of a single author, but reflects a delicate compromise among a plurality of actors with different interests, perspectives, and sensibilities. The authorial intent we see in literary works gets diluted at each round of revision, renegotiation, and redraft, and often ends up in a hodgepodge of competing voices.

Hence, the form of judicial writing is not dictated by the literary inclinations of any one individual, but rather by the collective dispositions of the international judicial community. As mentioned,[19] the community serves as the immediate audience of courts and tribunals and the final arbiter of (in)competence in the field. Its participants have shared expectations about the structure and style of judicial decisions. A ruling that conforms to those expectations is likely to be accepted as authoritative. As the 'quintessential form of authorized, public, official speech', it will wield a 'magical' power that no community member can resist or ignore.[20] Conversely, a decision that departs too radically from established canon will, at best, be derided as amateurish and, at worst, be deemed as arbitrary or illegitimate.

When it comes to *structure*, most courts have pre-formatted templates setting out the sequence of analytical steps that the drafters should follow.

Typically, a judgment begins with a number of introductory sections that pave the way for the court's analysis. This introductory portion (or 'front part', as it is called at the WTO) identifies the state conduct that gave rise to the case, recites the procedural history, outlines the parties' main claims and

---

[17] Intentionality is 'the power of minds … to be about, to represent, or to stand for, things, properties and states of affairs'. *Stanford Encyclopedia of Philosophy*, https://plato.stanford.edu/entries/intentionality/.

[18] Some authors, however, are using modern language analysis tools to identify the 'pens' of international courts. See e.g. Pauwelyn and Pelc, *Who Writes WTO Rulings*; D. Charlotin, 'Identifying the Voices of Unseen Actors in Investor-State Dispute Settlement', in F. Baetens (ed.), *Legitimacy of Unseen Actors in International Adjudication* (Cambridge University Press, 2019) 392.

[19] See *supra*, pp. 30–1.

[20] Bourdieu, 'The Force of Law', 838.

defences, and provides some undisputed factual background for the benefit of a wider readership. Compiling the introductory sections is relatively easy and often delegated to the junior members of the court's legal staff. 'Easy', of course, does not mean 'mindless' or 'automatic'. In fact, disagreements may arise about the elements that should be included and those that should be left out. *Which* background facts qualify as undisputed? *How* should the court characterize the parties' positions? *Why* would the introduction focus on certain aspects and not on others? As one might expect, there is no clear-cut answer to these questions. Any judicial statement, even one that purports to be uncontroversial, is laden with choices.

After setting the scene, the judgment turns to the court's own assessment (or 'back part' in WTO parlance). This portion of the text opens with a list of the issues that must be resolved to dispose of the case. The order in which the issues are listed is largely left to the drafters' discretion and, indeed, constitutes an important narrative tool in their hands. The court's assessment could, in principle, follow the order of claims and defences that appears in the submissions of either party. Yet, in practice, the drafters often tinker with the order and modify the flow of the analysis.[21] For example, they may identify threshold or definitional issues that must be dealt with upfront; tackle the easier issues at the beginning and keep the more controversial ones for the end, or vice versa; focus on the most salient aspects of the case and skimp on the rest; and so forth.

No order is inherently better than others, all combinations are possible. Everything depends on ingrained preferences and contingent preoccupations. Yet, the order chosen by the drafters has a tangible impact on the outcome of the case. A concatenation of thoughts is not a mere matter of organization. It is *also* a means to prioritize certain thoughts over others, select the most convenient logical connections, bypass conundrums, and build anticipation. That is why a judgment rarely tries to justify the court's chosen order of analysis.[22] Any attempt at explanation would force the drafters to reveal their hand and acknowledge that *other* concatenations could be possible.

Having set out the order, the drafters proceed to address the various issues in succession. For each issue, the text typically restates (again!) the most salient facts, summarizes the parties' specific arguments, and

---

[21] When this happens, the court imposes its own '*syuzhet*' over that of the parties. Gasbarri, 'Courtspeak', 97–9.

[22] And, when it does, the results are convoluted, bordering on incomprehensible. See e.g. Panel Report, *US – Animals*, paras. 7.1–7.20.

identifies the legal sources on which the analysis will be based. Then, at last, the drafters get to the court's analysis proper. While the content of the analysis varies depending on the circumstances, its general sequence remains the same. The court usually starts with the interpretation of the relevant norms – which, as discussed in Chapters 11 and 12, includes both an ascertainment of their applicability to the case at hand and a determination of their meaning – before turning to the application of those norms to the disputed facts. Sometimes, interpretation and application are kept separate (e.g. under different subheadings), sometimes they are woven together into one uninterrupted flow of reasoning.

The analysis culminates in a statement of the court's findings and conclusions, which are later reproduced in the *dispositif*. This final part of the judgment, often amounting to no more than a few dry sentences, turns all the preceding reasoning into binding commands. Obviously, the court's findings are the central and most important part of the text. When the judgment is first delivered orally, as at the ICJ, the declaration of the *dispositif* is preceded by a tense silence and followed by murmurs of relief or disappointment. When the judgment is delivered in writing, as at the WTO, the parties' counsel frantically flip through the last pages to check if they have won or lost. In due course, they will then digest the remainder of the court's analysis to better understand the reasoning and advise their clients on what is to come.

Hence, we could say that the structure of an international judgment consists of endless variations on the same theme. The templates that guide the drafting enable and, at the same time, delimit a range of possible solutions. On the one hand, the existence of a theme prevents the drafters from floating adrift or getting stuck. If judicial writing was a free-form exercise, the likely result would be paralysis. Craftsmanship flourishes under constraint, not freedom. That explains why a proactive judicial drafter can fill up 10 pages of text in a single day, while it took us almost 10 years to write this book.

On the other hand, the templates can straitjacket the flow of the reasoning, especially when the nature of the case, the parties' arguments, or the court's own views would invite a more flexible narrative structure. Judicial drafters often have a hard time shoehorning their thoughts into the required sequence. Of course, they can always *try* to adapt the structure and make it more original, just like a daring crime novelist can *try* to reveal the killer's identity upfront. Yet, in both cases, this makes for a harder sell. Adherence to the model is perceived by the international judicial community as the hallmark of a persuasive judgment.

The *style* of judicial writing is equally patterned. The community holds expectations about how a court's analysis should read, but tolerates minor deviations from the standard.

Through recursive interactions among its drafters, each court develops a signature style that makes its decisions easily recognizable to the trained eye. Some courts, like the ICJ and the ECtHR, tend to intersperse dry legal language with emotionally charged statements. For example, in *Diplomatic and Consular Staff in Tehran*, the World Court offered a technical review of the law of diplomatic immunities[23] before declaring, emphatically, that the principle of diplomatic inviolability 'is one of the very foundations of this long-established regime, to the evolution of which the traditions of Islam made a substantial contribution'.[24] Similarly, in *Delfi* v. *Estonia*, the ECtHR introduced its assessment by stating the underlying conflict in rather dramatic terms: on the one hand, 'user-generated expressive activity on the Internet provides an unprecedented platform for the exercise of freedom of expression'; on the other hand, '[d]efamatory and other types of clearly unlawful speech ... can be disseminated like never before, worldwide, in a matter of seconds.'[25]

Other courts, like the WTO Appellate Body, are averse to vivid language and carefully purge their judgments of any expressions that may convey emotion. Admittedly, some early WTO rulings did contain mildly evocative images. For instance, the report in *Japan – Alcoholic Beverages II* explained the variable geometry of product 'likeness' by comparing it to an 'accordion'.[26] Likewise, in *EC – Hormones*, the Appellate Body cautioned that a scientific risk assessment should not refer to the conditions of a science laboratory, but to those of 'the real world where people live and work and die'.[27] Still, these are but exceptions to the impersonal and technocratic register that dominates WTO jurisprudence. Such a dull tone may be due to the drafting role of the secretariat.[28] If the adjudicators wrote the rulings themselves, we could see 'stronger, livelier language'[29] – but at the risk of undermining collegiality and complicating the review process.

---

[23] *United States Diplomatic and Consular Staff in Tehran (United States of America* v. *Iran)*, Judgment of 24 May 1980, ICJ Rep. 1980, 3, paras. 84–5.
[24] Ibid., para. 86. See also Gasbarri, 'Courtspeak', 107.
[25] *Delfi* v. *Estonia*, ECtHR Judgment (Grand Chamber), No. 64569/09 (16 June 2015), para. 110.
[26] Appellate Body Report, *Japan – Alcoholic Beverages II*, p. 21.
[27] Appellate Body Report, *EC – Hormones*, para. 187.
[28] Pauwelyn and Pelc, *Who Writes WTO Rulings*, 27–30.
[29] Ehlermann, 'Revisiting the Appellate Body', 498.

Variations aside, the core model of judicial writing remains firmly rooted in legal formalism. The text of a decision must express the court's views in 'seemingly authoritative, conclusory, syllogistically ordered' terms, leaving no room for doubt or countervailing arguments.[30] The 'dialogical, conversational, analogical, and argumentative style'[31] typical of common law opinions is rarely found in international judgments, which opt instead for irrefutable and self-legitimating hermeneutics.[32] Of course, few nowadays would expect blind or mechanical obedience to syllogistic reasoning. Most logicians agree that no human discourse can be held to such a standard.[33] Even so, the assumption remains that a judgment should be rigorous, analytically coherent, and impeccably 'rule-following'.[34] Adjudicators are 'to make known the content of the law, that is, to work upon it from within, or logically, arranging and distributing it, in order, from its *summum genus* to its *infima species*, so far as practicable'.[35]

However, these formal strictures burden judicial writing with 'aspirations it cannot meet'.[36] They prevent the text of the decision from reflecting the myriad of legal communications that occurred up to that point, the countless choices made along the way, the persistent hesitations that punctuated the process.[37] The grammar of formal legal argument makes certain points *incommunicable*, as it is designed to obscure the indeterminate and purposeful nature of adjudication. A drafter cannot write something like: 'We find outcomes A and B equally viable, but we *choose* outcome A for reasons X and Y.' Such an overt acknowledgment would unmask the court's discretion and meet resistance in the community. Therefore, what ends up on paper reads more like this: 'The text and context of the relevant treaty provisions, coupled with their negotiating history and the operation of general principles of law, militate in favour of outcome A.'

---

[30] M. Rosenfeld, 'Comparing Constitutional Review by the European Court of Justice and the US Supreme Court' (2006) 4(4) ICON 618, 639.
[31] Ibid., 634–5.
[32] J. H. H. Weiler, 'The Political and Legal Culture of European Integration: An Exploratory Essay' (2011) 9(3&4) ICON 678, 682.
[33] See e.g. M. Troper, 'La Motivation des Décisions Constitutionnelles', in C. Perelman and P. Foriers, *La Motivation des Décisions de Justice: Études* (Bruylant, 1978) 287; Jouannet, 'La Motivation', 266–70.
[34] Venzke, 'The Role of International Courts', 106.
[35] O. W. Holmes, *The Common Law* (Little, Brown and Co., 1881), 219. See also e.g. Burniat and Delforge, 'Le Syllogisme Dialectique', 436.
[36] Venzke, 'The Role of International Courts', 102.
[37] W. M. Reisman, 'International Lawmaking: A Process of Communication – The Harold D. Lasswell Memorial Lecture' (1981) 75 ASILPROC 101, 107.

Hence, there exists an inescapable tension between the formal style in which a judgment must be written and the socially constructed nature of the court's reasoning.[38] How do the drafters ease this tension? Through technique. A host of narrative tools are available which allow to hide the messy realities of judicial practice behind the apparent smoothness of judicial writing. Mastery of these tools requires craftsmanship and constitutes a core skill in the business.

For instance, when the judges are uncertain or divided over the outcome of the case, the drafters can bridge the gap by couching the reasoning in elliptic terms. They can paper over controversial points by excising them from the text or burying them in footnotes;[39] use loose connectors to transition from one paragraph to another; blur the relationships between legal concepts; or strike a sensible balance between the said and the unsaid.[40] While this exercise in obfuscation promises to narrow the scope for criticism, it often achieves the opposite result. For instance, ICJ judgments are savagely criticized for their 'frequent lack of intellectual or logical cohesion';[41] their tendency to be 'so brief and sibylline as to be more productive of perplexity than of clarification';[42] their 'pastiche quality'; and their fragmentation into sentences that bear little relation to each other.[43] Similarly, some WTO Appellate Body reports have been accused of being 'crammed with judicial bureaucratese' and lacking 'reasoning with which a broader audience can engage'.[44]

---

[38] See Jouannet, 'La Motivation', 266.

[39] The relationship between the main text and the footnotes is highly symbolic of the power relationships in the field. Relegating a certain point to a footnote instead of deleting it altogether often signals that at least one drafter strongly supported it, but did not succeed in persuading the other drafters of its validity.

[40] The relationship between said and unsaid is, in principle, measurable by comparing the number of words contained in the Memo to the number of words that end up in the text of the final judgment. We would not be surprised if the ratio exceeded 5:1.

[41] Hernández, *The ICJ*, 108.

[42] H. Lauterpacht, cit. in Hernández, *The ICJ*, 108.

[43] Lillich and White, 'Deliberative Process', 36.

[44] G. Shaffer and D. Pabian, 'Case Note: *European Communities – Measures Prohibiting the Importation and Marketing of Seal Products*, WT/DS400/AB/R, WT/DS401/AB/R' (2015) 109 AJIL 154, 158–9. See also e.g. M. Cartland, G. Depayre, and J. Woznowski, 'Is Something Going Wrong in the WTO Dispute Settlement?' (2012) 46(5) JWT 979; T. P. Stewart et al., 'The Increasing Recognition of Problems with WTO Appellate Body Decision-Making: Will the Message Be Heard?' (2013) 8(11&12) GTCJ 390.

As a related technique, the drafters can steer clear of broad statements of principle and, instead, focus narrowly on the specifics of the case at hand. They can, for instance, strictly limit the analysis to the parties' arguments, liberally resort to judicial economy, and deliberately ignore possible analogies between the case at hand and past disputes. By showing restraint and avoiding systemic reasoning, a judgment can more easily dodge complex questions[45] and come across as rigorously 'dispute-oriented'.[46] However, too much caution can also signal 'a loss of judicial confidence',[47] which in turn may call into question the authority of the decision.

The use of apodictic language also helps conceal hesitation. We are all familiar with this dynamic in our everyday discussions. The less confident we are about the merits of our position, the less likely we are to question it in front of others. International adjudication is no different. The more 'plagued with doubt and uncertainty' the deliberative process, the harder the drafters' efforts to 'present the outcome as the only possible solution and all alternatives as next to absurd'.[48] Sometimes, this leads to a funny paradox. An 'easy' judgment – one that knows where it is going – may be eloquently worded, open to countervailing viewpoints, and amenable to exploring systemic implications. A 'difficult' judgment – one that is unsure about its overall direction – may be more averse to taking risks, prone to attacking straw men, and tinged with 'oracularity'.[49] A tortured decision can be spotted by the technical and cryptic jargon used by the drafters, who scatter the core reasoning across multiple paragraphs or pages to make it less quotable.

The 'angst' that leads to apodictic reasoning may not be the best long-term strategy.[50] Like any other decision, a narrow-minded or poorly expressed ruling informs subsequent jurisprudence, adds to the archive of collective knowledge, and contributes to the 'discursive system' that establishes what can be said and what can not.[51] The same assertiveness

---

[45] See e.g. the ECtHR's coyness in *Nada* v. *Switzerland*, discussed *supra*, pp. 217–18.
[46] Fauchald, 'Legal Reasoning', 307. See also Thirlway, 'Drafting ICJ Decisions', 24–5 (stating that litigants before the ICJ do not wish the judgment to 'deal with all the arguments they have presented to it beyond what is necessary to the decision').
[47] Shaffer and Pabian, '*Seal Products*', 160.
[48] Venzke, 'The Role of International Courts', 102.
[49] A. Cassese, 'The *Nicaragua* and *Tadić* Tests Revisited in Light of the ICJ Judgment on Genocide in Bosnia' (2008) 18(4) EJIL 649, 651.
[50] Venzke, 'The Role of International Courts', 102.
[51] M. Foucault, *The Archaeology of Knowledge and the Discourse on Language*, trans. A. M. Sheridan Smith (Pantheon Books, 1972), 129.

used to hide hesitation today can turn into a burden tomorrow. A court will have to engage in legal gymnastics to distinguish its future decisions from an unwieldy precedent. In turn, those efforts will probably produce more tortured reasoning, more needless circumlocutions, and ultimately more confusion among the audience. This, we believe, is the meaning of 'hard cases make bad law':[52] the more judicial reasoning drifts away from anything remotely intelligible, the harder it gets to retrace the path of the law, pinpoint what went wrong, and where.

To be sure, the drafters are not always aware that they are deploying a narrative strategy; nor do they stick rigorously to any particular one. Most of the times, they remain *fiercely unmethodical*, stitching their narratives together with whatever materials are at hand. A certain precedent bothers you? Paraphrase it. You are struggling with the legal status of a rule under the VCLT? Simply 'take note' of that rule and move on. The parties' logical constructs are giving you a headache? Shift the emphasis from abstract reasoning to the factual context. Rigid textualism, open-ended reasoning, invocation of general principles, matter-of-factual analysis – anything goes, provided it sustains the flow of your argument. *Bricolage* in all its glory.

Pull the strings together, iron out the last wrinkles, and *voilà*, your Fijian mat... sorry, your international judgment is ready for display. If you have done your job properly, your product will effectively eclipse the countless practices, interactions, and confrontations described in this book. Your judgment *will be all there is*. Granted, some fussy readers may still manage to spot the cracks in your narrative – those little discrepancies, those slight *non sequiturs*, those imperceptible logical leaps that you worked so hard to conceal, but which capture the whole essence of international adjudication. Most readers, however, will be content with what they see. They will go on for months discussing the technical implications of this or that point of law, systematize your text under some grand theory, draw connections with cases you were not even aware of, and eventually come to the proud conclusion that 'the position of the Court is safeguarded'.[53] Curtain calls.

•

---

[52] *Northern Securities Co. v. United States*, 193 US 197 (1904), dissenting opinion of Justice Holmes.
[53] D. Akande, 'Nuclear Weapons, Unclear Law? Deciphering the *Nuclear Weapons* Advisory Opinion of the International Court' (1998) 68(1) BYBIL 165, 217.

It is time to conclude our story. By drafting their respective judgments, our versatile protagonists undergo one last transformation. After being *consiglieri*, *bricoleurs*, explorers, and brokers, they now turn into weavers. As we narrate the final phase of their work, let us take the opportunity to bid them farewell. Soon, they will enjoy a well-deserved vacation in the imaginary realm from whence they came.

Sophie first. The drafting of the ICJ judgment in the *North Borneo* case is providing a steady supply of drama and excitement. After Judge Lehmann's appointment to the Drafting Committee,[54] two things quickly became apparent. First, that he and his fellow Committee members, President Rosas and Judge Quintana, all agree that the territory of North Borneo should remain under Malaysia's jurisdiction. Second, that they hold completely different views on how to reach that outcome.

As the reader might recall,[55] Jürgen Lehmann's opinion hinges on the 1963 consultation held by the UN Secretary-General, in response to which the North Bornean people expressed a clear intent to be part of Malaysia. A fervent supporter of the right to self-determination, Judge Lehmann wants to seize this chance to wipe the slate clean of the colonial past of South-East Asia.

Marcos Quintana, by contrast, has strong reservations about mentioning the principle of self-determination – perhaps, who knows, for fear that similar considerations may apply to Chiapas' claims of independence from his native Mexico. According to Judge Quintana, the cornerstone of the Court's reasoning should be the meaning of the term *'padjak'* in the Sultan of Sulu's deed. Whether one interprets that term as 'lease' or as 'grant', the fact remains that the cession of rights was in perpetuity. Therefore, as the Sultan's successors, the Philippines cannot reclaim North Borneo.

So far, President Rosas has remained quite vague about his own reasons to support Malaysia. Could he be concerned that stripping Malaysia of a substantial portion of its territory would stir the water too much? Or, maybe, could he have in mind the strong commercial ties between Malaysia and his home country, Peru? Sophie cannot tell.

Either way, Judge Lehmann is not happy. Back in his office after the first Committee meeting, he lights a cigarette and stares out of the window.

'This ain't good, young lady. We can't base our whole judgment on an ambiguous term in a godforsaken document.'

'I thought Judge Quintana agreed with you.'

---

[54] See *supra*, p. 283.
[55] See *supra*, pp. 253–5.

'People can agree on something for very different reasons. In our line of work, what matters is not the agreement, but the reasons. The endgame will see a lot of action. We'll need to raise our voice if we want this decision to *mean* something.'

'Sounds fun.'

'Right, fun,' Judge Lehmann sighs. 'Anyway, here's what we are going to do. Tomorrow, during the second meeting, I'll suggest that we divide up the drafting into two chunks. Marcos can deal with the Sultan's deed. Perhaps you can give his clerk that old memo you drafted. You and I take care of the Secretary-General's consultation and the principle of self-determination. José will be the overseer. Hopefully, we can harmonize the two sections of the draft and ground the decision on both. It's a hard sell, but worth a try'.

'Are you sure President Rosas will agree not to write a line? He and his special assistant are quite … how would I put it … proactive.'

'You mean annoying?'

'*You* said that, Sir.'

'We'll see how it goes tomorrow. José is very busy with conferences these days, so I wouldn't be surprised if he liked the idea of delegating the drafting to someone else.'

'Ok Sir. How can I assist you?'

'Let's start with listing past cases where the principle of self-determination was endorsed by international courts. Arbitral tribunals, too. There must be something from the PCA. I've done my own share of research, I'll send you what I have this evening. Then, we move on to non-judicial sources. General Assembly resolutions, treaties, reports, whatever we can find. Probably we'll not include any of that in the draft, but it's good to have them in the drawer if the need arises.'

'I see. What kind of input do you expect from me? A chart, a memo …'

'No, young lady. You draft the *judgment*.'

'Are you joking, Sir?'

'I'm dead serious.'

'I'm not sure I can do that. It's the first time that you ask v…'

'You've now been here for, what, three years? You're perfectly capable of doing this. There's not much to learn, really.' There it is, that false modesty again! 'And no worries: I'll review your draft word by word. The Committee will review my review. Why, the whole Court will examine the draft! You'll see: by the time we send out this judgment, your initial text will have changed so many times you'll hardly recognize it.'

'Alright, Sir. When do I start?'

'You should have started two minutes ago.'

Judge Lehmann's plan proves successful, at least initially. The next day, during the preliminary discussion about the 'overall plan' and the 'general economy' of the decision,[56] President Rosas agrees with the proposed splitting of the draft. He, however, reserves the right to change his mind if the section on self-determination 'goes too far'. Judge Quintana is forced to concede to this work allocation. The three judges, their clerks, the Registrar, and a handful of registry staff all get ready at the starting blocks. On your marks, go.

The first stretch of the marathon is exhausting. Day after day, Judge Lehmann and Sophie painstakingly stitch together their section of the draft. Given that the Peace Palace closes its doors at 7:00 PM, they often meet for dinner at a nearby restaurant to continue their work. At every new round of discussion, new lines of inquiry emerge which could be explored to make the text more persuasive. As weeks go by, Sophie feels increasingly empowered. She is grateful to her mentor for trusting her and to Norma for being supportive of her busy schedule.

Twenty days later, Judge Lehmann submits the fruit of their labour to the Committee. The draft clearly spells out the right of the North Bornean people to choose their state of affiliation but, at the same time, tries not to make too much fuss about the principle of self-determination. Despite the careful wording, Judge Quintana objects to the inclusion of that line of reasoning into the final judgment.

'I don't see any reason to put so much meat on the plate. Let's just stick to the *legal* sources and keep *wishful thinking* out of the room!'

With contrived ecumenism, President Rosas suggests to keep the draft section in the text for the time being, and see what the rest of the Court has to say about it.

The Committee then circulates the consolidated draft to the other judges, inviting them to submit amendments in writing.[57] Familiar fault lines emerge, mirroring the disagreements expressed during deliberations. Judges in the 'majority' are quite proactive, as they wish to ensure that the final decision reflects their views. 'Minority' judges are more cautious: why try to improve a draft they are ultimately going to oppose?

Once the Committee has considered the various amendments, it is time for the first plenary reading. As per common practice, it is for Judge

---

[56] R. Ranjeva, 'La Genèse d'un Arrêt de la Cour Internationale de Justice', in C. Apostolidis (ed.), *Les Arrêts de la Cour Internationale de Justice* (Édition de l'Université de Dijon, 2005) 83, 88. See also Kolb, *The ICJ*, 1009.

[57] See Article 7(i) of the ICJ Note on Judicial Practice. See also e.g. Lillich and White, 'Deliberative Process', 36.

Lehmann, the senior elected member of the Committee,[58] to defend the whole text before the whole Court. This is a tricky task. On the one hand, Judge Lehmann wishes to have his arguments on self-determination fully heard by his colleagues. On the other hand, he has to tread carefully not to overshadow Judge Quintana's section. Sophie, her fellow clerks, and the registry staff sit in the back while Judge Lehmann delivers his presentation, ready to correct any possible inaccuracies in his exposé.

The plenary Court then goes through the English and French versions of the draft line by line, paragraph by paragraph.[59] This is a delicate moment, for it is now that the minority judges must formalize their dissenting opinions.[60] Once again, different tactics are deployed across the table. Some dissenters charge head down, framing their opinions in stark oppositional terms. Others are more amenable to compromise, and propose *quid pro quos* with the majority. The clerks and registry staff liaise between the rival factions. Sometimes, they advise the Drafting Committee on how to incorporate the dissenters' arguments. Sometimes, they suggest ways to strengthen the majority judgment against them.[61]

It is here, during the first plenary reading, that Jürgen Lehmann's plan starts to go awry. To his dismay, the judges' comments are not limited to 'drafting issues or the flow of the argument'[62] but, instead, cut to the essence of the reasoning. At least four of his colleagues in the majority express concerns about the mention of the 1963 consultation, and suggest to leave that portion out of the final text. Apparently, Judge Quintana has been pulling strings behind the scenes. Worse still, President Rosas now seems convinced that the judgment should hinge exclusively on the Sultan's deed.

As the debate unfolds, Judge Lehmann and Sophie exchange worried looks. Once the first reading is over, it will become almost impossible to alter the core tenets of the judgment. The Committee will have to incorporate the plenary's comments into an amended version of the text, which will then undergo a second and final reading.[63] By then, the positions will have crystallized and any further changes will be only editorial. In short, this is Jürgen and Sophie's last shot to salvage the draft.

Time for some serious talk.

---

[58] Thirlway, 'Drafting ICJ Decisions', 19.
[59] See Kolb, *The ICJ*, 1009.
[60] Ibid.
[61] Thirlway, 'Drafting ICJ Decisions', 19.
[62] See Kolb, *The ICJ*, 1009.
[63] See Articles 7(i) and (iii) of the ICJ Note on Judicial Practice. See also e.g. Lillich and White, 'Deliberative Process', 36.

'Mr. President. My friends. I've been thinking carefully about your concerns. As you all know, I hate the idea of keeping the world a hostage of its colonial past. But …'

Judge Lehmann lingers on the 'but'. 'I am willing to reach a compromise with you. So here is my final offer. We begin with the term *'padjak'* in the Sultan's deed, and suggest that it means 'grant' rather than 'lease'. VCLT analysis, examination of the evidence, etc. Everything you already have in the draft. Then …'

Judge Lehmann pauses again, gazing around the room.

'… Then we recognize that some constructive ambiguity remains because, when the Sultan's deed was made, the normative categories of modern international law had not yet fully formed. However, we conclude, that ambiguity is resolved by the 1963 consultation, through which the people of North Borneo expressed their will to be part of Malaysia. No reference to the principle of self-determination. No repudiation of colonialism. Nothing. Just a little … splash of colour at the end. Do we have a deal?'

President Rosas stares silently at Judge Lehmann. All of a sudden, the old German Lion looks like an impassioned boy asking for his parents' permission to go out.

'Jürgen, I know how much you care about this, and you know I'm sceptical. Is there any way I can change your mind?'

'No, Mr. President. If the Committee doesn't include my proposed reasoning in the final text, I will issue a separate opinion going full throttle on self-determination. Let me remind you and our distinguished colleagues that I'm one of the most widely cited judges of the Court.' Jürgen smiles allusively. 'Wouldn't you rather keep me at bay for once?'

President Rosas and Judge Quintana nod imperceptibly at each other.

'Fine, Jürgen. The Committee will keep your bit on the 1963 consultation in the text for the second reading. Just give us something workable, will you?'

'I will, Mr. President. Thank you.'

Sophie exults in victory. Barring any major surprises, the Committee's text should survive the second reading mostly unscathed. Now, it is just a matter of tweaking that text to meet President Rosas' demands. For another two weeks, Sophie and Judge Lehmann rework their portion of the draft, shorten it, soften its tone, and harmonize it with the rest of the opinion. The 'splash of colour' advocated by Judge Lehmann passes the scrutiny of his fellow Committee members. Once consolidated, the text is edited by two registry staff who even out the peaks and troughs in the drafters' language and ensure uniformity with standard ICJ terminology. Finally, the Registrar appends the *dispositif* at the end of the Court's analysis.

At last, the ICJ's judgment in *North Borneo* is on the 'launching pad'.[64] As Sophie expected, the second reading goes smoothly. The plenary Court runs once again through the text and the *dispositif* line by line. Some sentences are turned around, a couple of paragraphs are expanded, a few others shortened. At the end, a final vote is cast. Taking the floor in reverse order of seniority, each judge formalizes their agreement or disagreement with the judgment.[65]

The result of three years of work is almost brutal in its brevity.

THE COURT:

(1) By fourteen votes to three,

*Finds* that Malaysia has sovereignty over the 'disputed territory', as defined by the Court in paragraphs 28–29 of the present Judgment;

IN FAVOUR: *President* Rosas; *Vice-President* Dvorak; *Judges* Quintana, Stephenson, Kyeong, Huyghebaert, Aristide, Grigorova, Swanepoel, Madsen, Ben Ahmed, Malacrida, Lehmann; *Judge* ad hoc Badawi;

AGAINST: *Judges* Zardari, Rajković; *Judge* ad hoc Jimeno;

(2) By fourteen votes to three,

*Rejects* all submissions made by the Republic of the Philippines in respect of the interpretation of the 1878 deed by the Sultan of Sulu concerning rights over the 'disputed territory';

IN FAVOUR: *President* Rosas; *Vice-President* Dvorak; *Judges* Quintana, Stephenson, Kyeong, Huyghebaert, Aristide, Grigorova, Swanepoel, Madsen, Ben Ahmed, Malacrida, Lehmann; *Judge* ad hoc Badawi;

AGAINST: *Judges* Zardari, Rajković; *Judge* ad hoc Jimeno;

(3) By ten votes to seven,

*Rejects* all submissions made by the Republic of the Philippines in respect of the outcomes of the 1963 consultation held in the 'disputed territory' by the Secretary-General of the United Nations;

IN FAVOUR: *President* Rosas; *Judges* Stephenson, Kyeong, Huyghebaert, Aristide, Swanepoel, Madsen, Malacrida, Lehmann; *Judge* ad hoc Badawi;

AGAINST: *Vice-President* Dvorak; *Judges* Zardari, Rajković, Grigorova, Ben Ahmed, Quintana; *Judge* ad hoc Jimeno.

---

[64] Kolb, *The ICJ*, 1009.
[65] See Article 8 of the ICJ Note on Judicial Practice.

As the high priests and priestesses of international law stand up one by one to say their last word, Sophie is overcome by conflicting emotions. Judge Lehmann's satisfaction moves her deeply. Once again, the German Lion has lived up to his nickname. 'He could not have made it without my help', Sophie thinks, only to immediately correct her thought: 'No, he could not have made it without the help of all those who, directly or indirectly, participated in the construction of this judgment. Filibert, Lionel, the other counsel; the judges, their clerks, the registry; and, why not, the late Thomas Franck, whose legacy Jürgen has tried to honour in deeds if not in words. This is also *their* decision.'

Yet, something does not feel quite right. For some reason, Sophie finds the pathos of the moment slightly artificial, like a bittersweet reminder that the preconstructed is everywhere.[66] She cannot tell if the judgment embodies 'ideals of peace, social justice and progress'[67] or is simply… well… a *something that has been done*. But then what? Once the last vote is cast, all the emotions and the doubts that marked the last three years of Sophie's life will be put to rest. The dust will finally settle, giving way to the timeless voice of The Law. In time, Sophie will shake off the feeling that it was all a carefully staged masquerade. She will forget those tiny, unextraordinary dust particles whirling in the air.

Sophie sighs in relief. At least, according to the weather forecast, the oral delivery of the judgment will happen on a sunny day.

•

For Carlos, the finalization of the arbitral award in *Kingsland Mining Corp. v. Turkey* is far less dramatic. Based on the input of the three arbitrators, he wrote the ruling swiftly and without hiccups, and is now going through the cathartic experience of shredding the piles of paper that had accumulated on his desk. The additional instructions Professor Gal gave him after deliberations were short and clear:

'Give Guillermo something to show for. If we don't humiliate him, we have him in the bag.'

The resulting draft is a textbook example of adherence to the orthodoxy of legitimate expectations in investment law.

Concerning the *interpretation* of the relevant legal sources, the Tribunal notes that Article 5 of the Canada-Turkey BIT requires each Party to accord

---

[66] Bourdieu and Wacquant, *Reflexive Sociology*, 235.
[67] M. Z. Khan, 'Address on the 50th Anniversary of the International Judicial System' (1972) 6(3) IntlLawyer 449, 457.

fair and equitable treatment to the covered investments in accordance with customary international law. In turn, customary international law seeks to strike an appropriate balance between, on the one hand, a state's sovereignty over its natural resources[68] and, on the other hand, the principle of good faith, whereby unilateral representations communicated by a state to an investor, on which the investor relied in making its investment, may create legally protected expectations as to the viability of an investment.[69]

The identification of which state representations are sufficient to create legally protected expectations cannot be made in the abstract, but must be based on the totality of circumstances of a particular case. A number of indicators may guide the interpreter's assessment. First, the degree of *authority* of the state agent making the representation may shed light on the official or unofficial nature of the representation itself. Second, the degree of *specificity* of the representation being made may bear on the extent of the legitimate expectation it creates. A generic commitment to attract foreign investments may be less binding on a state than the specific assurance made to an individual investor as to the viability of his investment.[70] Finally, it is well established under international law that a change in government does not exempt a state from the international obligations it entered into under the previous government.

*Applying* this standard to the facts of the case, the Tribunal observes, first, that on dates A and B, the Turkish prime minister delivered two televised speeches inviting foreign companies to invest in the mining sector, on promise that they would be accorded favourable conditions and full legal protection under national and international law. While those speeches came from a highly authoritative source, they were not specific enough to create legitimate expectations with particular investors. Therefore, the Tribunal *rejects* Claimant's argument that it relied on the speeches in question in deciding whether or not to continue its investment in Turkey.

Second, the Tribunal notes that, on dates C and D, two officials of the Turkish government held private meetings with representatives of Claimant. Based on its examination of the evidence and witness testimony, the Tribunal finds that, during the course of those meetings, those government officials made assurances to Claimant that, despite the upcoming

---

[68] Here, Carlos dropped a footnote referring to *some* case law.
[69] Another footnote, this time referring to *a plethora* of case law.
[70] This footnote, which spans three-quarters of a page, may well be Carlos' masterpiece. He carefully selected the cases supporting his view, paraphrasing where necessary, depending on the desired outcome of his analysis. Then he *also* cited a few adverse precedents to convey the impression of thoroughness and strengthen the credibility of the award.

change in government, Claimant's mining rights would remain protected. The Tribunal takes the view that these representations, albeit made by lower-ranking state officials, were nonetheless specific enough for Claimant reasonably to rely on them in good faith when deciding whether to continue or discontinue its investment. Therefore, the Tribunal *finds* that the Turkish government's subsequent refusal to renew Claimant's mining rights frustrated Claimant's legitimate expectations, contrary to the requirement, set forth in Article 5 of the BIT, to accord fair and equitable treatment to the covered investments.

Having so found, the Tribunal *does not find it necessary* to address Claimant's remaining claims concerning fair and equitable treatment. It also *considers* that the non-contractual character of Turkey's violation of Article 5 should be taken into account in determining the *quantum* of reparation due to Claimant.

*Et voilà.* As he runs the final check, Carlos is proud of himself. The flow of the argument is impeccable, the language nuanced, and the outcome in line with his mentor's wishes. Not surprisingly, Professor Gal's comments are terse and unsubstantial. The draft is then circulated to the co-arbitrators who, in turn, have little to say. Evgeny Mamatov replies to the email with: 'Excellent. Go ahead. E.' Guillermo Richler-Benitez is only marginally more reactive. Besides a few linguistic edits, his main suggestion is to beef up some footnotes with additional ICJ jurisprudence – probably to show his friends in The Hague that he has done his homework. It seems that Professor Richler has accepted defeat with dignity. He is probably already at work on other disputes with other frenemies. Now, all that remains is to coordinate with the ICSID secretariat for the editing of the award: typos, terminology, etc. Once that is done, the ICSID itself will take care of issuing the award to the parties.

Carlos pauses for a moment to imagine the parties' reactions. Kingsland and its counsel will be pleased with the outcome. Of course, they could have won more – for example, a fuller consideration of their residual claims on fair and equitable treatment. Even so, their gains are more than enough reason to celebrate. Since they had decided to disinvest from Turkey anyway, they might as well do so with some extra cash to spare. As for the government, Carlos doubts they will be too upset. Once again, a little slap on the wrist is better than a debacle.

The parties, of course, are just the tip of the iceberg. Carlos eagerly anticipates the favour with which the investment law community will receive the fruit of his labour. Arbitrators, party counsel, and law school professors will regard the award in *Kingsland Mining Corp.* v. *Turkey* as a balanced and well reasoned decision: one that resonates with the ethos of the discipline while subtly refining its doctrines. Few will suspect that the *natural* tone of the award conceals a brutal confrontation between opposed social forces, competing professional factions, and divergent worldviews. That turmoil has now subsided. The heterogeneous conflicts that agitate the community have found a fragile point of equilibrium, ready to be tilted again in the next battle.

But most of all, Carlos is keen to please Professor Gal, the man who made his dream job come true. After more than ten cases together, it is time for Carlos to seek appointments as an arbitrator himself. Who knows, maybe a small commercial dispute to begin with. Sole arbitrator. Easy stuff. Emboldened by his brilliant results, Carlos decides to knock on his boss' door.

'Not now, Carlos. I'm very busy.'

From what Carlos can tell, François Gal is playing a game on his phone.

'Sorry for disturbing you, Professor. When you have time, one of these days I'd like to talk to you about plans for the future.'

'Huh, you mean the next files? You already have three in the pipeline, don't you?'

'Well, I was thinking more about the possibility to … to have some cases of my own.'

François Gal raises his eyes from the screen and stares at him.

'I see. And *what* cases, if I may ask?'

'I don't have any yet. But perhaps I could see if someone in Argentina is interested in appointing me as an arbitrator in some small disputes. I have family connections there, you know.'

François Gal stands up and slowly walks towards his pupil.

'I don't think that's a good idea. If you were appointed by Argentina, I would have a hard time presiding disputes where Argentina is a party. Conflict of interest, you see. Or at least the appearance of a conflict.' Professor Gal mimics a journalist taking photos.

'But … I thought you had *no* appointments from Argentina.'

'I don't, but God knows if that's not going to happen in the future. It's a matter of keeping my options open. By the way, it would be very kind of you to use your connections to help me get a case. We pay you a fortune for something, don't we?' Professor Gal laughs.

'I understand your concerns, Professor. But I am asking you to consider that Argentine clients are the only ones I'm likely to get in the initial stages of my career. I need to build up my reputation if I'm to make it in the arbitration world.'

François Gal squints his eyes at Carlos and hisses:

'You're making it in the arbitration world by working with *me*. When I'm gone, you'll no doubt be a superstar. But for now, your job is to bring *me* new clients. Do that, and I'll be happy to discuss your career prospects.'

Then, he softens his tone: 'Oh, wait! I do have a small commercial arbitration in Ukraine next July. I was already thinking of dropping out. Would you like to replace me?'

'That would be an honour, Professor.'

'Great. I'll tell the parties, I am sure they'll be happy to pay a little less. Of course, by contract, your arbitrator fees belong to the firm. You only get the billable hours you spend on the case.'

'I know, that's fine with me.'

'You are a good lawyer, Carlos.'

'Thank you, Professor.'

'You don't want to rock the boat just yet. Patience and passion is all you need. Patience and passion. Now, if you don't mind.'

Without another word, Carlos leaves and walks back to his office. He will need some time to process what has just happened. For lack of better ideas, he puts on his headphones and plays *Lost in the Supermarket*.[71]

•

Aphrodite hardly ever experiences the catharsis of finalizing a draft. As we know,[72] by the time an ECtHR section deliberates on a case, she and her judge rapporteur have *already* written the preliminary judgment, which is then amended in light of the judges' comments and edits. In other words, the decision of a case and the drafting of the decision itself proceed in parallel. Moreover, the sheer number of files to which Aphrodite is assigned every year does not leave much time to savour victory. Sure, there is a certain satisfaction in wrapping up a particularly complex dispute. However, it is likely that the dispute in question will be taken up to the Grand Chamber, where it will sit for another couple of years before being finally resolved.

By and large, Aphrodite copes well with this perpetual lack of closure. After all, she repeats to herself, a Court with almost a billion potential complainants cannot rest on its laurels. However, sometimes, she regrets not having the time to take a step back and observe her professional

---

[71] The Clash, *Lost in the Supermarket*.
[72] See *supra*, pp. 289–92.

world with some detachment. Aphrodite's commitment to the protection of fundamental freedoms across Europe is beyond question. Still, in her breakneck rush for efficiency, she sometimes feels excluded from the fundamental 'questions of distribution and preference'[73] that lie at the heart of the system. What does it *really* mean to consider the European Convention as a 'living instrument', or to give human rights 'practical and effective' protection?[74] Is it true that the 'new politics' of human rights has moved away from the traditional left/right dichotomy, and revolves instead around the opposition between proactive integration vs. sovereign deference?[75] Would it be heresy to say that the ECtHR was not born out of 'moral altruism', but rather as a Cold-War tool to 'lock in democratic governance against future opponents'?[76]

To Aphrodite's consternation, these questions have already been decided elsewhere. All that remain are 'technical questions'[77] to be incessantly processed, digested, and managed by legions of experts. Aphrodite doubts she will ever see a change in her condition – even if, one day, she were to join the Jurisconsult's team. The 'relentless pressures of everyday life' prevent any individual from unearthing the deep structures of the system and challenging its core 'institutional arrangements'.[78] If this is true, thinks Aphrodite, the most she can do is to perform her duties to the best of her abilities. Perhaps, her commitment will carry enough force to leave a positive trace on the system as a whole. Perhaps, good old Candide got it right: '*il faut cultiver nôtre jardin*' (we must cultivate our garden).[79]

---

[73] Koskenniemi, '20 Years Later', 16.
[74] *Airey v. Ireland*, Judgment of 9 October 1979, No. 6289/73, ECtHR-1979, para. 24; *Imbrioscia v. Switzerland*, Judgment of 24 November 1993, No. 13972/88, ECtHR-1993, para. 38; *Bellet v. France*, Judgment of 4 December 1995, No. 23805/94, ECtHR-1995, para. 38; *Salduz v. Turkey*, Grand Chamber Judgment of 27 November 2008, No. 36391/02, ECtHR-2008, para. 51.
[75] L. Hooghe, G. Marks, and C. Wilson, 'Does Left/Right Structure Party Positions on European Integration?' (2002) 35(8) CompPolStud 965. See also E. Voeten, 'Politics, Judicial Behaviour, and Institutional Design', in J. Christoffersen and M. R. Madsen (eds.), *The European Court of Human Rights between Law and Politics* (Oxford University Press, 2011) 61, 64.
[76] A. Moravcsik, 'The Origins of Human Rights Regimes: Democratic Delegation in Postwar Europe' (2000) 54(2) IntlOrg 217, 248–9. See also e.g. M. R. Madsen, 'The Protracted Institutionalization of the Strasbourg Court: From Legal Diplomacy to Integrationist Jurisprudence', in J. Christoffersen and M. R. Madsen (eds.), *The European Court of Human Rights between Law and Politics* (Oxford University Press, 2011) 43, 43–4.
[77] Koskenniemi, '20 Years Later', 16.
[78] Unger, *What Should Legal Analysis Become?*, 98.
[79] Voltaire, *Candide: Ou, l'Optimiste* (La Sirène, 1759), 245.

Meanwhile, on the other side of the Atlantic, Soledad is trying her best to cheer up one of her junior colleagues. After six years of intense and emotion-laden work, the IACtHR has just issued a lengthy decision on a case concerning *desaparecidos*. Besides doing the heavy lifting, conducting research, collecting evidence, and drafting hundreds of pages of memos, the secretariat team led by Soledad played a pivotal role in strengthening the judge-rapporteur's draft and overcoming the diffidence of the six other judges.

Now that the ordeal is over, Soledad's 26-year-old supervisee is simply not ready to move on and is sobbing on her shoulder.

'It's so weird, Sol! One spends days and nights trying to make the world a better place, and one day, like that, it's gone.'

Soledad smiles maternally: 'I know, Louise. I felt the same way when I completed my first case. If you work here long enough, you'll learn when it is time to let go.'

'I don't want to let go! All this work for a piece of paper the state will not even read!'

Soledad is forced to recognize that it is unlikely that the responding state will promptly comply with the judgment and accord compensation to the victims' families.

'But hey, see it this way: our decision will, at least, empower the human rights community across the continent. NGOs, civil society organizations, like-minded academics will all rely on it to strengthen their advocacy and to demand the truth from their governments. Our audience is not the state: it's *them*.'

As Louise dries her tears, Soledad ponders. Her staff deserves a word of encouragement. Later that afternoon, she calls a meeting with the whole team, from seniors to interns. She waits until everyone has taken a seat and savours the silence of the room. Her folks are waiting for an inspirational speech of sorts. She asks everyone to hold hands.

'Guys, I want you to know how proud I am of the work we've done. It has been a true privilege to witness the sheer talent and the utter dedication of this group of lawyers. We've come up with a very good judgment, I believe. It is not for us to decide what the judges will do with it, whether the state will implement it, in fact whether anyone will remember it in ten years from now. The world is way too complex for us to control. Our job is done, and we must look forward to the next challenges. Now, as you let go of each other's hands, I want you to think that those hands *are the judgment*. Release it, let it fly, and rest assured that it will land where good people can put it to good use. Ready? Go.'

•

TRUTH WOVEN TOGETHER 329

Finally, Matt. Something odd is happening to him. Through years of WTO practice and acculturation, he has become a very skilful player in the game. His issues papers are invariably excellent. His ability to discreetly nudge the discussion during deliberations is praised by Appellate Body members and ABS lawyers alike. Interns love him. As his career progressed, Matt has developed the ability to remain detached, lucid, and even a bit cynical towards the object of disputes. He prides himself in not being carried away by emotions and not creating problems when an easy solution is readily available.

Thanks to these qualities, Matt's sailing through the *EU – Palm Oil* appeal has been rather smooth. Remember his characterization of the measure at issue?[80] The Division did not question it in the slightest. His 'likeness' assessment?[81] It was incorporated into the report almost *tel quel*. The same goes with many other aspects of the case, including: (a) the discriminatory nature of the EU palm oil regime under Article III:4 of the GATT and Article 2.1 of the TBT Agreement; (b) the European Union's failure to meet the requirements of Article XX of the GATT; and (c) the European Union's inability to show that the discriminatory nature of the EU palm oil regime stems exclusively from a legitimate regulatory distinction for purposes of Article 2.1 of the TBT Agreement. Technicalities aside, this means that the Division agreed with Matt's suggestions on most scores. Business as usual.

But here is the odd thing: for the first time in years, Matt has made the mistake of *caring* about a legal issue. That issue is whether the Indonesia-European Union free trade agreement (FTA), which authorizes the latter to keep its palm oil regulation in place, should affect the outcome of the case. As the reader may recall,[82] Matt found Jasper's – sorry, the European Union's – position quite compelling. As he prepared the issues paper, Matt anticipated that the Division would not be keen to venture outside the scope of the WTO agreements, but was prepared for the battle. What he did not expect was Björn's scepticism. The day before deliberations, Björn burst into his office:

'Matteo, your issues paper is excellent, as usual. But, honestly, I don't think we should insist on this FTA business.'

'Why not? Indonesia and the European Union have entered an FTA that authorizes the maintenance of the measure at issue. Arguably, the

---

[80] See *supra*, Chapter 9.
[81] See *supra*, Chapter 12.
[82] See *supra*, pp. 218–23.

European Union made concessions during the FTA negotiations in exchange for this carve-out. Shortly after ratification of the FTA, Indonesia sues the European Union at the WTO, where the carve-out does not apply. That is quite sketchy, don't you think?'

'Not really. Both Indonesia and the European Union are WTO members. They knew what obligations they would incur when they signed the WTO agreements. Whatever they negotiate on the side cannot add to or diminish from their WTO rights and obligations.'

'Well, what about subsequent agreements under Article 31.3(a) of the VCLT? Or other rules of international law applicable between the parties under Article 31.3(c)?'

'You know the answer. 'The parties' means *all* WTO members. Two members cannot agree to lesser obligations *inter se*.'

'Well, I know the panel in *Biotech* said that.[83] But the Appellate Body has never had a chance to rule on this. In *Airbus* …'

'In *Airbus*, *we* did not find it necessary to rule on the issue, because the non-WTO treaty was not yet in force.[84] However, even if it were in force, *we knew* that we couldn't dismiss the case on that basis alone.'

'You may have *known*, but you did not say it. Don't you think that the current case is the closest WTO law will ever get to an estoppel-type scenario?'

'You are mixing the issues here. Article 31.3 of the VCLT is about interpretation, not about estoppel. Even assuming that the FTA is relevant as a means of interpretation, the permission contained in the FTA cannot be used to upend the prohibition contained in the WTO agreements. A 'no' cannot be interpreted as a 'yes'. Remember *Peru – Agricultural Products*.'[85]

'Alright. But what about estoppel itself, then? In *Soft Drinks*, the Appellate Body left the door open to 'legal impediments' that would 'preclude a panel from ruling on the merits of the claims that are before it'.[86] Also, as I wrote in the issues paper, the panel in *Argentina – Poultry* came close to recognizing estoppel.[87] Isn't a blatant violation of good faith enough to dismiss a claim?'

'Those reports were issued more than ten years ago. That was *another era*, Matteo. We have closed that door. Again, think about *Peru – Agricultural Products*.'

---

[83] Panel Report, *EC – Approval and Marketing of Biotech Products*, para. 7.68.
[84] Appellate Body Report, *EC and certain member States – Large Civil Aircraft*, paras. 844–5.
[85] Appellate Body Report, *Peru – Agricultural Products*, paras. 5.93–5.117.
[86] Appellate Body Report, *Mexico – Taxes on Soft Drinks*, para. 54.
[87] Panel Report, *Argentina – Poultry Anti-Dumping Duties*, paras. 7.36–7.38.

'Yes, yes, I *do* know that report. I'm afraid we are talking past each other. Consider this scenario. Today, we say that the FTA is irrelevant and the European Union loses under WTO rules. Tomorrow, the European Union sues Indonesia under the FTA's dispute settlement clause, claims that its expectations under the agreement have been frustrated by Indonesia, and wins the case. At this point, you have the WTO saying that the European Union's measure is unlawful, and the FTA court saying that the *same* measure is lawful. Isn't this the nightmare scenario the ILC envisaged in its 2006 Fragmentation Report?'

'I am not sure I follow you. But, frankly, I don't care much about the ILC. Our *allegiance* is to the WTO membership, not to some academics writing about fragmentation.'

'I thought you were sensitive about scholarly opinions.'

'Not when they stand in our way.'

'Are we playing the wolf and the lamb?'

'Ha!' Björn scoffs, 'Don't tell me you're taking Keiko's side. I'm not the devil, as she always says: I'm just a good-intentioned civil servant.'

'The road to hell is paved with good intentions, Björn.'

Matt regretted these last words as soon as they came out of his mouth. He should not have said that. It is one thing to disagree with your boss, another to accuse your boss of tyranny. Indeed, Björn was taken aback by Matt's impudence.

'I barely recognize you, Matteo. Usually, you are not this feisty. Clearly, you took this issue at heart. Look, if you really want to go ahead with your FTA shenanigans, so be it. But be warned: the Division will not even listen to you.'

'Thank you, Björn. We'll see about that.'

Björn's prediction proved only partially true. During deliberations, two Division members dismissed the relevance of the FTA outright. The third Division member, however, showed a certain interest in Matt's line of argument. That adjudicator did not necessarily share Matt's systemic concerns about fragmentation. More simply, he seemed to agree on the unfairness of ruling against the European Union in light of the FTA. As the debate unfolded, Matt nervously gazed at Björn, who sat silently in a corner. During breaks, he saw the two orthodox Division members rush to the heretic's office, closing the door behind them.

At the end of deliberations, the Division chairman cleared his throat and said:

'On the issue of the FTA, we suggest that the secretariat prepare two drafts: one articulating the reasons to take the treaty into account, the other dismissing its relevance. We will decide the issue once we have seen both.'

Matt immediately understood what that meant. First, all attempts to convince the heretic to retract had failed. Second, the judges wanted the secretariat to draft both the majority ruling *and* the tentative dissent. This way, they sought to ensure linguistic consistency between the two texts and avoid what they feared would be inappropriate colloquialisms. This was the opening Matt was hoping for.

And so here we are, one month later. The three Division members and the secretariat team have taken their seats around the oval table, ready to go through the draft judgment that Matt and his teammates have prepared. Every Appellate Body report undergoes three readings before it is signed by the Division members, sent to translation, and finally circulated. The amount of comments diminishes with each round of review, such that the third reading is mostly editorial in nature.

To Matt's delight, the bulk of the draft fully conforms to the Division's expectations. Despite a few minor tweaks to the reasoning, the findings of inconsistency with Articles III:4 of the GATT and 2.1 of the TBT Agreement are quickly disposed of. The discussion gets a bit more lively when it comes to the European Union's defence under Article XX and the existence of a legitimate regulatory distinction under Article 2.1. One Division member, in particular, requests that the standard for the allocation of the burden of proof under Article 2.1 be made clearer than in prior jurisprudence.[88] The secretariat retorts that the current formulation of the standard, while confusing, was nonetheless the fruit of a delicate compromise among competing views, and begs the Division not to reopen that can of worms. No objections.

Finally, it is the turn of the FTA issue. As the judges flip through the pages of the two alternative drafts side by side, Matt can hardly hide his excitement. Who would have thought that, one day, he would take off the hat of the technical adviser and don that of the militant lawyer! Even if his position does not prevail, at least he will have penned an eloquent dissent for the benefit of future generations. What today is a simple minority opinion may plant the seed of doubt in the minds of tomorrow's adjudicators, and eventually take over as the new paradigm. 'I wish Professor Jackson could see this', thinks Matt.

After a long silence, the Division chairman prepares to take the floor. Matt gives Björn a quick sideways glance. His director looks strangely relaxed. Uh-oh.

---

[88] See the extraordinarily confusing wording in Appellate Body Report, *US – Tuna II (Mexico) (Article 21.5 – Mexico)*, paras. 7.32–7.35.

'First of all, let me thank the secretariat for its commendable work on this difficult issue. Having carefully considered both drafts, the Division has *unanimously* decided to go with the first. We will not, therefore, ascribe any relevance to the Indonesia-European Union FTA for the purposes of this case.'

So long, change of paradigm. You lasted the span of three sentences. Dispirited, Matt turns his eyes to the judge who had previously expressed sympathy with his views. Why did he chicken out? Matt feels entitled to an explanation, which arrives promptly.

'At first, I was quite taken by Matteo's idea that Indonesia acted in bad faith and should therefore be estopped from pursuing this dispute at the WTO. But, upon reflection, I realized that deciding the issue this way would send the wrong message to the international community. The WTO must remain an open house, where any state who believes that its trade rights have been impaired is able to seek redress. Who are we to question anyone's good faith, anyway? Let us stick to what the WTO agreements say, as the DSU requires us to do, and look no further.'

That is it. Not another word. If Matt were not so fond of his job, if his newfound principles were not the caprice of a day, he would answer something like this:

'Who are you to question someone's good faith? You are the *judges*, for heaven's sake! Good faith is not a vague moral precept: it is one of the cornerstone principles of international *law*. If you were not so busy navel gazing, you would know. And *what* international community are you talking about? I doubt that the world at large gives a penny about our discussions. And even if it did, wouldn't it prefer a decision that fosters the coherence of international law over one that breaks it into a million fragments? Apparently not. With your cowardly ruling, you are perpetuating the "clinical isolation" of the multilateral trade regime from the rest of international law, thus betraying the promise made by the Appellate Body twenty years ago.[89] Today, you are ignoring an FTA. Tomorrow, you will ignore a human rights convention, an environmental treaty, who knows what else. Is this what the "international community" really wants? No, my friend: we both know that your imaginary 'international community' is nothing but a close-knit, self-referential group of professionals with their ingrained ideology, dominant habits, and deep-seated idiosyncrasies. You are speaking to *them*, catering to *their* taste, naturalizing *their* dominant

---

[89] Appellate Body Report, *United States – Standards for Reformulated and Conventional Gasoline*, WT/DS2/AB/R (29 April 1996), p. 17.

position under the garb of rationality and technique. Even worse, *we* are giving you the weapons to do so. Without our expertise and our drafting skills, your conservative project would not go far. We are enablers. But beware, my dear judge: even if your don't hear them, new voices are emerging within our community. In one camp, many are questioning the system from the Left, calling for greater consideration of the political, ethical, and economic pluralism of our societies. In the other camp, the Right is packing punch, advocating for a return to trade protectionism and closure. In your blind efforts to preserve the status quo, you are lending ammunition to both sides. So go ahead, hold dearly to your "open house": it may soon be on fire.'

Of course, none of these words comes out of Matt's mouth. Instead, he inhales deeply and says:

'Very well. The first draft be it. Shall we discuss the footnotes?'

The next day at noon, the Division invites the rest of the Appellate Body and the whole secretariat for the signing ceremony. Sitting around the oval table, the three adjudicators sign the report in turn, while Björn takes photos with his smartphone. Following usual practice, the presiding judge distributes gifts themed after the products at issue: in this case, packs of palm oil cookies.

The atmosphere is jolly. Matt is nowhere to be found. Michelle, the intern, says he called out sick, but she is hiding the truth. Actually, she saw Matt sunbathing at the Bains des Pâquis, a fresh beer in hand, with his friend Jane Weaver. The two were happily catching up after months spent on opposite sides of the fence, joking about the case and making predictions about the future. Apparently, at some point, Matt asked Jane if her law firm is currently accepting applications.

# 17

## Spijkermakersstraat 9, 8:00 PM

As she walks up the steep staircase to her apartment, Sophie hears *The Ecstasy of Gold* by Ennio Morricone playing from the speakers. Once inside, she finds Norma sitting on the living room couch, a laptop on her knees and a glass of red wine at her side. She is so immersed in editing the footnotes of her latest paper that she does not notice Sophie approaching for a kiss.

'Hey hon!' Norma jumps up and hugs her girlfriend. 'How did it go?'

'It went ok.'

'What do you mean, "ok"? I watched the webcast, it was glorious! Did you have your victory lap?'

'Yes, kind of. We sat at the *Restaurant des Juges* the whole afternoon. It was cool, I guess.'

'What's wrong, love? You've just finished a massive case: this calls for celebration!'

'Nothing's wrong, I am just a little tired.'

'If it wasn't raining cats and dogs, I'd say let's go grab a drink outside, but ... Here, have some wine.'

'You opened the bottle of *primitivo*, well done. Maybe later, now I just need a shower.'

'I know you. Something is bothering you. Spill the beans.'

Sophie takes off her raincoat and sits on the couch.

'Hard to tell. I've been working on this case since before I met you. It's been a great ride for the most part. Jürgen really trusted me, I met lots of interesting people, you've been caring and supportive throughout. I could not have hoped for a better experience. And yet ...'

'Yet ...?'

'Yet, something still escapes me. Somehow, I expected *more* from this experience, from those people, from myself. Not that I'd know how to define "more" ...'

'Well, try. You're not sure the Court made the right decision?'

'It's not that. I do agree with the judgment. Well, to be honest, I don't know if I agreed with it from the outset or was *led* to agree with it ... But I'm persuaded that we did a good job, and that's what counts. No, I guess it's more about the *process* that led to the judgment. As a student, I had always thought of international adjudication as the pinnacle of world justice, the living embodiment of higher ideals, the Law's emancipatory response to the pettiness and self-interest of Politics ...'

'Yep, got the point. And it's not like that, is it?'

'Not from what I saw. For three years, I helped out digest fuzzy submissions replete with obscure language, circular arguments, partisan interpretations, and deliberate attempts at confusing the Court. On that shaky basis, I spent weeks, months, years guessing the truth of facts too remote to be truly knowable; determining the exact meaning of legal sources too open-ended to be exactly determinable; drafting a text too composite, too bitterly negotiated to be coherent. Throughout the process, I kept searching for a guiding principle, something greater than me, some firm baseline I could rest on ... Nothing. I wonder how the others go about this. Jürgen, the other judges, the counsel, my fellow clerks: they all seem so confident! How do they manage to understand what they are doing? What am I missing?'

'Either they're pretending, hon, or they've been in the game long enough to have come to terms with their doubts. No job ever truly allows you to understand what you are doing.'

'That's exactly the problem. I did not expect this to be just another job. I thought I was working in the service of a higher *vision*, but as it turns out, I was merely contributing to a *practice*. What's worse, as months went by, I started to doubt my own motivations, as if they did not fit in the rules of the game, as if they could not be expressed in the language I was supposed to speak. Remember that book, *Flatland*, you gave me for my birthday? That's *exactly* how I feel.'

Sophie reaches for the shelf, grabs the book, and flips the pages until she finds the passage she was looking for. The protagonist, a Square living in a two-dimensional universe, is suddenly lifted onto a three-dimensional plane. From this new perspective, he contemplates his home world from the outside, free from the limitations that had previously affected his vision.[1] Once back home, the Square commits to revealing the mysteries of the third dimension to his fellow Flatlanders.[2] However, as days go by,

---

[1] E. Abbott, *Flatland: A Romance of Many Dimensions* (Seeley and Co., 1884), 77–82.
[2] Ibid., 90.

this intuition, which at first 'had appeared as patent as Arithmetic', slowly starts fading away in his *own mind* and, as a result, becomes more and more difficult to communicate to his peers.

'I felt that all that I had seen … was in some strange way slipping away from me, like the image of a half-grasped, tantalizing dream.'[3]

'Going literary, I see.'

'Sorry for that. But the question remains: If universal justice and high principles are nowhere to be found, what is the third dimension?'

'Do you really need to find one? Think about doctors: their knowledge of the human body is grossly incomplete; they make mistakes; why, some of them are in the pocket of pharmaceutical companies. But we still believe in medicine, don't we?'

'Yes, but doctors serve an actual purpose in society. All I did was contributing to a piece of paper.'

'You're bordering on self-pity now. That piece of paper, as you call it, has very important real-world implications. Those are your third dimension: the social, political, and economic forces that pushed and pulled the Court and are now being affected by the judicial outcome. External factors, if you know what I mean.'

'I know what you mean, but *I didn't see* them. I was not there when the dispute arose, I won't be there when it ends. If external forces were ever at work, they largely remained outside the door, as part of an ever-elusive *context*. The rare times where they entered the room, they did so in disguise: dressed as legal arguments, as technical claims, as normative stances. They were not there naked, in their pure form: but processed and digested by our inner circle of professionals. No, Norma: if that's the third dimension, it is an invisible one. All I saw was a tentative, hesitant, and contingent quest for meaning. A quest that follows its own codes, sealed off from the world, conducted by a community that hardly ever lets external reality unsettle the rules of its game.'

'Well, welcome to *my* world: I wanted to change it, and now I am fixing footnotes.'

'But you are changing it, somehow! Or, at least, you can see beyond the two-dimensional universe of international adjudication …'

'… Yeah, and contemplate the two-dimensional universe of academia. Great. What I do is no less contingent than what you do. My contingency is simply organized along different structures than yours, follows different rules. But the disorientation remains, believe me. Besides, what's wrong

---

[3] Ibid., 94–5.

with international courts leaving context outside the door? Isn't that a guarantee of impartiality?'

'Yes, it is. Most of the people I worked with were unbiased and deeply committed to what they were doing. They were just ... a little clueless.'

'Did you just call the most renowned international lawyers in the world "clueless"?'

'Not in the sense that they don't know their stuff. Just that, in coming to a case, they have to grapple with it, make impossible decisions and pretend they are rational, get stuck in the cobwebs that you, I, and who knows how many other spiders weave around them. They decide, and yet they do not decide. I don't know, it's just all very messy in my head right now.'

'Don't worry about the mess, my love. Remember: law, politics, sociology, history – none will ever give you a firm ground on which reality stands. We are all transient at the end of the day. Well, all except Morricone: he's probably eternal.'

'Perhaps you're right.'

'If this whole business takes itself a little too seriously, so what? We both know that adjudication is about making choices, and that choices do not originate only from within ourselves, but are shaped by the people we encounter, the conversations we have, the things we fall in love with and those that repulse us. For all the transcendence we project in it, it's all just very small. And perhaps it's best so. Look, I can go literary, too. Hear this.'

Norma grabs another book from the shelf and ceremoniously clears her throat.

'What is the origin of the kind of defeatism that compels us to believe that ... a thundering voice must always emerge from nowhere – the voice of nature or the voice of Law – to dictate [our] behaviour and [our] convictions? Are we poor earthlings really so impoverished? The way in which unquestionable truths are gradually constructed through human interactions has always seemed to me to be more interesting, more enduring and more dignified.'[4]

'...'
'...'

'*Laudate hominem*?'
'That's about right.'
'I love you. Can you pass the wine?'

---

[4] Latour, *The Making of Law*, 197.

# INDEX

Academics
　critique of judicial decisions, 3–4, 6, 27, 51, 175, 217, 227, 304
　grammarians, as, 6, 25, 37, 57, 63–4, 131
　proximity to courts and tribunals, 29, 30, 39, 57, 59, 62, 118–19, 145–6, 151–2
Advisory Centre on WTO Law, 61
*Agreement on Technical Barriers to Trade*, 80–1, 100, 158, 233–4, 329, 332
Akin Gump, 61
*American Convention on Human Rights*, 90, 208, 209
*Amicus curiae*, 28, 154, 272, 280
Arguments of the parties
　adaptiveness of the parties' positions, 82–4, 190–1, 272–4
　creative lawyering, 70, 88, 92, 98, 218
　factual narratives, 84–9, 159–60, 192, 195–7
　framing of the case, 90, 94–5, 158–61, 176–7, 181
　legal narratives, 89–93, 224, 245–7
　preparations, 72–7, 79–82
　tailoring of the argument, 70–1, 76, 93–9, 272–3
Articles on State Responsibility, 121, 177, 216
Assistants to ISDS tribunals
　arbitral institution, 135
　generally, 131–5
　tribunal secretaries, 134–5
　undisclosed assistants, 135

Backlash against international courts and tribunals, 12, 31–2, 102, 147–8
Bourdieu, Pierre, 35, 197
Buonarroti, Michelangelo, 303
Bureaucracies, international judicial
　employment conditions, 39, 115, 172
　functions, 6, 29, 45, 46, 114–15
　recruitment, 111–13, 115, 120–1, 126–7, 131–2
　relationship with adjudicators, 38, 96, 115, 137–8, 146–51, 166–8, 170–2, 185, 252–5, 257, 262, 284–9, 291–2, 301–2, 316–17, 325–6, 332–3
　structure, 36, 114–16
Byrne, David, 45

Cardozo, Benjamin, 307
Community, international judicial
　autonomy, 4–5, 15–17, 27–31, 150–1
　competition, 34–40, 51–2, 60, 58–67, 83, 172, 197, 274, 285–90, 296–301, 319–20
　hierarchies, 35–40, 55–6, 72, 87, 172, 254–5, 276, 302, 325–6, 333
　revolving door, 29–30, 69, 151
Confidentiality of proceedings
　access to information, xiv–xvii
　conspiracy of silence, 139–40, 143–5, 150–2
　generally, 140–3
　invisible governance, 148–50
　legitimacy concerns, 146–8
　open secret, 145–6
Counsel, international
　composition of legal teams, 54–6, 60, 61, 81
　diversity, 67–8, 257–8

339

340        INDEX

Counsel, international (cont.)
  human rights courts, at, 65–7
  ICJ, at the, 58–60
  ISDS, in, 62–5
  oligopoly, 30, 55, 57–67
  proximity to courts and tribunals, 69–70, 257–8
  relationship with clients, 37, 56–7, 68–9, 72–8, 274
  specialization, 27, 58, 67, 71–2
  WTO, at the, 60–2
Court of Justice of the European Union, 174, 179, 180, 291
Critical Legal Studies, xi, 149, 237

Deliberations
  ECtHR, at the, 290–1
  generally, 278–81
  IACtHR, at the, 292–4
  ICJ, at the, 281–3
  ISDS, in, 276–8, 294–302
  WTO, at the, 283–9
Derrida, Jacques, 230, 238
Dezalay, Yves, xv–xvi
*Dispute Settlement Understanding*, 17, 87, 106, 189, 221, 287
Drafting of judgments
  collective effort, as a, 306–7
  craft, as a, 303–6
  discursive techniques, 313–15
  ECtHR, at the, 291–2, 326–7
  formalism, 311–13
  IACtHR, at the, 292–3, 327–8
  ICJ, at the, 316–22
  ISDS, in, 322–6
  literary production, as, 307–8, 311
  open-ended exercise, as an, 279, 305
  templates, 308–10
  WTO, at the, 328–4

Earnings of legal professionals, 38–9, 65, 113, 121
Eco, Umberto, 45, 230, 278
ECtHR registry
  divisions, 125–6
  generally, 122–8
  Jurisconsult, 127–8
Ethnographic method, xii–xiii

*European Convention on Human Rights*, 90, 123–4, 208–9, 327
European Court of Human Rights. *See* ECtHR

Fact-finding
  capacity, 86–7, 185–92
  conduct at issue, 174–6, 182–3
  human rights courts, at, 186–7
  ICJ, at the, 186, 188–9
  ISDS, in, 191–5
  municipal law, 69, 183–4
  scientific evidence, 187–8, 196–9
  WTO, at the, 189–91, 195–200
Fairness in international adjudication, 220, 257, 331
Fish, Stanley, 48
Foley Hoag, 54
Fragmentation of international law
  competition among courts and tribunals, 41–2, 178–82
  epistemic limitations, 13, 19, 96–8, 214–18, 334
  openings and convergence, 10, 98–101, 218–23
Free trade agreements, 100–1, 105, 218–23, 329–33
Freshfields, 54

Garth, Bryant, xv–xvi
*General Agreement on Tariffs and Trade*, 62, 80, 100, 158, 209, 216, 224–5, 239–40, 329, 332
*General Agreement on Trade in Services*, 180–1
Good faith
  Article 3.7 of the DSU, under, 221–2
  estoppel, 222–3, 330–4
  generally, 100–1, 218–19, 296, 299–300

Haas, Peter, 49
Hearings
  counsel, and, 272–4
  ECtHR, at the, 264–5
  IACtHR, at the, 265–7
  ICJ, at the, 267–8
  information gathering, 261
  ISDS, in, 256–61

performative acts, as, 268–70
script, 259–62
transparency, and, 270–2
WTO, at the, 261–3

IACtHR secretariat, 128–31
ICJ registry
  clerks, 118–20
  Department of Legal Matters, 117–18
  *experts fantômes*, 189, 247
  generally, 116–22
Inter-American Court of Human Rights. See IACtHR
International Centre for Settlement of Investment Disputes, 38, 64, 135, 324
International Court of Justice. See ICJ
International Criminal Tribunal for Former Yugoslavia, 8, 97, 138, 181
International Labour Organization, 102
International Law Commission, 27, 331
International Tribunal for the Law of the Sea, 8, 20, 34
Interpretation (content-determination)
  emotions, and, 129–30, 245–55, 329
  generally, 7–8, 44, 92, 202–3, 224–8
  indeterminacy, 203, 225, 227, 230–1, 238, 246–9
  political discretion, and, 13, 15, 148–9, 227, 249–51, 254, 282, 316–17
  social constraints on interpretation, 18, 48, 228, 238–44, 251–2
  VCLT rules of interpretation, 3, 8, 92, 203, 209, 220–1, 225–7, 229–37, 252
Interpretation (law-ascertainment)
  collective exercise, as a, 203–6, 223
  contextual norms, 91–2, 208–9, 232
  formal sources of international law, 17, 202, 204, 211
  generally, 202–7
  hierarchies of international norms, 206–7
  precedent, 209–14, 240, 314–15
  principal norms, 90–1, 207–8
  systemic integration, 10, 120–1, 220–1, 330
Investor-state arbitration. See ISDS

Judicialization of international law, 8–10, 26–7
*Jura novit curia*, 83, 207, 266

Kennedy, Duncan, 149
King & Spalding, 61

Latour, Bruno, xvi
Law and Literature, 307
Legitimacy of international courts and tribunals, 11–12, 28, 146–8, 203, 223, 286–7
Legitimate expectations of investors, 192, 294–301, 322–4
Literary fiction, ix–xi, xvii–xix
London Court of International Arbitration, 38

Marcuse, Herbert, 26
Marx, Karl, 51
Memoranda, internal
  generally, 165, 170–3
  internal draft (ECtHR), 166–7, 289–90
  internal draft (IACtHR), 167, 292
  issues paper (WTO), 165–6
  memo (ISDS), 163–5
  note (ICJ), 169–70
Morricone, Ennio, 335
*Multi-Party Interim Appeal Arbitration Arrangement*, 32, 62
Multi-sourced equivalent norms, 230–1
Music, 45, 163, 195, 268–70, 301, 326, 335

*Non liquet*, 156, 247
Non-governmental organizations, 28, 57, 151, 271, 280

Permanent Court of Arbitration, 55, 116, 133, 135
Permanent Court of International Justice, 26, 67, 168, 183
Pilot judgment procedure, 210
Practices, international judicial
  background knowledge, 26–7, 30, 47–51, 92, 200, 228, 238–9, 308, 311
  *bricolage*, 49–50, 88, 93, 194–5, 315

Practices (cont.)
　freedom and constraint, 18–19, 50–2, 83–4, 92–3, 177–8, 213, 244, 278–81, 305
　patterns, 46–7, 51, 165, 216, 240, 307–13
　performances, 44–6, 229, 268–73
　practice theory, 17–18, 24–5, 43–4

Qualitative methods, xiv–xv

Schachter, Oscar, 25
Seats of international courts
　Centre William Rappard (WTO), 102–4, 283
　Human Rights Building (ECtHR), 122–3
　IACtHR building, 128
　Peace Palace (ICJ), 1, 116–17, 281
Self-determination, right to, 160, 254, 316–20
Sidley Austin, 61
Steptoe & Johnson, 61
Summaries of the parties' arguments
　competing logics, 158–60, 176–8
　generally, 156–7, 161–2
　ICJ, at the, 159–61
　reduction and essentialization, 153–6
　WTO, at the, 157–9

The Clash, 301, 326
Transformation of context into a case
　by judicial bureaucrats, 154–5
　by the parties' counsel, 6, 82–4
　during deliberations, 278–9
　during the drafting of judgments, 304–5

United Nations Commission on International Trade Law, 32–3
United Nations Security Council, 177, 217–18

*Vienna Convention on Consular Relations*, 98, 232, 233
*Vienna Convention on the Law of Treaties. See* VCLT

Weber, Max, 38, 149, 156
White & Case, 54, 61
Wittgenstein, Ludwig, 230
World Trade Organization. *See* WTO
WTO secretariat
　Appellate Body Secretariat, 108
　generally, 102–13
　Legal Affairs and Rules Divisions, 108–10

## CAMBRIDGE STUDIES IN INTERNATIONAL AND COMPARATIVE LAW

*Books in the Series*

170 *The Everyday Makers of International Law: From Great Halls to Back Rooms*
Tommaso Soave

169 *The Effects of Armed Conflict on Investment Treaties*
Tobias Ackermann

168 *Investment Law's Alibis: Colonialism, Imperialism, Debt and Development*
David Schneiderman

167 *Negative Comparative Law: A Strong Programme for Weak Thought*
Pierre Legrand

166 *Detention by Non-State Armed Groups under International Law*
Ezequiel Heffes

165 *Rebellions and Civil Wars: State Responsibility for the Conduct of Insurgents*
Patrick Dumberry

164 *The International Law of Energy*
Jorge Viñuales

163 *The Three Ages of International Commercial Arbitration*
Mikaël Schinazi

162 *Repetition and International Law*
Wouter Werner

161 *State Responsibility and Rebels: The History and Legacy of Protecting Investment Against Revolution*
Kathryn Greenman

160 *Rewriting Histories of the Use of Force: The Narrative of 'Indifference'*
Agatha Verdebout

159 *The League of Nations and the Protection of the Environment*
Omer Aloni

158 *International Investment Law and Legal Theory: Expropriation and the Fragmentation of Sources*
Jörg Kammerhofer

157 *Legal Barbarians: Identity, Modern Comparative Law and the Global South*
Daniel Bonilla Maldonado

156 *International Human Rights Law Beyond State Territorial Control*
Antal Berkes

155 *The Crime of Aggression under the Rome Statute of the International Criminal Court*
Carrie McDougall

154 *Minorities and the Making of Postcolonial States in International Law*
Mohammad Shahabuddin

153 *Preclassical Conflict of Laws*
Nikitas E. Hatzimihail

152 *International Law and History: Modern Interfaces*
    Ignacio de la Rasilla

151 *Marketing Global Justice: The Political Economy of International Criminal Law*
    Christine Schwöbel-Patel

150 *International Status in the Shadow of Empire*
    Cait Storr

149 *Treaties in Motion: The Evolution of Treaties from Formation to Termination*
    Edited by Malgosia Fitzmaurice and Panos Merkouris

148 *Humanitarian Disarmament: An Historical Enquiry*
    Treasa Dunworth

147 *Complementarity, Catalysts, Compliance: The International Criminal Court in Uganda, Kenya, and the Democratic Republic of Congo*
    Christian M. De Vos

146 *Cyber Operations and International Law*
    François Delerue

145 *Comparative Reasoning in International Courts and Tribunals*
    Daniel Peat

144 *Maritime Delimitation as a Judicial Process*
    Massimo Lando

143 *Prosecuting Sexual and Gender-Based Crimes at the International Criminal Court: Practice, Progress and Potential*
    Rosemary Grey

142 *Capitalism As Civilisation: A History of International Law*
    Ntina Tzouvala

141 *Sovereignty in China: A Genealogy of a Concept Since 1840*
    Adele Carrai

140 *Narratives of Hunger in International Law: Feeding the World in Times of Climate Change*
    Anne Saab

139 *Victim Reparation under the Ius Post Bellum: An Historical and Normative Perspective*
    Shavana Musa

138 *The Analogy between States and International Organizations*
    Fernando Lusa Bordin

137 *The Process of International Legal Reproduction: Inequality, Historiography, Resistance*
    Rose Parfitt

136 *State Responsibility for Breaches of Investment Contracts*
    Jean Ho

135 *Coalitions of the Willing and International Law: The Interplay between Formality and Informality*
    Alejandro Rodiles

134 *Self-Determination in Disputed Colonial Territories*
    Jamie Trinidad

133 *International Law as a Belief System*
    Jean d'Aspremont

132 *Legal Consequences of Peremptory Norms in International Law*
    Daniel Costelloe

131 *Third-Party Countermeasures in International Law*
    Martin Dawidowicz

130 *Justification and Excuse in International Law:
    Concept and Theory of General Defences*
    Federica Paddeu

129 *Exclusion from Public Space: A Comparative Constitutional Analysis*
    Daniel Moeckli

128 *Provisional Measures before International Courts and Tribunals*
    Cameron A. Miles

127 *Humanity at Sea: Maritime Migration and the Foundations of International Law*
    Itamar Mann

126 *Beyond Human Rights: The Legal Status of the Individual in International Law*
    Anne Peters

125 *The Doctrine of Odious Debt in International Law: A Restatement*
    Jeff King

124 *Static and Evolutive Treaty Interpretation: A Functional Reconstruction*
    Christian Djeffal

123 *Civil Liability in Europe for Terrorism-Related Risk*
    Lucas Bergkamp, Michael Faure, Monika Hinteregger and Niels Philipsen

122 *Proportionality and Deference in Investor-State Arbitration: Balancing Investment
    Protection and Regulatory Autonomy*
    Caroline Henckels

121 *International Law and Governance of Natural Resources in Conflict and
    Post-Conflict Situations*
    Daniëlla Dam-de Jong

120 *Proof of Causation in Tort Law*
    Sandy Steel

119 *The Formation and Identification of Rules of Customary International Law in
    International Investment Law*
    Patrick Dumberry

118 *Religious Hatred and International Law: The Prohibition of Incitement to
    Violence or Discrimination*
    Jeroen Temperman

117 *Taking Economic, Social and Cultural Rights Seriously in International
    Criminal Law*
    Evelyne Schmid

116 *Climate Change Litigation: Regulatory Pathways to Cleaner Energy*
Jacqueline Peel and Hari M. Osofsky

115 *Mestizo International Law: A Global Intellectual History 1842–1933*
Arnulf Becker Lorca

114 *Sugar and the Making of International Trade Law*
Michael Fakhri

113 *Strategically Created Treaty Conflicts and the Politics of International Law*
Surabhi Ranganathan

112 *Investment Treaty Arbitration As Public International Law: Procedural Aspects and Implications*
Eric De Brabandere

111 *The New Entrants Problem in International Fisheries Law*
Andrew Serdy

110 *Substantive Protection under Investment Treaties: A Legal and Economic Analysis*
Jonathan Bonnitcha

109 *Popular Governance of Post-Conflict Reconstruction: The Role of International Law*
Matthew Saul

108 *Evolution of International Environmental Regimes: The Case of Climate Change*
Simone Schiele

107 *Judges, Law and War: The Judicial Development of International Humanitarian Law*
Shane Darcy

106 *Religious Offence and Human Rights: The Implications of Defamation of Religions*
Lorenz Langer

105 *Forum Shopping in International Adjudication: The Role of Preliminary Objections*
Luiz Eduardo Salles

104 *Domestic Politics and International Human Rights Tribunals: The Problem of Compliance*
Courtney Hillebrecht

103 *International Law and the Arctic*
Michael Byers

102 *Cooperation in the Law of Transboundary Water Resources*
Christina Leb

101 *Underwater Cultural Heritage and International Law*
Sarah Dromgoole

100 *State Responsibility: The General Part*
James Crawford

99 *The Origins of International Investment Law: Empire, Environment and the Safeguarding of Capital*
Kate Miles

98 *The Crime of Aggression under the Rome Statute of the International Criminal Court*
Carrie McDougall

97 *'Crimes against Peace' and International Law*
   Kirsten Sellars

96 *Non-Legality in International Law: Unruly Law*
   Fleur Johns

95 *Armed Conflict and Displacement: The Protection of Refugees and Displaced Persons under International Humanitarian Law*
   Mélanie Jacques

94 *Foreign Investment and the Environment in International Law*
   Jorge E. Viñuales

93 *The Human Rights Treaty Obligations of Peacekeepers*
   Kjetil Mujezinović Larsen

92 *Cyber Warfare and the Laws of War*
   Heather Harrison Dinniss

91 *The Right to Reparation in International Law for Victims of Armed Conflict*
   Christine Evans

90 *Global Public Interest in International Investment Law*
   Andreas Kulick

89 *State Immunity in International Law*
   Xiaodong Yang

88 *Reparations and Victim Support in the International Criminal Court*
   Conor McCarthy

87 *Reducing Genocide to Law: Definition, Meaning, and the Ultimate Crime*
   Payam Akhavan

86 *Decolonising International Law: Development, Economic Growth and the Politics of Universality*
   Sundhya Pahuja

85 *Complicity and the Law of State Responsibility*
   Helmut Philipp Aust

84 *State Control over Private Military and Security Companies in Armed Conflict*
   Hannah Tonkin

83 *'Fair and Equitable Treatment' in International Investment Law*
   Roland Kläger

82 *The UN and Human Rights: Who Guards the Guardians?*
   Guglielmo Verdirame

81 *Sovereign Defaults before International Courts and Tribunals*
   Michael Waibel

80 *Making the Law of the Sea: A Study in the Development of International Law*
   James Harrison

79 *Science and the Precautionary Principle in International Courts and Tribunals: Expert Evidence, Burden of Proof and Finality*
   Caroline E. Foster

78 *Transition from Illegal Regimes under International Law*
   Yaël Ronen

77 *Access to Asylum: International Refugee Law and the Globalisation of Migration Control*
   Thomas Gammeltoft-Hansen

76 *Trading Fish, Saving Fish: The Interaction between Regimes in International Law*
   Margaret A. Young

75 *The Individual in the International Legal System: Continuity and Change in International Law*
   Kate Parlett

74 *'Armed Attack' and Article 51 of the UN Charter: Evolutions in Customary Law and Practice*
   Tom Ruys

73 *Theatre of the Rule of Law: Transnational Legal Intervention in Theory and Practice*
   Stephen Humphreys

72 *Science and Risk Regulation in International Law*
   Jacqueline Peel

71 *The Participation of States in International Organisations: The Role of Human Rights and Democracy*
   Alison Duxbury

70 *Legal Personality in International Law*
   Roland Portmann

69 *Vicarious Liability in Tort: A Comparative Perspective*
   Paula Giliker

68 *The Public International Law Theory of Hans Kelsen: Believing in Universal Law*
   Jochen von Bernstorff

67 *Legitimacy and Legality in International Law: An Interactional Account*
   Jutta Brunnée and Stephen J. Toope

66 *The Concept of Non-International Armed Conflict in International Humanitarian Law*
   Anthony Cullen

65 *The Principle of Legality in International and Comparative Criminal Law*
   Kenneth S. Gallant

64 *The Challenge of Child Labour in International Law*
   Franziska Humbert

63 *Shipping Interdiction and the Law of the Sea*
   Douglas Guilfoyle

62 *International Courts and Environmental Protection*
   Tim Stephens

61 *Legal Principles in WTO Disputes*
   Andrew D. Mitchell

60 *War Crimes in Internal Armed Conflicts*
   Eve La Haye

59 *Humanitarian Occupation*
   Gregory H. Fox
58 *The International Law of Environmental Impact Assessment: Process, Substance and Integration*
   Neil Craik
57 *The Law and Practice of International Territorial Administration: Versailles to Iraq and Beyond*
   Carsten Stahn
56 *United Nations Sanctions and the Rule of Law*
   Jeremy Matam Farrall
55 *National Law in WTO Law: Effectiveness and Good Governance in the World Trading System*
   Sharif Bhuiyan
54 *Cultural Products and the World Trade Organization*
   Tania Voon
53 *The Threat of Force in International Law*
   Nikolas Stürchler
52 *Indigenous Rights and United Nations Standards: Self-Determination, Culture and Land*
   Alexandra Xanthaki
51 *International Refugee Law and Socio-Economic Rights: Refuge from Deprivation*
   Michelle Foster
50 *The Protection of Cultural Property in Armed Conflict*
   Roger O'Keefe
49 *Interpretation and Revision of International Boundary Decisions*
   Kaiyan Homi Kaikobad
48 *Multinationals and Corporate Social Responsibility: Limitations and Opportunities in International Law*
   Jennifer A. Zerk
47 *Judiciaries within Europe: A Comparative Review*
   John Bell
46 *Law in Times of Crisis: Emergency Powers in Theory and Practice*
   Oren Gross and Fionnuala Ní Aoláin
45 *Vessel-Source Marine Pollution: The Law and Politics of International Regulation*
   Alan Khee-Jin Tan
44 *Enforcing Obligations Erga Omnes in International Law*
   Christian J. Tams
43 *Non-Governmental Organisations in International Law*
   Anna-Karin Lindblom
42 *Democracy, Minorities and International Law*
   Steven Wheatley
41 *Prosecuting International Crimes: Selectivity and the International Criminal Law Regime*
   Robert Cryer

40 *Compensation for Personal Injury in English, German and Italian Law: A Comparative Outline*
   Basil Markesinis, Michael Coester, Guido Alpa
   and Augustus Ullstein

39 *Dispute Settlement in the UN Convention on the Law of the Sea*
   Natalie Klein

38 *The International Protection of Internally Displaced Persons*
   Catherine Phuong

37 *Imperialism, Sovereignty and the Making of International Law*
   Antony Anghie

36 *Principles of the Institutional Law of International Organizations*
   C. F. Amerasinghe

35 *Necessity, Proportionality and the Use of Force by States*
   Judith Gardam

34 *International Legal Argument in the Permanent Court of International Justice: The Rise of the International Judiciary*
   Ole Spiermann

33 –

32 *Great Powers and Outlaw States: Unequal Sovereigns in the International Legal Order*
   Gerry Simpson

31 *Local Remedies in International Law (second edition)*
   Chittharanjan Felix Amerasinghe

30 *Reading Humanitarian Intervention: Human Rights and the Use of Force in International Law*
   Anne Orford

29 *Conflict of Norms in Public International Law: How WTO Law Relates to Other Rules of International Law*
   Joost Pauwelyn

28 –

27 *Transboundary Damage in International Law*
   Hanqin Xue

26 –

25 *European Criminal Procedures*
   Edited by Mireille Delmas-Marty and J. R. Spencer

24 *Accountability of Armed Opposition Groups in International Law*
   Liesbeth Zegveld

23 *Sharing Transboundary Resources: International Law and Optimal Resource Use*
   Eyal Benvenisti

22 *International Human Rights and Humanitarian Law*
   René Provost

21 *Remedies against International Organisations*
   Karel Wellens

20  *Diversity and Self-Determination in International Law*
    Karen Knop
19  *The Law of Internal Armed Conflict*
    Lindsay Moir
18  *International Commercial Arbitration and African States: Practice, Participation and Institutional Development*
    Amazu A. Asouzu
17  *The Enforceability of Promises in European Contract Law*
    James Gordley
16  *International Law in Antiquity*
    David J. Bederman
15  *Money Laundering: A New International Law Enforcement Model*
    Guy Stessens
14  *Good Faith in European Contract Law*
    Reinhard Zimmermann and Simon Whittaker
13  *On Civil Procedure*
    J. A. Jolowicz
12  *Trusts: A Comparative Study*
    Maurizio Lupoi and Simon Dix
11  *The Right to Property in Commonwealth Constitutions*
    Tom Allen
10  *International Organizations before National Courts*
    August Reinisch
9   *The Changing International Law of High Seas Fisheries*
    Francisco Orrego Vicuña
8   *Trade and the Environment: A Comparative Study of EC and US Law*
    Damien Geradin
7   *Unjust Enrichment: A Study of Private Law and Public Values*
    Hanoch Dagan
6   *Religious Liberty and International Law in Europe*
    Malcolm D. Evans
5   *Ethics and Authority in International Law*
    Alfred P. Rubin
4   *Sovereignty over Natural Resources: Balancing Rights and Duties*
    Nico Schrijver
3   *The Polar Regions and the Development of International Law*
    Donald R. Rothwell
2   *Fragmentation and the International Relations of Micro-States: Self-Determination and Statehood*
    Jorri C. Duursma
1   *Principles of the Institutional Law of International Organizations*
    C. F. Amerasinghe